Creating Compositions

Third Edition

HARVEY S. WIENER
LaGuardia Community College

McGraw-Hill Book Company
New York St. Louis San Francisco Auckland Bogotá
Hamburg Johannesburg London Madrid Mexico
Montreal New Delhi Panama Paris São Paulo
Singapore Sydney Tokyo Toronto

TO THE MEMORY OF DON MARION WOLFE
whose ideas take on new power with each generation
of young writers

AND TO MY STUDENTS
who illustrate with every theme they write the
eternal freshness of those ideas

Creating Compositions
Copyright © 1981, 1977, 1973 by Harvey S. Wiener.
All rights reserved. Printed in the United States of
America. No part of this publication may be re-
produced, stored in a retrieval system, or transmitted,
in any form or by any means, electronic, mechanical,
photocopying, recording, or otherwise, without the
prior written permission of the publisher.

4 5 6 7 8 9 0 D O D O 8 9 8 7 6 5 4 3

See Acknowledgments on page 431. Copyrights included on this page by reference.

This book was set in Trump by Progressive Typogra-
phers. The editors were William A. Talkington, Phillip
A. Butcher, and David Dunham; the production supervisor was Diane Renda. The cover was designed by
Joan E. O'Connor.
R. R. Donnelley & Sons Company was printer and
binder.

Library of Congress Cataloging in Publication Data

Wiener, Harvey S
        Creating compositions.

        Includes index.
        1.   English language—Rhetoric.   I.   Title.
PE1408.W5819   1981   808'.042   80-15833
ISBN 0-07-070160-1

CONTENTS

CONTENTS: SKILLS IN GRAMMAR AND MECHANICS

PREFACE

The third edition of *Creating Compositions* continues to affirm that if you live by feeling and looking and hearing and responding, then you can write. The individual's life is the most important source for writing; your experiences—the countless moments of pleasure and sorrow and surprise that fill each day—make the best compositions. After you learn, through this book, to recreate your experiences in written words, then you can move easily into the world of abstract ideas where details other than those based upon experience are often needed to support a written assignment. Moving gradually into the formal college "essay," the text examines first the well-developed paragraph. As in previous editions, each chapter of the book explores a topic whose meaning your own life can dramatize: moments with friends, a room or a street alive in your memory, the role in your life of the liberated woman, to name a few. Most chapters urge class discussions about the quality of your own experience so that well before actual writing begins, you can share ideas and can listen to other people's thoughts about a topic.

I have made important changes in this third edition. Each chapter now contains instruction in *prewriting* (steps to take in discovering and fleshing out a topic) and in *sentence expanding, combining,* or *embedding* (techniques for improving style and clarity of expression). Many chapters have new themes and offer challenging topics for discussion and for writing. Most of the exercises are new. There are many new student compositions that appear along with several of the successful student themes from the last edition. Selections in The Professionals Speak sections have been updated, and the Reaching Higher sections have been expanded in most cases. Part III, the Minibook, offers several new sections and a variety of different activities.

But the basic format of *Creating Compositions* remains the same. In each chapter, vocabulary exercises present words helpful for the writing assignment at hand, words you might want to use in your own composition. These words are clearly and easily presented, and you will have the chance to figure out definitions without always having to look first in a dictionary. Further, correct definitions appear for your convenience in Appendix A.

A section in each chapter called Building Composition Skills explains different techniques in the construction of paragraphs and essays. You will also learn about and practice with the different kinds of details required to support a topic idea—from details alive with sense experience to details built upon statistics and quotations from reliable sources.

The section called Solving Problems in Writing looks at typical problems in written communication: the run-on error, the sentence fragment, problems with subject and verb agreement, punctuation skills, and a number of others. In all the explanations the stress is upon clear presentation. Charts and clearly marked model sentences illustrate principles by example more often than by rule and without the often confusing language of grammar. And the exercises often require that you apply each skill in the language of your own sentences. You probably will not need to do all the exercises and you can probably leave out those activities which deal with skills that you and your instructor agree you already know. Perforated pages make it possible for your instructor to collect the work you do directly in the book.

In each chapter a section called Writing the Paragraph offers specific goals for the writing exercise. Before you have to write your own composition, you will read some examples of what other students wrote in response to the same assignment. The questions that appear after these student models suggest directions for your own writing; so does the checklist of goals that remind you of the specific skills you are trying to build. Suggested topics will give you additional ideas for your own themes.

The section The Professionals Speak gives you writing samples to illustrate how professionals deal with the same kinds of materials you treat in your writing. And to provide a special challenge either through review or through more practice in composition, there is at the end of each chapter a section called Reaching Higher for students who want to advance further their skills in writing. Part III at the end of the text contains A Minibook of Special Skills that presents briefly several important areas of communication for successful college work, including how to write a business letter, how to prepare footnotes and bibliographies, how to take notes and write a summary, and several other skills.

As in the past, I have a number of debts to friends and colleagues without whose support and encouragement *Creating Compositions* could not have progressed. From Don Marion Wolfe comes the whole philosophy of sensory language and the need for exploring individual moments in order to write with meaning. His too are the ideas for using model paragraphs as the heart of any composition program and for using activities in language that require students to call upon their own resources in communication. To Don Wolfe my gratitude is limitless. His death in April, 1976, robs all of us who knew him of a brilliant teacher and a warm, faithful friend. To my wife Barbara Koster Wiener go thanks for her patience during the preparation of the materials and for her skills as a teacher of reading, which made her assistance invaluable. Don Linder and Jeffrey Kaplan assisted me ably in producing the manuscript. To my colleagues at La Guardia Community College who used *Creating Compositions* and who made valuable suggestions for improvement I am deeply indebted, as I am to those colleagues in colleges across the country who wrote to me with new ideas. Robert Esch at the University of Texas at El Paso read the manuscript with more care and attention than any writer dare hope for. I thank him and Barbara Clouse, Youngstown State University, and Tom Miles, West Virginia University, who offered their advice on the third edition. Finally, it is to the students in my composition courses who proved each term anew the infinite resources of their own lives and their ability to commit those vital elements into words—it is to them I owe special thanks.

Harvey S. Wiener

part I
PARAGRAPHS

chapter 1

ROOMS THAT LINGER, ROOMS THAT BREATHE: WRITING DESCRIPTION

INTRODUCTION TO DESCRIPTION

A kitchen in a warm apartment, a hospital room that smells of alcohol and ether, an attic in a lonely house—each of us knows some indoor place that has fixed itself clearly in our minds. To reproduce such a place in words is to describe for others the details that make it come alive. Because many writing tasks demand the reproduction of details, description is a basic element in the writer's craft. As a writer, you have to observe a scene around you with great care; and you have to present it faithfully so readers know exactly what you see.

This first paragraph assignment in description requires that you make a room come to life through your writing. Selecting some place filled with colors, noises, and people in the midst of actions, you will present a scene which is clear and vivid for any reader to appreciate. You will call upon your sense impressions of sound, color, smell, touch, and action to illustrate your major reaction to this room. Before you write your paragraph, you will read what students before you have written in response to the same assignment.

VOCABULARY

Step 1. Words to Describe Situations. These words specify reactions you may have to the room you want to describe. For any words you do not know, check a dictionary or Appendix A of this book. Write definitions on the blank lines below.

1. boisterous _____

2. amiable _____

3. regal _____

4. malevolent _____

5. dismal _____

6. hushed _____

7. hectic _____

8. tranquil _____

9. cluttered _____

10. effervescent _____

Step 2. Applying Vocabulary. After you are sure of the meanings of the above words, write:

1. a word to describe a friendly place _____

2. a word that means peaceful _____

3. a word to describe rough noisiness _____

4. a word to indicate deep silence _____

5. a word to describe a gloomy place _____

6. a word that means stately and royal _____

7. a word that means showing bad will _____

8. a word that would describe a lively, bubbling place _____

9. a word to describe a place of great excitement _____

10. a word to show things heaped in a disorderly way _____

Step 3. Words that Name Sounds. For the writer of description, words that indicate sounds are very important. For each word in italics below write a definition that explains the word accurately. Use a dictionary when you need one; check Appendix A for more help.

Example:
1. He *guffawed* at the jokes, his whole body shaking with delight.   *laughed in a loud burst*
   _____

2. The official tried to speak over the *clamor* of the students.
   _____
   _____

3. She spoke so low that her words were *inaudible.*
   _____
   _____

4. His uncle's deep, loud voice *bellowed* with laughter.
   _____
   _____

5. Wild applause *resonated* throughout the theater.
   _____
   _____

BUILDING COMPOSITION SKILLS

Sensory Language

Step 1. Listening Well. Listen a moment to the sound of the room in which you are now sitting. Write three sentences that tell sounds you hear. Use a color in each sentence.

*Examples: I hear the clamor of rush-hour traffic beyond the blue shutters.
Pink gum cracks as Paul blows a bubble at his seat.*

1. _____

   _____

2. _____

_____

3. _____

_____

Step 2. Action and Color. Look around. Write three sentences that show some action in the room. Use a specific color in each sentence.

Examples: *In front of me Marina munches on yellow corn chips.*
A green fly circles lazily above the window sill.

1. _____

_____

2. _____

_____

3. _____

_____

Step 3. What You Feel. Touch your desk, your shirt or sweater, your pen, or your wristwatch. Move around and touch the walls, the doors, the windows, and other objects in your room. Write a sentence that includes a word to show what you feel. Use a color or a sound as well.

Examples: *My forehead is hot and sweaty.*
I hear the squeak of my chair as I touch its smooth wooden sides.

1. _____

_____

2. _____

_____

3. _____

_____

The practices above demonstrate an important technique in writing: *concrete sensory detail*. *Concrete* means specific, solid; *sensory* means relating to any of the senses. The highly specific pictures that result are called *images*. Notice in the two columns below how the images in Column I are general and have little sensory appeal, while those in Column II are concrete because they appeal strongly to the senses.

I   *II*

1. the door   *a brown door with peeling paint and a broken glass*

2. a chair   *a mahogany rocking chair that clacks and groans*

3. the window   _____

4. an old book   _____

5. the chalkboard   _____

Step 4. Concrete Details.   In the blank spaces under Column II, write concrete sensory details for the general pictures in Column I.

Step 5. Naming Specifically.   One way to create pictures is to use the exact word you want rather than a general term that needs too many descriptive words to make the picture specific. Readers prefer the word *elm* or *oak* to *tree* because they get an added identification for the object through the exactness of the name.

   For each general term in Column I, write in Column II three different *specific* terms to replace it.

I   *II*

Example:
1. tool   *hammer, pliers, screwdriver*

2. car   _____

3. book   _____

4. animal   _____

5. food   _____

6. drink   _____

Topic Sentences

The key to a good paragraph is its topic sentence. For your purposes at this point, the topic sentence should always come as the first sentence of the paragraph.

   Look at these three sentences and try to judge which you think most effective as the opening topic sentence in a paragraph:

1. It all happened last night.
2. My room is on the second floor of our house.
3. My room is the messiest room on the second floor of our house.

   If you selected 3, you rejected 1 and 2 for good reason. Sentence 1, though typical of many papers by beginning writers, lacks a clear statement of topic. What is the *it*? What small element of suspense the writer tries to achieve is usually lost in a drift away from the topic. Not having stated it clearly at the beginning, the writer easily loses control. Besides, the "It all happened. . . ." opening is so familiar and overused by now that it pays to avoid it.

Sentences 2 and 3 are superior because they both state the topic immediately: it's clear to readers that they will be reading descriptions of rooms. Sentence 2, however, is merely a statement of fact. It gives the writer too little control over the topic. What details can be included? What details can be left out? Sentence 3, on the other hand, by introducing the word *messiest,* states the writer's opinion about the room and gives a means for determining which details to use in the description. Any image not contributing to the overall effect of *messiness* would be omitted.

The most effective topic sentences are those that state both the topic and the writer's opinion of or attitude toward that topic. The box below highlights the qualities of strong topic sentences.

A TOPIC SENTENCE REMINDER

Good Topic Sentences:

1. Introduce the topic immediately.

2. Limit the topic.

3. Give an opinion or an attitude or a reaction or an impression that the writer has about the topic.

Why:

So your reader knows what you will write about.
So you know what you will write about.

Hint: Do not surprise your readers. Tell them immediately what you want to write about.

So you will not have too much to write about.
So you will have enough to write about.
So you will focus on only one major feature or point.

You get readers interested in the topic: they will want to find out why you feel the way you do about your subject.
You can introduce a key word that will help you relate all your supporting ideas to one dominant impression.

Here are two more topic sentences, which are successful because they introduce a limited topic clearly *and* give the writer's opinion about that topic. Each is explained for you.

1. Everyone in my writing class this Monday morning looks restless and uncomfortable.

   Topic: people in the writing class Monday morning
   Opinion: restlessness

2. Last Friday night I realized the bitterness that exists in my husband's character.

   Topic: my husband last Friday night
   Opinion: bitterness

The writer of sentence 1 above would need to show in the sentences that follow it just why everyone appears to be restless.

The writer of sentence 2 would need to show specific details of her husband's bitterness.

Step 1. Determining Topics and Opinions. In the following topic sentences, underline the topic and circle the word(s) that tell the opinion or attitude.

Example:

1. Most new students are (shocked) at college registration procedures.
2. I'll always regret the day when the large oak tree fell in front of my house.
3. My old typewriter is my most valuable possession.
4. My family always loved Uncle Yee's sense of humor and wit.
5. On this chilly October morning I am sitting in the students' cafeteria, watching the commotion around me.

Step 2. Improving Topic Sentences. The following topic sentences need words of opinion or attitude, words which will help limit and specify the topic. Rewrite the sentences in the space provided. You may wish to change the idea of some of the sentences as you introduce opinions. Try to avoid overused words like *good, nice, pleasant, enjoyable* by using some of the vocabulary on pages 4–5.

Example:

1. I have a collection of old coins. *My collection of old coins is the envy of my Uncle Dave.*

2. This car is more than fifty years old. _____

_____

3. I go to the movies on Saturday nights. _____

_____

4. My father called me from Florida late last night. _____

_____

5. I revisited my high school last week. _____

_____

6. I spent many summer afternoons in my grandmother's attic. _____

_____

7. Letters of the alphabet sponsor commercials on the children's television program *Sesame Street.* _____

_____

8. My uncle taught me carpentry. _____

_____

9. Mel Brooks is a film director and writer of comedies. _____

_____

10. An increase in oil prices causes inflation. _____

_____

Step 3. Clearing Up Topics. The topic sentences below fail to specify the topic to be developed in the paragraph. Many lack key words to express opinions. Others give important details but fail to clarify exactly what the topic will be. On separate paper rewrite the sentences to make them clearer and more effective paragraph openings.

Example:
1. I will never forget what happened last winter. *One evening last winter I watched in amazement the birth of a calf.*
2. On the train I saw several people arguing.
3. I will write about my childhood train set.
4. I spent last summer with my college roommate.
5. Light streams through the window and leaves spots of yellow on the living room floor.

Step 4. Details and Topic Sentences. The most effective way to construct your sentence is to decide beforehand those details you wish to discuss. Suppose you wanted to write a paragraph on pollution and you wanted to discuss these two issues:

1. machines, such as cars and trains and lawn mowers, as major pollutants
2. humans as careless destroyers of our air and water

Here is a topic sentence that would permit the writer to discuss those two issues:

Both machines and human beings share the awful guilt of polluting our air and water.

The topic is clearly stated. Which words give the opinion or attitude?
   Suppose the topic sentence were:

Pollution is a terrible problem.

The writer would then have presented too broad a topic for treatment in a composition of limited length. There are just too many possibilities to consider with such a topic sentence, and the writer would tend to treat too quickly many points without examining closely two or three that are especially important.

For each group of three details in Column I, write a topic sentence (including opinion and limited topic) in Column II.

I Details in Paragraph   *II Topic Sentence*

1. On our vacation in San Francisco it   1. _____
   rained for three days.
   The cable car operators went on strike.   _____
   My wife had the flu.
   My luggage was lost.   _____

2. Inflation hurts old people who are living   2. _____
   on fixed incomes.
   Inflation affects the poor who are strug-   _____
   gling to pay their bills.
   Inflation hurts young people raising a   _____
   family.

3. Late night television programs fill time   3. _____
   for people who cannot sleep.
   Late night programs offer lively talk on   _____
   key world problems.
   Late night programs are fun in an adult   _____
   way.

Step 5. Predicting Topics. A good topic sentence suggests for the reader some of the details to be found in the paragraph. For each topic sentence below, write two kinds of information you might expect to find in the paragraph.

Topic Sentence   *Details in Paragraph*

Example:

1. In this complex society there are many   1. *a.* *pressure by friends*
   vital reasons to explain why teenagers   *to cut classes*
   drop out of school.
                                                  b. *personal problems*
                                                      at home

2. The Fourth of July is a day of special plea- 2. *a.* _____
   sure for me.
                                                      _____

                                                  b. _____

                                                      _____

3. Owning a car often presents many problems.

    3. *a.* _____

                   _____

                   _____

                  b. _____

                   _____

                   _____

4. Housing conditions in today's urban centers are disgraceful.

    4. *a.* _____

                   _____

                   _____

                  b. _____

                   _____

                   _____

Step 6. More Topic Sentence Practice.   For each general topic, note in Column II details that you might develop in a paragraph. Then write a good topic sentence in Column III.

I General Topic	II Details for Paragraph	III Topic Sentence
Example: 1. diets	*a crash diet I went on to lose weight always left me hungry. It made me very sick. I gained back all the weight I lost anyhow.*	*I learned from a crash diet I foolishly followed to lose weight that serious problems may result from an unwise eating program.*
2. a college diploma		
3. roller skating		

4. a first date

Getting It All Together: Transitions I

In a descriptive composition, the writer can move smoothly from one feature of the description to another by using *transitional expressions.* A transitional expression is a connector; it is a bridge between statements and ideas in paragraphs. Here are some transition words, which can relate ideas in a paragraph that describes a place; they will be valuable as you write your theme because they help move your reader's eye from one part of the room to another.

there	next to
behind	in the rear
up above	in front of
to the left	up front
to the right	over
nearby	around
below	surrounding
against	beyond
on	near the back
at the . . .	forward
beside	through the . . .
far off	from the
inside	
alongside	

Step 1. Seeing Transitions at Work. Examine the sentences in Column I below. The ideas seem unrelated and unclear. By adding transitional expressions in the blank spaces in the same sentences under Column II, make the relationship between ideas clearer. You may want to add a word or two after the transition as well.

I

As I cleaned Paul's bedroom, I realized what a sad and lonely place it had become since my brother had joined the army last November. I saw his dusty football trophies, which he had polished so carefully. I passed his blue and gold football jacket, which hung proudly. I picked up one of several detective novels Paul loved to read; the tattered bookmark indicated that he had never finished

II

As I cleaned Paul's bedroom, I realized what a sad and lonely place it had become since my brother had joined the army last November. _____ I saw his dusty football trophies, which he had polished so carefully. _____ I passed his blue and gold football jacket, which hung proudly _____. _____ I picked up one of several detective novels Paul loved to read; the tattered

the story. I suddenly heard my mother call me. Taking one last look, I slowly closed the door.

bookmark indicated that he had never finished the story. _____ I suddenly heard my mother call me. Taking one last look, I slowly closed the door _____.

A Sentence Review

Writers need to know how to build and to analyze sentences. The review chart below will help you write strong, complete sentences.

WRITING COMPLETE THOUGHTS: A SENTENCE REVIEW CHART

1. To be a sentence, a word group must contain a subject and a verb and must express a complete thought. In the following sentences, the verb is underlined twice, and the subject once.

   Our teacher gave us an assignment.

   The men work hard.

Hint: To find a verb, try these tests.

   A. Put *yesterday, today,* or *tomorrow* in front of the sentence. The word that changes is the verb, because only verbs show tense—time change.

   The children *laugh* while playing hide-and-seek.
   Yesterday the children *laughed* while playing hide-and-seek.

   Laugh changed to *laughed* with the word *yesterday.* Only verbs change in this way. *Laugh* is the verb.

   Tomorrow the children *will laugh* while playing hide-and-seek.

   Laugh changed to *will laugh* with the word *tomorrow.* Only verbs change this way. *Laugh* is the verb.

   B. When you have the word you think is a verb, put *he, she, we, it, you, I,* or *they* in front of the word. If you've created a word group that makes sense with one of these subject pronouns (see page 342), you have a verb.

Word	Test	
work	I work, they work	Verb
sings	he sings, it sings	Verb
laughter	I laughter, they laughter	No verb
is	she is, he is	Verb
seldom	I seldom, you seldom	No verb

   C. Some words are *always* verbs, no matter how they are used in a sentence. Often working along with other verbs, these *auxiliaries*—helping verbs—are worth memorizing. When you see them, you know that they are verbs; and you know that they may also be signaling other verbs soon to follow in a sentence. Here are some of the most important helping verbs:

have	has	will	might	had	am	was
may	does	can	do	should	is	were
could	did	shall		must	are	been
would						

2. Some sentences have verbs made up of more than one word. Notice how *had*, *should have*, and *were* are helping other verbs in these sentences:

Our teacher had given us an assignment.

Those men should have worked hard.

They were laughing aloud.

3. Some sentences have more than one verb for the same subject.

Those men worked and laughed.

4. Some sentences have several sets of subjects and verbs joined together.

Those men worked, but because they laughed, the job was finished late.

5. Some word groups, although very brief, are grammatically correct and are considered complete sentences because they express complete thoughts.

He ran.

It fell.

You might logically say, "We do not know who *he* is nor what *it* is. Aren't those sentences incomplete?" However, from a grammatical point of view, these word groups, because they contain subjects and verbs and express complete thoughts, *are* sentences. You might need more information to understand fully the correct meaning the sentence tries to offer, but often that information appears in sentences that come earlier or later on.

6. Some sentences have more than one subject for the same verb or verbs.

My brother and sister attended the concert.

Mr. Holmes and his son went to Boston but returned today.

7. Some sentences express complete thoughts, although the subject does not actually appear in the sentence.

Walk!

Go down the steps quickly!

In both these sentences, the subject is understood to be the word *you*.

8. Some words can be either a subject or a verb, depending upon how they are used in a sentence. However, the guidelines above will help you to decide if the word is a verb. If you are still uncertain, check a dictionary.

Cats cry outside my window at night.   (Here *cry* is the verb: yesterday, cats *cried*.)

A cry awoke me.   (Here *awoke* is the verb; tomorrow the cry *will awake* me. *Cry* is the subject: What awoke me? The cry.)

9. Some describing words often separate parts of a verb when the verb is more than one word. Don't be confused into thinking that words like *only*, *not*, *never* and others are verbs simply because they appear near or because they break up verbs. Look at the word in italics in the examples below:

The crow could *not* flap its wing.

They had *never* seen so strange a sight.

> In the first sentence *could flap* is the verb. (*Could* is one of the helpers; and both *could* and *flap* work in the test with subject pronouns: *I could, I flap.*) The word *not*, though it appears between the two words that serve as verbs in the sentence, is not a verb: *I not? They not?* Similarly, in the second sentence *had seen* is the verb; *never*, despite its position in the sentence, is not a verb. Both *not* and *never* describe the verb and are called *adverbs*.

Step 1. Sentence or Nonsentence? Only some of the word groups below are complete sentences. Read each item aloud; then, using the principles suggested in the Sentence Review Chart, pages 14–16, write *S* before each word group that makes a complete sentence and *NS* before each word group that is not a complete sentence. For each *NS* you write, explain how you would make the word group complete so that it qualifies as a sentence.

1. Across an empty field.
2. Grooming the horses.
3. Joaquin fed the chickens before dawn.
4. Singing and laughing in loud voices from across the yard on Cameo Drive.
5. The instructor and her students held class on the lawn and discussed the election heatedly.
6. Based on important facts.
7. They whistled.
8. Stop!
9. Leave these premises immediately.
10. A very intelligent child.

Step 2. Verbs and Subjects. Among the words below, only seven may serve as verbs. Circle them. From the words remaining, select subjects that make sense with the verbs. Then write six sentences of your own, including in each a correct subject-verb combination. Use separate paper.

Example: Sparrows fly swiftly.

mouse	study	vanish
tarnishes	squeaks	silverware
lion	listen	roars
children	sparrows	airplanes
(fly)	scientists	engine
door	noises	audiences

Step 3. Finding Subjects and Verbs in Sentences. Using the pointers in the Sentence Review Chart, find the subjects and verbs in each sentence below. Underline the subjects once and the verbs twice.

Example:

After I had fallen, an old man helped me to my feet.

1. Because of the heavy rain, Roger lost control of his car and swerved into a truck.

2. Always revise your writing, or your paper may contain several grammatical errors.
3. Before Mary had finished her song, the director clapped his hands and another girl came on stage, ready for singing.
4. The children were yelling so loudly outside that Elizabeth and Ray could not study for their final exams.
5. Hanging on the line, the red sweater flapped lazily in the summer breeze as Pedro put out the rest of the clothes.

Sentence Combining: Coordination

Read the sentences below. Then write on the blank line your first reaction to the way the sentences sound.

The Nursery

(1) My baby's room is the happiest room in our home. (2) I love to spend time there. (3) The walls are painted a sunny yellow. (4) Above the crib hangs a musical mobile. (5) It plays Brahms' Lullaby. (6) Stuffed dogs and cats rest on the floor. (7) The sweet smell of talcum powder is in the air. (8) A brown rocking horse sits in the corner. (9) My baby sucks his little pink thumb. (10) He suddenly awakens. (11) He doesn't see me in the corner. (12) He rests his head on the pillow. (13) I tiptoe quietly to the door.

_____

Did you write *choppy* or *childish*? If you did, you probably sensed that some of the sentences needed to be joined in some way. Although very brief statements as sentences are often effective in writing, there are several other ways of structuring sentences for a clear development of ideas.

One way is to use *coordination.* The words

and, but, or, for, nor (called *conjunctions*), and the semicolon (;)

are called coordinators. Coordinators help ideas flow smoothly in a paragraph by joining two complete thoughts together so that they both are equal in importance and strength. When you use *and, but, or, for,* or *nor* to join complete sentences, always use a comma before the coordinators.

	What They Mean	*How to Use Them*	
and	The information that follows in the second complete thought is true along with, in addition to, the related information in the first complete thought.	The boys sat in the schoolyard with their shirts off, **and** they enjoyed sunning themselves.	[comma] This part of the sentence tells what the boys do in addition to sitting in the schoolyard with their shirts off.

but	The information that follows in the second complete thought is something you would not expect to happen, according to the information in the first complete thought. Idea two tells an *exception* to idea one.	I wanted to see the *Late Show* on television, but I had too much homework. [comma] — You wouldn't expect someone who wanted to watch the program (as stated in the first part of the sentence) to miss it.
for	The information in the second complete thought tells why the events in the first complete thought happened or should happen.	We were not permitted to visit the baby, **for** we both had colds. [comma] — This tells why the visit (stated in the first thought) could not occur.
or	The information in the second complete thought is an alternative—another possibility—to the information in the first. *Or* suggests that only one of the two ideas will be possible.	You must arrive on time, **or** you will miss the first part of the examination. [comma] — This will occur only if what is told in the first part of the sentence does not occur.
nor	*Nor* continues into the second complete thought some negative idea begun in the first.	He never ate candy, **nor** did he miss the taste of sweetness. [This word begins the negative idea] [comma] — This continues the negative idea.
;	The semicolon indicates close relationship between both complete thoughts.	It was time for a new car; even his father agreed to that. [semicolon] — This thought depends for its sense on the thought before the semicolon.

Hint: Remember to use a comma whenever you use a conjunction to connect two complete thoughts.

Notice how well sentences 1 and 2 in the paragraph called "The Nursery" may be coordinated:

My baby's room is the happiest room in our home, *and* I love to spend time there.

Similarly, sentences 10 and 11 may be united:

He suddenly awakens, *but* he doesn't see me in the corner.

What other sentences might be coordinated effectively?

Three Important Hints:
1. Too many coordinated sentences can weaken prose style. Use coordination sparingly.
2. Don't coordinate a whole string of complete sentences with conjunctions. Your paragraph will be just as dull as if you had not used any coordinators. Sometimes semicolons or a combination of semicolon and conjunction may be used effectively to coordinate *three* complete thoughts: *We drove carefully through the strange neighborhood; all of us watched the street signs, but nothing looked familiar.*
3. Make sure that the two complete thoughts you coordinate make sense together.

Step 1. You Pick the Coordinator. Here are five coordinated sentences written by professional writers. The coordinator in each case is left out. Write in the blank space the best coordinator from the choices given on the right.

1. The big patch of shadow might be a hut certainly, _____ it might be a cave leading down into the very depths of the earth.
—Leo Tolstoy
    for   ;   but

2. A breeze must have blown outside, _____ the net on the basket moved . . . .
—Philip Roth
    or   for   nor

3. Small children and babies perched on every lap available, _____ men leaned on the shelves or on each other.
—Maya Angelou
    for   and   but

4. Now and then pigeons flutter _____ birds glide in and sing gay songs _____ both birds and pigeons are drinking from the beautiful fountains.
—Woodie King, Jr.
    but   ;   for
    but   ;   nor

5. At my father's funeral I had nothing black to wear, _____ this posed a nagging problem all day long.
—James Baldwin
    for   but   and

Step 2. Completing Sentences. Basing your choice upon the coordinator used in each statement below, add a complete thought to the beginning word group that appears. Make sure that your final sentence makes sense. Look at the example.

1. Jimmy found five dollars, but *he tried not to spend it.*
2. We stopped for lunch at a cheap hamburger stand, for

_____ .

3. The child darted out in front of our car; _____ .

4. A husband should never take his wife's love for granted, nor _____

_____ .

5. Many students have great difficulty adjusting to college life, but

_____ .

6. You can hand your paper in on time, or _____ !

Step 3. Coordinators in Your Sentences. Using any of the methods of coordination, write a sentence about the topics listed below. Use each type of coordinator at least once. Be sure a complete thought (containing subject and verb) follows each coordinator.

1. autumn _____

_____

2. the telephone _____

_____

3. your desk _____

_____

4. television _____

_____

5. swimming _____

_____

6. nuclear energy _____

_____

7. college instructors _____

_____

8. working mothers _____

_____

9. my father _____

_____

10. inflation _____

_____

SOLVING PROBLEMS IN WRITING
The Mirror Words I

The following exercises focus upon five groups of words that are especially difficult to spell because they look and sound so much like other words with different meanings.

it's its it's: it is it has	*It's* too quiet. Tell us if *it's* true. *It's* been a week since I saw her. **Hint:** You must be able to use the words *it is* or *it has* whenever you want to use *it's*.
its: possession or ownership by some non-human thing	The Raggedy-Ann doll lost *its* stuffing. As winter approached, the tree lost *its* leaves. **Hint:** If you can use *his* or *her* and the sentence gives a sense of ownership, you can use *its*. The tree lost *his* leaves. *His* gives the sense of ownership; since trees have no male or female qualities, *its* should be used.
~~its'~~	This form does not exist! *Do not use it.*

Step 1. *It's* or *Its*?   Write the correct word, *it's* or *its*, in the blank spaces below.

1. _____ sunny now, but _____ supposed to rain this afternoon.

2. Although _____ easy to read a poem, _____ meaning is often difficult to understand.

3. _____ been a long time since the end of World War II, but

_____ disastrous effects still linger in the minds of _____ survivors.

two   too   to
two: the number 2
too: 1. One meaning is *very, more than enough, excessively,* or *in a great degree.*
     The color is *too* dull.
     My cousin is *too* tall.	

---

2. *Too* means *also* as well.
Let me go *too.*
Will the mayor, *too,* speak at the luncheon?

Hint: When you use *too* (meaning *also*) at the end of a sentence, you may use a comma before it to indicate a pause and to give emphasis to your statement.

I shook Senator Carter's hand, too.

to: 1. *To* is used to show direction. It means *toward, for,* or *at.*
Carry the milk *to* the refrigerator.
To me he is always fair.
2. *To* is used as part of the infinitive. An infinitive is the starting point of any verb used in a sentence. In the sentence "He likes food," *likes* is the verb whose infinitive is *to like.* All infinitives are preceded by the word *to.* These two sentences use infinitives correctly: notice the word *to.*

[infinitive]
They like to fish in a stream.

To run in track meets, you must begin to train your legs.
[infinitive]   [infinitive]

Step 2. *To, Two, Too.* Fill in the blanks below with the correct form: *too, two,* or *to.*

Listening _____ the _____ howling German shepherds was _____ much _____ bear. It was bad enough having _____ stay in bed for _____ whole days without even being able _____ watch television, but the constant barking was starting _____ drive me crazy _____ . I was _____ old _____ have the measles. _____-year olds got the measles, not people who were going off _____ college in _____ months.

Step 3. Using *To, Two, Too* Correctly. Follow directions.

1. Write a sentence that uses *too* to mean *very.* _____

_____

2. Write a sentence that uses *to* as an infinitive. _____

_____

3. Write a sentence using the word *two.* _____

_____

4. Write a sentence using *too* to mean *also.* _____

_____

5. Write a sentence that uses *to* as a direction word. _____

_____

---

there   their   they're

there: a place   Was it *there?*

Hint: *There* often starts a sentence. It is sometimes followed by *are, were, is,* or some other verb.

   There are three birds.
   There was a good movie at the Rialto.
   There sat two children playing.

their: ownership (possession) by a group   It's *their* car.
                                               Was it *their* house that burned?

they're: they are

Hint: If you can say *they are*, you can use *they're.*

   They're late again!
   If *they're* tired, they should sleep.

Step 4. Listening for *Their, They're,* and *There*.   Read the brief paragraph below, noting the use of *their, they're,* and *there*. Then on separate paper write the paragraph as your instructor dictates it.

In the past my mother and father loved their apartment, but they're just not happy there anymore. There is no longer room for all of Dad's trophies, and Mom's plants lie cluttered over the entire living room. My folks are starting to look for a new place that they're both going to enjoy as much as their old apartment. There must be an apartment building in their area that has large rooms to hold many precious belongings. I'm going to look in today's paper. An apartment must be listed there that my parents will find right for their needs.

---

your   you're

your: ownership. It means *belonging to you.*
      Is that *your* car? Give *your* theme a lively title.

you're: you are

Hint: If you can say *you are*, you can use *you're.*

   You're late.
   When *you're* out of town, call.

Step 5. *Your* and *You're*.   Circle the correct words in the parentheses.

1. (Your, You're) not the student I sent for.
2. (Your, You're) theory is worthy of further research.

3. If (your, you're) uncertain of the date, check (your, you're) calendar.
4. (Your, You're) wit is as keen as (your, you're) intellect.
5. (Your, You're) bill can be mailed if (your, you're) in a hurry.

---

who's   whose

who's: the contraction for *who is* or *who has*

  Who's at the door?
  Tell him *who's* on the phone.
  Who's been to El Paso?

Hint: If you can say *who is* or *who has,* you can use *who's.*

whose: possession. It asks a question (*Belonging to whom?*) or it refers to some person or thing named earlier in the sentence.

  Whose dime is that?
  The man *whose* briefcase was lost offered a reward.

Step 6. Sentences with *Who's* and *Whose.*   Complete the following sentences so that they make sense.

1. I will announce whose _____ .

2. I will announce who's _____ .

3. My uncle, whose _____ , arrived late at the airport.

4. Whose _____ ?

5. Who's _____ ?

Run-on Sentences

As you remember from the review chart, pages 14–16, every sentence must have a subject and a verb to be complete. Run-on sentences are word groups that mistakenly push two or more sentences together as one. Find the "sentence collisions" in the following example:

I ran to the door my sister stormed in suddenly she burst into tears.

HOW TO FIX THE RUN-ON ERROR

1. The easiest way to fix the run-on is to use a correct end mark between sentences: a period, a question mark, or an exclamation mark. *A comma is not an end mark. It does not separate complete sentences.* If you read aloud the run-on sentence above, listen to the sound of your own voice. Where your voice stops and drops, use a period.

[capital letter]   [capital letter]

I ran to the door. My sister stormed in. Suddenly she burst into tears.

[period]

Of course, you need to use a capital letter to start each new sentence. If you had used a comma after *door* or *in* in the sentences above, you would have incorrectly separated two sentences (the subjects and verbs are underlined for you to help you see how the standards for completeness are met). A comma is too weak a punctuation mark to separate complete thoughts. Some instructors like to call the run-on error which uses a comma to separate complete thoughts a *comma splice*. A *comma splice* is merely two or more sentences run together with a comma between them.

2. When two run-on word groups, each complete with subject and verb, are very closely related in meaning, these word groups may be separated by a semi-colon. A semicolon, which includes both a period and a comma in its structure, indicates a stronger pause than a comma: the semicolon can separate complete thoughts. If you choose to use a semicolon, always begin the word group after the semicolon with a small letter.

[small letter]

I ran to the door. My sister stormed in; suddenly she burst into tears.

[semicolon]

Hint: A subject and a verb must come both before and after the semicolon. The structure of the sentence looks like this : *Complete thought; complete thought.*

3. Instead of keeping complete word groups apart, you may join them together with suitable joining words (*conjunctions*) and proper punctuation.
   a. When the two sentences have equal importance in your mind, use one of these joining words: *and, but, or, for, nor.* Use a comma before the conjunction. (You learned about combining sentences in this way—called coordination—on pages 17–20.)

   [conjunction]

   I ran to the door, and my sister stormed in. Suddenly she burst into tears.

   [comma]

   [conjunction]

   I ran to the door. My sister stormed in, and suddenly she burst into tears.

   [comma]

   b. You may also join the run-on sentences by making one complete word group less important than the other (see pages 89–95). Many different conjunctions perform that function. Here are a few: *because, while, although, since, when, if, as.* Use a comma after you complete the word group that begins with one of these joining words. Sometimes you need to add a new word or two, to take away words, or to change the position of words when you correct the run-on with one of these conjunctions.

   [less important
   word group]

   As I ran to the door, my sister stormed in. Suddenly she burst into tears.

   [comma]

[less important word group]   [word *suddenly* left out]

I ran to the door. When my sister stormed in, she burst into tears.

[comma]

Step 1. One Error, Five Corrections. Here are two complete sentences run on as one:

The fire alarm had begun to ring the workers dashed from the burning building.

Fix the run-on error on the blank lines below. The words and punctuation will tell you which methods to use.

1. The fire alarm had begun to ring; _____

   _____

2. Since _____ , _____

   _____

3. The fire alarm had begun to ring. _____

   _____

4. The fire alarm had begun to ring, _____

   _____

5. When _____

   _____

Step 2. One Error, Five Corrections. Here are two complete thoughts joined by a comma. On separate paper correct the comma splice in five different ways.

The train was about to leave, Juan darted toward the closing doors.

How to Find Run-on Errors

Repairing the run-on mistake is easy, once your instructor points out the error by writing in the margin of your paragraph "RO" for run-on or "CS" for comma splice. The trick is, of course, to find the run-on errors yourself.

1. Here are some simple hints to help you find run-on sentences:

   Read your paragraph aloud. When your voice stops and drops, use a period.

   Read your paragraph from the last sentence to the first sentence. That will help you keep apart complete thoughts.

Count your sentences. In this way, you will be looking for end marks, and you will be aware that a small number of sentences probably means run-ons in your paragraph.

2. The best way to recognize the run-on is to learn carefully two groups of *run-on stop signs.* These words, used at the start of complete-thought word groups, mean trouble to you because they, more than any other words, frequently cause run-on errors. Each time you use one of the words in either group, you must stop to think of the possibility that you may be writing a run-on sentence.

RUN-ON STOP SIGNS: GROUP I

then	there	consequently
now		moreover
finally		therefore
suddenly		however

Hint: These words are not conjunctions. They do *not* join sentences correctly. If they open complete-thought word groups, they must be preceded by a period or a semicolon. At times, a conjunction and a comma work as well.

In this word group, the run-on stop sign starts a complete-thought word group, and must have either a semicolon or a period before it:

[run-on
stop sign]
↓
We drove for a long time. However, we rested afterward.
We drove for a long time; however, we rested afterward.

In this word group, the run-on stop sign is used correctly in the middle of the sentence; *however* does *not* start a complete-thought word group here:

We drove, however, for a long time.

Step 1. Correct Punctuation for Run-ons. Correct the run-on errors below by inserting correct punctuation or by changing incorrect punctuation. One sentence is already correct.

Hint: If you have doubts about where your voice stops and drops, check for subjects and verbs to test sentence completeness.

1. I ran to the beach, finally the sun came out.
2. I love to wander through rows of corn there is a peacefulness that I enjoy.
3. The water was a clear blue color, however, the sand was filled with pebbles and litter.
4. We should try, therefore, to find a restaurant that serves food without preservatives.
5. The experiment was a failure, therefore, we must start over again.

RUN-ON STOP SIGNS: GROUP II

it	we	**Hint:** Although these words are frequently used in the middle of sentences, they are also used as sentence openers. If one of these words opens a complete-thought word group, the word must be preceded by a period or a semicolon.
she	he	
you	they	
	I	

Step 2. Rewriting the Run-on. Fix the run-on errors below by rewriting the word groups correctly on the blank lines. Use any of the methods explained on pages 24–26. All the run-on mistakes are caused by Group II *stop signs*. Write the letter *C* if the sentence is correct.

1. Roy found the missing wheel, it had rolled under the bed. _____

   _____

2. Jane ran all the way home, she couldn't wait to see if her package had

   arrived. _____

   _____

3. Professor Kent entered the classroom frowning he held the final exams

   in his hand. _____

   _____

4. Although the weather in Juarez looked fine, it started to rain. _____

   _____

5. Rosa told us the news we could not believe it. _____

   _____

   Use the two brief run-on review charts below to help you complete Steps 3 to 5 correctly.

RUN-ON REVIEW CHARTS

Run-on Finder

1. Read word groups aloud. At stop and drop of voice, use a period.
2. Read word groups from the last complete thought to the first complete thought. Look for subject and verb to test completeness.
3. Count sentences.
4. Recognize run-on stop signs:

Run-on Fixer

1. Use end marks between complete sentences. Use capital letter for next word after period.
2. Use a semicolon. Start next word with small letter.
3. Use a conjunction:
   a. With one of these, use a comma directly before: *and, or, nor, but, for.*

> a. Group I: *then, now, however, finally, there, consequently, moreover, therefore.*
> b. Group II: *it, she, you, I, we, he, they.*
>
> b. With one of these, use the comma after the whole word group is completed and when the word group opens a sentence: *because, since, while, although, as, when.*
> 4. Never use only a comma to separate complete sentences.

Step. 3. Avoiding the Run-on Mistake. Follow directions given in each statement below.

1. Write two sentences about jogging in the park. Start the second sentence with the word *it.* _____

   _____

   _____

2. Write two complete thoughts about your best friend, separating them with a semicolon. Open the second thought with the word *however.*

   _____

   _____

   _____

3. Write a pair of sentences about pollution, opening the second sentence with the word *there* or *now.* _____

   _____

   _____

   _____

4. Write three sentences about television violence. Use the word *it* to start the second sentence. Use the word *moreover* to start the third sentence.

   _____

   _____

   _____

   _____

Step 4. Stop-sign Words in Sentences. Use correctly in the blank space the *stop sign* that appears in parentheses before each set of word groups. Use correct punctuation and capitals when needed.

(however)   1. Barry hoped _____ that you would accept his apology.

(then)   2. Hans hailed a taxi _____ the bus came.

(they)   3. When you ride the horses _____ must be wiped down afterwards.

(there)   4. The young boys licked their lips _____ were two apple pies on the counter before them.

(however)   5. I love to cook _____ I hate to wash the dishes afterwards.

(finally)   6. She waited by the phone for an hour _____ it rang.

(there)   7. If you want to learn how to cut the wheat properly _____ are several steps to follow.

(consequently)   8. I watched soap operas instead of studying for the final exam _____ I failed the course.

(I)   9. As I turned the corner, I saw the ambulance in front of my house _____ was so scared!

(therefore)   10. Many college students need extra money to help meet expenses _____ they have part-time jobs.

Step 5. Correcting Sentence Errors. In the blank lines after these run-on errors, rewrite the sentences correctly in any way you wish. Write *C* if the sentence is already correct.

1. I watch the stars from my bedroom window it's such a peaceful sight.

_____

_____

2. In my tea I prefer lemon it destroys the bitter taste. _____

_____

3. Skiing is an exciting, stimulating sport however, on an icy slope skiing can be dangerous. _____

_____

4. Cattle, moreover, would not be able to graze in such a dry climate.

_____

_____

5. My sister spent her junior year studying in France then she returned to Boston to finish her degree. _____

_____

6. I stood there in the hospital waiting room, my mind went blank for a second then details of the wreck started coming back to me. _____

_____

7. Since he was my cousin, I trusted him however I found out that he had lied to me. _____

_____

8. Because my mother was ill, we called an ambulance it came immediately. _____

_____

9. What did he tell you I am younger than his sister? _____

_____

10. It was no longer a feeling of friendship that was inside me, it was a feeling of love, I adored Ellen. _____

_____

WRITING THE PARAGRAPH

Student Samples

Your first assignment is to write a paragraph of at least ten sentences that bring a room to life. Read the paragraph below, written by a student in response to the same assignment. When you finish reading, write the answers to the questions about the topic sentence and about concrete sensory detail.

The Gloom Room

On this dreary October afternoon in my writing class here on the second floor of Boylan Hall at Brooklyn College, a shadow of gloom hangs over the people and things that surround me. The atmosphere is depressing. There is an old brown chair beside the teacher's desk, a mahogany bookcase with a missing shelf, and this ugly desk of mine filled with holes and scratches. As I rub my hand across its surface, there is a feeling of coldness. Even the grey walls and the rumble of thunder outside reflect the atmosphere of seriousness as we write our first theme of the semester. When some air sails through an open window beside me, there is the annoying smell of coffee grounds from a garbage pail not far off. My classmates, too, show this mood of tension. Mary, a slim blonde at my right, chews frantically the inside of her lower lip. Only one or two words in blue ink stand upon her clean white page. David Harris, slouched in his seat in the third row, nibbles each finger of each hand. Then he plays inaudibly with a black collar button that stands open on the top of his red plaid shirt. There is a thump as he uncrosses his legs and his scuffed shoe hits the floor. A painful cough slices the air from behind me. I hear a woman's heels click from the hall beyond the closed door and a car engine whine annoyingly from Bedford Avenue. If a college classroom should be a place of delight and pleasure, that could never be proved by the tension in this room.

—Harry Golden

Step 1. Understanding the Selection.

1. Underline the topic sentence.
2. What key word (or words) shows Harry Golden's opinion of the subject he is writing about?
3. There are two things in particular that Harry Golden will discuss about his writing class, and he announces them both in the topic sentence. What are they?
4. Pick out three groups of words that describe sounds.
5. Pick out three word groups that use color to paint a picture.
6. Tell in your own words two specific actions you see in Harry Golden's theme.
7. Which sentence appeals to the sense of smell?
8. Which words include an appeal to the sense of touch?
9. Which word picture, in your opinion, is most vivid?
10. Why does Harry Golden mention the time of year and time of day in the first sentence?

Step 2. More Sample Themes.

As you read the themes below, make note of the vivid pictures the writer paints of the room she is describing. Underline the topic sentence. Circle words that show color, sound, smell, or touch. Put a check in the margin next to the line that you think contains the best word picture in the paragraph. Afterwards, answer the questions.

SOME WORDS TO KNOW BEFORE YOU READ

sulky: gloomy
stark: harsh, stiff, rigid
loom: to come into sight with an appearance of great size
menacing: threatening to cause evil or harm
anesthetist: a physician who administers the drug that lets a patient lose the
        sensation of pain during an operation
reel: to sway or rock from dizziness

A Birth Room

At General Hospital there I lay on stark white sheets in a stark white room, only a large clock with black hands, a worm-eaten chair, and a window in my view, as I waited with fear for the arrival of my first born. While the sulky, snowy January dawn rolled lazily through the window, I could see the wind making snow drifts outside and could feel it blow crystals through the rotting window sill. Overhead loomed a menacing light pressed to a vast white ceiling. In front of me an orderly in a green nylon gown cheerily imprisoned my ankles in metal stirrups. "Don't fret none honey," she said. "You ain't the first to have a baby." I forced a smile, but then a sharp pain in my back made me twitch. It passed in a moment although I swore I saw black spots growing on the empty walls. I looked to my left as I ran my fingers over the worn leather straps that held my wrists. The thin second hand moved swiftly on the clock near the door. It was five after seven. Behind me the anesthetist, all in white with mask in hand, fussed with some metal tools, and I saw his intense black eyes darting swiftly. The sudden smell of alcohol nauseated me. In the distance I heard moans reverberating down the corridors—moans of women in labor. I felt reassured about this, for I was one step higher. I was in the delivery room; they still suffered in the labor rooms. To my right Dr. Kassop paced inaudibly, his rubber shoes sliding on the polished green tiles. Then he moved close and with warm fingers touched my brow. How such a small thing can be so comforting! Near my feet Nurse Day bustled about adjusting the tubes from a bottle hanging upside down on a metal stand. No sympathy for a frightened person from her, I thought. To her it was just another birth. Then as I stared at those erupting black spots on the walls I heard a liquid splashing. Suddenly I felt the icy coldness of antiseptic between my thighs as a cry of "Oye!" from a Spanish woman far off rang in my ears. A great pain made me scream and the stark white room reeled. Was that my new baby's cry? That's all I remember. The anesthetist covered my nose with the sharp, welcome smell of his medicine as everything went blank, my fears and the white birth room lost in sleep.

—Gwendolyn Wellington

My Bedroom

My tranquil bedroom is my favorite room in the house. As I stand at the door looking in, the first thing I see on the far side of the room is a yellow wall, its soft color framing a computer printout picture of my boyfriend Clyde and me. Underneath it is a bed covered with a flowered bedspread and, to the left, my night table, holding a beige telephone, a small lamp, and a radio alarm clock. Behind the night table fresh air from my window gently rustles the yellow and green curtains back and forth. A toy red snake lying on top of the curtain rod smiles down at me. When I pull the door behind me, it squeaks. I feel a burst of air sailing through, carrying with it the scent of lemon soap from the bathroom down the hall. As I turn to examine the wall where the door is, I see my twelve drawer bureau. The polished mahogany glistens, showing me my reflection. To protect the wood from scratches, a white dresser scarf sits on top in a neat square. On top of it are a black and white television set, a wooden jewelry box, three bottles of perfume, and a baby picture of me in a silver frame. Hanging on the wall beside my dresser is a calendar with large black numbers. For October there is a picture of a brown and white kitten playing gently with a ball of wool. When I hear a hissing sound, I realize that the steam is coming up; in the corner below the calendar my lavender-painted radiator clamors for attention. Above it on the adjacent wall are three bookshelves. The top shelf holds some dusty hardcover novels and my history books on the Civil War; the middle shelf holds the paperback novels, plays, and biographies I've collected over the years; and the bottom shelf supports stacks of disco record albums, copies of *Ebony, People,* and *TV Guide,* loose papers, and all my samples of lipstick and nail polish. After I select a book from one of the shelves, pull off my socks and shoes, and run my toes through the soft shag carpet, I lie down on the bed to enjoy my peaceful room.

—Tanya M. Fitzgerald

1. What words in each closing sentence go back to the topic and attitude expressed in the topic sentence?
2. What are some transitions the writers use? Make a list of at least ten.
3. Why does Gwendolyn Wellington call the room *stark*? Why does she say "Overhead *loomed* a *menacing* light" instead of "Overhead *was* a light"?
4. What words in Tanya Fitzgerald's theme best name sounds? smells? actions?

Some Topics for Your Paragraphs on a Room

Select some indoor place you know well and plan to write a paragraph that describes the place clearly. You might want to choose one of these topics:

1. a concert auditorium
2. a college classroom
3. a locker room
4. your kitchen
5. a favorite restaurant
6. a doctor's (or a dentist's) office
7. your place of worship
8. the library
9. the place where you work
10. a pet shop
11. a garage
12. a railroad car
13. a hardware store
14. your bedroom
15. the waiting room in an airline terminal
16. a record shop
17. a movie house
18. a basement
19. a biology or a chemistry laboratory
20. a clothing store

Prewriting: Overcoming the Mental Block

Handing in a paper written for someone else to read is the last in a series of steps writers take to produce their work. Writing begins long before writers put pens to paper. A convenient word to describe many of the steps that lead up to the actual writing of a first draft is *prewriting.*

WHAT IS PREWRITING?

Prewriting is a set of activities writers use to shake loose ideas and details before writing begins. In order to limit a topic and to uncover possible ideas about it, you have to let your thoughts take shape informally. When you actually begin writing a paragraph, then you can develop and refine ideas you have already had a chance to examine.

Some prewriting techniques many writers use include:

1. making lists
2. brainstorming
3. making subject trees
4. preparing scratch outlines or other kinds of groupings for ideas
5. looking at what other writers have written on the same topic
6. doing timed writing
7. limiting broad topics
8. doing free association
9. doing research
10. conducting interviews

Various chapters in this book define and explain these techniques so that you will have a chance to practice them for different writing tasks.

Making Lists

Since good descriptive writing requires a number of strong sensory images, recording those images in lists is a valuable prewriting technique. With a list of many images before you, you can build a description alive in detail.

PREWRITING: MAKING LISTS OF SENSORY IMAGES

Topic: Gino's Pizza Parlor

Sight	Sound	Smell
fingers kneading white dough	ring of a cash register	tangy smell of garlic and pepper
bubbling mozzarella cheese	quarters and dimes clinking on the blue counter	cigarette smoke
red tomato paste		hot dough
		sweet orange soda

crisp brown crust

cries of "One
slice and a coke

rumble of the
juke box

Touch

wave of heat from
the oven
hot olive oil
on my fingers
cool ceramic counter
icy cup of Coke
greasy dollar

Taste

spicy sauce
fiery sausage
hot, bland cheese

—Lisa Roth

Step 1. Exploring Lists of Images. Look at Lisa Roth's lists of sensory images. Answer these questions about them.

1. Which image do you find most original? Where does the writer combine senses to create especially clear pictures?
2. Using any one or a combination of images on her list, write a complete sentence alive in sensory language.
3. What single dominant impression could you suggest to help the writer organize her details? How would you incorporate that impression in a topic sentence?

Step 2. Listing Ideas in Groups. Once you have selected the place you want to describe, develop images (see page 6) under various sense headings. Write *sight, sound, smell, touch,* and *taste* above five columns on a blank sheet of paper. Under each heading develop images about the place you are describing. (Remember, images of action and color go under *sight.* And you may not be able to come up with images under *taste,* the most difficult of the senses to convey in language.)

Practice making lists of this kind with one of the topics suggested below if you are not yet sure about your own topic. Study Lisa Roth's example on page 36.

1. your kitchen at breakfast
2. a local grocery
3. the college library
4. a dance in a gym or in a ballroom
5. a fast-food restaurant

Manuscript Form

A manuscript is the final copy of an author's created work. It should be carefully prepared before it is submitted. Mess up your first and later copies all you like. Draw arrows. Cross out words. Draw pictures. Use purple ink or crayon or pencil. Use scissors to cut out words and sentences. Paste or tape the words in new positions where they make more sense. Rip up pages you don't like and start again. Your first effort, called a *draft,* is a worksheet for you, the writer. But as soon as you expect someone to read and to react to what you have written, you have to prepare your work so it follows correct manuscript form. Your instructor will insist that your paper be clean and easy to read and that you follow procedures most professional writers follow before they submit their manuscripts.

1. Leave wide margins (1 to 1½ inches) on all four sides.
2. Write in ink on one side of each page only. Use regulation theme paper if you write by hand. If you type, use sturdy bond 8½- by 11-inch typing paper. Do not use onionskin. Use blue or black ink: nothing fancy.
3. Make sure your name, your class, and the date appear where your instructor asks for them.
4. If you write by hand, *print* all your capital letters (this makes them easier to read). Leave a large space after each end mark. Make periods firm and clear. They remind you that you are starting a new idea in a new sentence.
5. Check your theme by proofreading (look ahead to pages 38–39) for careless errors.
6. Occasional errors may be corrected with correction fluid or with a good ink or typewriter eraser.

IF YOU WRITE THE COMPOSITION IN CLASS

1. Do not plan on rewriting: you will not have time.
2. Think for several minutes about the topic. Spend a minute or two examining the topic sentence you write.
3. Jot down some ideas on scrap paper. If an outline helps you, draw one up quickly (see pages 152–153).
4. You are still responsible for errors. Check your theme by proofreading (see

below for careless mistakes. Save at least five minutes at the end of the session to proofread.

5. Most instructors encourage you to use a dictionary and thesaurus even when you write your composition in class. Check with your teacher, and if it is all right, look up words to check spelling errors. See pages 383–384 and 389–390 for reminders on using the dictionary and thesaurus.

Proofreading

Proofreading is a convenient term to name what writers do when they look over their work for errors.

As a writer you should not expect to proofread your writing at all stages of creation. There's not much point in worrying about being correct when you are trying to develop ideas in a rough draft. In fact, the *last* thing you want to think about as your ideas first take shape on paper is correctness. Drafts are for putting thoughts down clearly and logically.

When you revise each draft you look especially for ways of improving your language and the structure of your sentences. Part of that process will involve correcting major sentence errors of the kinds explained in this chapter and in other parts of the book.

Productive proofreading takes place at two critical stages in the writing of any paper. First, you need to check for errors in the draft that you will turn into a final manuscript. Next, you need to check over your final manuscript itself to make sure that no errors have slipped by.

The suggestions below will help you locate careless mistakes that may appear in your writing.

TIPS FOR EFFECTIVE PROOFREADING

1. Read *slowly.* This is not a job done by skimming. Look at—and read aloud, if necessary—every word. Don't let your eyes move too swiftly from one word to the next.
2. Use a ruler or a blank sheet of paper below each line; this will help you locate spelling errors by cutting off later words from your line of vision. Block any words that may distract you on the line you are checking. The fewer words you examine at a time, the easier it is to find spelling errors.
3. Examine each syllable of each word. Try pointing at each word as you pronounce it to see if it is correct.
4. Be aware of your own usual errors. A glance at your Progress Sheet (page 429) before you do any written work puts you on your guard. If you're a chronic run-on writer, know the run-on Stop Signs. If you write fragments, know the fragment Stop Signs. (See pages 61 and 101.) If you usually confuse *its* and *it's* and you have used one of those words in your paragraph, stop for a second to analyze the spelling you've chosen.
5. If you are writing in class, cross out errors neatly or erase them neatly. Some students like to skip lines in order to insert any words or ideas left out through

carelessness. If you've left out a word or words, draw a caret (∧) below the line and insert what was omitted. Do it this way:

So we awakened early and ∧ˢᵗᵒ ᵗʰᵉ went ᵗᵒ ᵗʰᵉ beach

6. You can't look up every word to check spelling, but you do know which words you are unsure of. *Look them up in the dictionary.* And keep a record of the words you usually spell wrong (see Your Own Demon List, page 382).
7. You can make minor corrections on your final manuscript, but if too many errors require corrections there, you should consider it as a draft and should write another manuscript to submit.

Step 1. Practice with Proofreading. Correct these errors by following the suggestions above.

The nicist think about raining dayes at our country home was the opportunite to play in in the attic. Are attic was with old stage costums witch are grandparents wore many years a go. There collection of wiggs an beeded dresses kept us busie for hours, for instance, i was always pretended that I was a beatiful princes who would be rescud by a hansome Prince, I whish I could relieve those child hood days.

FOLLOW-UP: AFTER YOUR INSTRUCTOR RETURNS YOUR GRADED THEME

1. Check your paper to make sure that you understand your instructor's writing and any correction symbols used in the margin.
2. Correct all errors in mechanics—grammar, spelling, and punctuation.
3. Rewrite your entire paper if your instructor suggests that you do so. Correct

> problems in content and thought development, using the comments in the margin to guide you.
> 4. Enter on page 382 all the words you misspelled.
> 5. Enter on the Theme Progress Sheet (Appendix B) the total number of errors you made in each category listed on top of the page. In that way you can see before you write the next theme just what kinds of mistakes you usually make.

Requirements

Make your theme lively, vivid, and well organized by following carefully the directions given in the checklist below.

A Checklist of Requirements: Theme 1

1. Think carefully about the topic. Select for description some place that is especially clear in your mind, a place you can make alive with concrete sensory detail. If you select a place that you can visit again before you write, so much the better. In that way you can gather fresh sensory responses.
2. Do prewriting (see page 35) that works best for you. You might want to try listing sensory images in groups. Read on pages 31–34 the student themes as models for your own writing.
3. From your prewriting activities prepare a rough draft in which you write consecutive sentences that describe as best you can the place you have selected.
4. Write as many other drafts as you need to shape your ideas clearly. When you prepare your final draft, be sure to follow the guidelines on pages 37–38.
5. Proofread your paper twice: once *before* you prepare your final manuscript and once *after* you prepare it. (See pages 38–39.)
6. Write a topic sentence that includes an opinion and states clearly what your topic will be. Make sure the topic is properly limited.
7. Mention time and place as early as possible in the paragraph.
8. Use at least three words that appeal to the sense of *sound.* See page 5 for some new "sound" vocabulary.
9. Use at least three *colors* in different places throughout the theme.
10. If you can, mention the names of people you see. Show people as they perform some action: Harry Golden says that Mary chews the inside of her lip. Gwendolyn Wellington shows Dr. Kassop pacing the floor.
11. Give the reader an idea of your surroundings by describing parts of the room. Try to make the details support the opinion word you state in the topic sentence.
12. Use at least one group of words to appeal to the sense of *touch* and one group of words to appeal to the sense of *smell.*
13. Give your paragraph a title. *A title is not a topic sentence. If you can use part of the topic in your title, you must still repeat the topic in the topic sentence* (see pages 95–97).

14. *a.* Write one sentence that uses the semicolon correctly. See pages 17–20.
    b. Use at least one of the *run-on stop signs* to open a complete-thought word group. See pages 27–28.
    c. Try to use one or two words from the vocabulary introduced at the beginning of the chapter.
15. Check your theme for errors, especially for run-ons and for the spelling problems noted in this chapter.
16. Don't jump too quickly from one feature of your subject to another. As you describe some person or thing, take two or three sentences to show clearly what you see before you move on to another aspect of your subject.
17. Use words like *up front, to my left, nearby, across the room, far away, above, beside, in the corner* to help you move from one thing you wish to describe to another.
18. In the last sentence of your paper, be sure to let your reader know that your paragraph is coming to an end (see pages 178–180).

THE PROFESSIONALS SPEAK

The details of a room are essential parts of good fiction. Writers know that to make a firm impression on the reader's mind, they must give lively sensory images so that the scene may be easily visualized.

Step 1. A Vivid Kitchen.   Read the selection below and answer the questions on sensory language.

SOME WORDS TO KNOW BEFORE YOU READ

contend: to struggle in opposition
recessed: set back
mantelpiece: the shelf above a fireplace
hearthstone: a stone forming the place where fire can be made
partition: something that divides
rubbly: rough
inflexibly: in a way that is rigid
welt: a swelling on the surface of the body
perpetual: happening all the time

The Kitchen

   The kitchen was living room, dining room, and cooking room. There were two long narrow windows in one wall. An iron coalrange was recessed in another wall. Above the stove the recess was made of coral-colored bricks and creamy white plaster. It had a stone mantelpiece and a slate hearthstone on which Francie could draw pictures with chalk. Next to the stove was a water boiler which got hot when the fire was going. Often on a cold day, Francie came in chilled and put her arms around the boiler and pressed her frosty cheek gratefully against its warm silveriness. Next to the boiler was a pair of soapstone washtubs with a hinged wooden cover. The partition could be removed and the two thrown into one for a bath tub. It didn't make a very good bath tub. Sometimes when Francie sat in it, the cover banged down on her head. The bottom was rubbly and she came out of what should have been a refreshing bath, all sore from sitting on that wet roughness. Then there were four faucets to contend with. No matter how the child tried to remember that they were inflexibly there and wouldn't give way, she would jump up suddenly out of the soapy water and get her back whacked good on a faucet. Francie had a perpetual angry welt on her back.

—Betty Smith
A Tree Grows in Brooklyn

1. Which two word groups identify colors?
2. Name two verbs that tell a sound.
3. Underline the one sentence that you think shows the liveliest action.
4. Lines 7 and 8 contain four words that appeal to touch. What are they? What other sentences use touch words?
5. Circle any words that show transition.

Step 2. A Room in a Boarding House. In the selection below, the writer creates a mood in the place he describes by mixing his own thoughts with specific images of the room. How would you say the writer's inner feelings compare with the physical environment he describes? When you finish reading, answer the questions that follow.

My Room at the Lilac Inn

As I look around this room in this third-rate boarding house, my eyes are greeted first by the entrance to its gloomy interior. The door is painted a dirty cream color. There is a crack in one panel. The ceiling is the same dingy color with pieces of adhesive tape holding some of the plaster in place. The walls are streaked and cracked here and there. Also on the walls are pieces of Scotch tape that once held, I presume, some sexy girls, pictures of *Esquire Magazine* origin. Across the room runs a line; upon it hang a shirt, a grimy towel, and washed stump socks belonging to my roommate, Jack Nager. By the door near the top sash juts a piece of wood on which is hung—it looks like an old spread. It is calico, dirty, and a sickly green color.

Behind that is a space which serves as our closet; next to that is the radiator, painted the same ghastly color. The landlady must have got the paint for nothing. On top is Jack's black suitcase, his green soap dish, and a brightly colored box containing his hair tonic. Over by the cracked window are a poorly made table and chair. On top of the table, a pencil, shaving talcum, a glass, a nail file; one of my socks hangs over the side. Above the table is our window, the curtains of cheese cloth held back by a string. There is also a black, fairly whole paper shade to dim such little sunlight as might enter.

This window is my only promise of a better future. Through it, I can see the well-lit and nicely furnished living room of a modern apartment house across the street. Someday I'll live like that.

There, next to the window, leaning against an aged bureau, as if resting, are my faithful crutches. On the oilcloth covering the top of the bureau lie some seventeen odd books. These I used at the _____ University here in Washington, D.C. I am attending a six-month course, getting the fundamentals needed to be a Service Officer for veterans. There are enough books on that bureau to take at least a year's reading for absorption. Beard's *American Government and Policy, Anatomy, How to Interview, Soldier to Civilian,* government laws, manuals, textbooks, a public speaking guide and what-have-you are all reflected in the cloudy mirror. On the bureau stands a picture of my love, my faithful wife. I think of her. I wish I were with her tonight.

Standing alongside this bureau is this *thing*. A leather cup, straps and buckles dropping from it. Below this cup, the flesh-colored *thing* and calf, and on its foot a brown sock and oxblood shoe. This is a prosthesis. I've called this wooden leg a lot of other things. This is the replacement for the real one that was shot off in France. O, what the hell! A leg isn't everything. You've got to keep living. There are a lot worse things in this world to reckon with than an artificial leg.

On the parlor chair, here probably because there's no other place for it, my brown pants are thrown, together with my old khaki shirt. On the floor my recently painted foot locker that was in many an army camp with me is still doing service.

Jack Nager grunts alongside me in the double bed as he turns over; he is getting a good sleep tonight. His below-the-knee stump quivers as he touches some close-to-the-skin nerve on the bed. His foot was also a donation for democracy. I reach to turn out the twenty-five watt bulb on the shadeless lamp; I find the light switch. The room is in darkness. From the street three stories below comes the sound of a motor car; it fades away. Occasionally a click, click of heels hitting the pavement as someone passes by. Within the house the sound of muffled voices, the flushing of a toilet, someone blowing his nose.

I forget everything and concentrate on sleep.

—John J. Regan in
The Purple Testament,
ed. Don M. Wolfe

1. What key word or words in the first sentence show the writer's attitude toward the place he is describing? In the first paragraph and a half, there are several words that repeat this attitude.
2. Which images best appeal to your senses of sight and sound?
3. Where do the writer's thoughts take over from the actual description of the place?
4. What is a prosthesis? Notice how John Regan gives you the definition of the word in the sentence after he uses it.
5. In the first two paragraphs what hints do you find that suggest who and what the writer is? Where do you actually learn that he is a veteran and that he is wounded?
6. How does the physical setting of the room compare with the writer's inner thoughts and feelings?

REACHING HIGHER

Step 1. Photo into Words.   Look at the photograph on page 3. Decide what kind of room it shows; then, decide on your own attitude toward the room as it is represented. Write a topic sentence. In a paragraph of fifteen to twenty sentences, support the opinion in your topic sentence with lively sensory details. Use a variety of words to show color and action. Imagine the sounds you might hear and some of the touch sensations you would experience: include these as well in the paragraph. Identify people you might see by using clear images.

Step 2. Run-ons in a Paragraph. Correct the run-on errors by changing some of the punctuation in the paragraph below. Capitalize the first letter of any word that starts a sentence. You may add words if you wish. Study the charts on pages 28–29 for review.

The Living Room

On this clear, crisp October afternoon I lie on the brown carpet with my back resting against an over-stuffed armchair, I survey my comfortable living room. Frayed upholstery covers the chair and the matching couch next to me from the fireplace on my right drifts the aroma of burning wood, however the smell of pot roast and mushroom gravy is in strong competition. The warmth emitted from the first fire of the season pervades the room suddenly with a crack and a sputter a few glowing cinders elude the wire screen and jump onto the smooth red brick beside me. Nearby, my four year old daughter, Lisa, lounges on the floor lazily she draws pictures with orange and red crayons. To my left a maroon velvet chair and three polished wood nesting tables cast soft shadows onto the pink walls above them hangs a large portrait of a kind looking old man he has luxurious blue eyes and his dark mustache curls upwards at the corners. A little to the left, on the white mantle-piece, sits the walnut clock it whirs, then it chimes the hour in ringing tones, six times, as I struggle up from the floor.

Step 3. Describing a Person. For further practice in description focus a paragraph on a person you observe. Ask one of the people in the class to stand in front of the room as a model. As you watch the person up front, decide on one single impression that the person creates: is the man or woman *handsome, nervous, playful, cheerful, charming, serious, strange, relaxed, confident*? After you state the impression in the topic sentence, describe the details that you feel contribute to that impression. Use images (see page 6) to discuss the person's face, clothing, stance, gestures, and way of speaking to the class. Read your brief paragraphs aloud, as your instructor directs. But before you write, study the following sample and the chart of hints.

Richard

Richie Fries sits confidently atop the brown desk before us on this English theme day in late November. He speaks immediately, brown eyes sparkling at his audience of fellow classmates. His pressed blue shirt stresses his tall straight posture as his hand motions express words. He scratches his neat black hair as if in thought.

"Next question!" he says. "Gotta wake you up. Ya look like you're falling asleep." The class watches his every expression, but there is no sign of nervousness in Richard, not a drop of sweat falling from his brow. "Look at me," his apple cheeks shout, "Look at me," his smile says. "Look," his position at the edge of the table screams. "Look at me. This is my moment of glory." His actual words race by at record pace. "My father tells me I should think in seventy-eight and talk in thirty-three," Rich speedily adds. Susan asks him to smile and change his position. Propping himself upon his elbow, he leans back on the desk. "Hey, why isn't this guy in Hollywood?" I think to myself. His eyes dance. They illuminate when he talks and glow softly when he is silent. His exciting brown eyes hold the class in a strong grip. They are only brown, same as so many other eyes, but they twinkle and they bubble and they look squarely at their audience without so much as a nervous blink. His eyes smile even when his lips fall. The girls like him: he is lively, has a good physique—I suppose it is understandable. Michelle asks where he goes to meet girls and the class giggles squeamishly. After a long, funny answer, Richie leans back, the edges of his lips pushing his cheeks up. His brown eyes now stare at no one. Everybody is writing. He takes a deep breath. Then, in a sudden leap from the table Richie returns to his seat like a conqueror.

—Debbie Osher

HINTS FOR SUCCESSFUL PARAGRAPHS ABOUT A CLASSMATE

1. Mention in the first sentence the time, place, and the single impression you have of the student.
2. Use some details of setting. Debbie Osher says "brown desk."
3. Use only those details in the rest of the paragraph that contribute to the single impression. *Leave out any details that do not help create the impression.*
4. Mention the person's size, color of hair and eyes, clothing. Use images of sound, color, and touch.
5. Write a sentence that tells what the model says. Richard says, "My father tells me I should think in seventy-eight and talk in thirty-three."
6. Toward the end of the paragraph, describe the one feature of the person's face that gives you the impression you have. Notice how in "Richard" the writer concentrates on the eyes of her subject.

Step 4. Your Own Photo Essay. With an Instamatic camera or a Polaroid, take several pictures of some room. Try to take pictures that will convey *one* dominant impression you have about the room. You may want to show that the room is a *lively* place or one that is *tense, happy, dull, hectic,* or *somber.* When you get the photos back, mount them and present them to the class. Can other students determine from your pictures the impression you are trying to create?

chapter 2

THE BODY IN ACTION:
TELLING A STORY

INTRODUCTION: WRITING A NARRATIVE PAPER

If you ever screamed yourself hoarse watching a football game, if you ever ran miles along a river bank, or if you ever slid into home plate to break a tie, you know the delight of sports and exercise and their hold on our lives. Both as spectator and participant you can, no doubt, recall many experiences, some joyful, others bitter. Maybe you remember the fear you felt at learning to ride a bicycle, or the spirit of teamwork that allowed you to win the freestyle relay at the town pool. Perhaps you still hear your coach's shrill voice yelling at you, or recall your father's consoling words, "Well, you did your best." Perhaps some moments in sports gave you a better understanding of your character, such as the time you tried to hurt your opponent while playing soccer or the time you let a friend score a basket when you yourself might just as easily have made the points. Maybe you are one of those enthusiasts of lifetime sports, running or swimming or biking to keep your heart healthy. For you it is not simply competition that excites your blood: you enjoy the thrill of your body in action and the joy of mental release that accompanies vigorous exercise.

These moments that stand out vividly in your lives are the subjects for your next theme. The paragraph you write will narrate (tell a story about) a brief, meaningful event which you experienced with sports or exercise.

VOCABULARY

Step 1. Words for Actions. These words are useful in describing people's actions and help create specific pictures. Check a dictionary and write in the definitions in the blank spaces. See Appendix A for more help.

1. grimace _____

2. stagger _____

3. trot _____

4. swagger _____

5. saunter _____

6. plunge _____

7. careen _____

8. mutter _____

9. squirm _____

10. spurn _____

Step 2. Using New Vocabulary. Fill in each blank with a word from the list in Step 1 so that the sentences make sense.

1. In a voice so low we couldn't understand her, she _____ her answer.

2. Running leisurely down Main Street, Bob _____ over to the post office to mail his letter.

3. Balancing herself carefully on the high diving board, Mary suddenly _____ into the icy water.

4. Hurt, exhausted, and dirty, the defeated football players _____ into the dressing room.

5. The wrestler _____ across the room, boasting that no one could match his strength.

6. Enjoying his slow, relaxed walk, the old man _____ around the block.

7. Because the driver was tired, his Pontiac _____ from one side of the road to the other.

8. With a quick slap across his face, the young woman _____ her date's advances.

9. Discovering his error, he reddened and _____ with embarrassment.

10. At the thought of spending a day with the man she hated so, Leslie _____, and we could all see her face twisted with annoyance.

Step 3. How People Do or Say Things. The following words, all ending in -ly, are helpful in showing how people do or say things. Check them in a dictionary and write definitions. For more help, see Appendix A.

1. irresponsibly _____

2. contemptuously _____

3. sullenly _____

4. spontaneously _____

5. irritably _____

6. brazenly _____

7. precariously _____

8. painstakingly _____

9. meekly _____

10. vehemently _____

Step 4. Seeing the Words at Work.

1. When would you do something *vehemently*? _____
   _____

2. If someone behaved *meekly*, what would you expect him to do? _____
   _____

3. How could you tell if something was being done *spontaneously*? ____
   _____

4. Why might a child be behaving *sullenly*? _____

5. What types of workers would perform their jobs *precariously*? _____
   _____

6. If someone spoke *contemptuously*, how would you expect him to
   sound? _____

7. What kind of job would you do *painstakingly*? _____
   _____

8. How could you tell if someone acted *brazenly*? _____
   _____

9. How could someone tell if you were speaking *irritably*? _____
   _____

10. What would a group of children have to do for you to say that they were
    behaving *irresponsibly*? _____

BUILDING COMPOSITION SKILLS

Finding the Topic

One of the best ways to get ideas on any topic is to talk about and listen to
the ideas of the people around you. You can thus air out your own thoughts
and see how they sound before you begin to put them on paper. You also
get ideas about your own experiences when you hear the ideas your friends
may have.

Step 1. Talking about the Topic.   Pick any word group below and read it
aloud, adding your own ending. Then, in a few more sentences, explain what
you said. Or, if your instructor suggests, write down in a few brief sentences
your completion for any of the statements. Of course, you may use the name
of any sport in place of the one used in the sentences below.

1. I played well when . . . .
2. I lost the game to . . . .
3. A dangerous sport I like is . . . .
4. A game I'll never forget was . . . .
5. The value of sports is . . . .
6. Jogging makes me feel . . . .
7. One thing I hate about sports is . . . .
8. When I won my first game, I felt . . . .
9. When my coach yelled at me, I was . . . .
10. I wish my son (daughter) would play . . . .
11. When I swim, I . . . .
12. When it comes to riding horses, I . . . .
13. Watching a football game at a stadium is . . . .
14. When I learned to water ski, I . . . .
15. For bodily fitness my exercise is _____ because . . . .

Here are some students' responses:

A dangerous sport I like is skiing because the cold mountain air, the steep slopes, and the heart-pounding speed make me feel alive.

—Richard Young

I wish my son would play basketball more for enjoyment rather than for a victory over the other team. He takes the sport too seriously, and he broods over a loss for days.

—Willa Brown

I'll never forget the day I went fishing with my Uncle Seth on Lake Champlain. I remember he said, "Greg, today you're going to see the real me."

—Gregory Henderson

Expanding the Topic Sentence

An effective topic sentence is nicely limited when it mentions a topic specifically and gives your opinion about the topic that you want to discuss. (If you need a quick review, see Chapter 1.) But you can further limit the topic sentence—especially when you write a paragraph that tells a story—by showing where and when the event you are writing about takes place. By *where* we mean the room, the outdoor setting, the physical location in which the moment happened. By *when* we mean not the date but the season or month of the year, the part of the day, the day of the week. Sometimes a word of color or sound or touch helps the *when* and *where* details come to life. Here are two topic sentences that give the topic and opinion, tell when or where, and use a sense word.

     [time]   [place]   [opinion]

One winter evening in our school gymnasium I learned the importance of teamwork in basketball as the final bell clanged to end the game.

                                                                 [sound]

Topic: teamwork in basketball

     [time]   [place]   [opinion]

Every morning in the park I experience the agony of the long distance runner as I jog ten miles through the grey dawn.

                          [color]

Topic: jogging ten miles

Step 1. Adding Details. Add details of time or place or both to the topic sentences listed in Column I and rewrite them under Column II. If possible, use a sound, color, or touch word.

I

Example:

1. My husband loves the excitement of watching hockey.

2. Cheerleaders always helped our teams to win.
3. My coach embarrassed me in front of the other football players.
4. My father enjoys the peacefulness of trout fishing.

II

On weekend evenings in our living room my husband, lying on our green sofa, loves the excitement of watching hockey.

Step 2. Writing Sentence Openers. In each subject in Column I write a topic sentence that includes time and place, gives an opinion, and appeals in some way to one of the senses. Try to put the words that tell *where* or *when* right at the beginning of the sentence.

I

Example:

1. team practice sessions

2. watching a champion boxer
3. learning to swim
4. a terrible defeat

II

Every Saturday morning I hate dragging my football equipment to Washington Field to practice for the next week's game.

Step 3. Analyzing the Topic Sentence. Turn to the bottom of page 8. Look at the topic sentences numbered 1 and 2. What words tell the time of the event? Which of the topic sentences tells *place*?

Using Chronology: Time Order in Sequence of Events

Whenever you relate a moment, the events are easily understood when you write of them in the time order in which they happened. The arrangement of details or events according to time is *chronology.* Look at the two paragraphs below. The sentences on the right present the events in their order of occurrence, while those on the left jump around without logic from event to event.

Confused

On Wednesday evenings my uncle and I spend an enjoyable hour playing racquetball. On the way home we sometimes stop for a beer or ice cream; of course, the loser always pays the bill. We usually go into the sauna for ten minutes before hitting the showers. We change our clothing in the locker room, and play an exciting but exhausting hour of racquetball. My uncle picks me up in his station wagon and we zoom over to the Bethpage Racquetball Center. When I get home, I'm ready for a good night's sleep.

Chronological

On Wednesday evenings my uncle and I spend an enjoyable hour playing racquetball. After dinner, my uncle picks me up in his station wagon and we zoom over to the Bethpage Racquetball Center. After a quick change of clothing in the locker room, we play an exciting but exhausting hour of racquetball. Then we usually go into the sauna for ten minutes before hitting the showers. On the way home, we sometimes stop for beer or ice cream; of course, the loser always pays the bill. When I get home, I'm ready for a good night's sleep.

Step 1. Chronology. Write four sentences in chronological order about each subject named below.

1. catching a fish

    a. _____

    b. _____

    c. _____

    d. _____

2. brushing your teeth

    a. _____

    b. _____

    c. _____

    d. _____

3. studying for an exam

 a. _____

 b. _____

 c. _____

 d. _____

Step 2. Telling the Order.   Here is a good topic sentence that calls for a paragraph in *chronological order*. Write six or seven sentences after it in which you tell details in the order in which they might have occurred. Use a separate sheet of paper.

Camping out in a tent in Yellowstone National Park can be a very unpleasant experience in the early spring.

Expanding Sentences: -ly Openers for Variety

One way to avoid writing a paragraph whose sentences are too much alike is to start one or two of them with a word that ends in *-ly*. You have a number of these words (called *adverbs*) in your vocabulary already (*swiftly, slowly, annoyingly, suddenly*). Step 3 on page 48, introduces some new and more difficult *-ly* words.

Step 1. -ly Words for Variety.   On a separate sheet of paper use each *-ly* word in Step 3, page 48, to open a sentence of your own.

Example: Irritably my cousin screamed, "Beat it!"

Step 2. Two -ly Openers.   A very effective technique for opening sentences is to use two *-ly* words at the beginning. Separate the *-ly* words either with a comma or with *and* or *but*. Don't use two *-ly* words that mean exactly the same thing.

Slowly, annoyingly, the actor's voice filled the theater.
Strongly and cautiously, the lion stalked its prey.

   Write a sentence about each subject indicated below, starting each sentence with two *-ly* words. Use words from your own vocabulary and from the words in Step 3, page 48. Use a separate sheet of paper.

1. the sun shining after a rainstorm
2. an automobile speeding down the highway
3. getting out of bed in the morning
4. a cat licking its fur
5. sneaking twenty minutes late into a classroom.

SOLVING PROBLEMS IN WRITING

Using Quotations Correctly

One way of adding life to your narrative is to use the words spoken by a person who plays some part in your paragraph. It's usually more realistic and more lively to use the person's specific words rather than an indirect quotation, a statement which only summarizes what was said. Look at the difference:

1. My father said that I might be a good basketball player, but that he wanted me to study for my exam tomorrow.
2. My father shouted, "You might be a hot-shot basketball player, but I want you to study for that exam tomorrow!"

Sentence 2 has more force because it is a direct quotation; it lets the reader hear the person's exact words. Now, of course, if you are writing about a moment that occurred a while ago, it's impossible to remember *exactly* what a person said. Still, if you recall the general idea of the person's words, construct your sentence so that the reader hears it as a quotation.

Correct punctuation of quotations—exact words—is sometimes tricky. Remember that most quotation sentences have two parts: one part tells who is talking and how the person says the words; another part tells what is being said. These parts must be separated by punctuation. Study the charts below.

I. EXACT WORDS AT THE END

[quotation marks]
[capitalize first spoken word]

My father shouted, "You might be a hot-shot basketball player, but I want you to study for that exam tomorrow!"
[quotation marks]

[comma]   [end mark inside: period, question mark, or exclamation point]

Hint: If the same person speaks another sentence—without being interrupted—right after the first one, *don't* use another quotation mark. Put the last quotation mark after the very *last* word any one person speaks.

My father shouted, "You might be a hot-shot basketball player, but I want you to study for that exam tomorrow. I won't put up with any more failing grades."

Step 1. Correct Quotations.   Put in the correct punctuation for these sentences.

1. The defendant shouted I am innocent of all these charges
2. Will Rogers said I never met a man I didn't like

II. EXACT WORDS AT THE BEGINNING

[quotation marks]

[capital letter]   [small letter]

"You might be a hot-shot basketball player, but I want you to study for that exam tomorrow," my father shouted. ←——[period]

[comma, question mark, or exclamation point inside
[quotation marks]   quotation mark: no period]

Step 2. Writing Quotations.   Put in the correct punctuation for these sentences.

1. This will teach you a sense of responsibility my father snapped
2. I hope Dad comes home soon my sister said

III. EXACT WORDS BROKEN UP

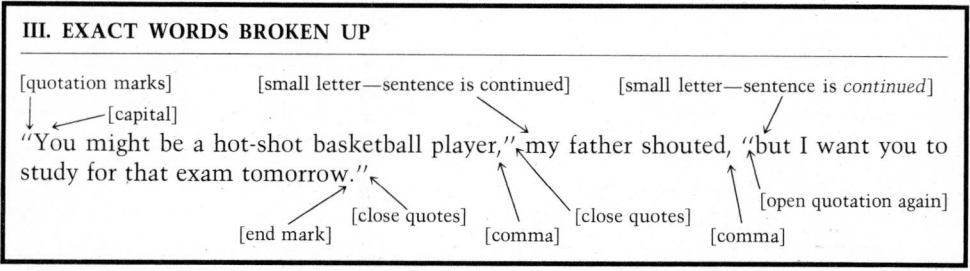

[quotation marks]   [small letter—sentence is continued]   [small letter—sentence is *continued*]

[capital]

"You might be a hot-shot basketball player," my father shouted, "but I want you to study for that exam tomorrow."

[open quotation again]

[close quotes]   [close quotes]

[end mark]   [comma]   [comma]

Step 3. Punctuating Quotations.   Punctuate these sentences correctly.

1. Didn't you know Barbara asked that Jim is in the hospital
2. If Paul were here Richard said he would know what to do

Hint: The question mark goes at the end of the complete question.

Step 4. Practice with Exact Words.   In Column I, write three sentences you have heard spoken recently. In Column II, rewrite each sentence with correct punctuation to show who did the talking. Sometimes a word like *shouted, muttered, whispered,* or *cried* is more vivid than *said.* In other sentences, *said* is adequate because the words in the quotation itself tell the tone the speaker is using. In one sentence, use the spoken words at the beginning; in another, use the spoken words at the end. In one sentence, break up the spoken words as in Chart III, above. One of each appears in the examples below.

I

Examples:

"Are you serious about joining the track team?"

"Hey, we'd better move or we'll be late for class."

"This cafeteria coffee is poisonous!"

1. _____

_____

_____

_____

2. _____

_____

_____

_____

3. _____

_____

_____

_____

II

Trying to stifle a laugh, my friend asked, "Are you serious about joining the track team?"

"Hey, we'd better move," someone insisted, "or we'll be late for class."

"This cafeteria coffee is poisonous!" gasped Peter, frowning.

_____

_____

_____

_____

_____

_____

_____

_____

_____

_____

_____

_____

Sentence Fragments: Phase I

The *fragment* is an incomplete part of a sentence used as though it were a sentence itself. Here are some fragments that are easy to recognize.

1. Over the curb and into the street.
2. Pushing angrily through the crowds.
3. Just to play his radio quietly.
4. Usually exhausted from lifting heavy cartons.

None of these fragments makes any real sense. Since a sentence contains a complete thought and has a subject and a verb (see the sentence review on pages 14–16) the word groups above are not sentences.

Fragment 1 has no subject or verb. *What* is being done over the curb and into the street? *Who* is doing it?

Fragment 2 has no subject (*Who* does the pushing?) and only a part of a verb—the word *pushing.*

Fragment 3 has no subject (*Who* plays the radio?) and only part of a verb—the words *to play*. (You may recall that when *to* is used like this, what results is merely the starting point of the verb: it is not a verb itself.)

Fragment 4 has no subject (*Who* was exhausted after lifting heavy cartons?). The word group would also need a word like *is* or *was* in order to be complete. Here *exhausted* without a helper is no verb.

Each fragment, 1, 2, 3, 4 above, separated from the sentence that comes before it, is easy to recognize because it really makes no sense. But now look at the fragments as they appear as parts of paragraphs and read the explanations alongside.

Fragment

1. *a.* In a square of pavement down the block a small dog played with a rubber ball, but it rolled out of his reach. *b.* He rushed after it. *c.* Over the curb and into the street.

2. *a.* Holiday shopping is always a difficult task. *b.* Every store I visit overflows with noisy shoppers. *c.* Pushing angrily through the crowds. *d.* I'll try to shop earlier next year.

3. *a.* It is important to understand that teenagers often require privacy. *b.* For an hour or two a boy wishes to be left alone in his room. *c.* Just to play his radio quietly.

4. *a.* My mother works very long hours to support our family. *b.* She trudges home at eight o'clock every evening. *c.* Usually exhausted from lifting heavy cartons. She falls asleep by nine-thirty.

Explanation

Here a student might think that the subject *he* and the verb *rushed* in sentence *b* would also serve as subject and verb in word group *c*. But that is not the case. Word group *c* is a fragment because it lacks its own subject and verb. The capital letter in *over* and the period after *street* indicate that the writer thought the sentence a complete one.

Here, a student might think that the word *shoppers* in sentence *b* would serve as the subject in word group *c*. But word group *c* must have its own subject. Furthermore, the word *pushing* is not a verb: if *is* or *was* appeared before it, or if the word were *pushed* instead of *pushing*, it would be a verb. But as it stands, word group *c* is also a fragment because it lacks a verb.

Here, it is possible that an inexperienced writer would imagine the word *boy* in sentence *b* serves as the subject in word group *c*. But word group *c* must have its own subject to be complete. In addition, *to play* is no verb. We need to add a word such as *wants* or *likes* before the infinitive. Sometimes the infinitive can be changed to a verb: *plays, played*, or *is playing*. But as it stands, word group *c* is also a fragment because it lacks a verb.

Here, the writer gives no subject in word group *c*. Furthermore, *exhausted*—as it is used—is only a part of a verb. It must have *is* or *was* or some such word before it. So, word group *c* is also a fragment because it lacks a verb.

Fixing Fragments. Knowing that sentence fragments lack subjects, complete verbs, or both, you should not find this kind of sentence error difficult to correct.

1. Add a subject and a verb to make the sentence complete.

Correct this Fragment

Over the curb and into the street.

This Way

[added subject]
The dog jumped over the curb and into the street. [added verb]

Pushing angrily through the crowds.

[subject]
They are pushing angrily through the crowds. [word added to make verb]
They push angrily through the crowds. [-*ing* word changed to verb]

Just to play his radio quietly.

[subject]
He just wants to play his radio quietly. [word added to make verb]
He just plays his radio quietly. [infinitive changed to verb]

Usually exhausted from lifting heavy cartons.

[subject]
She is usually exhausted from lifting heavy cartons. [word added to make verb]

Step 1. Completing Sentences. The last word group in each item below is a fragment. Rewrite the fragment in the space provided and add a subject, a verb, or both in order to make the sentence complete. You may wish to change an -*ing* word or an infinitive to a verb; or you may wish to add a new verb as a helper.

1. I swaggered out of the classroom. Knowing that I passed the exam.

   _____
   _____
   _____

2. Imagine my disappointment when I went to the refrigerator and looked for the apples. Already eaten by my brother Juan.

   _____
   _____
   _____
   _____

3. Millions of people are jogging. To stay fit and healthy.

   _____
   _____

_____

_____

2. Another way to fix the fragment is to connect it to the sentence that comes before it. In that way you legitimately give the fragment the subject and verb it needs by using words of another sentence. Notice how the last two sentences in 1, 2, and 3 on page 57 may be joined together to eliminate the fragment:

Correct the Fragment

He rushed after it. Over the curb and into the street.

Every store I visit overflows with noisy shoppers. Pushing angrily through the crowds.

For an hour or two a boy wishes to be left alone in his room. Just to play his radio quietly.

This Way

He rushed after it, over the curb and into the street. [small letter] [no period]

Every store I visit overflows with noisy shoppers, pushing angrily through the crowds. [no period] [small letter]

For an hour or two a boy wishes to be left alone in his room just to play his radio quietly. [no period] [small letter]

3. A fragment may be corrected effectively by attaching it to the sentence that comes after it.

Correct the Fragment
Usually exhausted from lifting heavy cartons. She falls asleep by nine-thirty.

This Way
Usually exhausted from lifting heavy cartons, she falls asleep by nine-thirty. [comma] [small letter]

Here is another example:

Correct the Fragment
Hearing the photographer talk about his travels through Alaska. Audiences responded with enthusiasm.

This Way
Hearing the photographer talk about his travels through Alaska, audiences responded with enthusiasm. [comma] [small letter]

Hint: When you open a sentence with a fragment that contains an *-ing* verb part or an *-ed* verb part, follow the fragment with a comma.

Step 2. Correcting the Fragment. Each of these groups contains at least one fragment. Correct the error by adding the fragment either to the sentence that comes before or to the sentence that comes after. Write your new sentence in the blank spaces alongside.

Hint: Make sure that the new sentence you have written makes sense.

1. Professor Porter's voice droned on in front of the lecture hall. Gazing lazily out the window at a cluster of clouds. I day-dreamed about my future summer vacation on Martha's Vineyard.

   _____
   _____
   _____
   _____

2. Jogging is my favorite activity. Running down deserted streets in the early morning hours. I am not even aware of the strain on my heart and lungs.

   _____
   _____
   _____
   _____

3. It's no wonder people find it hard to be independent. Everywhere we turn someone gives us orders. At home, in school, on the job.

   _____
   _____
   _____
   _____

4. The large, gas-guzzling automobile will soon disappear. Replaced by smaller, more economical cars. Large vehicles are already losing popularity.

   _____
   _____
   _____
   _____

5. In America everyone recognizes the extent of poverty. Even the President and the members of Congress. But they cannot agree how to end it.

   _____
   _____
   _____
   _____

Finding Fragments. Here are some suggestions for learning to recognize sentence fragments of the type described in this chapter.

1. Read your paragraph aloud. Learn to tell the difference between pauses between words and stops between sentences. A pause often requires a comma. A full stop requires a period or one of the other end marks, a question mark or an exclamation point. A semicolon may also indicate a complete stop between sentences.
2. Read the sentences of your paragraph from the last to the first. In that way you'll be listening for complete thoughts that make sense.
3. Look for an -*ing* word used incorrectly as the verb in a sentence.
4. Make sure every sentence has its own subject and its own verb. (See item 7 in the sentence review, page 15, for "understood" subjects.)

5. Make sure every sentence expresses a complete thought by itself.
6. Watch out for these "Fragment Stop Signs: Group I" because they are expressions which often open word groups that fail to include subjects and verbs.

Fragment Stop Signs: Group I

just	especially
for instance	for example
such as	like
also	mainly

If you open a sentence with one of these words or word combinations, be sure a subject and verb come later on in the sentence.

Study the review chart below before moving on to the next steps.

A FRAGMENT FINDER	**A FRAGMENT FIXER**
1. Read aloud. Listen for incomplete thoughts.	1. Add subject, verb, or both.
2. Look out for *-ing* words, especially when they start sentences.	2. Add fragment to sentence that comes before or sentence that comes after. Make sure final sentence makes sense.
3. Look for subject and verb in each sentence.	3. Change an *-ing* word to a verb by using *is, was, are, were, am* in front of it. Or, change *-ing* word to a verb.
4. Read paragraph from last sentence to first. Stop after each sentence and ask: Is it a complete thought?	4. If you put an *-ing* fragment or another "verb-part" fragment in front of a complete sentence, use a comma after the fragment.
5. Know Group I of the Fragment Stop Signs: just mainly especially for instance for example like also such as	5. Change an infinitive to a verb by removing "to" and using the correct form of the verb. Or, put one of these verbs before the infinitive: *like(s), want(s), plan(s), try (tries), is, was, were, are, am.*

Example:

Fragment	*Corrected*
John works weekends. To earn money for college.	John works weekends. He *earns* money for college.
	or
	John works weekends. He *likes* to earn money for college.

Step 1. Eliminating Fragments. The sentence groups below contain *one or more* sentence fragments. Correct the fragments by using any of the methods you have learned so far. Cross out words, add words, change or remove punctuation. If the set of sentences is correct, mark it *C*. Use a separate sheet of paper.

1. I dashed into the brightly lit emergency room. Searching frantically for my son among the other patients. Finally I spotted him in a corner. Lying on a cot.
2. Watch out for words said in anger. They can hurt people. Especially the ones you love.
3. Avitar XRC. A sports car to set you free. See it at your nearest dealer.
4. Old people face many terrible problems. For example, their dependence on fixed incomes. Poor medical care in nursing homes. Also, neglected by their own relatives.
5. The sun set slowly over Hilton Head Island. At the edge of the water two children sat quietly, staring at their completed sandcastle and waiting for the evening tide.
6. I love Sunday mornings in my uncle's home. For instance, the smell of bacon cooking on the stove. The aroma drifts slowly into my bedroom. Making my stomach churn and my mouth water.
7. We gained much in the few months we were apart. Together vowing never to take each other for granted again.
8. Many athletic events attract large crowds only because the sports are violent and bloody. Such as ice hockey and boxing.
9. She lifted herself painfully from the chair. Like an old woman of eighty. She sighed and let her breath out slowly. To make us believe that she was really in pain.
10. The South is unlike the other sections of our country. In many ways. Its magnificent architecture is a blend of the past and the present. Modern skyscrapers soaring over quaint, wooden townhouses.

Step 2. Avoiding the Fragment Error. Use each of these word groups to open a sentence of your own. Complete the sentence in the space provided.

Hint: If you follow the word group with a complete sentence, use a comma after the opening word group.

1. Smoking a cigarette

_____

_____

2. Stopped by a police officer

_____

_____

3. Bleeding from the cut on her leg

_____

_____

4. Storming into the classroom

_____

_____

5. Depressed by low grades

_____

_____

WRITING THE PARAGRAPH

Your assignment for this theme is to write a paragraph of at least twelve to fifteen sentences to show one moment in which you reveal some experience you had with exercise or with sports.

WHAT IS A "MOMENT"?

1. A "moment" is a memorable instance in your life that illustrates some opinion or idea you want to write about.
2. A "moment" is limited as much as possible in time; it is a brief span of time which you recall sharply.
3. You must make this "moment" as vivid for your reader as it was for you when you experienced it. In order to do this, you need to fill in details with concrete sensory language. Remember that you create pictures (images) by using sensory words that will let the reader share your experience.
4. What kinds of details do you need to make the moment come alive? Show some images of the setting (where the moment occurs) through color, smell, touch, and sound; describe the people who participate in the moment (show their faces and actions); use bits of important dialogue that people speak as the moment develops.

Step 1. Reading Samples. Read the paragraphs below, written by students in response to the same assignment. When you finish reading each paragraph, answer the questions on expanded topic sentences, sensory language, chronological order, and sentence variety.

Chicken

One hot July afternoon at Hecksher State Park Pool I finally tried diving but suffered defeat. I was in the water when I suddenly noticed someone on the diving platform. Quickly and gracefully the muscular young man bounced off the blue board. As he hit the water, a small splash leaped up. He made it seem so simple and so much fun that suddenly I wanted to try it. I could do it; I knew I could. Brazenly I scampered out of the water and ran across the hot concrete floor to the ladder, stepping in small puddles that I passed. As I looked up, I saw someone in a bright yellow bikini stepping down. She looked into my eyes and confessed, "I've changed my mind. That's too high and the water's too deep for me." "Chicken," I thought to myself and slowly climbed the steps one by one. Suddenly I thought to myself, "What if I don't make it? What if I drown? Think positive; you'll do it, and then you'll be able to dive every time you come to the pool." I kept repeating those words to myself as I nervously reached the top. I stood there proudly, yards above everyone at the pool. "Hey, everybody, look at me, I'm going to dive." Placing one foot in front of the other, I inched my way to the tip of the board. Looking down into the clear blue water, I saw my faint reflection. The water looked so cool and inviting as I felt the hot sun burning my back. The smell of chlorine drifted up as I heard the screams and laughter of the young children below me. As I glanced around, red and blue sun umbrellas whirled together in front of my eyes. "Hurry it up, will you," someone behind me said. "Okay, okay," I said, "here I go." I bounced once, then twice. I smiled as I swung my arms in front of me, still not daring to jump. I counted aloud, "One, two, three." Then suddenly I stopped bouncing, quickly balanced myself and did an about-face. Staggering back to the ladder, I pushed everyone aside as I stepped down. When I reached the hot pool deck, I realized what I had done. I looked into a pair of brown, sympathetic eyes and muttered, "I couldn't do it." Touching my shoulder, my sister replied, "Maybe some other time, Liz." "Yes, maybe," I said, but I thought to myself, "Chicken."

—Elizabeth Santiago

1. What is the topic of this paragraph? What is the writer's opinion about the topic?
2. Which quotation sentence is most realistic, one that includes words you think a person might really say in the situation?
3. Which image in the paragraph is most clear? Where has Elizabeth Santiago used color most effectively? Which actions are especially well presented?
4. Why is the title a good one?
5. What does *scampered* mean? Why does the writer say "scampered out of the water" instead of "went out of the water"?
6. Which sentence opens with two -*ly* words?
7. The events in the selection you read follow a strict chronological arrangement. Below, several important details from the selection are listed. But they appear in the wrong time sequence. Put number 1 in front of the first event that occurred; number 2 in front of the second; and so on.

_____ Liz pushed everyone aside as she stepped down.

_____ Liz heard the screams and laughter of the young children.

_____ Liz scampered out of the water and ran quickly over to the ladder.

_____ Liz said to her sister, "I couldn't do it."

_____ Liz saw the muscular young man bounce off the diving board.

Fishing with My Father

On an exciting summer day in mid-July in the middle of Sabago Lake my father helped me reel in my very first catch. At first, everything was quiet around us. There were no human voices, cars, or planes to break the silence of the still pond. It was a perfect day for fishing. The sky was a brighter blue than usual, and puffs of white clouds raced overhead. We sat hushed, afraid to talk, thinking that the fish would hear us and would stay away. As we sat there, my father, holding his pole in one hand, passed me some lunch. I put down my brown chipped rod to take a sandwich wrapped in tin foil from him. The foil reflected the bright sunlight onto the water. With my mouth filled with peanut butter, I whined, "When do you think the fish will bite? We've been in this boat forever." It was terribly hot, for the sun hung directly over us, and the mosquitoes had told me hours ago that they favored my blood the best. Buzz. Smack! Another body dropped to the bottom of the boat. "These things are eating me alive," I complained to my father. Suddenly my line tightened and my sinker moved. "Dad, it moved; what do I do now?" My father, now as excited as I was, crawled over to my side of the boat. Everything rocked. Little circles with white bubbles formed on the water. Dad took the rod from me and, grasping it firmly like a champion fisherman, pulled and reeled the line in. "First you pull a little to let it know who's boss," he explained excitedly. "Then you bring it in gradually." In complete control of the pole he alternately reeled and jerked the line. Finally, a six-inch silvery blue perch sailed through the air, dangling on my line. The fish landed on the seat of the boat, flapping wildly and gasping for air. I picked the perch up, looked into its gaping mouth, and then plopped the struggling body into a pail of water. The fish regained consciousness and swam around unharmed for the moment. I think it knew that it would be part of our dinner that night.

—Lenora Hines

1. What words in the topic sentence show Lenora Hines' attitude toward her fishing experience with her father?
2. Why does the writer say "on a warm summer day" and "in the middle of Sabago Lake" in the first sentence?
3. Why are the quotations particularly effective in this narration?
4. Which action words make this theme come alive?
5. Which words appeal to the reader's sense of sound and color?

Some Topics to Think About

In case you need some help in finding a moment about which to write, perhaps one of these titles will give you an idea.

1. My Coach's Temper
2. Training for Victory
3. An Unforgettable Game
4. Feeling Proud
5. A Crushing Defeat
6. The Meaning of Sportsmanship
7. Try-Outs
8. My Moment of Glory
9. A Bicycle Ride I Won't Forget
10. Watching the Action
11. Proving Myself
12. Alone on a Run

13. The Agony of Jogging
14. Skiing Thrills
15. Soccer and Me
16. Fishing with Friends

17. From the Grandstand
18. Tennis Madness
19. Riding the Surf
20. In the Swim

For some more topic ideas turn to pages 49–50 and reread the sentences in Step 1.

Prewriting: Brainstorming for Ideas

Another prewriting technique (see page 35) to loosen up ideas on a topic is *brainstorming*. Brainstorming is usually a technique in which a group of people meet in order to stimulate thinking on some idea or problem. People who brainstorm ask lots of questions about the problem at hand, trying then to answer them. To brainstorm on your own about some topic you are considering, make up questions that can generate information and details. On a scratch page write the words *Who? What? Where? When? Why?* and *How?* Then, try to answer the questions in short word groups or in full sentences.

BRAINSTORMING

Topic: baseball game

Who? my brother Pete and I

What? helped lose the game

Where? Highland Park in Fairfield, New Jersey

When? last July, a humid afternoon

Why? both poor players, inexperienced, clumsy, nervous

How? I struck out 3 times, Pete dropped 2 fly balls

— Jerome Haag

Another kind of brainstorming involves the writer in more detailed questioning about the topic. You think on paper in question form about all the various things you want to ask in regard to the subject you have identified.

BRAINSTORMING

Topic: learning to swim

When did I learn to swim? I was eight years old, and I remember being scared. Why? Fell into the creek at Cole's Farm three years before. Who helped me learn? My sister Bertie. How did she get me to do it? Why was I stupid enough to try again, being so scared? She dared me. When was this? June afternoon on the way home from school on the very last day. We were at the creek again. What did the scene look like? What did Bertie say? How did I feel when she held me under my stomach, making me kick my feet and move my arms? How did the water feel? What did I smell, feel, hear at my first swimming lesson?

— Wilma Hanson

Hint: In brainstorming activities concentrate on getting ideas down on paper. Don't worry about spelling or other matters of correctness.

As with any other prewriting activity, the exercise in brainstorming allows you to develop from it a rough draft that expands on some or all of the ideas you have generated. You might need to group some of the thoughts you've written in brainstorming before you attempt your first draft.

Step 1. Stirring up Ideas. Write your exercise or sports topic in a word or two on the top of a blank page. Next, list at 2- or 3-inch intervals along the left-hand margin the questions *Who? What? Where? When? Why?* and *How?* Then start filling in your responses. Or, you might wish to generate more detailed questions about the topic, questions you try to answer after you write them. Look at the two samples above.

Requirements

Follow these suggestions as you write a one paragraph theme about an experience with exercise or sports. Reread the samples on the preceding pages before you begin.

A CHECKLIST OF REQUIREMENTS

1. Think carefully about the topic. Select for narration a brief moment, one that is clear in your mind, one that you can expand into a scene rich in sensory detail. (Review the definition of *moment* in this sense on page 63.)
2. Do prewriting that works for you. You might want to try brainstorming (see above) for this assignment.

3. From your prewriting activities prepare a rough draft in which you write consecutive sentences that narrate a moment with exercise activity.

4. Write as many drafts as you need in order to make your ideas clear and your details specific. When you prepare your final draft, follow correct manuscript form. (See page 37.)

5. Proofread your paper twice: once *before* you prepare your final manuscript, and once *after* it.

6. Write a topic sentence that states a limited topic through some opinion or attitude word.

7. Try to include time and place in the topic sentence. If you find this impossible, tell time (month, part of the day, or season) and place (a special room, some street whose name you mention) as soon as possible.

8. Use several *colors* in various places in the paragraph. Elizabeth Santiago says "red and blue sun umbrellas whirled together."

9. Show a person as he or she performs some action. Use a lively verb. Elizabeth Santiago shows how she bounced on the diving board, and Lenora Hines shows her father reeling in the fish.

10. Show the faces of the people you're writing about. Elizabeth Santiago says, "I looked into a pair of brown, sympathetic eyes." The eyes are particularly easy to write about; you can combine color with another sense like touch (*moist, hard, soft,* and so on).

11. Use several word groups that appeal to the sense of *sound.* "Chicken" includes "screams and laughter of young children," and "Fishing with My Father" contains words such as "buzz" and "smack."

12. Show details of the scene in which the moment occurs; use a detail of *touch* and one of *smell.*

13. Start one sentence with an *-ly* word. Start another sentence with two *-ly* words separated by a comma or *and.*

14. Write one quotation sentence which gives someone's exact words. Check the review charts on pages 54–55 for correct punctuation.

15. Tell your story in clear chronological order. See pages 52–53.

16. If you can, use some of the new words on pages 47–49.

17. Check your theme for errors, especially the fragment mistake explained earlier in this chapter, and the run-on error, explained in Chapter 1. See also your Theme Progress Sheet (page 429) and your Individual Spelling List (page 382).

18. Give your paragraph a lively title. See pages 95–97 for some help.

THE PROFESSIONALS SPEAK

Significant experiences with sports or exercise are often the basis for dramatic narratives by professional writers. These writers work from the same kinds of experiences you have been asked to write from in this theme.

Step 1. Reading Two Professional Samples.   Read the excerpts below and answer the questions after each selection.

SOME WORDS TO KNOW BEFORE YOU READ

sadistically: cruelly
discernible: capable of being seen
resilience: ability to bounce back, to return to original form
adept: skilled
osmosis: the gradual movement of a substance through some kind of barrier

An Important Lesson

It was an early September day, cool and bright and just right for running, and I was in the first few miles of a 10½-mile race over a course sadistically boobytrapped with steep, exhausting hills. Still, I felt rested and springy; despite the hills it was going to be a fine run.

Just ahead of me was Peggy Mimno, a teacher from Mount Kisco, New York. She too was running easily, moving along efficiently at my speed. The pace felt comfortable, so I decided to stay where I was; why bother concentrating on pace when she was setting such a nice one? I'd overtake her later on when she tired.

So I tucked in behind her. The course headed north for five miles, wandered west for a hilly mile, then turned south again along a winding road. The race was getting tougher. We had four miles left and already it was beginning to be real work. I was breathing hard, and my legs were turning to mush.

Peggy overtook a young male runner. Apparently she knew him, for they exchanged a few cheerful words as she passed him. Their exchange worried me. You don't chat during a race unless you are feeling good, and Peggy plainly was. There was still a discernible bounce in her stride, but whatever resilience I'd once possessed had long since left me.

Still, I was close enough to overtake her if she tired, so I didn't give up hope completely. We were approaching a long, punishing hill now and it would be the test. We were a mile from the finish line, so whatever happened on the hill would almost certainly determine who crossed it first.

As I moved up the hill, working hard, my attention wandered for a few minutes. When I looked up, Peggy was moving away—first five yards, then ten, then more. Finally it was clear that there was no hope of catching her. She beat me decisively.

There is an important lesson in that race. Much of what you read about running makes a sharp distinction between the sexes. Women are assumed to be weaker, slower and not nearly as adept athletically. (For example, women are always being told how to place their feet and hold their arms; the assumption is that any man simply knows such things, perhaps through some kind of male osmosis.) Yet as Peggy Mimno so clearly demonstrated, the similarities between male and female runners are more important than the differences. I have run with a number of women, both in training and in competition, and I can testify that it is often hard work.

—James F. Fixx
The Complete Book of Running

1. Why does James Fixx use the narrative technique in the above excerpt?
2. Which sentence best states the main point of this selection?

3. Which words show most effectively the hard work involved in running a race?
4. Why is the first sentence an effective one?
5. What important lesson did Fixx learn from his race?

SOME WORDS TO KNOW BEFORE YOU READ

entourage: followers and friends
theoretically: in theory, not in reality
pseudopsychological: pertaining to false psychology
ferocity: fierceness
unanimous: complete agreement

"Let's Call It a Day"

The blood was flowing from inside Joe Frazier's mouth and trickling from his nose. The skin was puffed under the right eye and both above and below the left eye, and as Frazier made his way back to his corner at the end of the fourteenth round, Eddie Futch, his manager, his trainer, and his friend, came to an immediate decision. "Let's call it a day," Futch said.

"Don't," Frazier said, "don't stop it." But there was no conviction in his words. Joe Frazier always listens to Eddie Futch, and now Futch was telling his fighter that his bid to become the third man ever to regain the heavyweight championship was ended, that once again, despite a display of courage that was awesome, Frazier had lost to the man he calls Cassius Clay.

Futch leaned over Frazier and pulled one of his strong fists toward him and took out a pair of scissors and began to cut away at Frazier's red eight-ounce boxing gloves. In front of the challenger, the referee, Carlos Padilla, Jr., saw Futch's action and waved his arms, signaling the end. Across the ring, Angelo Dundee caught the signal and shouted, "It's all over," and reached down and lifted his man, Muhammad Ali, off his stool.

And then as chaos broke loose in his corner, as the members of his entourage jostled for position the way they always do, Muhammad Ali lay down on the floor of the ring and caught his breath. He was still the champion of the world, the winner on a technical knockout in 14 rounds.

For the fourth time in this calendar year, he had successfully defended the title he took from George Foreman a year ago, but all the other victims together—Chuck Wepner, Ron Lyle, and Joe Bugner—didn't put up half the struggle Joe Frazier did in a magnificent prenoon battle in the sweltering heat of the theoretically air-conditioned Philippine Coliseum.

"I don't know how he stood up," said Ali after the fight. "I know I would have gone down under all those punches I threw. He is greater than I thought he was."

A few days ago, Ali was saying that the fight would end early, possibly even in the first round, that Frazier was slow and soft and finished, that the fight would not even be close. But this fight was close. There wasn't a knockdown, and even though all three officials, the Filipino referee and the two Filipino judges, had Ali ahead on points by a comfortable margin after 14 rounds, there were many at ringside who thought Frazier, the underdog, outweighed by about nine pounds, was leading or at least even.

A crowd of 25,000 that paid $1.5 million—both records for an indoor fight—watched a fight that began with pseudopsychological warfare and ended with street slugging.

Frazier entered the ring first, wearing blue trunks with a dull finish and white piping. By the time he reached his corner, he was already drenched with sweat.

Then Ali came in, his trunks a shiny white with black piping, the glitter of his trunks and the dullness of Frazier's a perfect symbolic contrast. There was not a drop of sweat on Ali. He did not sweat at all until the fight began.

Someone brought into the ring a handsome trophy, and the ring announcer said that the trophy would be presented by President Ferdinand Marcos, who was in the audience, to the winner. Ali didn't wait. He scampered into the center of the ring, grabbed the trophy, and lugged it back to his corner, looking at Frazier defiantly, as if daring the challenger to come take it back.

And then the fight began and in the early rounds, the first two or three, Ali seemed to be in complete command, almost toying with Frazier, giving a boxing lesson. In the last 30 seconds of the first round, Ali rocked Frazier with a left hook and a few seconds later, connected with a straight right. When the round ended, Frazier gave the champion a little tap on the rear and walked back to his own corner with a sort of goofy smile on his face.

In the third round, for the first time, Frazier rocked Ali with a left hook, and the sound and ferocity of the blow drew oohs from the crowd. Ali, responding more to the crowd than to the punch, turned and made a face, opening his mouth wide, as if to say that sounded a lot tougher than it felt. He was making fun, Angelo Dundee said later. But it hurt him. I saw his legs when it landed.

In the middle rounds, from about the fourth through the eighth, Frazier was in charge most of the time. He was the aggressor, and even when Ali flurried and pounded him with combinations, Frazier kept boring in, kept punching. The goofy look was gone.

And in those middle rounds, a strange thing happened: Ali lost the crowd. Before the fifth round, he led his followers in chants of, "Ali, Ali, Ali," but the men in Frazier's corner came back with chants of "Joe, Joe, Joe," and then the crowd, basically Filipino, started shouting, "Frazier, Frazier, Frazier."

The feeling was by no means unanimous, but enough of the Filipinos felt that Ali was too *mayabang,* too cocky, for their tastes, and so they wanted the underdog, the less boastful man to win. Apparently, Filipinos admire cockiness when two cocks fight—not when two men fight.

By the eighth round, the blood began to roll out of Frazier's mouth, some of it staining Ali's white trunks. But Ali was accomplishing little in those rounds, often allowing Frazier to back him into a corner and pound away at him. His corner yelled instructions, "Stay there," meaning in the middle of the ring, and "Don't hook"—you never hook with a hooker, Dundee said later—but Ali seemed to ignore the counsel.

By the twelfth round, Ali was definitely running the show again, manipulating Frazier, dictating the pace and the fury of the fight. "We had an extra gas tank in the corner," said Dundee later, kidding. Then he turned serious and said, "Nobody can suck it up like my man."

Ali sucked it up, found new strength, and sapped Frazier's. The thirteenth and fourteenth rounds were exercises in punishment. Several times, Ali landed six, seven, eight punches in a row, rights and lefts, shattering combinations that sent the sweat flying off Frazier's face, the mouthpiece flying from his mouth, but couldn't send him down to the floor.

In the thirteenth round, Frazier slipped—helped by a flurry of Ali punches—and almost went down, but regained his balance. His eyes were beginning to close, and in the following round, he was squinting at Ali, making out mostly the form of red gloves, coming at his face, bouncing off his nose and his forehead and his cheeks, pounding and pounding and pounding.

"No," said Frazier at the end, facing the press with sunglasses hiding his eye, "I wouldn't say I was hurt. No, I wasn't hurt. Just banged up. Tomorrow, I'll be all good."

Then Joe Frazier took off his glasses, and the bumps under the right eye and over the left looked enormous. They looked almost as big as Joe Frazier's heart.

—Dick Schaap
"That Thrilla in Manila"

1. In this selection by Dick Schaap there are several narrative elements. The piece starts with the story of the fourteenth round in a fight between Frazier and Muhammad Ali. Then, Schaap returns to the beginning of the fight and narrates it from start to finish. Why has the writer selected this method of presentation? Schaap writes for newspapers and sports magazines. What might that have to do with the way he presents his material?
2. What image of the fight stands out most vividly for you?
3. Read aloud several images that mention colors, that describe actions, that name sensations of touch.
4. What is Schaap's attitude toward Joe Frazier? How does the last sentence contribute to this attitude?
5. Why has Schaap written such short paragraphs? Try developing a topic and an opinion word for a topic sentence that could organize some of the short paragraphs into one longer paragraph.

REACHING HIGHER

Step 1. Photo into Words.   Look at the photograph on page 46. Write a paragraph of at least ten sentences that explain the feelings of the people you see. Use details of color, of sound, of touch, of smell to make the scene come alive.

Step 2. Review.   Read this paragraph for the kinds of errors with fragments you have learned about so far. Correct the mistakes directly on the page. There are nine sentence fragments.

The Last Ski Run

A light December snow speckles my ski goggles as I gaze down the expert's slope on Buttermilk Mountain. At the powdery whiteness below. The sun is dipping behind the jagged mountains. Surrounded by feathery clouds. Like a peacock's tail. The skiers in blue and red ahead of me start their graceful slide down the slope. Quickly disappearing in the late afternoon shadows. Exhausted after a full day on the slopes. I watch my warm breath turn into vapor in the brisk mountain air. To start my last run of the day. I finally plant my poles in the soft powder and surge forward. Realizing that my wife is probably beginning to worry about me. My legs stiffen in fear and sweat drips from under my hat. Especially at an icy patch or a sudden bump. At last I reach the bottom of the lift. To discover that I am the last skier on the mountain.

—Mark Kent

Step 3. Expanding a Poetic Moment. A valuable exercise in writing narrative is to select a poem that crystallizes a moment in time and to flesh out in your own language the scene the poet sketches. One of the outstanding qualities of good poetry is its ability to suggest scenes through economical use of language. Poets strive for *compression*; that is, they try to use as few and as carefully chosen words as possible to set scenes and to create emotional reactions in readers. Since all of us have different emotional states and different kinds of imaginations, what one person sees or feels after reading a poem is often quite unlike another person's responses.

As you read each of the following poems, think about the character of the person who speaks and of the other people in the poem. Then, by using sensory language, expand the moment the poet presents in a paragraph of your own. Try to suggest in the opening sentence or two the most important meaning of the poem. Describe the people as you see them, whether or not the poet has shown them clearly. Through color, sound, action, and images of smell and touch, paint a scene rich in details that your own imagination creates. Use comparisons (simile, metaphor, personification: look ahead to pages 120–122) for special vividness.

Read the poem below and then the paragraph written by a student as an example.

Lament

Listen, children:
Your father is dead.
From his old coats
I'll make you little jackets;
I'll make you little trousers
From his old pants.
There'll be in his pockets
Things he used to put there,

Keys and pennies
Covered with tobacco;
Dan shall have the pennies
To save in his bank;
Anne shall have the keys
To make a pretty noise with.
Life must go on,
And the dead be forgotten;
Life must go on,
Though good men die;
Anne, eat your breakfast;
Dan, take your medicine;
Life must go on;
I forget just why.
　　—Edna St. Vincent Millay

The Meaning of Death

In "Lament" I see a sad mother (who has lost her husband) unsuccessfully trying to explain the meaning of death to her children in a cold dark kitchen. Sitting at the breakfast table one December morning, the mother in a faded robe runs her hand up and down the yellow plastic tablecloth. There are the morning smells of instant coffee, cereal, and orange juice, but she does not notice them. Her sorrowful brown eyes are small like little stones. Tiny lines of age and worry fill her face, and her hair, speckled with gray, falls sloppily onto her forehead. When she speaks to her ten-year-old son Dan, he stops tapping the table with his fork and listens. "Dan, even though your father is dead, I'll make you trousers from his old brown pants. You can keep the pennies in his pockets for your bank." Quickly, Dan looks away staring at a vitamin pill and his cough medicine, a red syrup in a clear glass bottle. "Anne," the mother says, "I'll give you Daddy's keys to play with." But the three-year-old in a wooden high chair just frowns and plays with the oatmeal in her little dish. The mother cannot soothe the children, though, because she herself is confused about the meaning of death. First she tries to comfort the children by keeping alive the father's memory. (That is why she talks of his keys with the pretty noise and his coins covered with tobacco.) But then she says just the opposite when she explains that the dead must be forgotten so life can go on. This contradiction is, I believe, the feeling many people experience in the loss of loved ones. We want to forget the person who died and to remember him as well. All the mother's sadness, bitterness, and confusion about death show in the last two lines: "Life must go on; I forget just why."

　　　　　　　　　　　　　　　　　　　　—Sheila O'Connor

Now read to yourself or listen as your instructor reads aloud the following poems. Then, using Sheila O'Connor's theme as an example, write your own paragraph that expands the scene from any one poem as you see it. You may wish to write about "Lament," if you prefer it to one of these.

Mother to Son

Well, son, I'll tell you:
Life for me ain't been no crystal stair.
It's had tacks in it,
And splinters,
And boards torn up,
And places with no carpet on the floor—
Bare.
But all the time
I'se been a-climbin' on,
And reachin' landin's,
And turnin' corners,
And sometimes goin' in the dark
Where there ain't been no light.
So, boy, don't you turn back.
Don't you set down on the steps
'Cause you finds it kinder hard.
Don't you fall now—
For I'se still goin', honey,
I'se still climbin',
And life for me ain't been no crystal stair.
                              —Langston Hughes

The Mole

"There goes The Mole!" Mother cried.
"You children look quick or you'll miss
him!" It was Father, disappearing down
the cellar stairs. Every day he'd retreat
to his radio shack, stay past midnight.

He'd built a rig others envied, came
from miles around to see. Every day
he'd jam the airwaves, ruin the block's TV.
Every day we'd hear him sit before the mike
calling "CQ, CQ, calling CQ" to whoever

listened at the other end. He once
claimed to reach Moscow. "Ralph's the handle,
calling from W3CAT, the Old Cat Station—
W-3-Cat-Alley-Tail." He *was* a handsome
cat; Mother once adored him, I know.

But what I'll never know is: Why he'd talk
to any stranger far away and not once
climb back up the stairs to the five of us
to say, "Hello . . . Hello . . . Hello . . . Hello."
                              —Robert Phillips

Mag

I wish to God I never saw you, Mag.
I wish you never quit your job and came along with me.
I wish we never bought a license and a white dress
For you to get married in the day we ran off to a minister
And told him we would love each other and take care of each other
Always and always long as the sun and the rain lasts anywhere.
Yes, I'm wishing now you lived somewhere away from here
And I was a bum on the bumpers a thousand miles away dead broke.
   I wish the kids had never come
   And rent and coal and clothes to pay for
   And a grocery man calling for cash,
   Every day cash for beans and prunes.
   I wish to God I never saw you, Mag.
   I wish to God the kids had never come.

—Carl Sandburg

chapter 3

**STREET SCENES AND SANDLOTS:
MEMORIES OF YOUTH**

INTRODUCTION: USING EXAMPLES TO DEVELOP A PARAGRAPH

Each of us builds up unforgettable memories from childhood. These memories grow from experiences at school, from weekend trips in buses or cars or subways, from days in the country sun, or from sights on the city streets.

Often these events fall into a pattern so that we join together certain experiences under a single impression in our memories. We can recall, for example, a number of things that frightened us as children; we can point to a few occasions in which we learned how to speak up for what we wanted; we can remember the events that brought joy or pain or fear in our early years. Sometimes that single impression, which repeated experiences support, becomes a central thread in our own personalities. Because of a string of events, we may view ourselves forever as *insecure, shy, unloved, confident, independent, happy, angry.*

The scars and joys of your younger days will be the substance of the theme explored in this chapter. For this assignment you will present in a paragraph a number of experiences from your memories in order to suggest some general impression about your early life. To do so you will learn how to develop a paragraph by using *several* examples. Since each example represents an incident from your own experience, you will again turn to concrete sensory detail (see pages 5–7) to support your general statements, but not with as much completeness as you can achieve in a paragraph that narrates an event of a single moment (see page 63). When you use a number of examples to support a topic idea, you need to move the reader smoothly from one instance to another; therefore, you will examine further some important transition words.

VOCABULARY

Step 1. Words for the Past. Each of the underlined words below can be helpful to you in writing about your childhood experiences. Try to determine the meaning of the word from the way it is used in the sentence. Circle the letter next to what you think is the best definition. Check the correct definitions in Appendix A.

1. When I <u>reminisce</u> about my childhood, I recall all my wonderful birthday parties.
   a. remember the past   *b.* ignore   *c.* think   *d.* cry
2. For example, my mother's pictures of my sweet sixteen party give me strong feelings of <u>nostalgia.</u>
   a. sorrow   *b.* desire to return to the past   *c.* illness   *d.* happiness
3. My tenth birthday was certainly my most <u>memorable</u> one, for my father presented me with a brown and white puppy named "Skippy."
   a. troublesome   *b.* exciting   *c.* happy   *d.* notable

4. The thought of Skippy licking my face with his hot, wet tongue <u>evokes</u> fond memories.
   a. produces   *b.* transfers   *c.* strikes   *d.* wipes away

5. I <u>recollect</u> how hilarious my tenth birthday party was; my school friends tossed balls of whipped cream at each other.
   a. forget   *b.* remember   *c.* become collected   *d.* fantasize

6. Surprisingly, I cannot clearly <u>discern</u> my eighteenth birthday party per-haps because both my parents had recently passed away.
   a. discuss   *b.* identify   *c.* forget   *d.* mention

7. There was a brief <u>interlude</u> after my eighteenth birthday when I thought it was silly and childish to celebrate any more of my birthdays.
   a. intermission   *b.* argument   *c.* period of time   *d.* event

8. Now that I am thirty, I realize that the <u>remembrance</u> of our past is a precious and important part of our lives.
   a. idea   *b.* discussion   *c.* situation   *d.* memory

9. Some people find it painful to <u>contemplate</u> the past because they are then more aware of the passing of the years.
   a. consider   *b.* talk about   *c.* sacrifice   *d.* manage

10. In <u>retrospect</u>, my past is indeed full of happy, tender memories that I will never forget.
    a. to come back   *b.* conclusion   *c.* tribute   *d.* review of ear-lier experiences

Step 2. Words for Unforgettable Personalities. These words are useful in describing those unforgettable personalities of your youth. Check them in the dictionary and write in definitions. For more help, see Appendix A.

1. compulsive _____

2. domineering _____

3. reticent _____

4. gregarious _____

5. volatile _____

Step 3. Using New Vocabulary. Fill in each blank with a word from the list in Step 2 so that the sentences make sense.

1. His wife's _____ temper erupted violently when he came home at 4:00 A.M.

2. The _____ politician darted around the room, shaking hands and talking to small clusters of guests.

3. The timid child was so _____ that he refused to speak to his new classmates.

4. My father is very _____ ; he checks the locks frequently each day and he won't allow anyone except him to secure the doors of our house.

5. My boss is so _____ that three secretaries quit their jobs last week rather than submit to the tyranny.

BUILDING COMPOSITION SKILLS

Finding the Topic

Step 1. Getting Ideas. Complete any word group below by reading it aloud with your own ending. Then, in a few more sentences, explain what you said by giving two or three examples. Or, if your instructor suggests it, write down in a few brief sentences your completion for any of the statements and then read aloud what you have written. Look at the examples.

1. The times I cut classes I . . . .
2. I lose my temper when . . . .
3. The things that frightened me as a child were . . . .
4. I'm easily embarrassed when . . . .
5. I can always please my parents (wife, husband) when . . . .
6. I got into trouble when . . . .
7. My insecurity shows when I . . . .
8. My childhood was unusual because . . . .
9. The first job I had taught me . . . .
10. My confidence showed when . . . .
11. As a youngster, I admired . . . .
12. I remember learning about loneliness when . . . .
13. Happy memories of my adolescence were . . . .
14. When I returned to my old neighborhood, I . . . .
15. My basic personality trait is . . . .

Examples:

My childhood was unusual because I lived in so many strange places. Since my father was an air force colonel, I lived for a time in Japan and Turkey. One summer I lived on a houseboat with my uncle, and the following winter at a remote radar station complex in Alaska.

—Karen Youngman

I'm easily embarrassed when I have to stand up in front of a group to speak. In science class when I had to make a report on the nervous system, I stammered nervously and felt my knees shake. And once in high school English I was so nervous that I dropped my note cards to the floor and had to slip back to my seat without finishing the report.

—Helen Cendrowski

Paragraph Unity: Using Subtopic Sentences

It's often helpful, especially when you use several examples to support your point, to remind the reader of the topic in several places in the paragraph. The subtopic sentence serves that function.

Here is a topic sentence that will obviously introduce a paragraph which uses several instances to support the topic:

When I was seven years old and the family moved from a small village in Puerto Rico to Manhattan, everyday city occasions frightened me.

This topic will deal with selected events of city life; the writer's opinion is that these events were frightening. The very next sentence would present the first subtopic:

The traffic noises scared me.

The word *scared* repeats the opinion of the topic sentence; *traffic noises* introduce one specific aspect of the topic for discussion. The next three or four sentences would explain how the traffic noises were frightening. Images filled with sensory language in those sentences would support this first unit of thought. After finishing this thought group, the writer would write another subtopic sentence:

I also didn't like the people I saw on the streets.

The words *people I saw on the streets* introduce another part of the topic for the writer to discuss. The words *didn't like* refer back to the opinion in the topic sentence. The next few sentences would illustrate the point of the subtopic with colors and sounds and actions. After this thought unit ends, another subtopic sentence would appear:

And every new thing I saw in Manhattan looked oversized and ugly.

The words *every new thing I saw in Manhattan* refer the reader back to the original topic; the words *oversized and ugly* repeat the writer's opinion toward the topic discussed in the paragraph. In this way the paragraph achieves unity—all the sentences will build upon the main idea.

Even paragraphs that do not give several incidents can benefit from subtopic sentences. Paragraphs of description (Chapter 1) and narration (Chapter 2) achieve unity too when subtopic sentences introduce major blocks of thought. Each subtopic sentence needs several sentences of support for whatever aspect of the topic the writer introduces. Here a topic sentence introduces a paragraph that narrates:

On a cold, December morning, I learned how dangerous skiing can be.

Here are two subtopic sentences:

Subtopic sentence 1: *As I rode up the chairlift, the sun reflected off the icy surface of the slope.*
Subtopic sentence 2: *Suddenly the hazardous rock loomed in front of me.*

What kind of information would you expect to find in the seven or eight sentences after subtopic sentence 1 above? After subtopic sentence 2? What words in each of the subtopic sentences remind the reader of the opinion expressed in the topic sentence?

SUBTOPIC SENTENCE CHART _____

Subtopic Sentence	*Why*
1. Introduces one aspect of the topic you want to discuss	So it's clear to the reader what proof you will use at a given point in the paragraph So it's clear to you what part of the topic you are treating at a given point in the paragraph
2. Uses a word similar to the "opinion" word in the topic sentence	So the reader is reminded of your position on the topic So that you remember that you're trying to prove only a certain feature about the topic So that the details in the sentences that follow the subtopic sentence all try to support the key impression you have given about the topic in the topic sentence

---

Step 1. Finding Subtopics.   Reread "The Gloom Room" on pages 31–32.

1. Copy here the first subtopic sentence, the sentence that introduces the one aspect of the topic that the writer will discuss first. _____

_____

2. Copy the second subtopic sentence. _____

_____

3. What details does Mr. Golden use to support the first subtopic sentence?

_____

4. What details does he use to support the second subtopic sentence?

_____

_____

Step 2. Writing Subtopic Sentences.   For each topic sentence below, write subtopic sentences. The numbers in parentheses tell you how many subtopic sentences to write. Use your own paper.

Hint: Each subtopic sentence:
a. introduces some aspect of the topic that can be discussed in a few sentences
b. may repeat some idea of the opinion word
c. must be followed by supporting details.

Example: At Springfield Gardens High School, trouble and I were never far away from each other! (3)

Subtopic sentence 1:   Once I "borrowed" my homeroom teacher's key for a practical joke.

Subtopic sentence 2: To protest the awful cafeteria food, I caused a commotion.

Subtopic sentence 3: The Dean of Boys summoned me when he learned I had cut history eighteen times.

1. When I was seventeen, two friends had major effects on my way of thinking and behaving. (2)
2. During our trip to Washington, D.C., I had two unforgettable experiences. (2)
3. On the bus ride downtown yesterday, several passengers and the driver suffered in the rush-hour traffic. (2)
4. My first date was a disastrous experience. (3)
5. I learned early how to survive in a rough neighborhood. (3)
6. Most people are unaware of the physical and mental benefits of disco dancing. (2)
7. For me the first day back at school is always filled with excitement. (2)

Hint: There is no set number of subtopic sentences to use for each paragraph. If you write only two subtopic sentences, each subtopic (thought unit) will need to be developed in greater detail. Write three subtopic sentences, and you will need to use fewer supporting details for each thought unit.

Several Examples without Subtopic Sentences

Sometimes a writer wishes to propose many instances to support the topic sentence in a paragraph. In that case, each instance is not highly developed—it is told in just a sentence or two—and a subtopic sentence to introduce each example is unnecessary. The paragraph below uses several instances to support the attitude in the topic sentence, but does not need subtopic sentences. The unity in the paragraph comes from repetition of key words (see pages 87–88).

SOME WORDS TO KNOW BEFORE YOU READ:

downs: an area of low hills in South England
cricket: a popular English game; it is played by two teams, the ball hit along the ground with a kind of bat
sixpence: an English coin
newt: a salamander, a small lizardlike animal

Memories of Crossgates School

I have good memories of Crossgates, among a horde of bad ones. Sometimes on summer afternoons there were wonderful expeditions across the Downs, or to Beachy Head, where one bathed dangerously among the chalk boulders and came home covered with cuts. And there were still more wonderful midsummer evenings when, as a special treat, we were not driven off to bed as usual but allowed to wander about the grounds in the long twilight, ending up with a plunge into the swimming bath at about nine o'clock. There was the joy of waking early on summer mornings and getting in an hour's undisturbed reading (Ian Hay, Thackeray, Kipling and H. G. Wells were the favourite authors of my boyhood) in the sunlit, sleeping dormitory. There was also cricket, which I was no good at but with which I conducted a sort of hopeless love affair up to the age of about eighteen. And there was the pleasure of keeping caterpillars—the silky green and purple puss-moth, the ghostly green poplar-hawk, the privet hawk, large as one's third finger, specimens of which could be illicitly purchased for sixpence at a shop in the town—and, when one could escape long enough from the master who was "taking the walk," there was the excitement of dredging the dew-ponds on the Downs for enormous newts with orange-coloured bellies. This business of being out for a walk, coming across something of fascinating interest and then being dragged away from it by a yell from the master, like a dog jerked onwards by the leash, is an important feature of school life, and helps to build up the conviction, so strong in many children, that the things you most want to do are always unattainable.

—George Orwell
Such, Such Were the Joys

Arrangement by Importance

In telling about an event, you know that the clearest way to present the moment is to give the details in chronological order—the order in which things occur. If you write a paragraph that gives several instances or examples to support the topic sentence, you can certainly write about them in the order in which they occurred. But another method is to tell the details in the order of their importance: tell about the least important thing first and the most important thing last. In this way you build up to the proof that has the most significance.

Suppose you wanted to write a paragraph for this topic sentence:

When I returned to my old neighborhood, I was sad to see how many things had changed.

Let's assume that you would develop these three incidents as illustrations in the paragraph:

1. *Mr. Lewis, my old history teacher, had died in a car accident.*
2. *Mike's Pizzeria, a local hangout, was destroyed in a fire.*
3. *The park bench where I spent hours reading was gone.*

From these incidents, although item 1 might have occurred first in time, because it seems to be the most important it would best be discussed last in the paragraph. Item 3 seems least important so it could be the first event discussed. Of course, only the writer himself could determine which was most or least significant.

Step 1. Making the Order Count. In Column I, jot down three instances you might discuss and expand for each of these topic sentences. In Column II, arrange the details in order of importance.

I Instances
1. Several good experiences in high school made me like my years there.

   a. _____
   b. _____
   c. _____

2. Many things frightened me easily as a child.

   a. _____
   b. _____
   c. _____

II Order of importance

1. _____
2. _____
3. _____

1. _____
2. _____
3. _____

Step 2. Arranging Details by Importance. Instead of writing in detail about two or three instances, you can mention seven or eight instances, each in just a sentence or two. In Column I, list seven events that could be written to support the topic sentence as given. In Column II, arrange the details according to importance as *you* see it.

I Events
1. Choosing the kind of person to marry is a very difficult and important decision.

   a. _____
   b. _____
   c. _____
   d. _____
   e. _____
   f. _____
   g. _____

2. Living in cities has many advantages over living in other parts of the United States.

   a. _____
   b. _____
   c. _____
   d. _____
   e. _____

II Order of Importance

1. _____
2. _____
3. _____
4. _____
5. _____
6. _____
7. _____

1. _____
2. _____
3. _____
4. _____
5. _____

f. _____   6. _____

g. _____   7. _____

Getting It All Together: Transitions II

In Chapter 1 you learned about bridging thoughts through transitions—idea
connectors—that move the reader from place to place. But you can also join
ideas by means of other types of connecting words.

Connecting through Time

later on	suddenly	former
afterward	now	latter
years ago	some time later	in the first place
earlier	once	in the next place
before	often	further
next	yesterday	furthermore
first	today	meanwhile
second	tomorrow	previously
third	then	when
	in the past	at last
	thereafter	

Hint: These words help refer the reader to the idea that came directly before. The words
suggest that the ideas are numbered.

Step 1. Using Time Connectors.   Here are several ideas that could be used
one after the other in a paragraph. They are not sentences. Using these
details, connect the ideas with some of the time transitions above and write
complete sentences in a paragraph. Use a separate sheet of paper.

means of effective transportation important to Americans
horses and single riders popular
covered wagons and carriages for more complex travel
go long distance with family's belongings
mass transportation by train important in travel history
bus, ship, airplane develop
automobile single most popular form of transportation
relatively inexpensive means of going from one place to another
families everywhere consider car necessity
rising costs of oil question auto's continued use
turn to mass transportation

Connecting through Coordinators
and, but, for, or, nor, yet

You learned in an earlier chapter that these words could join sentences together. The words also serve to connect ideas in separate sentences. Notice

how the sentence on the left below—a correct sentence grammatically—
may be written as two sentences, the second of which makes a powerful
transition to a new thought group.

He tried everything he could to make me like him, but I just could not bear the way he treated my mother.

He tried everything he could to make me like him. But I just could not bear the way he treated my mother.

Hint: *And, but, for, or, nor,* or *yet* may be used at the beginning of a sentence. In your early years of school, you were probably warned against doing so because you may have started too many sentences with *and* or *so.* But, used carefully, coordinators open sentences effectively. Make sure a complete thought follows the coordinator. Make sure the sentence before is logically related to the sentence that follows the coordinator. Don't open more than one or two sentences in each paragraph in this way.

Step 2. Coordinators for Transition. Use a coordinator that makes sense as a sentence opener in each blank space below.

1. Many young people live for today. _____ who can tell what tomorrow may bring?

2. My sister pleaded with my father to allow her to go camping. _____ my father still refused to give her permission.

3. Tom refused to apologize to Michael. _____ Michael was as stubborn as Tom in refusing to settle their argument.

4. You can choose the chocolate cake for dessert. _____, if you want something even richer, ask for banana cream pie.

Hint: See pages 17–18 for explanations of the meaning of coordinators such as *and, but, for, or, nor.*

Connecting through Repetition

Sometimes the repetition of a word or two at the beginning of or within a sentence helps join ideas together. Notice the repetition of the words *who* and *what* in the use of the angry questions below.

Who Are These Men?

Who are these men who defile the grassy borders of our roads and lanes, who pollute our ponds, who spoil the purity of our ocean beaches with the empty vessels of their thirst? Who are the men who make these vessels in millions and then say, "Drink—and discard"? What society is this that can afford to cast away a million tons of metal and to make of wild and fruitful land a garbage heap? What manner of men and women need thirty feet of steel and two hundred horsepower to take them, singly, to their small destinations? Who demand that what they eat is wrapped so that forests are cut down to make the paper that is thrown away, and what they smoke and chew is sealed so that the sealers can be tossed in gutters and caught in twigs and grass?

—Marya Mannes
More in Anger

Step 3. Finding Connectors. Read "Memories of Crossgates School" on pages 83–84. Circle the words repeated at the beginning of several sentences, words that help connect ideas through repetition.

Connecting through Pronouns

he	you	its
she	who	our
it	whom	their
we	his	your
they	her	whose

A pronoun takes the place of a noun. When you use a noun in one sentence, a pronoun that occurs later on in another sentence automatically refers the reader back to the original noun. In that way, you can help ideas move smoothly from one to the other.

Step 4. Pronouns as Connectors. Circle the pronouns that help connect the sentences in this paragraph.

The Tailor Arrives

Almost instantly there was the sound of soft steady footsteps through the open doors, and from the back of the house through the hall following the manservant there came the tailor. He was a tall man, taller than the servant, middle-aged, his face quiet with a sort of closed tranquility. He wore a long robe of faded blue grasscloth, patched neatly at the elbows and very clean. Under his arm he carried a bundle wrapped in a white cloth. He bowed to the two white women and then squatting down put his bundle upon the floor of the veranda and untied its knots. Inside was a worn and frayed fashion book from some American company and a half-finished dress of a spotted blue-and-white silk. This dress he shook out carefully and held up for Mrs. Lowe to see.

—Pearl S. Buck
"The Frill"

Step 5. A Brief Paragraph with Pronoun Connectors. Write five sentences to describe the person sitting next to you in class. Mention the person's name in the first sentence. Connect the ideas in each succeeding sentence by using pronouns to bridge each complete thought. Use a separate sheet of paper.

Hint: It must always be clear to the reader just which noun the pronoun replaces. Consider this sentence:

The mother held the baby and she laughed at her.

We don't know—because the pronouns are unclear—just who did the laughing at whom.

Sentence Combining: Subordination for Sentence Variety

In Chapter 1, pages 17–20, you learned how to combine sentences using co-ordination. Another way to join thoughts in paragraphs is to set up a relationship between two thoughts, a relationship in which one of the two ideas is stressed more than the other. For example, you can join two short sentences so that one of the thoughts gets more emphasis. Look at these two sentences (from "The Nursery" on page 17), which are then joined using subordination:

He rests his head on the pillow. I tiptoe quietly to the door.

a. Because he rests his head on the pillow, I tiptoe quietly to the door.

The words *I tiptoe quietly to the door* express a complete thought and, as such, give the part of the sentence that has the most stress.

The words *because he rests his head on the pillow* are not a complete thought and, therefore, get less emphasis than the rest of the sentence. Those words give "background information": they tell *why* the writer tiptoed quietly to the door. But clearly, it is the tiptoeing to the door that the sentence stresses, and the writer shows that the baby's falling asleep brought about the action of leaving the child's room.

Now look at the sentences joined together in another way:

b. Because I tiptoe quietly to the door, he rests his head on the pillow.

Here, the words *he rests his head on the pillow* are the stressed part of the sentence because they can stand alone as a complete thought.

The words *Because I tiptoe quietly to the door* are not a complete thought. As "background information," they tell *why* the baby fell asleep. But it is the fact that the baby rests his head on the pillow that the sentence stresses. The writer shows that the action of tiptoeing to the door made the baby do what he did.

The technique that gives one part of a sentence more stress than another is *subordination.* Only the writer can decide which part of the sentence is less or more important. Completely different meanings are achieved by subordinating different word groups within a sentence: this is clear in sentences *a* and *b* above.

It's obvious that the word *because* is the word that brings about the subordination in sentences *a* and *b*. It is one word among many which are called *subordinators.* Although all subordinators connect the unstressed part of a sentence to the part that gets the emphasis, they explain different things about the emphasized part of the sentence.

> If you want to show *why* the stressed part of the sentence occurred, use one of these to subordinate:
>
> as
> since
> because
> in order that
> so that
> as long as
>
>   [This tells why the lateness occurred.]
> *Example:* Because the train was delayed, I arrived late to work.
>   [This is the stressed part
>   of the sentence. It expresses
>   a complete thought.]

Step 1. Subordination to Tell Why. Make up a correct subordinate part to tell *why* for each of these complete thoughts. Use one of the subordinators above. Be sure a subject and a verb come after the subordinator:

1. _____ , I called for an ambulance.

2. _____ , Mr. Bogan raced across the street.

> If you want to show *when* the stressed part of the sentence occurred, use one of these to subordinate.
>
> after   whenever
> as   while
> as soon as   until
> before   once
> since   provided
> when
>
>   [This tells *when* the wish for
>   popcorn occurred.]
> *Example:* After the movie began, we decided we wanted popcorn.
>   [This is the stressed part of the sentence.
>   It expresses a complete thought.]

Step 2. Subordination to Tell When. Make up a correct subordinate part to tell *when* for each of these complete thoughts. Use a subordinator from the chart above. Be sure a subject and verb follow the subordinator.

1. _____ , the students gathered their books and bolted from the classroom.

2. _____ , she locked the front door and trudged wearily up the stairs.

If you want to show *where* or *how* the stressed part of the sentence occurred, use one of these to subordinate:

wherever   if   as if
where   how   as though

[This tells *where* forces of good work.]

Examples: Wherever evil appears, the forces of good will work against it.

[This stressed part of the sentence is a complete thought.]

[This tells *how* Susan acted.]

As if she had never seen snow before, Susan dived madly into the drifts.

[The stressed part of the sentence: it is a complete thought.]

Step 3. Completing Subordinated Sentences. Write the stressed part of the sentence for each subordinated word group below.

1. Wherever William looked, _____ .

2. As though he had not eaten in a week, _____ .

If you want to show *under what condition* the stressed part of the sentence occurred, use one of these to subordinate:

although   unless
if   provided
though   once

[You would not expect a tired person to run.]   [This complete thought is what the sentence stresses.]

Examples: Although I was tired, I ran the ten blocks home.

[This tells *under what condition* the bills will be paid.]

Unless the check comes, I will not be able to pay my bills.

[This, a complete thought, is what the sentence stresses.]

Hint: *Although* introduces an idea that you would not expect to happen because of the information in the stressed part.

Step 4. Subordinators Tell Conditions. Complete the sentences below by adding a subordinated section that tells under what conditions the main part of the sentence occurs. Use the subordinator as indicated.

1. Although _____, she still refuses.

2. Once _____, I can feed the baby.

3. If _____, I will fail my psychology course.

Hint: Always use a comma after the subordinate part of the sentence when the subordinate part comes first.

[subordinate
 part]

As she arrived, we left.

[comma here]

Step 5. Subordinating Your Sentences. For each topic below, write a sentence that uses subordination at the beginning of the sentence. Use as many subordinators as you can from the four groups in Steps 1 to 4. Don't forget commas after the subordinated part.

Example:

1. music *After the music stopped, Carol and I sat down for a drink.*

2. a suntan _____

3. raising a family _____

4. a person you admire _____

5. playing tennis _____

Subordinated portions like the ones you've been writing may also appear at the ends of sentences. You generally do not use a comma before the subordinated section if it comes at the end.

Example: I watched every game of the World Series because I love baseball.

Step 6. Subordination to Join. Each item in Column I below contains two brief sentences. Subordinate one of the two sentences, and rewrite your new sentence in Column II. Then, subordinate the other sentence, and write the new sentence in Column III. Look at the example.

I

1. I felt faint.
   John grabbed me.

2. It began to rain.
   We rushed for shelter.

3. The cat hid under the bed.
   The dog barked.

4. I wrote a letter to him.
   He sent a postcard to me.

II

As I felt faint, John grabbed me.

_____

_____

_____

_____

_____

_____

_____

_____

_____

III

As John grabbed me, I felt faint.

_____

_____

_____

_____

_____

_____

_____

_____

_____

Hint: If the subordinated part—placed at the end—starts with *though* or *although,* use a comma.
Example: We read the whole book, though we were bored by it.
[comma]

If in the subordinate part of the sentence you want to describe someone or something you have mentioned in the stressed part, use one of these:

who
whose   that
which

[This identifies the woman.]
1. The woman whose purse was stolen called the police.

[This identifies the book.]
2. We bought the book which had the most pictures.

[This identifies the man.]
3. The man who enjoys his work does the best job.

4. The Empire State Building, which is in New York, is no longer the tallest building.

Hint: The word *which* never refers to a person, only places and things. Use *who, whom,* and *whose* to refer to people. **Wrong:** The people which eat fast will be ill.

Correct: Those people $\begin{Bmatrix} who \\ that \end{Bmatrix}$ eat fast will be ill.

The meat *which* we ate was tasty.

A HINT ABOUT COMMAS

Sentences 1 to 3 above do not use commas with the subordinate part because the subordinating sections identify some subject. Without the words *whose purse was stolen,* we cannot identify the woman. Without *which had the most pictures,* we cannot identify the book in sentence 2. Without *who enjoys his work* we have no idea of which man is being identified. *Because they are essential for proper meaning, subordinate sections that identify the subject don't need commas.*

However, when information is added in a subordinate section to describe further a subject already identified, you need to use commas as in sentence 4 above. This material is *nonessential:* the subordinate section merely adds information about a subject already named. (See pages 236–239 for more information on commas.)

[comma]   [comma]
Professor Barton, who teaches here, is ill.
[This *adds* information;
the person is already
identified.]

The girl who won the contest received $100.
[This identifies the girl:
no commas.]

I admire John Steinbeck's novels, which are full of rich imagery.
[comma]   [This *adds* information; the novels
have already been identified.]

Step 7. Practice with *Who, Whose, Which, What, That.* Add words to complete the subordinate section in each sentence below. Use commas where necessary.

1. The basketball star *who* _____
   rammed the ball through the basket.

2. I live in a small town *that* _____.

3. The Golden Gate Bridge *which* _____
   is one of the major tourist attractions on the West Coast.

4. They are the only circus people *who* _____.

5. The injured woman *whose* _____
   waited for help more than an hour.

Step 8. Writing Sentences that Subordinate. For each of these subordinate word groups, write a complete sentence that makes sense. Put the subordinated part in the middle or at the end of the sentence; remember to put in commas when necessary. Use a separate sheet of paper.

1. who never smiles
2. whose father makes clocks
3. that was destroyed by fire
4. that made me happy
5. who loves me deeply
6. that crashed into the gorge
7. which he purchased
8. who never forgets my birthday
9. whose speech was lively
10. which disturbed our sleep

Step 9. Rewriting Coordinated Sentences. Although coordination is often effective, subordination of ideas allows for much greater sentence variety. Many beginning writers use coordination too frequently. Change each co-ordinated sentence below to a sentence that uses subordination.

Examples:

I like water skiing, but the speed frightens me.

Although I like water skiing, the speed frightens me.

1. The children began to cry, for their circus trip was canceled. _____

2. Paco finally arrived, and we sat down to dinner. _____

3. Mr. Wong telephoned for an ambulance, and the three police officers administered first aid. _____

4. The ketchup was on sale, but there were no more bottles on the shelf.

5. You must pay bills on time, or you may lose your credit. _____

Step 10. Rewriting a Paragraph. On a separate sheet of paper, rewrite the paragraph "The Nursery" that appears on page 17. Use coordination and subordination to vary the sentence length and structure. Use coordination only once; use subordination at least three times.

MAKING UP TITLES

The title is a helpful feature for the reader since titles give the first hint of what appears within the paragraph or essay.

<table>
<tr><td colspan="2">

HOW TO WRITE A STRONG TITLE

1. Give the main idea of your paragraph in the title.
2. If you don't want to tell the topic in your title, pick out a word or word group from the paragraph that will hint at the kind of topic you are treating.
3. Arouse the reader's curiosity by the title.
4. Write the title last, after you have finished the paragraph.
5. If you can write an interesting, exciting title, good. If not, don't worry. It's better to be clear and to give a title that suits the paragraph than to be brilliant, clever, or original.
6. When you write your title, put it on top of page one. Capitalize all important words.

Hint: Do not capitalize words like *and, the, an, a, but,* or any of the short direction words like *in, on, to, for* unless one of these words is the first or last word in your title.

</td><td>

WHAT NOT TO DO IN A TITLE

1. *Do not* make the title the only statement of the topic. *A title is not a topic sentence.* If you tell the topic in the title, repeat the topic in the topic sentence.
2. *Do not* try to be cute. If you want a funny title, be sure your paragraph deals with a humorous subject.
3. *Do not* use overworn expressions as your title: "A Stitch in Time Saves Nine" or "Love Makes the World Go Round" would be inappropriate titles for themes on prompt action and love because these titles are too familiar.
4. *Do not* write titles that are too long. A long full sentence is rarely used as a title.
5. *Do not* write a title that is too general.
6. *Do not* use quotation marks or underlining in your title when it appears on your composition.

</td></tr>
</table>

Step 1. Seeing Effective Titles. Each statement in Column I is the topic sentence of a paragraph. Column II gives a title which is poor for one of the reasons explained in the chart above. In Column III, write why you think the title is poor; in Column IV, try to write your own title.

I	II	III	IV
1. Many members of my family contributed to my happiness as a child.	Relatives	*too general*	*Relatives and Childhood Pleasure*
2. One frightening experience I recall is the awful time I was locked in a butcher's refrigerator for three hours.	Keeping Cool		
3. I will never forget the happy times I spent with Vicky at Camp Wabigon.	Vicky and I Spend Happy Summers at Camp Wabigon		

4. I learned the true   Shootin' the Hoops
   meaning of
   friendship while
   playing varsity
   basketball.

5. I remember the   Money Is the Root of
   awful troubles I   All Evil
   had working after
   school for Mr.
   Sanchez.

Step 2. More Practice with Titles.   List titles of several books, motion pictures, or television shows. Explain why you think the titles are effective or why they lack appeal for you. What might you add to the titles to make them stronger?

SOLVING PROBLEMS IN WRITING

Sentence Fragments: Phase II

The technique of subordination you learned earlier in this chapter is an essential characteristic of effective writing style. Used incorrectly, however, subordination gives rise to another type of *sentence fragment*. It's important to use the subordinating word group only when it can join on to a complete sentence, a word group that can make sense standing alone. These fragments appeared on student papers because the students forgot that subordinators must *join* ideas together:

1. **When** an empty shopping cart soared down the aisle.
2. **Who** really looked ridiculous.
3. **Unless** our government gives financial assistance.

The words in dark print are *subordinators*. Each one indicates that a major and complete idea will be expressed either earlier or later on in the sentence.

In number 1, the reader wants to know *what has happened* **when** that empty shopping cart soared down the aisle.

In number 2, the reader wants to know **who** *it was that* looked ridiculous.

In number 3, the reader wants to know *what will happen* **unless** the government gives financial assistance.

It is true that each of the word groups does contain a subject and a verb (they are underlined in each case). However, the use of the *subordinator* means that connection to a complete thought must be made for a correct sentence.

But those subordinator fragments are easy enough to recognize in isolation. Now look at them as they appear in parts of paragraphs.

Fragment

a. (1) Parents should leave their children at home when shopping must be done. (2) One afternoon at the A&P I stood minding my own business at the corn counter. (3) *When an empty shopping cart soared down the aisle.* (4) I knew some little brat was to blame.

b. (1) All the children in the third grade danced in snowflake costumes on the auditorium stage. (2) Over to the left stood my cousin Tyrone. (3) *Who really looked ridiculous.* (4) He was covered with a big white sheet and he moved more like a hippo than a snowflake.

c. (1) Our country's Olympic teams will be defeated. (2) *Unless our government gives financial assistance.* (3) American athletes cannot afford the time to train and compete.

Explanation

The word *when* here is a subordinator. It must connect all the words that follow it to a complete sentence. Since word group 3 is standing alone and *is not* connected to a complete thought, it is a *fragment*. The reader needs to know, within word group 3, what happened *when an empty shopping cart soared down the aisle.*

The word *who*, as it is used here, is a connector. It must join all the words that follow it to a complete sentence. In addition, the sentence that uses the word *who* must also identify the person that *who* refers to. It's not enough to use *Tyrone* at the end of sentence 2. Since word group 3 is standing alone and is not connected to a complete thought, it is a *fragment*.

The word *unless* is a subordinator. It must connect all the words that follow it to a complete sentence. Since word group 2 is standing alone and is not connected to a complete thought, it is a *fragment*. The reader needs to know, within word group 2, what will happen *unless our government gives financial assistance.*

FIXING THE SUBORDINATOR FRAGMENT: METHOD I

Join the fragment to the sentence before. In *a*, above join 2 and 3.

One afternoon at the A&P I stood minding my
[no period]
own business at the corn counter when an
[small letter]
empty shopping cart soared down the aisle.

In *b*, above, join 2 and 3.

Over to the left stood my cousin Tyrone, who
[comma]
[small letter]
really looked ridiculous.

In *c*, above, join 1 and 2.

Hint: A comma may be required when a subordinate word group is added at the end of a complete sentence. See page 93.

Our country's Olympic teams will be defeated
[small letter] [no period]
unless our government gives financial assistance.

Step 1. Adding Fragments On: I.   Correct the selections below by adding the fragment onto the sentence that comes before it.

1. Our country will face an energy crisis in the near future. Unless we develop new resources in this century.
2. I greatly admire my Uncle George. A man who taught me to love the simple things in life.

FIXING THE SUBORDINATOR FRAGMENT: METHOD II

Join the fragment to the sentence after.
In *c*, page 98, add 2 and 3.

Unless our government gives financial assist-
[comma]
ance, American athletes cannot afford the time to train and compete.

In *a*, page 98, add 3 and 4.

When an empty shopping cart soared down the aisle, I knew some little brat was to blame.
[comma]

Hint: When a subordinate word group comes first in a sentence, use a comma between it and the complete sentence that follows.

Step 2. Adding Fragments On: II.   Correct the selections below by adding the fragment to the sentence that follows it.

1. Before my first child was born. I was afraid that I would be a poor parent.
2. An event that I'll never forget. The day the astronauts landed on the moon was a great achievement for all citizens of the earth.

Hint: In trying to decide whether to add the fragment to the sentence before or after, first decide which way makes more sense. Add the fragment to the sentence to which it is most closely related in meaning.

FIXING THE SUBORDINATOR FRAGMENT: METHOD III

Add a new subject-verb word group to the fragment.
In *a*, page 98:

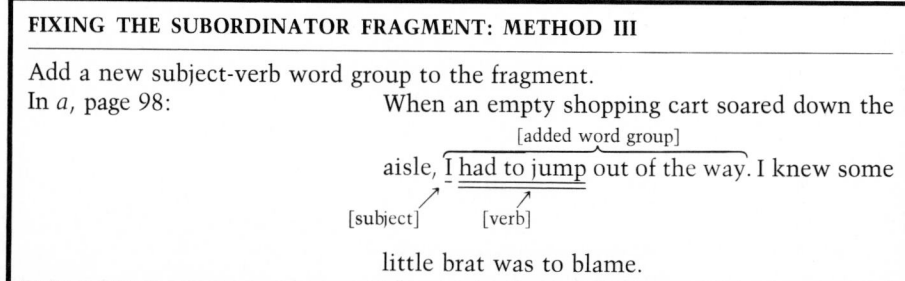

When an empty shopping cart soared down the
[added word group]
aisle, I had to jump out of the way. I knew some
[subject] [verb]

little brat was to blame.

Step 3. Adding Words to Fragments. Add the necessary words to these fragments and rewrite the correct sentence on the blank lines below. Remember punctuation.

1. If the drought continues. _____

_____

2. When the play begins. _____

_____

FIXING THE SUBORDINATOR FRAGMENT: METHOD IV

Sometimes you can take out the subordinator and some accompanying words in order to correct the fragment.

In *a*, page 98:

[remove subordinator]

~~When~~ An empty shopping cart soared down the

aisle.   [capital letter]

Sometimes it is necessary to add a new word, which will serve as the subject. In *c*, page 98.

[added word; subject of *looked*]

He

~~Who~~ really looked ridiculous.

[remove subordinator]

Hint: Use this method only when all others fail. It's best to incorporate the fragment into a complete sentence. In that way you will be improving your writing style by using subordination.

Step 4. Dropping the Subordinator. Correct these fragments by removing the subordinator.

1. Although I applauded the actors and actresses.
2. The boy who fell into the Hudson River.

FINDING THE FRAGMENT

You can see that the only way to spot the subordinator fragment is to be thoroughly familiar with the list of subordinators you were asked to experiment with earlier in this chapter. Here again are most of the subordinators, this time in Stop-Sign warning charts. If you memorize these words, you'll know what causes most students to write fragments.

FRAGMENT STOP SIGNS

I

as long as	how
after	provided
although	if
as	since
as if	so that
as soon as	though
because	unless
before	until
whenever	when
once	where
while	whether

II

what	whoever
which	whomever
who	whatever
whose	
that	

Hint: Remember, do not avoid using these words. When used correctly, they add variety and clarity to your style.

REVIEW CHARTS: THE SUBORDINATOR FRAGMENT

A Fragment Finder

1. Learn the list of subordinators that frequently give rise to fragments (see above).
2. Read the sentences aloud; do not confuse a pause for breath (which may or may not be indicated by a comma) with a complete stop (indicated by a period, a semicolon, or some other end mark).
3. Read your sentences from the last one to the first, stopping after each sentence to see if a complete thought has been expressed.

A Fragment Fixer

1. Join the fragment to the sentence that comes before.
2. Join the fragment to the sentence that comes after.
3. Add a new subject-verb word group.
4. Remove the subordinator. Add any new words.

Step 1. Correcting Fragments. Most of the selections below contain fragments of the subordinator type. Correct the fragments in any of the ways you have learned. If the selection is correct, mark the sentence *C*.

1. I consider myself to be a very handy person. Because whenever something breaks in the house I'm able to fix it.
2. We camped out at Moon Lake. Where we steered our canoe amid churning white water.
3. Travelers' checks are very safe. Wherever people travel. Their money is secure. Even if it is lost or stolen.
4. Many people praised WABC-TV. The station that first reported the story. That showed the events of the crime.

5. Diets high in sodium are unhealthy. A special problem for people who have high blood pressure. Who have to watch salt intake.
6. New York City has the reputation of being a dangerous city. Which it can be. But it is also a city of great business and culture.
7. Before I took the speed-reading course, I was a very slow reader. Now that I have finished the course, my reading speed has tripled.
8. My stepfather was late for dinner. Since he missed the bus. He had to walk home from work.
9. The weather in Seattle was great during our vacation. Although we encountered some rain. The temperature was ideal for sight-seeing.
10. Certain events stand out in my memory. Such as my first day in college. Which I will never forget.

Step 2. More Practice with Fragments. Study the fragment review charts on page 101. Then follow directions.

1. Write two sentences which tell something you do each morning when you wake up. Use the words *when I get out of bed* in one of your sentences. _____

   _____

   _____

   _____

2. Write one complete thought about a person who is always interrupting you. Use the words *who is always interrupting me* in your sentence.

   _____

   _____

3. Write two sentences that tell how you study for a final exam. Open one of your sentences with either of these word groups:
   Whenever I have a final exam or *Before a final exam.*

   _____

   _____

   _____

4. Write a sentence that tells what you do when you have to wait for a bus. Start your sentence with one of these words: *when, if, while.*

   _____

   _____

   _____

5. Write a sentence or two about farming. Use the words *to plant* or *to drive a tractor* or *to plow the fields* somewhere in your sentence.

_____

_____

_____

6. Write a sentence that tells your opinion of some course that you were asked to take in high school or college. Use the words *which is required*

in your sentence. _____

_____

_____

7. Write two sentences about the types of books you enjoy reading. Use the words *that I like* in one of your sentences. _____

_____

_____

8. Write three sentences about people you know. Use one of these word groups in *each* sentence:

who smiles easily
who always buys me coffee
whom I have not seen in a long time

_____

_____

_____

_____

9. Write a sentence about one of your teachers. Use this word group in your sentence: *whose ideas are helpful.* _____

_____

10. Write a sentence or two about some changes in your life style as a result of your learning to drive. Use one of these word groups somewhere in your sentence: *because I learned to drive* or *since I learned to drive.*

_____

_____

_____

_____

11. Write a sentence which tells of some exotic ethnic food you like. Use this word group somewhere in your sentence: *whether or not it is spicy.*

_____

_____

12. Write a sentence or two about people who sew their own clothes in order to save money. Start your sentence with these words: *When sewing to save money.* _____

_____

_____

_____

13. Write a sentence whose first word is *Whoever.* _____

_____

_____

14. Write two sentences, each one telling about a television show you like. Start the second sentence with *Also.* _____

_____

_____

15. Write two sentences about what you would do if you had to risk your life to save someone. Open one of the sentences with *If.* _____

_____

_____

_____

_____

Step 3. Look at Step 1 on page 16. For each word group that is not a sentence, write a complete one by adding and/or changing words.

Writing Plurals

Although the usual method of plural formation involves the addition of an -*s,* there are several variations. Study the review charts below which show examples and state rules.

Regular Plurals

Add -*s* to the singular for most plurals

boy + -*s* = boys
pencil + -*s* = pencils
tree + -*s* = trees

Words Ending in Y

1. If a consonant comes before the *y*, change the *y* to *i* and add -*es*.

   cit(y) + -*s* = cities
   part(y) + -*s* = parties
2. If a vowel comes before the *y*, add only -*s*.

   day + -*s* = days
   key + -*s* = keys

Words Ending in F

1. Most words ending in -*f* form plurals by adding *s*:

   roof—roofs
   chief—chiefs

2. Some words ending in *f* change to *v* and add -*es*:

leaf—leaves	wife—wives
elf—elves	self—selves
wolf—wolves	half—halves
knife—knives	calf—calves
shelf—shelves	loaf—loaves

Plurals That Stay the Same

Some words are the same in plural and singular:

cattle	series
deer	sheep
bass	wheat
corps	means
cod	dozen
	swine

one deer, many deer
a series, three series

Plurals That Add Syllables

If another syllable is added when you pronounce the plural, add -*es*. Words ending in *s*, *ss*, *ch*, *sh*, *tch*, *x*, *z* add another syllable and therefore add -*es*.

fox + -*es* = foxes
church + -*es* = churches
glass + -*es* = glasses

Words Ending in O

1. Add -*s* to most words ending in -*o*.

   piano + -*s* = pianos
   radio + -*s* = radios
2. Exceptions

echoes	heroes	mulattoes
potatoes	Negroes	mosquitoes
tomatoes	torpedoes	mottoes

-en Plurals

Some words add -*en* to make plurals

ox—oxen
child—children

Inside Plurals

Some words show plurals by changing letters within the word:

mouse—mice
man—men
louse—lice
foot—feet
tooth—teeth
goose—geese

Words from Other Languages

Some words still keep the plural of the foreign language from which they originated:

alga	algae
oasis	oases
alumnus	alumni
alumna	alumnae
parenthesis	parentheses
thesis	theses
basis	bases

bacterium	bacteria
medium	media
phenomenon	phenomena
axis	axes
criterion	criteria
radius	radii
fungus	fungi
datum	data
stratum	strata

Combination Words

1. If a word is formed by combining two or three words, make a plural of the main word.

   son-in-law = sons-in-law   man-of-war = men-of-war
   editor-in-chief = editors-in-chief
   commander in chief = commanders in chief

2. If the combination is written as one word, add *-s* or *-es* to the end.

   suitcase = suitcases
   cupful = cupfuls

Hint: Check a dictionary for plurals of combination words.

Step 1. Plurals.   Write the plurals of these words:

1. firefighter
2. desk
3. halo
4. wheat
5. patient
6. dwarf
7. watch
8. rodeo
9. bacterium

10. flash
11. lady
12. forkful
13. opportunity
14. mouse
15. locus
16. belief
17. child

18. soprano
19. loaf
20. medium
21. mosquito
22. crisis
23. passer-by
24. torpedo
25. monkey

Step 2. Selecting Plurals.   Change the words in parentheses to their plurals, and write them in the spaces provided.

1. Both (party) _____ served (cod) _____ with two (dozen)

   _____ different (loaf) _____ of bread.

2. Those (woman) _____ who are (alumna) _____ of the

   University of Texas are (editor-in-chief) _____
   of their county newspapers.

3. The ship-to-shore (radio) _____ informed the marine (corps)

   _____ of the (torpedo) _____ headed their way.

4. The scientific (datum) _____ on the study of (mouse) _____

show that they can kill (themself) _____ by eating (cupful) _____ of a known poison.

5. The (wolf) _____ attacked the (sheep) _____, but the ranchers leaped to their (foot) _____ and became (hero) _____ by scaring the (animal) _____ away.

WRITING THE PARAGRAPH

To develop your paragraph through examples, choose some memories from your childhood as the basis of this written assignment. Express them by means of details of people, places, and actions. Try to select memories that fall into a pattern and that suggest a single impression about your experiences. In that case you will develop your paragraph by offering several instances to support your topic sentence.

Using Subtopics: Student Samples

You may find it convenient to use subtopics if you offer a few well-detailed examples to support your topic. Read the student samples below; pay close attention to the use of subtopic sentences to introduce each new example. Then answer the questions that follow.

Childhood Mischief

I will never forget the mischievous things I used to do when my parents were not at home. Sliding across the beige linoleum floor on a cushion of talcum was one exciting bit of mischief. I shook baby powder all over my bedroom floor until it looked as if it was covered with snow and as slick as a sheet of ice. With white socks I became an ice skater gliding gracefully across a frozen pond. Feeling adventurous sometimes, I would run from the hall and slide into my room stopping within a few inches of my wooden dresser, which stands opposite the door. I did another really crazy thing on a night my older sisters babysat for my brother and me. Tired of minding us, Angela and Alethea sent us to bed but we were not the least bit tired. To make our sisters mad, my brother and I sneaked past them into the kitchen. We each took a little bit of laundry detergent and put it in our noses. Slipping back into bed, we kept sneezing uncontrollably for fifteen minutes. We thought this was funny, and every time a sneeze did not come we laughed. This made my oldest sister Angela very angry. Annoyed, she yelled at us, "You two better stop that sneezing, or when Ma comes home I am going to tell her how you were behaving!" From that moment on we had to cover up our sneezes so we would not get into trouble. But the most mischievous thing I did was to throw heavy rocks at passing cars. My friends, my sister Alethea, and I would go to Crotona Park and would climb to the top of a steep, rocky hill that overlooked an exit off the Cross Bronx Expressway. Whenever we hit one of the speeding cars, we would run off somewhere and hide. One day my sister hit a new brown and beige Mustang. She did not see a small angry man burst out of his car. All of us ran except Alethea. Cursing in a harsh voice, the man climbed up the hill behind her and almost grabbed her. She darted out of his reach just in time. That was the last time I ever threw rocks! In retrospect, all those mischievous things I did for fun could have caused me trouble not only with my parents but with other innocent people too.

—Elaine Dawkins

Horrors and High School Math

I will never forget my math teachers because I disliked most of them throughout my high school years. I remember my eleventh year math teacher vividly. She had a straight nose on which a pair of gold-rimmed glasses sat tightly at the end. Before each lesson began, she compelled me, her worst student, to erase long white columns from the chalkboards. Each day she gave pages of homework. I hated those assignments, so I just ignored them. In the end, of course, my reward was a *fifty* in red on my report card. Next, my geometry teacher stands out in my mind. Although Miss Carpenter was twenty-five, she acted like an old witch of a hundred. She wore the same dingy green dress each day. Sloppily, mousy brown hair hung in her eyes, and she scooped strands and curls off her forehead. Her voice, high-pitched, would screech across the classroom and down the hall. "Julius," I can still hear her squeak, her lips pinched in a little pink circle, "if you don't know about diameters, I'll have to fail you." But of all my math teachers, I disliked most the one who taught me algebra. A tall, lanky man, this teacher had an angry temper that kept most of us from asking questions. Once a girl in the last row asked timidly, "Will you explain that again please?" As Mr. Gilian's face grew scarlet, he plunged his hands into his black pants pockets. "Try paying attention," he barked, "and then you won't have to bother me with ridiculous questions." From my past unpleasant experiences with math teachers I have grown to dislike them all automatically; is it any wonder that my math grades never rise above C's and D's?

—Julius Passero

Step 1. Reviewing What You Read. Discuss these questions.

1. What is the topic in each paragraph? What is the writer's opinion about the topic in each case?
2. Read aloud the subtopic sentences for each paragraph.
3. How are the details in each case arranged, chronologically or by importance? How do you know?
4. Which details of color, sound, and action do you find most original?

Listing Details: Examples without Subtopics

In the words below from "There Was a Child Went Forth," Walt Whitman, the nineteenth-century American poet, suggests that every experience a person meets in life becomes part of that person.

There was a child went forth every day,
And the first object he look'd upon, that object he became,
And that object became part of him for the day or a certain part of the day,
Or for many years or stretching cycles of years.

The early lilacs became part of this child,
And grass and white and red morning glories, and red clover, and the song of the
  phoebe-bird.

>   —Walt Whitman
>   "There Was a Child Went Forth"

Some events play more important parts than others in contributing to our development. For the child in the poem, lilacs, morning glories, clover, and a bird's song became part of him. What experiences do you remember that became part of you? Can you capture them in images? What details can you list in order to answer the question "What Am I?"

Step 2. Using Details in Place of Subtopics. You need to recall the memories that are the deepest parts of yourself, the most vivid events (in your relations with people, parents, and the world) that you feel have become part of you. What you have seen and heard; what you have learned from others and seen in their faces; what smells you recall at unforgettable moments; the books you have read and the movies you watch: these all are the sources of defining your self.

In a paragraph that offers several details to support an idea you do not need to use subtopics because you are presenting, almost as a list, a series of examples.

Use the following paragraph by Andrew Siscaretti as a model before you write. As he does, use only images in your paragraph: mention people and places by name. Use color and sound.

You might wish to prepare this assignment along with Step 2 on pages 115–116; there you use Whitman's poem to make a collage.

What Am I? West, Clapton, and Flynn

I am the ringmaster of a three ring circus formally known as my family. I am the arguments between my brother and the whisperings of my sisters. I am the polluted, greyish-blue sky of Long Island City and the slimy, filthy waters of the East River and Newton's Creek. I am the limp in old Jack's leg or the large red girder that smashed down upon it. To my childhood companions, I was a real Casanova for going out with twin sisters at the same time and to those girls I am a devil. And I am the look that I still receive from their reddened blue eyes. To mom, I am still her blue-eyed bundle of joy, maybe growing up to wear the black robe of priesthood, while to pop, I am a future Jim Thorpe sprinting flat races, hurtling over large obstacles with a pole vault; and smacking through defenses for touchdowns. Or am I a future Jerry West, swishing the winning basket at the buzzer? On the football field, I am every player to hold a ball but after ripping my leg open, I change from a growling bear into a purring kitten waiting to die. In the hospital, I become the uncontaminated cleanliness and the antiseptic fragrance of the ward. I also become the lethal point of the syringe used to render me into the "world of nod" or the scent of flowers I receive from close friends. While listening to my stereo, I become Eric Clampton strumming "Layla" before close to thirty thousand screaming fans and I also become the tangy odor of marijuana that permeates Madison Square

Garden. I become one of the fans smoking a joint in the front row. My gang thinks of me as just another head in the crowd but I am still part of each one of them: one person's sneer, another one's smile, I am the hate and the love that exist among them. In the movies I become an Errol Flynn and a John Wayne who rescue the beautiful brown-eyed damsel and slay the cowardly rogue. I am the pebble in a little boy's shoe, a knife in a policeman's back, a dent on someone's car, a Hank Aaron homerun, my mother's teardrops, a bubble in Raquel Welch's bath, or a derelict stinking of alcohol. I am all of these things and many more. I am life.

—Andrew Siscaretti

Some Topics to Think About

In case you have trouble finding a topic, reread some of the sentences on page 80. Here are some other topics you might wish to write about:

1. doing things wrong (right)
2. my disposition
3. my triumphs
4. taking chances
5. athletics and me
6. insecurity: my personality key
7. my strengths
8. three rules I hated to obey
9. competing with a brother (sister)
10. religion in my life
11. my temper and my personality
12. trouble in the kitchen
13. being independent
14. learning important lessons
15. my dreams
16. young loves
17. experiences dating
18. embarrassment
19. outdoor life
20. teachers I liked (disliked)

Prewriting: Free Association to Get You Started

In free association, you choose a topic and jot down on a piece of paper everything and anything about that topic that pops up in your head. The ideas may be random and unrelated. The important thing is to let your thoughts run freely. Don't stop to correct the spelling of a word. When you are finished, look over your words and group related ideas together so that a pattern emerges. These ideas can serve as sources of details for your theme. Below is part of one student's attempt at free association. Examine his list of words and answer the questions that follow.

PREWRITING: FREE ASSOCIATION

Topic: my childhood behavior
sister's appendicitis: threw a tantrum in school
caught smoking in the junior high school bathroom

fishing trip with my father when I
    was five — I dumped all the bait
    overboard
happy Sunday mornings at home when
    I made pancakes and eggs for the
    whole family (pretty messy!)
bringing home stray parakeet
worm collection in a fish tank
draining a glass of wine from the
    dining room table (I was seven years
    old and I couldn't stop laughing)
Hallowe'en fun, howling like ghosts and
    waking all the neighborhood dogs
learning to swim at Riverhead
collecting money door-to-door for
    Muscular Dystrophy
sliding down Wilder Hill and knocking
    out a tooth
eating a whole bag of chocolate kisses.
                        — Michael D'Angelo

Step 1. Exploring a Student's Free Associations. Look at the list above to answer these questions:

1. What associations on Mr. D'Angelo's list might you group together because they seem related in some way?
2. What general word or words could you use to describe some of the groups

of details? Would you call any of the groups *dangerous? thoughtless? funny?*

3. What central personality thread might Mr. D'Angelo choose to develop on the basis of some of the items on this list?

Step 2. Your Own Free Associations. Select one of the topics on page 110 (or select a topic of your own), and practice prewriting by using free association to shake loose some ideas about the subject. Use separate paper.

Step 3. Associations on Tape. Some writers use a tape recorder for free-association techniques in prewriting. Once you have an idea of the topic you want to write about, speak for about twenty minutes into a tape recorder. Say whatever comes into your mind about the topic. Afterwards, with pencil and paper before you, play back the recording of your voice. Try to identify some thread running through your associations about your childhood. Then play the tape again, listening for those examples which support that central thread. Write down the examples with brief phrases; then try to arrange them in some order.

Requirements

Follow these suggestions as you write a one-paragraph theme that in some way reveals some memorable feature of your youth. Read the samples on pages 107–110 before you begin.

A Checklist: What to Do in Theme 3

1. Think carefully about your topic. Decide, with your instructor's help, whether to write a paragraph that employs two or three instances to show something about your youth, or one that offers a listing of details without subtopics. _____

2. Do prewriting (see page 35) to help you develop ideas. You might want to try free association as a prewriting technique for this theme. _____

3. After prewriting, prepare a rough draft that organizes your ideas clearly and logically. All the examples you offer—no matter how many— must support the personality thread you are trying to identify. _____

4. Write as many other drafts as you need to shape your ideas. When you prepare your final draft, be sure to follow the guidelines on page 37. _____

5. Proofread your paper twice: once *before* you prepare your final manuscript and once after you prepare it. (See pages 38–39). _____

6. Write a topic sentence (see page 8) that announces the subject of the paragraph and that gives your attitude toward the subject. _____

7. Use subtopic sentences where necessary (see pages 80–83) to introduce each new aspect of the topic. Notice how Elaine Dawkins and Julius Passero (pages 107–108) use subtopic sentences to tell in general terms the one specific part of the paragraph that will follow. _____

8. Use specific colors: "a new brown and beige Mustang." _____
9. Use words that tell sounds. Andrew Siscaretti (page 109) says, "swish- _____
ing the winning basket at the buzzer."
10. Use the words that show lively actions: "he plunged his hands into his _____
black pants pockets."
11. Use at least one line of someone's spoken words. Which spoken sen- _____
tence in Julius Passero's theme is most original?

Hint: See pages 54–55 for punctuating quotations.

12. Show details of scene; use a touch word and a word that appeals to the _____
sense of smell.
13. Use effective transitions to tie your sentences together: see pages 86– _____
87. You might want to try repeating a pronoun (page 88) and repeating
the same word at the beginning of several sentences (page 87).
14. Arrange your details either in chronological order or in order of impor- _____
tance, whichever suits your paragraph best.
15. Use some of the new vocabulary on pages 78–79. _____
16. Open one sentence with a word that ends in -ly (see page 53). _____
17. Start some sentences with different subordinators, given on pages _____
89–93.
18. Use a semicolon correctly (see pages 17–18). _____
19. As you proofread your paragraph, look especially for run-on errors (or _____
comma splices), sentence fragments, and errors in writing plurals.
20. Give your paragraph a strong, lively title (see page 95). _____

THE PROFESSIONALS SPEAK

Step 1. Authors Remember their Youth. The selections below develop
topics through the use of examples. Discuss the questions after you read
the excerpts.

Down South

Down South seemed like a dream when I was on the train going back to New York.
I saw a lot of things down South that I never saw in my whole life before and most of
them I didn't ever want to see again. I saw a great big old burly black man hit a pig in
the head with the back of an ax. The pig screamed, oink-oinked a few times, lay
down, and started kicking and bleeding . . . and died. When he was real little, I
used to chase him, catch him, pick him up, and play catch with him. He was a
greedy old pig, but I used to like him. One day when it was real cold, I ate a piece of
that pig, and I still liked him. One day I saw Grandma kill a rattlesnake with a hoe.
She chopped the snake's head off in the front yard, and I sat on the porch and
watched the snake's body keep wiggling till it was nighttime. And I saw an old brown

hound dog named Old Joe eat a rat one day, right out in the front yard. He caught the rat in the woodpile and started tearing him open. Old Joe was eating everything in the rat. He ate something that looked like the yellow part in an egg, and I didn't eat eggs for a long time after that. I saw a lady rat have a lot of little baby rats on a pile of tobacco leaves. She had to be a lady, because my first-grade teacher told a girl that ladies don't cry about little things, and the rat had eleven little hairless pink rats, and she didn't even squeak about it.

I made a gun down South out of a piece of wood, some tape, a piece of tire-tube rubber, a nail, some wire, a piece of pipe, and a piece of door hinge. And I saw nothing but blood where my right thumbnail used to be after I shot it for the first time. The nail grew back, little by little. I saw a lot of people who had roots worked on them, but I never saw anybody getting roots worked on them.

Down South sure was a crazy place, and it was good to be going back to New York.

—Claude Brown
Manchild in the Promised Land

Boyhood Farm Days

As I have said, I spent some part of every year at the farm until I was twelve or thirteen years old. The life which I led there with my cousins was full of charm, and so is the memory of it yet. I know how the wild blackberries looked, and how they tasted, and the same with the pawpaws, the hazelnuts, and the persimmons; and I can feel the thumping rain, upon my head, of hickory nuts and walnuts when we were out in the frosty dawn to scramble for them with the pigs, and the gusts of wind loosed them and sent them down. I know the stain of blackberries, and how pretty it is, and I know the stain of walnut hulls, and how little it minds soap and water, also what grudged experience it had of either of them. I know the taste of maple sap, and when to gather it, and how to arrange the troughs and the delivery tubes, and how to boil down the juice, and how to hook the sugar after it is made, also how much better hooked sugar tastes than any that is honestly come by, let bigots say what they will. I know how a prize watermelon looks when it is sunning its fat rotundity among pumpkin vines and "simblins"; I know how to tell when it is ripe without "plugging" it; I know how inviting it looks when it is cooling itself in a tub of water under the bed, waiting; I know how it looks when it lies on the table in the sheltered great floor space between house and kitchen, and the children gathered for the sacrifice and their mouths watering; I know the crackling sound it makes when the carving knife enters its end, and I can see the split fly along in front of the blade as the knife cleaves its way to the other end; I can see its halves fall apart and display the rich red meat and the black seeds, and the heart standing up, a luxury fit for the elect; I know how a boy looks behind a yard-long slice of that melon, and I know how he feels; for I have been there. I know the taste of the watermelon which has been honestly come by, and I know the taste of the watermelon which has been acquired by art. Both taste good, but the experienced know which tastes best. I know the look of green apples and peaches and pears on the trees, and I know how entertaining they are when they are inside of a person. I know how ripe ones look when they are piled in pyramids under the trees, and how pretty they are and how vivid their colors. I know how a frozen apple looks, in a barrel down cellar in the wintertime, and how hard it is to bite, and how the frost makes the teeth ache, and yet how good it is, notwithstanding. I know the disposition of elderly people to select the specked apples for the children, and I once knew ways to beat the game. I know the look of an apple that is roasting and sizzling on a hearth on a winter's evening, and I know the comfort that comes of eating it hot, along with some sugar and a drench of cream.

—Mark Twain
Autobiography

1. What topic does each writer attempt to support?
2. What examples does he present in order to develop the topic?
3. Which images of action are clearest?
4. What words serve as transitions through repetition in each selection?

Step 2. Reviewing a Professional Sample.   Reread "Memories of Cross-gates School" (pages 83–84) by George Orwell. What topic does the paragraph try to develop? What examples does the writer give in order to support his point? Which details are most lively and original?

REACHING HIGHER

Step 1. A Photo into Words.   Look at the photograph on page 77. Write a topic sentence that introduces the main subject of the picture and some opinion you have about the subject. Write subtopic sentences—if necessary—to introduce each aspect of the topic; add details of color, sound, smell, touch, and action to support each subtopic sentence.

Step 2. A Collage to Answer "What Am I?"   Read again the piece on pages 108–109 from Walt Whitman's poem "There Was a Child Went Forth." This time, using old magazines, newspapers, paint, ink, pieces of advertisements, various other materials (foil, string, macaroni, photographs), make a *collage* that you think will present to the class a visual answer to the question "What Am I?" Select from the sources you use things that you believe have become part of you. Look at the "What Am I?" collage on the next page by Jacqueline Boston.

After everyone has prepared collages, line them all up in front of the room so that nobody's name can be seen. One at a time, discuss the personality of the person who made each project. What specific feature of the collage tells you most about the person who made it?

Jacqueline Boston

chapter 4

PEOPLE YOU KNOW, SIDE BY SIDE

Howard Smithline

INTRODUCTION TO COMPARISON AND CONTRAST

Hundreds of people brush past our lives every day: crowds at the shopping malls; long lines at restaurants and movie houses; bodies on campus running, strolling, laughing, pushing, drifting between classes; men and women and children in the family, on the block, in the homes of friends. With many of these people nothing more develops than a meeting of the eyes, then a quick glance away and a rapid forgetting. With others, relationships build, some with our delight and thanks, others against our own wills. As our experiences and memories collect faces, appearances, personalities of the people around us, we cannot help making comparisons and drawing contrasts, almost automatically. One woman's smile reminds us of another's. One child's delights make us wonder at another child's pains. One man's kindness and patience we lay alongside another man's anger and cruelty. In our minds' eyes we see side by side our relatives, our friends, our teachers, our colleagues, our enemies, our loves.

One of the best ways we have to analyze, understand, and evaluate is through comparison and contrast. It is second nature for us to compare one experience with another to see points of resemblance and difference. In writing, such a process adds force to your presentation; the reader comes to understand the value of your experiences as you yourself weave together the strands of comparison or contrast.

VOCABULARY

Step 1. Words for Opposite Physical Qualities. These words will help you contrast people you may want to describe. In the blanks write definitions for the opposite—or nearly opposite—words in each set. Use a dictionary for assistance. (Check Appendix A for more help.)

1. *a.* dexterous _____   *b.* awkward _____

2. *a.* diminutive _____   *b.* massive _____

3. *a.* rotund _____   *b.* slender _____

4. *a.* swarthy _____   *b.* pallid _____

5. *a.* stately _____   *b.* undignified _____

Step 2. Applying Meanings. From the words above select one to describe a person who

1. has pale skin _____   6. is bulky and solid _____

2. is very tiny _____   7. is clumsy _____

3. shows no self-respect or nobility _____   8. is formal and dignified _____

4. has a plump shape _____

5. is gracefully thin _____

9. is skillful in the use of body or mind

_____

10. has a sunburned complexion _____

Step 3. Words for Contrasting Moods. Check the definitions of these words to describe moods. Write definitions you understand in the blank spaces (see Appendix A).

"Up" Moods

benevolent _____

confident _____

affectionate _____

serene _____

exuberant _____

"Down" Moods

irate _____

spiteful _____

sluggish _____

masochistic _____

depressed _____

Step 4. Listening in on Moods. Each statement made below identifies a mood named in Step 3. Identify the mood that the person who speaks seems to be experiencing.

_____ 1. "I just can't get going today. My feet feel like lead, and I'm so tired and lazy that I don't want to move!"

2. "Let me kiss you again. I love to hold you."

_____ 3. "If I get my hands on him, I'll kill him. I'll tear him limb from limb."

_____ 4. "I'll be happy to watch the children tomorrow so you can play tennis and then go to the beach."

_____ 5. "He hurt me when he broke off our engagement. I want to hurt him in return."

6. "I feel so calm and peaceful."

_____ 7. "I'll study until dawn. Unless I suffer, I'm not going to pass that final!"

8. "I know I can do the job right."

_____ 9. "I'm delighted at being alive. What a beautiful, wonderful, sunny day!"

_____ 10. "I never felt so rotten in all my life."

BUILDING COMPOSITION SKILLS

Finding the Topic

Step 1. Talking It Over. Using the suggestions below, speak for a minute or two about two people who are similar to or who are very different from each other. Show how your specific experiences with these people illustrate your point as Thomas Baim does in his talk below.

1. two friends you know
2. the way two relatives disciplined you
3. two math or science teachers you liked (or disliked)
4. how your parents are alike (or different)
5. how your brothers (sisters, cousins) are different
6. your husband's (wife's) behavior: two contrasting scenes
7. two employers you worked for
8. two different boy friends (girl friends)
9. a teacher who lectures as opposed to a teacher who guides class discussions
10. two helpful neighbors
11. two coworkers: likenesses and differences
12. high school teachers versus college teachers
13. your son (daughter) at one age compared with the same child at another age
14. two neighborhood storekeepers: how they treat customers
15. two physicians you have visited recently

To me lectures are worthless; group discussions make much better and more interesting class sessions. Mr. Goldman, my junior history teacher at Park Lane High, lectured to us all the time. Even though he had a lively booming voice and a good knowledge of his subject, after thirty minutes, feet would shuffle on the floor, pencils would drop, girls would whisper and yawn as the teacher turned his back to write on the board. I loved history, but I found myself staring out the window at the sky or the clouds. But Mr. Rudnicki, my psychology teacher here at State, never lectures. Sure, he contributes information to our discussions—sometimes he talks for ten minutes straight—but lots of other people talk as well. It's much more exciting to hear different voices and different opinions. We all sit around with our chairs in a circle and usually more than half the class talks at each session. I know it's much harder to learn in this kind of class because you never really know what's "right" since there is often no definite information. But I find I'm always thinking about what went on in my psych class, and I can't wait to forget what I scribbled in my notebook during a lecture!

—Thomas Baim

Comparisons for Clear Pictures: Using Figures of Speech

An important way to improve your written expression is to make comparisons so that the reader sees clearly some picture you are describing. Notice how the picture in Column I below takes on new life in Column II by means of a comparison.

I	II
Her blue eyes sparkled.	Her eyes sparkled *like small blue circles of ice.*

By using the word *like* (or, often, *as*) in II above, the writer compares *eyes* to *small blue circles of ice.* Such a comparison, using *like* or *as,* is called a *simile.*

A *metaphor* is a comparison that leaves out the comparing word *like* or *as*:

Her eyes were small blue circles of ice.

This kind of comparison is often very forceful because it shows that the object is so much like the thing to which it is being compared that it almost becomes that thing. Look again at the difference.

Her eyes were *like small blue circles of ice.*   Her eyes *were small blue circles of ice.*

Here, a woman's eyes are compared to circles of ice, and there are two distinct features of the comparison, *eyes* and *blue circles of ice.*

Here, the woman's eyes are said to *be* those *blue circles of ice.* It is as if the eyes and the icy blue circles were one and the same; the eyes take on all the qualities of the ice.

Sometimes, to add liveliness, a writer can give some nonhuman object living qualities. The comparison between a nonhuman object and a living thing is called *personification:*

The hot day dragged its weary feet into the evening.

In this sentence, the *day,* a nonhuman object, is given the qualities of a person who is tired: the words *dragged its weary feet* express the human quality.

Step 1. Reading Lively Comparisons.   Read aloud these comparisons by professional writers. Explain the meaning of the comparison. Which sentence lets you see most clearly what the writer had in mind? Which comparison is most original?

1. If dreams die, life is a broken-winged bird that cannot fly.
   —Langston Hughes

2. Greatly shining,
   The Autumn moon floats
      in the thin sky;
   And the fish-ponds shake
      their backs and flash
      their dragon scales
   As she passes over them.
            —Amy Lowell

3. Then, there was a crush of falling timbers nearby and Scarlett saw a thin tongue of flame lick up over the roof of the warehouse in whose sheltering shadow they sat.

   —Margaret Mitchell

4. His face was white as pie-dough and his arms were lank and white as peeled sticks.

—Robert Smith

5. The mysterious East faced me, perfumed like a flower, silent like death, dark like a grave.

—Joseph Conrad

Step 2. Comparisons of Your Own.   Using the word groups below, on separate paper write sentences that make a comparison in a vivid picture. Strive for originality, humor, beauty, clarity. Use any of the three types of comparisons you have learned so far—simile, metaphor, personification.

Example:

rain

The rain hissed on the hot cabin roof, then slithered down the window in streams like transparent snakes.

—Gerald Hull

1. a fire
2. a door
3. a woman's laugh
4. a smile
5. the moon
6. a river
7. the fall
8. an old automobile
9. a bus
10. snow

Step 3. Metaphors for Abstract Words.   Try to explain your view of some hard-to-define emotion, idea, or concept in a metaphor rich in sensory detail. Select a word such as *hope, love, fear, power, war, hate, hunger, life, sorrow, joy, death,* or any other abstract term. Look at the student samples on the next page. Use your own paper.

Life is a rosebush growing in my garden, full of thorns but fragrant and lovely.

—Alayne Finkelstein

Fear is sitting in a creaking dentist's chair and seeing only the top of Dr. Rifkin's bald head as his trembling hand tries to zero in on a cavity.

—Janet Hutter

Life is an elusive, black fly buzzing through cool air, slipping past the blue-eyed youngster stalking him with a fly swatter.

—Terry Sanders

Step 4. Avoiding Trite Comparisons.   When a comparison appears too frequently in language, it loses its originality. Any statement or expression that is overused is called *trite* or *hackneyed* because it is no longer original. Such expressions appear numbered from 1 to 10 below. For each one, rewrite the comparison to strengthen it. Use separate paper.

Example: quiet as a schoolyard in a Sunday morning rain.
1. quiet as a mouse
2. red as a beet
3. white as a ghost
or
white as a sheet

4. fresh as a daisy
5. as good as gold
6. dark as night
7. as different as night and day

8. busy as a bee
9. mad as a hornet
10. work like a horse

Getting It All Together: Transitions III

As you may recall, certain words help one idea in a paragraph flow smoothly into the next idea. The *transition* words below, cementing together ideas so that the thoughts are related clearly, show relationships you might want to indicate in your paragraph.

Transition Words That Add One Thought to Another

in addition	likewise
moreover	nor
and	further
and then	next
besides	last
again	also
too	
furthermore	

Transition Words to Compare Ideas (to Show Likenesses)

in the same way
similarly
likewise
resembling
alike
like

Transition Words to Contrast Ideas or to Admit a Point (to Show Differences)

but	although	dissimilar
still	on the other hand	unalike
however	in contrast	differ(s) from
nevertheless	otherwise	difference
on the contrary	conversely	different
after all	while this may be true	
notwithstanding	yet	
even though	granted	
though	in spite of	

Transition Words to Show that One Ideal Results from Another

as a result	accordingly
thus	therefore
because	consequently
since	then
hence	

Step 1. Transitions to Show Relationships. In this paragraph, fill in each blank with a transition word that will help move one idea smoothly into the next. The information at the left tells what kinds of transition words you need. Be sure that the word you select makes sense in the blank.

The True Musician

[Contrast] _____ Plato believed that music played a strong part in a man's education, he did not ignore other areas of learning. Music, through rhythm and

[Add] harmony, could bring grace to the soul _____ a man educated in

[Result] music could develop a true sense of judgment; _____ he would be able to recognize quality in art and nature and could respond with praise for

[Compare] good things. _____ a man who knew music could, without having to

[Contrast] think too long, give blame to any bad artistic works. _____ any man who devoted his life only to music risked the chance of becoming too soft-

[Result] ened and soothed. _____ such a man would be a feeble warrior and

[Contrast] of little use to the Greeks. Someone who practiced gymnastics, _____, could fill himself with pride and could become twice the man that he was.

[Compare]   [Admit point] _____ he could develop courage for battle. _____ athletics made an essential part of the educated man, Plato also knew that too much focus on physical training could make a man excessively violent and fierce.

[Add] _____ he might come to hate philosophy and the art of persuasion in

[Compare] preference to battle. _____ such a man would live in ignorance and

[Result] would not be civilized. _____ Plato showed that the man who learned music and athletics in good balance was best: "He who mingles music with gymnastics in the fairest proportions . . . may be rightly called the true musician. . . ."

Transition Words that Summarize

therefore	consequently
in conclusion	thus
finally	to sum up
as a result	accordingly
in short	in brief
as I have (shown)	in other words
(said)	all in all
(stated)	

Transition Words that Emphasize

surely	indeed
certainly	truly
to be sure	in fact
undoubtedly	without a doubt

Transition Words that Tell an Example Will Follow

for example	specifically
for instance	as an illustration
as proof	to illustrate

Step 2. Example, Summary, Emphasis: Transitions. From the three lists, select one word that will fit in the blank as a good transition. The words at the left tell the kinds of transition words you need.

[Emphasize]   1. Rock music is still extraordinarily popular. _____ it will continue its hold on young people over the next decade.

[Example]   2. Not all housework is tedious. _____ cooking, even though it can be a chore, is still an imaginative and creative one.

[Summarize]   3. He failed his driving test three times. _____ he could not use the family car all summer long.

[Emphasize]   4. _____ there are many ways to save energy around the house.

[Example]   _____ lowering the thermostat drops oil consumption remarkably.

Step 3. Checking More Transitions. Read "Different Roommates," pages 130–131. Circle the transition words that add, compare, contrast, show result, summarize, or indicate example.

Expanding Sentences: Building Lively Quotations

A sentence in which you tell the exact words someone is saying adds life to a paragraph. Often you can expand a quotation sentence by using sensory language in order to paint a vivid picture of the speaker or the circumstances under which the speaking is done. By adding action words and appeals to color, smell, touch, or sound, you can create a full and satisfying image for your reader.

HOW TO BUILD A QUOTATION SENTENCE

1. Start with a lively, realistic quotation:

   "Hurry up, you lazy slowpoke!"

2. Tell who talks:

   "Hurry up, you lazy slowpoke!" Vivian shouted.
   "Hurry up, you lazy slowpoke!" my sister said.

3. Tell *how, when,* or *where* the words were spoken:

   [where]
   "Hurry up, you lazy slowpoke!" Vivian shouted at the door.
   "Hurry up, you lazy slowpoke!" my sister said angrily.
   [how]

4. Add a detail to describe some action or movement:

   Pulling on her gloves at the door, Vivian shouted, "Hurry up, you lazy slow-
   [action]
   poke!"

"Hurry up, you lazy slowpoke!" my sister said angrily as she stamped her [action] foot on the floor.

5. Describe the speaker's face. Add a detail of color or touch or sound.

Pursing her lips and pulling on leather gloves at the door, Vivian shouted, [description of speaker] [touch word]
"Hurry up, you lazy slowpoke!"

"Hurry up, you lazy slowpoke!" my sister said angrily, her brown eyes flash- [color] [description of speaker]

ing as she stamped her foot on the floor.

Hint: Review the correct punctuation of quotations on pages 54–55.

Step 1. Expanding Quotation Sentences. Expand each of these quotations by adding details in several steps like those in the box above. Write your final sentence on the blank lines.

1. "I'm not interested in your opinion." _____

_____

2. "Close the door because it's freezing in here." _____

_____

3. "This work must be finished by this afternoon." _____

_____

4. "I'm trying to say I'm sorry." _____

_____

5. "Let's get moving!" _____

_____

Step 2. Building up Your Own Quotations. Return to Step 4 on pages 55–56. Expand in the manner described above each original sentence you wrote in Column II. Use separate paper.

THE COMPARISON-CONTRAST PARAGRAPH: THREE PATTERNS

A favorite method of paragraph and essay development involves comparison and contrast. *Comparison* means showing how things are alike, and *contrast* means showing how things are different. Sometimes a paragraph may be developed through illustrations of how things are *different;* other paragraphs discuss *similarities* only; still others may treat both *likenesses and differences.* The writer decides which approach to take.

Hint: If you are asked to *compare* two things, you usually need to *contrast* them as well.

Whatever approach you choose, there are some patterns you can follow to make the comparison effective.

Likenesses *or* Differences

Pattern 1. In this kind of paragraph, first you discuss one of the two objects; then you discuss the other object.

You can single out one basic way in which the two objects are alike or different in order to limit your topic effectively. For example, you might decide to compare two people at work by discussing the way they do their jobs. The first part of the paragraph would show something about one person's approach to work; the next part of the paragraph would show something about the other person's approach.

However, instead of deciding on one basic way by which to compare the two things, you can choose to discuss a *few* points or ideas about the first object; then you can discuss a *few* points or ideas about the second. Here you do not use a single focus of comparison. For example, in a paragraph comparing two people in this manner, you might want to discuss these points:

1. the way they dress
2. the way they talk
3. how they behave under pressure

First you would discuss all those ideas in regard to one person; then, in the next part of the paragraph, you would discuss the same points in regard to the other person. In each part, of course, you would need to offer details to support your ideas.

SOME HINTS ABOUT PATTERN 1

If you decide on a basic focus of comparison:
1. The subtopic sentence (see pages 80–83) will help you introduce the basic difference for each object.
2. You might wish to illustrate your point with *one specific instance* about one person and *one specific instance* about the other. Each instance would be a dramatic moment expanded by means of sensory language.
3. If you want to use more than one instance from your experience to illustrate each part of your point, you can also use sensory language. True, you will not be able to go into great detail for each instance, but you need to make the details as clear as possible.
4. You might wish to combine 2 and 3: state briefly several instances that illustrate your point about the first person; then focus on one dramatic moment that illustrates your point about the second person.

If you decide to discuss a few points about each object:

1. A subtopic sentence can help you introduce each of the two people you are comparing.
2. You will not be able to go into great detail for each of the points. However, make sure you can support each point with some kind of illustration.
3. You run the risk of writing a dull paragraph because each point is usually repeated twice, once for each object. Lively illustrations and varied vocabulary can help overcome dullness.

Step 1. A Student's Theme.   Read the student sample below. Answer the questions after the paragraph.

The Two Willies

Only five years old, my son Willie tickles the family with opposite sides to his behavior. One piece of him is quiet and shy, especially when he is with strangers. Last month I had to drag him up the steps at Presbyterian Nursery School for his first day in class. Willie clutched at my leg in silent terror as we stood at the doorway to his room. Two little boys sat at a table near the window and played with green clay as they giggled to each other. Nearby a boy and girl dressed and undressed two rag dolls. "Well, so this is Willie," said his teacher, Miss Natalie, with a bright smile. "Come, let's say hello to the rest of the class." But she had to pry his fingers one by one off my skirt as he stared without a sound. When Miss Natalie led Willie from child to child, saying his name, Willie never breathed a word. Though his teacher says now that he is coming along, he is still the quietest boy in the class. But just let him loose in the backyard of our house and he turns into a wild man! Yesterday, a warm fall afternoon, he hung by his ankles from a limb of our elm as my heart pounded. Calling like a monkey and beating his chest, he swung back and forth, back and forth. Leaping down, he raced to the grey wooden fence and barked through it at my neighbor's German shepherd, who howled and rattled his pen. Then like a squirrel Willie dug up a dozen holes in the lawn and buried whatever he could find, bottle caps, pieces of glass, leaves, cigarette butts, broken twigs. He's never quiet or shy! He chased flies, snorting through his nose. Off key he sang the *Sesame Street* song as he poked a pink worm with a rock. When Charlotte, my next-door neighbor's four-year-old, came to play, Willie screeched at her like a plane about to crash and pushed her to the grass. She cried miserably, but Willie showed no mercy. My psychology teacher assures me that my son is perfectly normal for his age, but he is not at all easy to understand at this stage.

—Mollie Boone

1. What is the basic focus Mollie Boone offers to show the different qualities in her son Willie?
2. What two moments does she use to illustrate her point?
3. Which, in your opinion, are the liveliest images of action? What details name sounds? Where is color used effectively?
4. Read each of the two subtopic sentences. What key words in the subtopic sentences suggest opposite meanings?

Step 2. Using a Focus for Comparison. Assume that you would develop each topic in Column I in a comparison-contrast paragraph like Pattern I where you would use a single focus of comparison. In Column II, write down the basic way in which the two ideas are either alike or similar. In Column III, name two specific moments you might use to illustrate each object. Look at the example.

I Topics to Compare	II Basic Focus of Comparison	III Two Illustrations
1. baseball and football	*level of excitement (baseball: dull; football: exciting)*	*a. time I sat through an eleven inning no-hitter. b. time I watched the Jets and Packers at Shea Stadium.*
2. two former teachers		
3. a blind date compared with a date I chose myself		

Step 3. Understanding Another Approach. Assume that you would develop each topic in Column I in a comparison-contrast paragraph that follows Pattern 1 where there is no basic focus but where, instead, a few points are discussed for each object. In Column II, list three significant points you might use to illustrate each part of the topic. Look at the example.

I Topic for Comparison	II Discussion Points
1. city and country winters	*a. transportation b. ways of having fun c. landscape*
2. waiters and waitresses	a. _____ b. _____ c. _____

3. two neighbors

a. _____

b. _____

c. _____

Pattern 2. This pattern does not separate the two objects you are discussing. Instead, it treats both objects together for each point of comparison. For example, in a paragraph comparing two roommates, let's assume that a writer wants to discuss these three points:

1. their physical appearances
2. their interests
3. their approaches to school work

After mentioning each point, the writer would discuss both roommates in relation to that point, in order to illustrate how they compare in physical appearance, how they compare in their interests, and, finally, how they compare in the way they do schoolwork.

HINTS ABOUT PATTERN 2

1. Ordering details by importance (see pages 84–86) is often the best plan for this pattern. You may wish, therefore, to discuss in less detail your first point or points so that you can concentrate more fully on the last point, the one that is most important to you.
2. The subtopic sentence helps you introduce each new point of comparison.
3. Transition words help you move easily from one point to the next.

Step 4. A Point-by-Point Comparison. Read the paragraph below, developed by means of Pattern 2. Answer the questions that come after it.

Different Roommates

I am amazed myself at how little trouble it is living with and liking two such different roommates. Their physical appearances differ greatly. With small brown eyes and straight black hair to her shoulders, Julie is tall, lean, and statuesque. Pat, on the other hand, is tiny. Under five feet tall, she keeps her blonde hair short and fluffy. Looking out over a small nose, her large grey eyes are "funny looking," according to her. "They're all right if you like cats," she says grinning. These two girls also have different kinds of interests. Julie likes reading or relaxing quietly in front of the television set. She likes talking too; she will speak to me for hours about a feature in *People Magazine* or about a Marx Brothers' film she watched on Channel 4 until dawn. Her voice quivers with excitement. "Just listen to this," she will say, her eyes glowing, her warm fingers pressed to my palm to hold my attention. But for Pat the outdoor life holds more interest than books or screens. At six each morning, in a bright orange sweat suit, she is jogging merrily down University Drive, crunching through leaves for her usual four miles. She swims. She plays tennis. She is a

terror at paddleball, smashing shots I have to groan to return. However, the most interesting difference between them is their approach to schoolwork. Julie grows
tense before an exam. At her desk a small fluorescent lamp throws a pale light on
her face as she sits for hours glaring nervously at a page in her biology book. She
underlines words noisily and scrawls notes to herself in the margin with a yellow felt
pen. Her lips say over and over some key words she wants to memorize. Because
only "A" grades satisfy her, she works tirelessly. Pat, on the contrary, takes everything easy, and exams are no exception. Sprawled on the red and white print couch,
she surrounds herself with cola, corn chips, chocolate bars, apples, and salted
nuts. She jabbers endlessly and jumps up every few minutes to stare out the window, to do a few sit-ups or to splash herself with spicy cologne. Without much effort
or anxiety she crams enough data into her head to earn grades that keep her happy.
Since I can live in harmony with my two roommates in spite of their differences, I
am confident that I will be able to get along with most people anywhere.

—Cecilia Richardson

1. Pick out the three subtopic sentences.
2. Which details let you see best what Julie looks like? what Pat looks like?
   Which images do you find clearest and most memorable?
3. What is the main difference in the approaches to schoolwork each of the
   writer's roommates takes? What specific details best show the difference?
4. What order has Cecilia Richardson used to arrange the points in this
   comparison? Why has she chosen such an order?

Likenesses *and* Differences

Pattern 3. In this comparison and contrast paragraph, you discuss both
likenesses *and* differences. You can decide on *one basic way* in which the
two objects may be compared, or you can discuss a number of points for the
two objects without naming some central focus (as in Pattern 1). The idea
here is that both similarities *and* dissimilarities appear in the paragraph. Of
course, you will have to illustrate just *how* these two objects have some
similar features and how they have different features. If you think the differences are more important, discuss the *similarities* first so that you may
give the reader the most important idea *last* (see pages 84–86 for order of
details). If you think the similarities are more important, discuss the differences first.

Let us assume that you want to compare two of your relatives and that
you select *the way they disciplined you as a child* as the one basic point of
comparison. Let's also assume that the differences in these methods of disciplining are what you think are most important. The first part of your paragraph could illustrate through vivid details one or more of these similarities:

1. your relatives' concern for your welfare
2. their strictness
3. their little speeches after you did something wrong

Then, you might focus on one or more of these differences:

1. the way the two relatives looked when they were angry
2. what they actually did to you
3. how long it took them to get over their anger

Determine the *number* of points you want to discuss by the nature of the details you wish to use. One dramatic, expanded illustration for *one* of the points would mean that fewer points would be treated in the paragraph.

HINTS ABOUT PATTERN 3

1. The topic sentence should indicate that your paragraph will treat *both* similarities and differences. Coordination or subordination may be effectively used in the topic sentence.

    [subordinator]

    Although my mother and father shared similar outlooks in rearing children and in disciplining them, mom took her responsibilities more seriously.
    [coordinator]

    Both of my parents were very liberal in the way they reared their children, but my father's sudden loss of temper in moments of anger always scared me.

2. Remember, if differences are more important to you, discuss similarities first; if likenesses are more important, talk first about differences. Topic sentence I below stresses the major area of difference; topic sentence II stresses the major areas of likeness. The sentences deal with similar topics.

    I

    Although my mother and my grandmother supported strict rules in rearing young children, I could always count on grandma's understanding when I got in trouble at school.

    This paragraph will stress the differences in the degree of understanding the relatives showed toward school problems.

    II

    Despite their different ways of showing approval or disapproval for my behavior, my mother and my grandmother supported strict rules in rearing children.

    This paragraph will stress the similarities in the support shown by the two relatives for strictness in raising children.

3. Sometimes you do not need to explain both similarities and differences, even though you wish to make the point that likenesses and differences exist. You can assume that the reader understands, appreciates, or agrees with the part that you do not wish to explain. In this way you can use the paragraph to develop the more important element of your comparison. For example, in topic sentence 1 above, the writer could assume that readers would accept this part of the sentence: "my mother and my grandmother supported strict rules in rearing young children." The writer would not have to discuss these strict rules but could move right on to illustrate the differences as he or she sees them.

Step 5. Understanding the Pattern. For each subject of comparison or contrast in Column I list in Column II two or three similarities that might be expanded with details in a paragraph. In Column III list two or three differences between the two objects, differences that might also be expanded with details in the paragraph. Look at the example.

I	II	III
Topic for Comparison	*Some Similarities*	*Some Differences*
1. cats and dogs as pets.	a. companionship b. owners develop a sense of responsibility c. amusement	a. cats are very easy to care for b. cats often get in trouble c. cats are moody and unpredictable
2. ice skaters and roller skaters		
3. city children and rural children		
4. riding a bicycle and riding a motorcycle		
5. one friend's temper versus another friend's temper		

Step 6. Comparison and Contrast. Pattern 3: A Student Model. Read the student's paragraph below, which discusses likenesses and differences in two people who are close friends. In the margins are explanations of the various parts of the paragraph. Answer the questions that appear after Stacy Kissenger's theme.

Birds of a Feather?

[topic sentence:
1. tells that similarities and differences will be discussed
2. tells that the *differences* are more important]

Despite their close relationship my two friends Tammy Smith and Laurie Potter provide striking contrasts in their dispositions. Granted, there are many ways in which these friends are similar. Both born on farms, Tammy

[subtopic sentence: tells that discussion of likenesses will follow]

[one similarity and instances to illustrate it]

and Laurie prefer fields of corn to buzzing city streets. Their love for farming unites them as together they lecture their city slicker friends like me about Guernseys and Holsteins or about the uses of cultivators. Both girls also share an interest in athletics. The two of them played on the high school basketball team and by their senior year had developed the flawless "Smith-Potter" rebounding method which included elbowing and stomping on anyone separating them and the ball. Off the basketball court their fun-loving natures further reinforce each other as they tease and joke, often to the dismay of those around them. Once they convinced the shop teacher's daughter

[another similarity (note transition "also" and reference to topic sentence with "Both girls share an interest") and a supporting example]

[more points to finish discussion on similarities]

that rubber crowbars and metric screwdrivers really existed. But the personality differences between these two friends are much more outstanding than the likenesses. Laurie is carefree and easygoing with a well of cheerfulness within her. Her sapphire eyes twinkle brightly and the corners of her lips curl upward into a smile as she chats with her friends in the college hallways. When I am feeling miserable, she jokes and giggles to chase away the depression. Her own anger rarely surfaces. When everyone else rages, Laurie rarely shows hostility, except perhaps in her face. Angry, she retreats within herself. Her chatter ceases as the twinkle disappears from her eyes. Her jaw locks tightly, and every muscle tenses. The soft brown crop of curls and the light sprinkling of freckles

[subtopic sentence: tells that discussion of differences will follow]

[details to show qualities for one person]

across her nose suddenly make her face look sharp. But the anger passes quickly, and Laurie once again radiates warmth and excitement. Tammy, in contrast, is much less even-tempered. Though she is a warm and generous person, her moods often change drastically. Frequently she grows depressed and sulks for days at a time. Her forehead wrinkles with anxiety; her hazel eyes glare disgustedly, even at best friends. If Laurie or I try to find out why she is so angry, she growls, "Just leave me alone!" and

[closing sentence:
1. uses transition "then"
2. restates main idea that two friends are alike yet have distinct personality differences
3. introduces a new but related idea: people do not have to have similar personalities in order to be close friends (See pages 178–180 for information on closing sentences.)]

stalks away. Once I watched her face flush with crimson as she snatched a phone book and hurled it, its pages flapping before it thudded against the floor like a dead bird. At another time I saw her kick the wall beside her bed, leaving a black heel mark just above her pillow. Neither people nor things are safe when one of her famous moods transforms Tammy into a monster! Despite some likenesses, then, these two contrasting personalities have convinced me that being birds of a feather is not essential for friendship; although their dispositions differ widely, Laurie and Tammy are each other's best friends.

[contrasting details to show qualities for other person (note transition "in contrast" and reminder of the differences between the two girls with "much less even-tempered")]

—Stacy Kissenger

1. What is the basic feature of contrast between the two friends?
2. In what two ways are the girls alike? What details does Stacy Kissenger offer to support those likenesses?

3. How does she illustrate the major difference she sees between the two people she is discussing? Do you find her illustrations effective? Why or why not?
4. Discuss the images in the paragraph. Which pictures best use color and sound?

SOLVING PROBLEMS IN WRITING

The Mirror Words: II

Here are several more words which cause confusion because they look and sound alike.

---

quit   quiet   quite
quit: to stop. I *quit* my job last week.
quiet: silent; without noise or movement. A *quiet* room is restful.
quite: completely; rather. He was *quite* disturbed at the accident.

Step 1. *Quit, Quiet, Quite?* Fill in the blank with *quit, quiet,* or *quite* so that the sentences make sense.

1. "That's _____ a _____ automobile you have there," the gas station attendant said with a grin.

2. In a _____ voice he mumbled that he would _____ as of tomorrow.

3. It's _____ a drive to Helena from Great Falls but perfect for a _____ Sunday morning.

4. When you _____ studying, take a long, _____ walk around the campus.

5. That was _____ a foolish thing to do.

---

principal   principle
principal: 1. a head person at a school. The *principal* speaks to the students each day.
2. a major sum of money. The *principal* he invested earned $1,250 interest.
3. a descriptive word that means *most important*. Rice is still the *principal* food for many people.

principle: a rule, a major belief, a basic idea or truth
One *principle* for success is hard work.
As a man of *principle,* he refused a bribe.
The *principle* of atoms and molecules goes back to the early Greeks.

Hint: Princip*le* and ru*le* both end in *-le*: if you use princip*le* make sure it means ru*le*.

Step 2. Using *Principle* and *Principal*. Fill in the blanks with the letters *l-e* or *a-l* so that the word *principle* or *principal* correctly suits the meaning of the word group.

1. a woman of princip_____s

2. the high school princip_____

3. princip_____s of algebra

4. return on the princip_____

5. princip_____ results of the investigation

6. the princip_____ act in the show

7. deep moral princip_____s

8. lost interest and princip_____

9. a speech from the princip_____

10. my princip_____ goal in life

---

loose   lose
loose: rhymes with *moose*. It means *not tight, free;* sometimes it means *set free*.
    A *loose* shoelace is dangerous.
    You should *loose* the brake before driving your car.
lose: rhymes with *whose*. It means *to misplace* or *not to win or keep*.
    If you *lose* the registration form, you will have to pay another fee.

Step 3. *Lose* or *Loose*? Write in the correct word, *lose* or *loose*, so the word groups make sense.

1. _____ the prize

2. a _____ leaf notebook

3. The child's tooth is _____.

4. He will _____ the swimming race.

5. _____ his nerve

6. _____ necktie

7. Turn it _____.

8. snakes set _____

9. _____ your temper

10. Don't _____ your way in the woods.

---

no   now   know
no: negative; not any
    I have *no* information about it.
now: at this time
    Now you can understand his reasons.
know: to understand, to be acquainted with
    I *know* the principles of chemistry.
    They *know* the family next door.

Step 4. *No, Now, Know* for Proper Meaning. Fill in the blank spaces with the correct word, *no, now,* or *know*.

Many people _____ do not _____ where their ancestors

came from. Yet _____ one can resist the urge to _____ his

or her true beginnings. Men and women everywhere _____ longer ignore the past and _____ that if they ask questions _____ amount of effort is too much _____ to uncover family origins. To _____ one's past is to _____ oneself.

---

were   where

were: the past tense plural form of the verb *to be*

Hint: *Were* rhymes with *her.*
We *were* searching for our car.
They *were* laughing.

where: a word that tells a place or asks "in what place?"

Hint: Pronounce the *wh* at the start of the word. *Where* rhymes with *care.*
In the city *where* I grew up many changes now appear.
Where did all that noise come from?

Step 5. *Were* and *Where* in Action.   Fill in the blanks with the correct word, *were* or *where.*

1. We _____ waiting for you to return.

2. The child did not know _____ to go.

3. Why _____ you late?

4. _____ all the computers broken?

5. A tulip grew _____ he planted the bulb.

6. It's a place _____ old people go to relax.

7. The mosquitoes _____ really biting last night!

8. _____ you trying to convince him to sing?

9. _____ did you send your payment?

10. _____ _____ you yesterday?

---

piece   peace
piece: a part or portion of something
         One *piece* of glass cut his finger.
peace: without war; a state of restfulness
         Peace is one of our noblest goals.

Step 6. *Piece* or *Peace*?   Fill in the blanks with *peace* or *piece.*

1. love and _____

2. _____ on the battlefield

3. a _____ of bread

4. a _____ mission

5. a _____ of meat

6. a _____ of writing

7. _____ in the Middle East

8. a _____ of cherry pie

9. need some _____ and quiet

10. a _____ officer

---

then   than
then: at a certain time
    The folksinger performed, and *then* we left the party.
than: a comparing word
    She is taller *than* her brother.

Step 7. Using *Then* and *Than*. Fill in the blank spaces with the letter *e* or *a* to make *then* or *than*, whichever the sentence requires.

1. prettier th___n a May sunrise

2. waited until th___n

3. Th___n she spoke

4. manners no better th___n children's

5. more votes th___n her opponent

6. could not leave just th___n

7. The mayor spoke th___n

8. taller th___n you

9. looked thinner th___n her sister

10. "I'll see you th___n."

---

lead   led
lead: 1. rhymes with *weed*. It means *to show the way*.
    A good instructor will *lead* you to discover important values.
    The boy who *leads* must know the forest path.
    2. rhymes with *fed*. It is a grayish metal.
    A *lead* pencil contains graphite and no *lead* at all.
led: rhymes with *fed*, too. This *led* is the past tense of *lead*. It means *showed the way*.
    He *led* us through the back alleys of Los Angeles.

Step 8. Making Sense with *Lead* or *Led*. Fill in the blank spaces with *lead* or *led*, whichever makes sense.

1. Who will _____ our country into the twenty-first century?

2. After he had _____ the expedition for two weeks, he collapsed with exhaustion.

3. Do felt-tip pens _____ the _____ pencil in popularity?

4. As she _____ the troop through the woods, thunderclouds the color of _____ covered the sky.

> **knew   new**
> knew: had knowledge about; was familiar with
>   They *knew* each other from childhood days.
> new: the opposite of old
>   That *new* car has all the safety features.

Step 9. *Knew* or *New* **in Word Groups.**   Write in *knew* or *new* so that each word group makes sense.

1. _____ the governor

2. my _____ friend.

3. nothing _____

4. _____ nothing

5. a _____ typewriter

6. _____ a shortcut

7. She gave us _____ ideas.

8. I _____ the directions.

9. _____ shoes

10. What's _____?

> **cloths   clothes   close**
> cloths: woven or knitted material used to make a variety of items
>   Dry the dish*cloths* before using them.
> clothes: what you wear
>   The *clothes* of today are lively and imaginative.
> close: to shut; near
>   Please *close* the door. Stand *close* to me.

Step 10. *Cloths, Clothes,* **or** *Close?*   Underline the correct word from the parentheses below.

1. Before you (clothes, close) the drawer, make sure your summer (cloths, clothes) are neatly in place.
2. Her (close, cloths, clothes) cost lots of money, but she never looks right in them.
3. If your (close, cloths, clothes) are dirty, light (cloths, clothes) may be used to wipe off the dust.

Step 11. Reviewing Troublesome Words.   Fill in the blanks with proper letters in the sentences below.

1. On a qui____ morning qui____ a few people w__re trying to see w____re the President's car would show between the trees.

2. The princip____ said, "You can rely on religious princip_____ to bring you more p____ce th__n you can imagine."

3. If you l__se your wallet, the princip____ thing to remember is w_____e

you w___e for most of the day.

4. If you want to l___d the team, you'll need __ew attitudes, not __ew

clo_____.

5. Qu_____ a few l___se p__ces of l___d lie on the floor __ow.

Agreement of Subject and Verb

You probably know already that a verb can tell time, so to speak, because it indicates whether an action has already happened, will happen soon, or is in the process of happening.

The girl spoke *in a loud voice* shows, through the verb *spoke,* that the action happened in the *past.*

The girl will speak *in a loud voice* shows, through the verb *will speak,* that the action is going to occur sometime in the *future.*

The girl speaks *in a loud voice* shows, through the verb *speaks,* that the action is happening at *present.*

The quality of time telling that verbs illustrate is called *tense:* past, future, and present are three of the main tenses in the English language. In using the present tense, problems in agreement arise.

AGREEMENT DEFINED

When a subject is singular, the verb must be singular.
When a subject is plural, the verb must be plural.
The girl speaks in a loud voice

[singular   [singular verb
(no -*s*   (-*s* ending)]
ending)]

The girls speak in a loud voice.

[plural   [plural verb
subject   (no -*s* ending)]
(-*s* ending)]

Hint: The letter *s* is often a clue to proper agreement.

---

(1) *Singular Subjects* {Go with} *Singular Verbs (which usually do not end in s)* {Go with} *(which usually do end in s)*

A teacher works hard.

[no *s* to show singular subject]

(2) *Plural Subjects (which usually do end in s)* {Go with} *Plural Verbs (which usually do not end in s)*

Teachers work hard.

[no *s* to show plural verb]

A safe <u>driver</u> <u>moves</u> carefully   Safe drivers move carefully
          ↖ [no *s* to show   ↖ [no *s* to show
            singular subject]   plural verb]

Remember: Some subjects form plurals in ways other than adding an -*s* (*children, men, mice*). See pages 104–106.

Step 1. Verb and Subject in Agreement. Select a subject from Column I and a verb that agrees with that subject from Column II. Write the words in Column III. In Column IV tell whether the subject and verb are singular or plural. Then write a sentence with each subject-verb combination. Look at the example.

I	II	III		IV
Example:		*Subject*	*Verb*	
women	grow	*daisies*	*grow*	*plural*
horses	laughs			
child	tick			
clocks	lose			
daisies	gallop			
river	flows			
people	speak			
students	study			
	dances			
	work			

1. *White daisies grow wild along Harden Creek.*

2. _____

3. _____

4. _____

5. _____

6. ————————————————————————————
————————————————————————————

7. ————————————————————————————
————————————————————————————

PRONOUNS AND AGREEMENT PROBLEMS

A singular pronoun works with a singular verb.
A plural pronoun works with a plural verb.
   Pronouns used as subjects do not end in **s**, so the letter **s** cannot serve as a clue to agreement as far as the subject is concerned. But because a singular *verb* in the present tense usually ends in **s**, look for an **s** at the end of the verb used with a singular pronoun subject.

Singular Pronoun Subjects		*Plural Pronoun Subjects*	
I	it	we	you
he	you	they	
she	who		

It crawls along the ground.   They crawl along the ground.
[singular   [s ending on verb]   [plural   [no s]
pronoun]   pronoun]

Exceptions
1. *I,* even though it is singular, is always used with a verb that does NOT have the singular **s,** at the end.
   I sing   not   I sings
   I run   not   I runs
2. *You,* even though it can be used as singular or plural, is always followed by a verb that does NOT have the singular **s** at the end.
   You sing   not   You sings
   You run   not   You runs

Step 2. Plural to Singular. Rewrite each sentence below, changing the plural subject to a singular pronoun subject. In most cases you will have to change the verb too so that it agrees with the new subject. *Do not add* -ed *to the verb:* that will *avoid* the agreement error by shifting into the past tense where there are few problems in agreement! Study the example. All subjects and verbs are underlined.

1. Cats run wild in the hot city streets.
   It runs wild in the hot city streets.

2. The children want dinner too early in the day.

————————————————————————————

3. For car repairs my <u>friends</u> <u>use</u> Anthony's Service Station.

_____

4. My <u>cousins</u> <u>buy</u> cherries from a farm stand.

_____

5. Those <u>men</u> <u>speak</u> softly.

_____

6. My <u>teachers</u> <u>try</u> to return papers quickly.

_____

Step 3. Verbs that Work with Pronouns. Draw a line through any verb which does not work correctly with the pronoun in each group below. Look at the example.

1. They
~~sings~~   laugh   speak   ~~listens~~   ~~votes~~   complain
2. He
question   read   acts   decide   appear   go   have
3. I
study   tries   work   plan   decides   asks   has
4. We
jump   eats   remain   swims   attends   want   does
5. You
explain   drives   try   work   finish   remembers   goes

Step 4. Sentences with Correct Verbs and Pronouns. For any *five* correct combinations of pronoun subject and verb that appear in Step 3 above write an original sentence. Use separate paper.

Example: They complain whenever the temperature drops below seventy degrees!

Some Special Pronouns and Agreement

Even though they may seem plural to you, some pronouns, when used as subjects, are singular and always go with singular verbs. Although people do not usually keep to this rule when they speak, formal writing still requires that you use singular verbs with these subjects.

Singular Pronouns

anybody	somebody	neither
anyone	everybody	either
nobody	someone	everything

| no one | everyone | nothing |
| none | each | something |

Examples: [singular verb (s ending)]

Singular ⎰ Anybody believes a sincere speaker.
Subject ⎱ Everyone tries hard.
              [singular verb (s ending)]

Step 5. Sentences of Your Own. On a separate sheet of paper write a sentence for each singular pronoun listed above. Be sure that the verb is singular (check for the s ending) and that the tense is present (don't add -ed).

Examples:

Each of the boys drifts off on his own.
Everyone buys a newspaper.

FOUR TROUBLESOME VERBS

I. *TO BE*

Singular Forms
am: Use with *I* only
is: use with all singular subjects (except *you*)
I *am* tired today.
It *is* late.
The wind *is* blowing.

Plural Form
are: use with all plural subjects and with *you*
You *are* attractive.
The students *are* busy.
They *are* all outside.

Hint: Do not use *be* with any subject.
It *is* late.   *not*   It *be* late.
They *are* at the movies.
        not
They *be* at the movies.

This verb has agreement problems in the past tense as well.

Past Singular
was: use with all singular subjects (including *I*)
    except *you*
I *was* awake early.
    not
I *were* awake early.
He *was* seated in the rear.
    not
He *were* seated in the rear.

Past Plural
were: use with all plural subjects and with *you*
They *were* singing.
        not
They *was* singing.

You *were* lucky to miss being drafted.
            not
You *was* lucky to miss being drafted.

II. *TO HAVE*

Singular Form

has: use with all singular subjects except *I* and *you*

He *has* a cold.

The book *has* a torn page.

It *has* a bright red cover.

Hint: If the subject is singular, the verb usually ends in *s*. If the subject is plural, the verb usually does not end in *s*.

Plural Form

have: use with all plural subjects and *I* and *you*

I *have* five dollars.

You *have* a cold.

The women *have* new cars.

III. *TO GO*

Singular Form

goes: use with all singular subjects except *I* and *you*

She *goes* to sleep early.

The dog *goes* out before dinner.

It *goes* to its favorite tree.

Hint: If the subject is singular, the verb usually ends in *s*. If the subject is plural, the verb usually does not end in *s*.

Plural Form

go: use with all plural subjects and *I* and *you*

I *go* to the garage daily.

The men *go* this way.

You *go* too far when you drive.

IV. *TO DO*

Singular Form

does: use with all singular subjects except *I* and *you*

She *does* important work.

It *does* not look right.

Hint: If the subject is singular, the verb usually ends in *s*. If the subject is plural, the verb usually does not end in *s*.

Plural Form

do: use with all plural subjects and *I* and *you*

You *do* the work!

I *do* too much driving.

Another Hint: Although you should usually avoid contractions in formal writing, contractions with some of these verbs and the word *not* can cause many agreement problems. To select the correct form of the verb, separate the contraction into two words.

doesn't: does not	Use with singular. He doesn't work. (does not)
don't: do not	Use with plurals, *I*, and *you*. They don't work. (do not)
wasn't: was not	Use with singular (and *I*). The doctor wasn't in. (was not)
weren't: were not	Use with plurals and *you*. You weren't ill. (were not)

Step 6. Picking Correct Verbs. Circle the correct form of the verb in each sentence below. Then write the subject and the verb in the appropriate columns alongside each sentence.

Subject   Verb

_____   _____

_____   _____

_____   _____

_____   _____

_____   _____

_____   _____

_____   _____

_____   _____

_____   _____

_____   _____

1. When I (be, am, is) alone, I (have, has) to listen to music or I (go, goes) crazy!

2. He (has, have) to go to school today, but if he (does, do), he (is, be) in trouble on his job.

3. If it (doesn't, don't) matter to you, tell us where you (was, were) before you (has, have) to leave again.

4. When she (go, goes) on a construction job, she (does, do) the work quickly; when her assistant (has, have) the job, though, he (doesn't, don't) ever work fast.

MORE THAN ONE SUBJECT (compound subjects)

[Subject is plural]   [plural verb]
A desk and an old lamp stand in the room.

Since *desk* and *lamp* both make up the subject, the subject is plural; therefore the sentence requires a plural verb.

When { either . . . or
        neither . . . nor
        or
        nor
        not only . . . but also }
join subjects, the verb agrees with the subject that stands close to the verb.

Either the manufacturers or the driver is at fault.
                [closer subject: singular]   [verb: singular]

Either the manufacturer or the drivers are at fault.
                [closer subject: plural]   [verb: plural]

Step 7. More than One Subject. Use the expressions indicated to open each sentence. Then use the correct form of the verb in parentheses in a sentence of your own. *Do not use the past tense:* use only the present.

Example:

1. Television or radio (to play)

   Television or radio plays in my house most of the day.

2. Not only my sisters but also my cousins (to be)

   _____

3. In my class neither the women nor the one man (to have)

   _____

4. Either the table or the chairs (to do)

   _____

5. A bed and a dresser (to stand)

   _____

IS, ARE, WAS, **AND** *WERE* **WITH** *IT, HERE, WHERE,* **AND** *THERE*

To start a sentence correctly with *Here is, There is,* or *Where is,* remember that *there, here,* and *where* are not subjects: subjects in these sentences always come after the verb.

[not the subject]   [subject (singular)]

Here is an old maple tree.

    [verb: singular]

[not the subject]   [plural]

There are dead lilacs on the lawn.

    [verb: plural]

It is followed by a singular verb, *is,* even when the word it refers to is plural.

It is an important idea.

    [singular]

It is ideas like these that we need.

    [plural]

Step 8. Special Openers. Use the words given below as the subject for each sentence. Open each sentence with *it, here, where,* or *there* and the verb that agrees with the subject: *is, are, was,* or *were.*

Example:

1. two open doors *There were two open doors in the hallway.*

2. a cactus _____

3. mountains _____

4. some apples _____

5. love _____

WORDS THAT GET IN THE WAY

Don't be confused by singular or plural words that appear between the subject and the verb in a sentence.

[Although this word is plural and close to the verb, it is *not* the subject.]

The rain (on the rooftops) is causing trouble.
[singular subject]   [singular verb]

[Although this word is plural and close to the verb, it is *not* the subject.]

A group (of students) was here before you.
[singular subject]   [singular verb]

Don't be confused by certain words that join with the subject: *together with, as well as, in addition to, along with* do not affect the subject.

[These words do not affect the subject.]

The banker, (together with his partners), was arrested for theft.
[singular verb]

Step 9. Verbs that Agree. Circle the correct form of the verb.

1. A set of fine glasses (look, looks) lovely on the shelf.
2. The talk about important Indian tribes (was, were) interesting.
3. The pieces of chocolate cake (has, have) icing.
4. The book as well as the magazines (was, were) ruined.
5. One of the girls (was, were) expected to drive.
6. Ideas, in addition to action, (require, requires) attention.

PLURAL WORDS THAT ACT AS SINGULAR

Some words, though they look plural, always take singular verbs:

physics	Amounts of weight, height or length, time and
economics	money:
civics	Three ounces *is* a small amount.
mathematics	Six feet *is* very tall.
news	Three hours *was* not enough time.
measles	Five dollars *is* what I am paid each day.

Economics *is* difficult.
Measles *is* a childhood disease.

Titles, though they may be plural, take singular verbs.

Star Wars was an exciting film.

Hint: These words are always plural and take plural verbs:

scissors	trousers
glasses	means
riches	pants

The scissors *are* on the table.

WORDS BOTH SINGULAR AND PLURAL

Words like *committee, group, team, family,* and *class,* when referring to an action by the group as a whole, take singular verbs.

When you want to stress that each individual in the group does something, use a plural verb.

The committee *are* leaving the work until tomorrow.	The committee *is* leaving the work until tomorrow.
The plural verb *are* stresses individuals leaving the work.	Here you are showing that the committee acts as a whole in leaving the work.

Step 10. Singular or Plural Verbs? Write the correct form of the verbs in parentheses.

(to fly)   1. Two hours _____ quickly when you are happy.

(to be)   2. The news _____ good from England.

(to look)   3. The scissors _____ sharp.

(to practice) 4. The team _____ on the parade ground every Saturday morning.

AGREEMENT WITH WHO, THAT, WHICH

The words *who, that,* and *which* are singular *or* plural depending on the words they refer to.

The boy who finds the money keeps it.

[*Who* is singular because it refers to *boy,* a singular word.] [singular because *who* is singular]

One of the pages that appear looked badly torn.

[*That* is plural because it refers to *pages,* a plural word.] [plural because *that* is plural]

Step 11. Agreement with *Who, That, Which*.   Circle the correct form of the verb.

1. My father is one of those people who (is, are) very strict.
2. One of the women who (work, works) with me received a promotion.
3. Darrel is one of the boys who never (come, comes) late.
4. Aspirin is one of the drugs that (require, requires) careful use.

Step 12. Reviewing Agreement Problems.   Finish each incomplete sentence below so that agreement is correct. Use the verbs in the columns.

is	go	speak
are	goes	speaks
was	do	stand
were	does	stands
looks	have	sit
look	has	sits
taste	laugh	feel
tastes	laughs	feels
want	speed	throw
wants	speeds	throws

Example:

1. A cup and saucer *sit on the table.*
2. Five minutes _____
3. One of my neighbors _____
4. Mathematics _____
5. A Siamese cat and a poodle _____
6. My husband, along with the children, _____
7. Anyone who _____
8. Either a car or a motorcycle _____
9. Neither frankfurters nor salami _____
10. Twenty-five cents _____

Step 13. More Review.   Circle the correct form of the verb.

1. Every Sunday she (goes, go) to the park.
2. One of the children (has, have) a cold.
3. Three bottles of milk (costs, cost) too much.
4. There (is, are) the sandwiches you ordered.
5. Neither the bicycle nor the toys (belongs, belong) here.
6. The teacher (doesn't, don't) accept themes written in pencil.

7. That (is, be, are) the strangest exercise I have ever seen.
8. In high school, economics (was, were) my best subject.
9. Fifty pounds (is, are) too much weight to lose.
10. The street (has, have) garbage everywhere.

WRITING THE PARAGRAPH

Think about some of the people you know, and, using any one of the several methods of paragraph development explained in this chapter, write a composition which in some way uses the technique of comparison and contrast. Read the student themes on pages 128, 130–131, and 133–134 in order to review the approaches you may use. Look at the suggested titles below and at the ideas on page 120 to help you along. If you would like to write about a topic that suggests comparisons between subjects other than people, see page 159 for suggestions.

Topic Ideas: Comparing People

Use any topic of your own, of course, but in case you are stuck for ideas, you might find one of these titles helpful as you think about comparing or contrasting two people.

1. My Daughter (Son): Two Different Personalities
2. Discipline: Mother's Style, Father's Style
3. How My Cousins Are Alike
4. Two Bosses: A Study in Contrasts
5. Two Teaching Styles
6. My Two Boy Friends (Girl Friends)
7. My Children Are So Different!
8. Roommates
9. How My Parents Compare
10. Two Classmates
11. Two Neighbors I Know
12. Good Friends
13. Two Children on the Block
14. Birds of a Feather
15. My Two Grandmothers (Grandfathers)
16. My Aunts Spoiled Me
17. Two Shopkeepers
18. My Brother: Before and After
19. A Doctor I Liked, A Doctor I Disliked
20. Good Service and Bad: Two Waiters in Contrast

Prewriting: The Informal Outline

As a way of exploring and of grouping information on a topic, the *informal outline* (sometimes called a rough or a scratch outline) can be helpful before you prepare your first draft. With an informal outline you lay out in groups or categories various thoughts you intend to develop in your paper. Under each group or category you jot down a few words or phrases which will help you expand ideas into sentences. For extensive assignments or for complicated topics the more formal *sentence outline* may serve you better. (See page 421 in the Minibook.)

Preparing an outline is not a prewriting activity like list making or brainstorming or free association. Those help you to uncover ideas about topics and to discover what you know or what you need to find out when you are stuck for ideas. Outlining, however, demands that you already know in some detail what you want to write about. Of course, an outline should be highly flexible so that you can eliminate idea groups or can add to them as you write your first draft.

Because a comparison-contrast theme usually involves balanced parts that can be separated easily—you deal with one object, then another; or you deal with one point as it relates to two objects before you go on to another point about the objects—informal outlines can help you, once you have stated and limited your topic. Look at this informal outline by Cecilia Richardson for her paragraph "Different Roommates" on pages 130–131. Notice how she uses numbers (1, 2, 3) and letters (a, b, c) to organize her material easily. Although numbers and letters are not *required* in a scratch outline, many writers find them convenient.

PREWRITING: A SCRATCH OUTLINE

Topic: Contrasts between my roommates Pat and Julie. —— [topic already limited]

1. Physical appearances —— [first thought group]

   [objects writer will discuss]

   a. Pat — small, blonde, funny-looking grey eyes —— [details to be developed in the paragraph]

   b. Julie — tall and lean, straight black hair

2. Attitude toward school work
   a. J.
       tense before exams
       studies for hours
       takes notes carefully
   b. P.
       takes things easy before tests
       surrounds herself with food

[second thought group divided into objects for discussion, details under each]

3. Interests
[third thought group]
   a. J.
       inactive type -- reads, watches T.V., likes talking
   b. P.
       "outdoors" type
       jogger, swimmer
       beats me at paddleball
            --Cecilia Richardson

Step 1. Comparing Paragraph to Outline. Reread "Different Roommates" on pages 130–131. Comparing it to the outline above, answer these questions. Use separate paper.

1. How does the topic sentence compare with the statement of topic in the outline?
2. What new order does the writer present in her paragraph for the thought

groups numbered 1, 2, and 3 in the outline? Why do you think she has made the change?

3. The outline is not consistent in the order of discussion of the two objects. Under 1, Pat comes first; under 2, Julie comes first. Why has Cecilia Richardson changed this situation in the paragraph so that she discusses the same person, Julie, first each time?

Step 2. Practice with Informal Outlines.   Look at the topics you developed in Step 2 or 3 on pages 129–130. On a separate page prepare a scratch outline for any of the topics and their accompanying illustrations or discussion points. Be sure to include in your outline some details you might use to develop the thought groups.

Step 3. An Outline for Your Paragraph.   If your instructor requests it, prepare an informal outline after you have decided on your own comparison and contrast topic and before you write your first draft. Use separate paper, and hand in your outline when you hand in your theme for evaluation. Use Cecilia Richardson's outline (pages 153–154) as a model, but take whatever liberties you need with it so that the outline works for you. Remember, this is a *rough* outline. Its main purpose is to help you write your paper successfully.

Checking Your Paragraph Quality

While preparing your outline and your first and later drafts, but before writing your final copy, use this checklist for your paragraph so that you will follow as many of the suggestions as possible. After you prepare your final copy, fill in the checklist and submit it to your instructor along with your theme.

1. Did I spend time thinking about the topic in some prewriting activity   _____
   that works well for me? (See page 35.)

2. Did I use a scratch outline to help me organize ideas?   _____

3. Did I write a rough draft and any other needed drafts before making my   _____
   final copy? Did I make changes in my rough drafts so that I expressed
   thoughts clearly and smoothly? Does my final copy follow correct manuscript form?

4. Did I write a topic sentence that makes clear what I want my para-   _____
   graph to deal with and that states some dominant impression I have
   about the subject (pages 7–8)?

5. Did I use subtopic sentences and transitional expressions or both to help   _____
   the ideas move smoothly from one to the other? (pages 80–81 and pages
   123–125). Here are two transitional expressions that appear in my
   theme.

a. _____

b. _____

6. Does my paragraph contain several word pictures that use sound, color,   _____
   smell, and touch?
     Here is one image that uses sound.

   _____

7. Did I use two or three comparisons (pages 120–122) in my paragraph?   _____

8. Did I try to use words from the new vocabulary on pages 118–119?   _____

     Here is one word I used. _____

9. After making changes in my drafts for clarity and smoothness, did I   _____
   check my Theme Progress Sheet (page 429) and proofread the draft before my final draft? Did I check especially for the run-on and fragment
   errors? Did I proofread again before I submitted my final draft?

10. Did I examine my theme for any mistakes in agreement? Have I checked   _____
    carefully for words I may have confused, like those explained on pages
    135–139?

11. Did I look in a dictionary for any words that troubled me as I spelled   _____
    them?

12. Did I use a variety of sentence types: subordination; coordination; sen-   _____
    tences that open with words that end in -*ly*?

13. Did I try to write one expanded quotation sentence that through strong   _____
    images includes details of the speaker? (See pages 125–126.) In "Dif-
    ferent Roommates," Cecilia Richardson writes: "Just listen to this," she
    will say, her eyes glowing, her warm fingers pressed to my palm to hold
    my attention.

14. Did I write at least twelve sentences, about three hundred words?   _____

THE PROFESSIONALS SPEAK

Read the selection below. It describes the experiences of two students at an
integrated high school where a riot closed the school. Keep in mind the use
of comparison-contrast techniques.

SOME WORDS TO KNOW BEFORE YOU READ

animosity: feeling of bad will
serene: peaceful
pun: a humorous use of a word which brings out unexpected meanings
verbatim: in exactly the same words
cytology: the study of cells
din: loud, confused noise
tonnage: the carrying capacity of a ship

Black and White at Madison High

Socially, the races have almost no contact. There are no school dances, no picnics, trips, clambakes. After school, the blacks troop over to Nostrand Avenue to wait for the city buses back to the ghetto. There is, of course, no interracial dating, and even an after-school friendship is something rare and unusual.

"When I first came here as a sophomore, I was petrified of them," says 16-year-old Pierre Socolow, a white senior who lives near the school. "If I'd see them all going out one exit, I'd find another one to go out of. But now I've gotten over that. If they're standing by a door, I just go out right past them. But maybe that's because I'm a senior." Other than the exits, just about the only place even to meet blacks in the school is the one period a day when everyone goes to gym. "In gym you get friendly with them and they become familiar faces," says David Chase, another white senior, who wants to study biochemistry at Cornell University. "Then, the next time in the hall if you see him, you can say, 'Hi, see you in gym.' But you wouldn't see them after school."

A majority of the blacks come to the school with crushing academic problems, many reading two to five years below grade level. And a lot of the separation has as much to do with class and educational differences as with race. "I looked at the black kids with the same regard as the whites in the business and commercial course," says Charles Schumer, a Madison graduate who was elected the district's State Assemblyman last fall, his first year out of law school. "There was no animosity or anything. They were just different; they were not the kinds of kids who were friends."

Assemblyman Schumer's younger brother, Robert, is a 17-year-old senior at Madison now and will graduate in June. He lives with his family half a block from the school in a tidy white stucco house on a serene, tree-lined street. Over the living-room fireplace is an 18-by-22-inch color photograph of the three Schumer children: Charles, who went to Harvard and Harvard Law School; Fran, also a Madison graduate, who went to Radcliffe and is now working in North Carolina as a reporter on *The Charlotte Observer;* and Robert. Robert, whose father runs an exterminator business in Bedford-Stuyvesant, ranks 26th in his class out of 850 but doesn't think he's going to make Harvard. He scored only 1150 on the Standard Achievement Test and might have to settle for the University of Michigan. His brother had scored 1535 out of a possible 1600, and Robert feels a certain pressure to succeed in similar fashion. "It's not overt, but it's there," he says. "They don't think I work hard enough. If my mother doesn't see me doing my homework all the time, she gets annoyed." For practice, Robert spent six weeks last summer taking college courses at Cornell. It was his brother's idea, he said, "but I really liked it."

Ernest Drew is also 17 and a classmate of Robert's. Ernest lives in Brownsville on a block of Bergen Street that has abandoned cars, a gutted factory and boarded-up tenements. He is one of seven children. His mother is from British Honduras and speaks halting English; his father, a Jamaican, has a job as an ironworker. Whereas Robert prepared for Madison at Cunningham Junior High School, which, academically, ranks ninth in the city out of 168, Ernest went to Intermediate School 55, which ranks 13th from the bottom and where only 9 per cent of the graduates can read at their proper grade level. To get to Madison, Ernest has to get up at 6 A.M. and spend nearly an hour on two different buses, standing all the way. His classes on the G track are mostly all black, while Robert's are Honors sections and almost totally white. But the color difference pales beside the one of content.

Robert's Honors English is a creative-writing class where students learn imagery from Dostoevski and D. H. Lawrence and read Carl Jung for his theory on the creative process. The teacher, Robert Anker, is chairman of the English department and a student favorite who dishes out a breezy lecture punctuated by cheerful if nauseating puns ("Yes, that's Shakespeare's omelet," he says of Ophelia's lover, "a good egg but a little yellow") that keep the class in stitches. The discussion rests on much of what the students have read on their own. At one point, for example, a student in the back says, yes, he agrees with Carl Jung and points out that it was only after Thomas Wolfe lived in Europe that he could write about his experience of growing up in America.

Ernest's G class is called Power English. There, the students plod through vocabulary books, pondering words like "vague" and "gesture." They, too, read books, but ones written for black high-school students such as "Black Pimps," "My Daddy Was a Numbers Runner" and "Mr. and Mrs. Bo Jones," which is a tale of high-school pregnancy. To pass the course, Ernest has to read five books and hand in a one-paragraph book report on each. Here is a report on "Black Pimps," in its entirety and verbatim, done by an 18-year-old girl in Ernest's class: "The book Black Pimps is about pimps, ho, prostitutes and hustler, the games they pull. How they commute with one another. Also how the contract their pimps or players. There use of slang words of the ghetto. What their style are or the way in which they are made."

The teacher is Robert Greenman, Ernest's favorite. "To go over every mistake on that paper, I'd have to spend a whole period," he says, "so what I do is pick out five mistakes and let it go at that. It's just not possible to grade some of these kids. They would never get a passing mark."

For science, Robert has already had introductory biology and this year is taking a college-level course that concentrates on physiology, cytology and genetics. Ernest takes "General Science," a sort of grab bag of information about everything from atoms to astronomy, much of it lost somewhere between the teacher and her students. "Ernest," asks the teacher, "what do you use to measure carpeting: meters, grams or liters?"

Ernest stares, mute.

"She's messing with you, man," whispers a classmate. After a bit, the teacher asks the question of another student.

"Some teachers you just have to speak up and say you don't know," says Ernest. "But with her, you just stare at her."

The class moves on to oxygen. "Would it be a good thing if all the plants in the world died?" the teacher asks a girl on the other side of the room.

"Yes," says the girl. Then, quickly, "No!"

"Why not?"

"Because . . . it just wouldn't," the girl replies.

In mathematics, Robert is up to calculus. That day the teacher is sick, so the class is taught by a fellow student. Ernest has two math classes. One, a math workshop, uses minicomputers paid for by the Federal Government to help students as they puzzle out 8 into 48 and 7 into 49. The teacher asks about a cut on his lip, and Ernest, who is in the class for his third go-around, explains that he was mugged over the weekend near his home. "Some of these kids are five years behind," says the teacher, "but we try to improve their skills. I say we try. We don't always succeed." Ernest's other math class is Business Math, where he learns the arithmetic of borrowing money and paying taxes.

Both youths take American History II, which deals with immigrant groups and foreign policy, but there the similarity ends. In Robert's—he has had to sign up for a Regular class, since the Honors section would interfere with calculus—the emphasis is on learning history. In Ernest's, it is on using history to have another go at reading, writing and arithmetic. That day, Ernest's teacher is trying over the general din to shout some information about a graph showing construction of American ship tonnage before and during World War II. The point here is not to learn about shipbuilding but to see how to read a graph.

Ernest's attention wanders to a friend outside the room who is making gestures through a window in the door, indicating that Ernest should cut his next class and "party" out on the sidewalk. The friend has a green jewel in his left ear and a rabbit-fur jacket which, Ernest explains later, cost $167 and was paid for by one of his girl friends. The teacher is now completely drowned out by boys and girls yelling at one another. A girl named Fern is quietly playing with jacks.

"What kind of religion did the Indians have?" the teacher shouts in desperation.

"Voodoo," one boy calls back.

The teacher asks Fern to *please* put away her jacks. The whistle sounds—an ear-goring electronic noise transmitted over a loudspeaker—and the class is dismissed.

Though at opposite academic poles, both boys say they're glad they went to Madison, Robert for its good college preparation and Ernest because it's a "together" school. It also provided Ernest a welcome alternative to Boys' High, an all-black school in Bedford-Stuyvesant that his mother was afraid would lead him into taking hard drugs. The two boys, of course, do not know each other, although both have acquaintances of the opposite race. Ernest knows a white boy named Kenny, he says, whom he "parties" with outside when both cut classes. Robert's black friends are mostly from his gym class. "It's an in-school relationship," he says. "I'm friendly with them, but after school it drops there."

After June, both will go their separate ways.

Robert, who worked in his brother's campaign last fall, hopes to go on to law school and then maybe into politics. Ernest has a six-course deficit from subjects he flunked but thinks he can make it up by going to night school in his neighborhood and still graduate in June. Students get a diploma from Madison if they pass enough courses and can show they read at the eighth-grade level. As for the future, Ernest is taking welding lessons from a friend and maybe, he says, he will become a welder.

—Bruce Porter
"It Was a Good School to Integrate . . ."

Step 1. Understanding the Selection. Discuss these questions.

1. How do the family and social backgrounds of the two boys, Robert Schumer and Ernest Drew, compare? What are the major differences between them?
2. How do the experiences in various high school classrooms show the sharp contrast in what and how the boys learn? Discuss the classes in English, science, mathematics, and history.
3. Why are both boys glad they chose Madison High?
4. How do you account for the differences in the boys' future plans?

5. The Human Rights Commission, in its investigation of Madison High School, said that the riots that erupted at the school were completely predictable and stemmed from the school's failure to assimilate—to take in and make as its own—black students into the life of the school. How does the author's contrast between the students demonstrate that failure?

REACHING HIGHER

Step 1. Pictures to Words. Look at the photographs on page 117. Write a paragraph that compares and contrasts any two of the faces you see there. Use concrete sensory language to fill in details. Write a topic sentence that states the comparison clearly.

Step 2. Other Topics. Several other topics for comparison and contrast appear below. Write a paragraph about any one of them.

1. two movies you saw
2. summer in the city and summer in the country
3. two female rock singers
4. driving and racing
5. football and soccer
6. two different dances you do
7. spring and autumn in the garden
8. marijuana and alcohol
9. high school classes and college classes
10. two television comedies (dramas, "specials," movies)
11. travel by train and travel by car
12. summer sports and winter sports
13. today's automobile and the automobile of the future
14. two poems you read
15. two political leaders: Carter and Kennedy; Kruschev and Stalin; Washington and Lincoln
16. poverty today and yesterday
17. children's dress today and yesterday
18. city ghettos and suburban ghettos
19. two concerts you heard
20. picnics and dinners at home

Step 3. Two Special Comparison and Contrast Papers.

1. The Mood Sketch

An imaginative paragraph is one in which you compare and contrast one of your inner moods with the actual moment in which you were experiencing that mood. In this type of paragraph, you set up a contrast between your inner emotions and the world around you. You need to use a number of concrete details to make the scene rich in sensory appeal; and you need to mix in those details with the thoughts and feelings which reflect the mood you are experiencing.

A mood, as you know, is some state of feeling at a given time. Each of us lives through a number of moods each day: happiness, boredom, loneliness, fear, excitement, depression, sorrow, anger, discomfort, relaxation, tiredness. The point of this writing assignment is to set the mood in a specific place at a specific time and to weave in the details of the setting with your own inner state.

Read the theme below as an example. Then look at the hints and the suggested topics.

Waking on a Monday Morning

I hear an innocent click and then, "It's seven fifteen on a bee-yoo-tiful Monday morning here on WABC" blares out of my clock radio on my bedroom dresser; "Oh damn, it's Monday!" I think with a groan. Lifting out of bed with the grace of a sick hippo, I manage to turn the volume down. Resting my weight on my dresser, I grope for the light switch. In an instant the bulb flashes on and knocks me with its glare right back into bed. I weigh in my mind what I have to do. "Damn, I don't feel like getting up, and I don't feel like going to work, and I don't feel like going to school." I smile to myself. I'd sure hate to have to put up with me in the morning! Finally pushing my better judgment to the top, I stumble into the bathroom, banging my knee on the door. After I wash with icy water, I return to the closet for a faded pair of dungarees and an ugly old sweatshirt. "The sun is out strong," the disc jockey screams, in a rapturous voice, "and it's a perfect November morning." Ugh! I look out the window; the early morning cloudiness hangs like a grey film on everything in sight. "How the hell can anyone enjoy Mondays?" I mutter to the plastic face of the radio. It sneers at me. "Sure, what does that announcer care?" I figure to myself. "He works four hours a day and earns fifty grand a year. No wonder he's so happy!" I notice I've buttoned my shirt wrong. I do it all over again, cursing. When I move lazily into the kitchen I grab a chipped bowl and a box of Rice Krispies from the cabinet above the sink. Setting my breakfast on the table, I try to pour the cereal into the plate, but the cereal has its own thoughts and tumbles onto the tablecloth, onto my lap, onto the floor. "Damn these rice thingees! We ought to declare war on China or Japan or wherever we get rice from!" Cleaning up the mess, I return hungry to my room where the skinny white hands of my clock tell the whole story. "Seven forty-five. I'd better move it." Scooping up a fistful of change, I release the nickels and quarters into my pocket with a jingle. I snatch my jacket and pull it around me, glancing at my face in the mirror. Awful! I look at the clothes and papers and books strewn haphazardly everywhere in my room. Awful! Quickly I zoom out the front door, slamming it behind me. A cool morning breeze and the sun rising above the roof across the street suddenly make me feel better. Trapping that ugly part of myself within, I say aloud, "Okay Monday, we're on neutral grounds now. I'm ready to take you on!"

—Ronald Gross

HINTS ABOUT THE MOOD PARAGRAPH

1. Tell the major feeling in the opening sentence.
2. Identify the setting as soon as possible. Ronald Gross mentions the clock radio on his bedroom dresser in order to locate the scene for the reader.
3. Show the thoughts that go through you mind as the mood develops. *At the same time,* show the details of the moment. These details of the outside world keep mixing in with your inner world of feelings. Notice in "Waking on a Monday Morning" how the voice of the disc jockey interrupts a mood.
4. Use eight or ten lively images of concrete details.
5. Use quotation sentences to identify thoughts.
6. Use comparisons like those explained on pages 120–123. Find a simile in the above theme.

Here are several moods which students have felt at some time. Perhaps one might suggest to you possibilities for a paragraph. The key in selecting a proper mood for writing is to try to remember a brief moment you experienced recently in which your feelings were all one major kind.

1. boredom in class
2. Sunday evening depression
3. fear at exam time
4. joy in being alive
5. rainy-day sadness
6. excitement at a concert
7. dislike of a teacher
8. waiting for a date
9. nervousness at the birth of a child
10. sleepiness when doing homework
11. alone at the beach
12. annoyance at waking up
13. love for a spouse
14. sorrow at a loss of a relative
15. pity for a beggar
16. pride at some achievement
17. tiredness after exercise
18. pleasure during a good meal
19. feeling important on the job
20. closeness to God in church or synagogue

2. The Analogy

An analogy is a special kind of comparison. It relates two things that seem to be very different on the surface by showing that there are many things these two objects have in common. The paragraph sample below is developed through analogy. What does the topic sentence announce as the terms of the analogy? Which details of color, sound, and touch make the comparison most vivid?

Biology Jailhouse

Professor Diedrich's biology class on the Monday morning of midterm day at Prep is a prison scene. First we convicts stand uncomfortably outside the classroom door in our dismal winter coats in brown and grey, whispering behind our hands or staring nervously down the empty hall. This is leisure time for the prisoners. Some men squat on the floor and frown; others lean against the ugly green walls near the lab; others drag deeply on stubs of cigarettes. A black film of unshaved whiskers sits like coal dust on every face. Sullenly, my friend Tony says "You wanna butt?" He pushes a pack of Lucky Strikes at me, but I shake my head no. Suddenly footsteps sound on the stairway around the bend. The warden, Professor Diedrich, marches firmly to the door and shouts, "Let's go!" We all snap to attention and, still slouching, march single file into the lecture hall. "Take every other seat. Skip two rows between you and the person in front of you. When the examination begins, there's to be no talking or smoking." I fall into my seat, thinking, "I wish I could break out of this place." But I know I'm just paying for my crime: everyone warned me not to take biology in my freshman year. Suddenly two guards—assistant examiners—burst through the doors with cartons of test booklets and question sheets. Taking a handful of books and question pages, the guards stamp between the rows, tossing out the equipment solemnly. "Nobody writes," barks the professor, "until eight o'clock sharp!" He scribbles in yellow chalk the time the exam begins, the time it ends, and the time it is now, measuring out a life's sentence for the prisoners before him. At eight o'clock the bell howls like a siren; everyone jumps and writes a name across the first page of the examination blue book. Occasionally, nervously, someone glances up at the beady-eyed guards who watch us without a smile. But I know my parole will begin just one hour from now. If I pass this awful exam, maybe I will not be a two-time loser like most of my friends, just an "ex-con" who learned his lessons and never returned to the biology jailhouse.

—Charles Gomez

Here are some other analogies you may wish to develop in a paragraph. As your instructor directs, select one of them for your theme assignment. Better yet, make up your *own* analogy to develop in a paragraph.

1. teachers are like firecrackers
2. learning is a baseball game
3. homework: my private war
4. campus personalities and colors
5. college as racetrack
6. books as people
7. the college exam room as hospital
8. the term paper as slave market
9. the principal's office as courtroom
10. a date is like a card game

Step 4. Exploring Contrasts Visually. Select two related objects which you might compare or contrast. With a camera, take several pictures which explore the relationship between the two objects. Mount your pictures and then arrange them in an effective order. Patterns 1, 2, and 3 on pages 126–134 will help you decide on an effective arrangement even though you are now working with visual images. You might want to select from this list of possible topics:

youth and old age
sun and rain
delight and pain
fear and courage
night and day
boys and men

wealth and poverty
work and play
men and women
heat and cold
dawn and dusk
city streets and country roads

chapter 5

THE CHILD'S WORLD:
ON THE HUNT FOR FACTS

INTRODUCTION TO STATISTICS AND EXPERT TESTIMONY

How do children learn? What forces are most crucial in shaping their lives: the family? the schools? the street? the playground? How can we understand their needs, their fears, their inner voices, their magical worlds? How should we teach them, discipline them, love them?

This theme assignment asks you to explore some aspect of child development which interests you. Instead of relying upon your own experiences to illustrate some impression you have about the world of children, for this paragraph you will turn to another vital tool for supporting ideas: research.

In earlier chapters you learned how to develop topics through sensory detail. Although your own experiences (told through the clear language of the senses) always make for exciting and informative paragraphs, often you must write about subjects outside your own life. Writing about World War I in history class, about the varieties of cell reproduction in biology, about the social status of the American Indian in sociology—for these kinds of assignments you need some source of detail other than your own experience. Research leads you to knowledge beyond your own life; the information you find in books, in periodicals (magazines and newspapers), or on the television or the movie screen serves well as the basis of support for ideas you wish to develop.

In this chapter you will learn how to use details based upon research. Instead of concentrating upon images—which you will certainly still be able to use—you will learn how to employ statistics and cases from reliable sources as supporting details. You will also see how to quote, directly or through paraphrase, information you have read or heard from someone else.

VOCABULARY

Step 1. Words for Growth. These words frequently appear in a discussion of child development. Write definitions next to words you already know. For any words whose meanings you do not remember, check a dictionary or see Appendix A for some help.

1. phase _____

2. retarded _____

3. accelerate _____

4. enrichment _____

5. maturation _____

Step 2. Words for a Child's World. The words in italics below will help you to write about children. Try to determine the meaning of the word from the way it is used in the sentence. Circle the letter next to what you think is the best definition. Then check the correct definitions in Appendix A.

1. The child was *naïve* enough to believe that the Cookie Monster on *Sesame Street* was a real animal.
   a. stupid   b. unsophisticated   c. unaware   d. foreign
2. Young children are especially *vulnerable* to measles, mumps, and chicken pox.
   a. susceptible to injury   b. valuable   c. protected   d. delicate
3. It is important to *nurture* children carefully so they will achieve their full potential.
   a. watch   b. nature   c. nourish   d. mature
4. When Tommy barked like a dog and crawled on the floor, Ms. Rivera scolded his *puerile* actions.
   a. pretty   b. funny   c. childish   d. imaginative
5. Children are sometimes influenced more by their friends and *peers* than by their parents.
   a. equals   b. teachers   c. television shows   d. brothers

Step 3. Writing Sentences with New Words. Write a sentence that shows clearly the meaning of each word below.

1. accelerate _____

2. phase _____

3. puerile _____

4. vulnerable _____

5. maturation _____

6. nurture _____

7. peers _____

8. retarded _____

9. enrichment _____

10. naïve _____

Step 4. *-ing* Words for Liveliness. These words, in their *-ing* forms, will help you improve your writing style (see pages 180–183). Check a dictionary for any you don't know; write the definition in the blank space (see Appendix A for more help).

Hint: Look up the word in its infinitive form. Look up *sputter*, not *sputtering*, for example.

1. sputtering _____

2. asserting _____

3. familiarizing _____

4. lauding _____

5. assenting _____

Step 5. Naming the Action. From the list above, write in each blank a word that would:

1. show that someone was praising something _____

2. show agreement _____

3. show someone becoming acquainted with information _____

4. show a manner of excited and unclear speech _____

5. show someone making a statement she thought was true _____

BUILDING COMPOSITION SKILLS

Finding the Topic

Step 1. Sharing Ideas. Here are several statements about different aspects of child development. Pick out one or two remarks with which you strongly agree or disagree and discuss your opinions briefly, giving reasons to support your point of view.

1. Children in low socioeconomic groups do not learn as easily as children in higher socioeconomic groups.
2. Women teachers are best for young children.
3. The mentally retarded can be educated within degrees.
4. Boys do not learn as quickly as girls.
5. Many children in American schools get poor instruction in reading.
6. Child abuse is a serious problem in American families.
7. Most children are not fed properly.
8. There is not enough disciplining of children in our society.
9. Busing has a harmful effect on children.
10. State governments should spend more money to support day-care centers.
11. Public schools do not stimulate the creativity of our children.
12. The youngest child in a family usually has the most difficult problems.
13. Television has a negative effect on a child's learning and development.
14. The public schools are not doing enough for the physically handicapped student.
15. The number of students who drop out of high school is increasing each year.
16. Adopted children are generally happy with their adoptive parents.
17. Public school children should receive sex education.
18. Most parents do not understand the emotional needs of their children.

Using Statistics and Cases

You might support many of the ideas in Step 1 by recalling instances from your own experiences. But another effective way to back up your position on a topic is to use statistics or cases as supporting evidence.

STATISTICS AND CASES FOR STRONG DETAIL

Statistics may be thought of as *facts*, the numbers and examples revealed through responsible investigation. By offering comparisons between figures in charts, tables, and graphs, statistics make impressive evidence for backing up ideas.

A *case* is a specific incident involving real people and events. It is another kind of factual evidence that writers offer to support topics.

Of course, you must realize that even when presenting facts, writers often weigh evidence in favor of a particular point of view. Writers who are *biased*—that is, who have strong opinions about an idea—sometimes do not present complete information; or, they may interpret the facts to suit a conclusion they have already reached.

In order to use statistics and cases wisely, make sure that you
1. select them from reliable, unbiased sources
2. present them in clear language
3. give information honestly; do not leave out important records because they do not agree with the point you wish to make

---

Step 1. Statistics as Supporting Detail.   Read the excerpt below in which the writer uses statistics to support his point that parents who neglect their children cause juvenile delinquency. Answer the questions after you read.

SOME WORDS TO KNOW BEFORE YOU READ

impoverishment: lack of strength or richness
apathy: uncaring
urbanization: the process by which rural areas become cities
anonymity: nameless or unknown

Our Lost Children

Although Americans in recent decades have grown richer, our children have grown poorer. Many families no longer adequately perform the nurturing and supporting function that children need, emotionally and intellectually.

The evil consequences for children are not in dispute. The rate of suicide among children aged ten to fourteen is twice as high as it was twenty years ago. For children aged fifteen to nineteen, the rate has tripled.

Since 1963, crimes by children have been rising at a faster rate than the juvenile population. About half of such crimes involve the traditional youthful offenses of theft, breaking and entry, and vandalism; but serious, violent crimes—though still involving a relatively small proportion of children—are going up at a startling rate. The rate of armed robbery, rape, and murder by juveniles has doubled in a decade.

The Senate Juvenile Delinquency Subcommittee surveyed 750 school districts and reported these changes between 1970 and 1973:

Dropouts increased by 11 percent, drug and alcohol offenses on school property were up 37 percent, burglaries of school buildings up 11 percent and assaults on teachers up 77 percent.

Among those who are thought of as normal children, lower reading scores and scholastic aptitude scores reveal intellectual impoverishment. Beyond all this loom the apathy and waste of the counterculture. Its existence is no longer news, but its ranks are still swelled each year by thousands of pathetic runaways and dropouts.

What forces are producing the increasingly severe stresses on today's children?

The phenomenon is complex and baffling, but several developments seem to be interacting. Urbanization is a factor. Children who might have made it on a farm or in a village—despite adverse family circumstances such as extreme poverty or a father's desertion—encounter disaster in a big city with its anonymity and diverse temptations.

Births by unwed mothers and divorce, two trends that are both rising steadily, result in depriving children of the stable, two-parent support that they need in their growing years. One out of every six children under eighteen today is living in a single-parent family. This is almost double the proportion in 1950.

Many divorced or widowed parents obviously succeed with their children. But, ideally, rearing a child is a two-person job. When one parent is missing, the risks of failure increase. Indeed, it is best if a child has grandparents or other supportive relatives on the scene as well.

Instead, what has happened is the near disappearance of the extended family and the substitution of television, the hopelessly inadequate electronic babysitter. One study, for example, revealed that fifty years ago half of the households in Massachusetts included at least one adult besides the parents; today the figure is only 4 per cent. In a small child's life, "Captain Kangaroo" is no substitute for a devoted grandmother.

—William V. Shannon
The New York Times

1. What statistics do you find most surprising, informative, or interesting?
2. What is the source for Shannon's statistics on school crime?
3. According to the author, what factors have resulted in the neglect and delinquency of children?

Step 2. Cases Make the Point. Read the following excerpt by a professor of child psychology, and answer the questions after it.

SOME WORDS TO KNOW BEFORE YOU READ

retaliation: getting back at someone for bad deeds or behavior
taunt: to anger someone with insults or sarcasm
shrilly: in a high-pitched and piercing manner
reprove: scold
recalcitrant: stubborn
bedlam: scene of wild uproar and confusion

Removing Privileges

It may be necessary at times for parents or teachers to deprive a child of a privilege following some demonstration of unacceptable behavior. Now the principle involved in such a punishment is not, or should not be, revenge or retaliation on the part of the educator. If this punishment is to teach then it must be set forth as a reasonable and logical consequence of misbehavior. Let's take a simple example: Margaret who is six is in one of her unreasonable moods. It's Sunday afternoon. She had wanted to go to the park with her parents and little sister, but rain is threatening and it seems best to stay home. Mother tries to get her occupied in drawing, then in sewing doll clothes, then in cutting and pasting pictures in her scrap-book. Any of these activities would normally have absorbed Margaret, but today nothing suits her. She grows more and more irritable and whiny. She taunts the baby and snatches toys from her. She tries to switch off the television set while her father is watching a program that interests him. She then tries to drown out the program through singing loudly and shrilly. When reproved, she becomes more whiny and more recalcitrant, invents fresh ways of annoying her parents and molesting the baby until the family living room has been turned into bedlam. Finally her father tells her severely that she will have to leave and go up to her room. When she thinks that she can control herself she can come down to join the family again.

Here the educational objective of the punishment is to demonstrate to Margaret that if she cannot control her behavior and must disturb the family she will have to be temporarily excluded from family activity. As a punishment it is a reasonable and logical consequence for the kind of conduct Margaret had demonstrated. It says in effect, "We cannot have you disturb the whole family with your negative and obstinate behavior (*whatever* the deeper meaning of this behavior can be) and you are asked to leave the room until you feel you can return as a reasonable member of the family, at which time you will be welcome to join us again." The logic will not be missed by Margaret at the age of six and the justice of the punishment should also be apparent to her, at least after she has calmed down.

—Selma Fraiberg
The Magic Years

1. What is the main idea of this excerpt?
2. What case does the author offer to support that main idea?
3. Why has the author used a case here instead of statistics?

HINTS FOR USING CASES AND STATISTICS

1. Statistics must often be read from charts or graphs. Be sure you understand what the various figures and numbers mean.
2. Don't just pile up a series of numbers as statistical information or your reader will lose interest. Make sure that you present your statistics in a clear and honest way. Often an image adds life to a paragraph built upon facts and figures.
3. In using cases, identify as much as possible the people, the events, the specific families or groups whose experiences support your idea.
4. Always select your statistics and cases from reliable sources. And be sure to name whatever sources you use for your information. The chart on pages 175–176 suggests ways for telling the reader what materials you used as the basis for your facts.

5. Make sure that your statistics are not one-sided. By leaving out information or by "loading" evidence to give an incomplete picture, a writer can bias information. See pages 298–300 for other propaganda techniques to avoid.

Charts, Graphs, and Numbers: Some Truths about Children

Here are various statistics about children's growth and development. After you examine the statistics, answer the questions in Step 3 about how you might use the data in a paragraph.

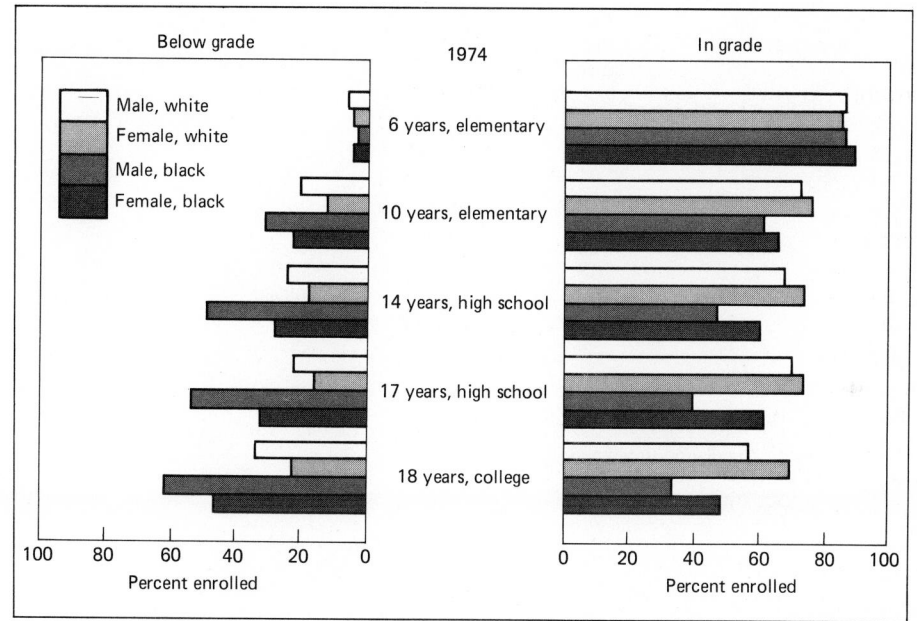

Expenditures for Public Elementary and Secondary School Education

School year	Total	Total per pupil	School year	Total	Total per pupil
1929/1930	$ 2,316,790,000	$108	1963/1964	$21,324,993,000	$ 559
1939/1940	2,344,049,000	106	1955/1966	26,248,026,000	654
1949/1950	5,837,643,000	259	1967/1968	32,977,182,000	786
1953/1954	9,092,449,000	351	1969/1970	40,683,428,000	955
1955/1956	10,955,047,000	388	1971/1972	48,050,283,000	1,128
1957/1958	13,569,163,000	449	1973/1974	56,970,355,000	1,364
1959/1960	15,613,255,000	472	1975/1976	70,829,345,000	1,699
1961/1962	18,373,339,000	530	1976/1977*	74,801,266,000	1,782

* Estimated.
Source: National Center for Education Statistics

Level of Education: White and Black Adults

| Race and Sex | Persons 25 years old or older (1,000) | Years of school completed 1977 (percent distribution) | | | | | | | Median school years completed |
| | | Elementary School | | | High School | | College | | |
		Less than 5 years	5–7 years	8 years	1–3 years	4 years	1–3 years	4 years or more	
Total, all races, March 1977	120,870	3.7	6.9	9.3	15.2	36.1	13.4	15.4	12.4
Male	56,917	4.0	7.0	9.4	14.0	32.1	14.2	19.2	12.5
Female	63,953	3.5	6.8	9.2	16.2	39.6	12.7	12.0	12.4
White	107,216	3.0	6.2	9.4	14.4	37.0	13.8	16.1	12.5
Male	50,782	3.1	6.3	9.6	13.5	32.7	14.6	20.2	12.5
Female	56,434	2.8	6.1	9.3	15.3	40.9	13.2	12.4	12.4
Negro	11,698	9.8	13.5	8.6	22.6	28.4	9.8	7.2	11.4
Male	5,205	12.0	14.1	8.3	20.1	27.6	11.0	7.0	11.3
Female	6,493	8.0	13.1	8.8	24.7	29.1	8.9	7.4	11.4

Source: U.S. Bureau of the Census

Child Mortality Rates in Selected Countries, 1970

| Country | Percent in age group who die each year | | Percent that die before 5th birthday (3) | Age at which same percent as in col. 3 die in | |
	Under 1* (1)	1–4 (2)		Taiwan (4)	United States (5)
India	13.9	4.40	28.1	61	63
Pakistan	14.2	5.30	31.0	63	66
Egypt	11.7	3.93	24.8	60	61
Guinea	21.6	5.20	36.7	66	68
Cameroon	13.7	3.93	26.5	61	62
Guatemala	8.9	2.75	18.5	55	57
Taiwan	2.0	0.43	3.6	5	20
Japan	1.5	0.14	1.9	1	1
United States	2.1	0.10	2.5	2	5
Sweden	1.3	0.07	1.7	1	1

* Live births.
Sources: UN, *Demographic Yearbook, 1963, 1967, 1969, and 1970;* Population Reference Bureau, "1970 World Population Data Sheet" (Washington: Population Reference Bureau).

How Teens are Spending Vacations (Percentages)*

| | Working | Traveling | Miscellaneous Activities | |
			At Home	Other
National	61	27	24	12
Boys—Total	67	24	21	10
13–15 years old	51	34	31	11
16–18 years old	81	15	11	9
Girls—Total	55	29	28	13
13–15 years old	34	38	42	16
16–18 years old	74	25	15	9
White-collar home	61	28	23	13
Blue-collar home	61	24	27	10
East	60	26	27	9
Midwest	61	28	24	13
South	63	24	20	12
West	58	28	30	12
Metro areas	62	30	17	12
Suburbs	57	30	24	10
Nonmetro areas	62	23	29	12

* Percentages add up to more than 100 because some teenagers take part in more than one activity.
Source: *Newsday,* August 8, 1979.

Name _____ Class _____ Date _____ 173

Total Arrests, by Age Groups, 1975 (Latest Available Figures)*

Age	Arrests	Age	Arrests	Age	Arrests	Age	Arrests	Age	Arrests
Under 15	716,206	18	475,515	22	311,059	30–34	611,474	50–54	286,036
15	409,297	19	424,982	23	279,641	35–39	467,240	55 & over	385,529
16	478,886	20	381,874	24	262,158	40–44	402,791	Not known	8,178
17	474,070	21	347,005	25–29	934,240	45–49	357,464	TOTAL	8,013,645

* Data based on reports furnished to the FBI by 8,051 agencies covering an estimated population of 179,191,000.
Source: Federal Bureau of Investigation.

SOME POINTERS FOR WRITING STATISTICS CORRECTLY

1. Use numbers for percent
   18% or 18 percent
2. Use numbers for dates
   May 15, 1971
3. To show sums of money:
   a. If you need two words or fewer (*not* counting the word *cents* or *dollars*) write out the words for the numbers.
      three hundred dollars
      forty-two cents an hour
      eight billion
   b. If you need three or more words, use the numbers.
      $8.76 $8,487 $62,908,433
   c. For a series of numbers, use the figures, not the words.
4. Two-word fractions are written like this:
   seven-tenths of all students
   one-ninth of student drivers

Step 3. You Use Statistics.   Examine the charts, tables, graphs, and statements on pages 171–173. What statistics or cases could you offer to support the following topics?

1. Over the years, expenses for children in public schools have climbed.
2. The majority of teenagers spend their vacations working.
3. Juvenile delinquency for teenagers under fifteen is extremely high.
4. Child mortality rates are very high in foreign countries.

QUOTATIONS AS DETAILS

Another source for supporting topic and subtopic sentences in your paragraph is quoted material from books, magazines, newspapers, radio, and television. By quoting, you use someone else's words and ideas to support your own opinion on a given subject. Of course, if you read something or hear it on the radio, it is not necessarily true; however, by using reliable sources, you can impress your reader with the strength of your position.

If, in your reading or listening, you discover some ideas that you want to use *exactly* as you have read or heard them, you can quote the material just as it was presented by giving the source of your information and by using quotation marks around the material. In that way you tell your reader that somebody else first stated the ideas you are writing about and that they are not original with you.

If you do not wish to use the information exactly as you have read or heard it, you may *paraphrase*—that is, you can use your own words to give an idea of what someone else wrote or said, especially if you want to summarize the idea. You do not need quotation marks, but here too you must identify the source of your information.

HINTS FOR USING QUOTATIONS AND PARAPHRASE

1. Review the correct use of quotation marks on pages 54–56 and on pages 405–406.
2. Do not load your paragraph with too many quotations or with one quotation that is too long. Usually, in paragraphs and essays based upon research, about one-fourth of the writing should be made up of quoted material.
3. Use your own clear language in preference to quoting dull or ordinary material. A sentence or two of your own to summarize a long or complicated point is often an effective way to offer important information.
4. Always select material from reliable sources. And whether you quote someone directly or paraphrase the ideas you have read, be certain to name whatever source you have used. The chart on pages 175–176 suggests ways for telling the reader what you took your information from.

Effective Quotations

Read the selection below (taken from a longer work) which uses quoted material. Answer the questions that appear after it.

SOME WORDS TO KNOW BEFORE YOU READ

propagate: spread a report or idea from person to person
assertion: an unsupported statement put forward as being true
distortion: a twisting out of shape; misrepresentation
prevalence: widespread or in general use or acceptance

Racism in Education

Since racism is the philosophy of the Establishment and is propagated in the institutions of higher learning and by the mass media which they control through ownership, it is not surprising to observe that "a vast majority of the white population south of the Mason-Dixon Line, and large numbers, probably a majority elsewhere, are firmly of the belief that Negroes are subhuman or only semi-human, despite the positive assertions of biology and anthropology to the contrary." (*The Rich and the Super-Rich,* by Ferdinand Lundberg).

The Black parent knows his child is "educable" in spite of all the funded programs and studies to the contrary. Dishonesty and distortions in intelligence tests are common. The literature on such tests shows that when "two groups of whites differ in their IQ's, the explanation of the difference is immediately sought in schooling, environment, economic position of parents. However, when Blacks and whites differ in precisely the same way the different is said to be genetic." (*The Study of Race,* by Sherwood L. Washburn). There are other instances which show the prevalence of racism. Trade schools (located in all industrial centers) have a long history of excluding Blacks. However, a Black occasionally slips through the net, after which the net is thoroughly examined to see how it happened. The trustees of these trade schools include the conservative officials of craft unions which exclude Blacks from membership. A classic example involved the Sheet Metal Workers Union Local 28 in New York. There were 3,300 white members in the union, but no Blacks. Apprenticeship was reserved almost exclusively for relatives of members. Finally, the State Commission on Human Rights found the local union guilty, and the union agreed that "henceforth every applicant for membership would be judged solely on an aptitude test administered by the New York Testing and Advisement Center."

—Maude White Katz
"End Racism in Education:
A Concerned Parent Speaks"

1. What is the source of each of the quotations in the above selection?
2. What *case* does the writer offer to make her point that racism spreads to trade unions? How is the writer's discussion of that case an example of *paraphrase*?
3. Why does the writer talk of a "net" in the second paragraph? How does the word help build an image?

How to Avoid Plagiarism

NAMING YOUR SOURCES

Any time you use someone else's words or ideas without giving credit to the person who first presented them, you are guilty of *plagiarism*. Although plagiarism is a serious offense, students often plagiarize merely through oversight or through a misunderstanding of the way to do research.

It is perfectly all right to use someone else's ideas, statements, or conclusions to support your own points in a paragraph or essay. However, you must always mention the source of your information. Leaving that out makes you guilty of plagiarism.

You can choose, with your instructor's guidance, one of these methods of naming your sources:

1. *Tell your source directly in the paragraph.* Make sure you mention the author; name the title of the book, newspaper, or magazine and underline it. Be sure to

include the date if you quote from, or paraphrase parts of, an article in a newspaper or a magazine. The title of an article is placed in quotation marks; you may name the source in parentheses—as was done in the selection by Maude White Katz on page 175—or you may mention it directly in a sentence.

Example:
John Holt, in <u>Freedom</u> <u>and</u> <u>Beyond</u>, writes, ". . . ."
A report on London schools in the <u>New</u> <u>York</u> <u>Times</u> of July 24, 1979, shows that . . . .
In the January, 1974, issue of <u>Today's</u> <u>Education</u>, Norman Cousins says, in his article "Truth in Government," ". . . ."

2. *Use footnotes directly after quoted or paraphrased material.* If your instructor requires footnotes, you must follow an accepted form for writing them. See the Minibook, "Writing Simple Footnotes," in Part 3, pages 404–405.
3. *Name your sources in a bibliography.* A bibliography is a list of books used in the preparation of a report. If your instructor requires a bibliography, use the correct form explained in "Preparing a Bibliography," pages 401–403 in the Minibook.

Finding Facts on Your Own

Because education has drawn so much criticism, individual and governmental groups have investigated many phases of the educational process. Here are a few places you can turn to for statistics, cases, and quotations on several aspects of child development.

Reference Books
  Encyclopedia Brittanica
  Compton's Encyclopedia
  The Associated Press Almanac
  The World Almanac and Book of Facts

Books
  Ames, Louise Bates. *Your Four-Year-Old: Wild and Wonderful.* New York: Delacorte, 1976.
  Ayrault, Evelyn West. *Growing Up Handicapped: A Guide for Parents and Professionals to Helping the Exceptional Child.* New York: Seabury Press, 1977.
  Bloom, Freddy. *Our Deaf Children.* London: Martins, 1974.
  Corsini, Raymond J. and Genevieve Painter. *The Practical Parent: ABCs of Child Discipline.* New York: Harper & Row, 1975.
  Fraiberg, Selma H. *The Magic Years: Understanding and Handling the Problems of Early Childhood.* New York: Scribner's, 1959.
  Gianini, Elena. *What Are Little Girls Made Of? The Roots of Feminine Stereotypes.* New York: Schocken Books, 1976.
  Glickman, Beatrice Marden. *Who Cares for the Baby?* New York: Schocken Books, 1978.
  Holt, John. *How Children Fail.* New York: Pitman, 1964.
  _____. *The Underachieving School.* New York: Pitman, 1969.
  Inglis, Ruth Langdon. *Sins of the Fathers: A Study of the Physical and Emotional Abuse of Children.* New York: St. Martin's, 1978.
  Keniston, Kenneth and the Carnegie Council on Children. *All Our Children: The American Family Under Pressure.* New York: Harcourt, 1977.
  Kozol, Jonathan. *Death at an Early Age.* Boston: Houghton Mifflin, 1967.

Maude White Katz on page 175—or you may mention it directly in a sentence.

_____. *Free Schools.* Boston: Houghton Mifflin, 1972.

Lamb, Michael E., ed. *The Role of Father in Child Development.* New York: Wiley, 1976.

Neill, A. S. *Summerhill: A Radical Approach to Child Rearing.* New York: Hart Publishing Company, 1960.

Pearce, Joseph Chilton. *Magical Child: Rediscovering Nature's Plan for Our Children.* New York: Dutton, 1977.

Porteous, Hedy S. *Sex and Identity: Your Child's Sexuality.* Indianapolis: Bobbs-Merrill, 1972.

Segal, Julius and Herbert Yahraes. *A Child's Journey: Forces that Shape the Lives of Our Young.* New York: McGraw-Hill, 1978.

Silberman, Charles E. *Crisis in the Classroom.* New York: Random House, 1970.

Stevens, Anita and Lucy Freeman. *"I Hate My Parents!" The Real and Unreal Reasons Why Youth Is Angry.* New York: Cowles Book Co., 1970.

Wiener, Harvey S. *Any Child Can Write.* New York: McGraw-Hill, 1978.

Pamphlets

United States Department of Commerce. *We the Americans: Our Education.* Washington, D.C.: U.S. Government Printing Office, 1973.

United States Department of Health, Education, and Welfare. *Annual Review of Child Abuse and Neglect Research.* Washington, D.C.: U.S. Government Printing Office, 1978.

United States Department of Health, Education, and Welfare. *On Being Educated in 1991,* Paper Prepared for the Conference of Associations of Student Government, by Terrel H. Bell. Washington, D.C.: U.S. Government Printing Office, 1970.

United States Department of Health, Education, and Welfare. *Education of the Gifted and Talented.* Washington, D.C.: U.S. Government Printing Office, 1971.

United States Department of Health, Education, and Welfare. *Positive Approaches to Dropout Prevention.* Washington, D.C.: U.S. Government Printing Office, 1973.

United States Department of Health, Education, and Welfare. *Ten Years of Progress.* Washington, D.C.: U.S. Government Printing Office, 1973.

United States Department of Health, Education, and Welfare. *Ten Years of Progress.* Washington, D.C.: U.S. Government Printing Office, 1973.

United States Department of Labor. *Trends in Educational Attainment of Women.* Washington, D.C.: U.S. Government Printing Office, 1970.

United States Department of Labor, Manpower Administration. *Relating General Educational Development to Career Planning.* Washington, D.C.: U.S. Government Printing Office, 1971.

Periodicals

Barnhouse, R. T. "Sex Roles and How Children Learn Them." *New Catholic World,* 220 (November, 1977), 280–283.

Boulding, E. "Children's Rights." *Society,* 15 (November, 1977), 39–43.

Brenton, M. "What Can Be Done about Child Abuse." *Today's Education,* 66 (September, 1977), 50.

Callard, E. D. "Developing Socially Valued Behavior in Young Children." *Education Digest,* 44 (May, 1979), 8–11.

"Child Abuse and Neglect in the American Society." *Center Magazine,* 11 (March, 1978), 70–77.

"Children in Jail: A Study by the Children's Defense Fund." *Progressive,* 43 (April, 1979), 22–25.

Coles, R. "Children of Affluence." *Atlantic,* 240 (September, 1977), 52–58.

"Declaration of the Rights of the Child." *UNESCO Courier,* 32 (January, 1979), 18–19.

"Education for the Handicapped." *Education Digest,* 43 (March, 1978), 12–15.

Fanshol, D. and E. B. Shinn, "New Light on Foster Homes." *Human Behavior,* 7 (August, 1978), 35.

Gerard, W. "Kids without Rights: Report of the Canadian Council on Children and Youth." *Macleans,* 91 (November 20, 1978), 40–43.

Mattill, J. "How High and Why? The Cost of Malnutrition." *Technology Review*, 81 (February, 1979), 83.

Mifflin, L. "Will Competitive Sports Hurt Your Child?" *Harper's Bazaar*, 110 (May, 1977), 90

Norman, M. "Substitutes for Mother: Effects of Day Care Centers." *Human Behavior*, 7 (February, 1978), 18–22.

Wightman, M. "Gifted, Talented Children: Programs in Texas to Help the Top 5 Percent." *Education Digest*, 43 (September, 1977), 51–53.

Wilcox, H. G. "Organized Child." *Human Behavior*, 7 (December, 1978), 49.

Witty, M., ed. "Child's Mind: A Symposium." *Harpers*, 256 (April, 1978), 43–58.

ENDING A PARAGRAPH

A paragraph must have some kind of closing, some indication that expression of the ideas is finished and that the writer has not just run out of things to say. In one-paragraph papers, the closing may be made effectively in just one sentence. Often two or three sentences may conclude the paragraph. Here are a few pointers to help you write closing sentences.

SOME CLOSING-SENTENCE POINTERS

1. The closing sentence should leave no doubt in the reader's mind that you are finished with the paragraph.
2. The closing sentence should leave the reader with a feeling that you have done what you intended to do. It should clinch the main point of your theme.
3. The closing sentence should perform one or a combination of these functions:
   a. Restate the main idea by referring back to the topic sentence

Hint: You do not have to use the same words that appear in the topic sentence. Find synonyms for the opinion word and the words that state the topic.

   b. Summarize one or more of the subtopics
   c. Give the dominant impression of the experience being described

4. Use transition words to help you conclude: *therefore, as a result, consequently,* and a number of others explained in previous chapters are good for concluding, summarizing, and showing results.
5. Make the conclusion fit the tone of the paragraph. A funny, brief, clever conclusion might suit a humorous paragraph about education. But a serious paragraph about learning problems would require something more formal.

WHAT NOT TO DO IN CLOSING SENTENCES

1. Don't start a new topic.
2. Don't contradict the point you have tried to make. A one-paragraph paper that tries to show why children dislike school should not end in the way that one student chose: "Some of them like school very much, however."
3. Don't make statements that are obvious or overused. A paragraph dealing with the high costs of education would gain little by a conclusion like this: "Money is the root of all evil."

4. Don't apologize for your lack of knowledge, lack of resources, or lack of interest. If you are not qualified to write about the topic, select a topic for which you are qualified.
5. Don't end with a quick statement that indicates that your paragraph is over. *Avoid* endings like these:

And that's all I have to say.	You see what I mean.
The end.	That's all.
That's how it happened.	It may sound unbelievable but it's true.
I hope you have enjoyed my story.	Therefore what I have said is true.

6. Don't use too many words. Be brief, to the point, and clear.
7. Don't make any sweeping statements that admit no possibilities of other ideas or actions. To conclude a paragraph with "Therefore, all children can learn to read at home with their parents' help" overstates your case by an *absolute* conclusion, that is, a conclusion that has no conditions or possible exceptions or limitations. Try to soften your point with words that permit other possibilities: *perhaps, it seems, we may conclude, I am in favor, a good suggestion is.*
8. Don't make your closing statement too obvious by saying things like: "As I have shown you in my paragraph . . . ." or "So my closing sentence is . . . ."

Step 1. Picking Good Endings. Column I gives the topic sentence of a paragraph. Circle, in Column II, the closing sentence you think would best suit the paragraph. Explain your choice.

I

1. A father should share in the discipline of his son as the child grows up.

2. Our society must realize that children have constitutional rights that must not be ignored.

3. The number of students who drop out of high school is increasing each year.

II

a. "Spare the rod, spoil the child!"
b. But the mother can do an excellent job in disciplining the child in the family.
c. So a boy needs a father who is a friend at times but who is a strong parent all the time.

a. Since I am not a lawyer, I don't know all the legal rights of children, but something should be done.
b. As I have shown you in the above paragraph, this is a serious problem.
c. Therefore, the legal rights of our children as American citizens must be upheld.

a. However, many students are realizing the value of a high school diploma and remain in school.
b. Our schools should change their approach to education in order to halt the high drop-out rates among high school students.
c. High school students must be forced to stay in school until they graduate.

Step 2. Rewriting Closing Sentences. Answer the following questions.

1. Reread "Childhood Mischief," pages 107–108. How does the closing sentence *summarize* the various subtopics? _____

   _____

   Write a different closing sentence which will *suggest some consequence of the actions told about in the paragraph.* _____

   _____

2. Reread "The Gloom Room," on pages 31–32. How does the closing sentence give the *dominant impression of the experience?* _____

   _____

   Write a different closing sentence which will *summarize* the main point. _____

   _____

3. Reread "Waking on Monday Morning," on page 160. How does the closing sentence *restate the main idea* and *suggest some action that could be taken* based upon the ideas expressed in the paragraph?

   _____

   Rewrite the closing sentences so that it *forms a judgment* based upon the information in the paragraph. _____

   _____

EXPANDING SENTENCES: VERB-PART OPENERS FOR VARIETY

You can improve sentence variety by opening a sentence with a verb part or with a group of words containing part of a verb. You have already dealt with two verb parts: the *infinitive* and the *-ing* word.

Using the *-ing* Opener

An *-ing* word—called a *present participle*—used without a helping word (see page 14) is not a verb, but it may be used effectively to open a sentence that contains a "legitimate" verb. Here is a complete sentence that contains a verb and subject:.

A young boy read *Robin Hood.*

An *-ing* word may be added at the beginning:

[comma here]
Whistling, a young boy read *Robin Hood.*

Hint: A comma must come after an introductory *-ing* word or an introductory group of words that contain an *-ing* word.

A word that tells *how, when,* or *where* may be placed after the *-ing* word.

           [how]   [comma here]
Whistling softly, a young boy read *Robin Hood.*

A group of words that tell *why* or *how* or *where* or *when* may now be added after the *-ly* word.

              [These words tell where]   [comma here]
Whistling softly *in a hard brown chair,* a young boy read *Robin Hood.*

Sometimes a subordinator (see pages 89–95) may appear as the first word in a verb-part opener:

   [subordinator]   [comma here]
While whistling softly in a hard brown chair, a young boy read *Robin Hood.*

Hint: Make sure that the first two or three words after the comma tell *who* or *what* is doing the action of the *-ing* word with which you have opened the sentence. See pages 184–186 for some work with incorrect verb-part openers.

Step 1. Opening a Sentence Strongly. Add opening word groups to the complete sentences below by selecting an item first from Column I, then from Column II, then from Column III. You should have three new sentences for each statement on the next page.

I	*II*	*III*
(*-ing* word)	(one word to tell *how, when, where*)	(a word group to tell *how, when, where, why*)
trembling	gracefully	in the sky
leaping	noisily	below the hill
soaring	clumsily	near me
roaring	there	through an open window
speeding	yesterday	in darkness
moaning	above	on a warm summer night
creeping	innocently	with a whine
dancing	swiftly	beyond the gray mountains
cheering	today	at noon
speaking	slowly	beneath a pale cloud
crying	excitedly	across a stream
hurtling	softly	from their seats
		at the campfire
		beside an old oak

Example:

The boat returned home.

a. *Speeding, the boat returned home.* _____

b. *Trembling noisily, the boat returned home.* _____

c. *Drifting slowly across the stream, the boat returned home.*

1. A truck rumbled down Route 84.

   a. _____

   b. _____

   c. _____

2. The children laughed loudly.

   a. _____

   b. _____

   c. _____

3. The cat sprang quickly away.

   a. _____

   b. _____

   c. _____

Step 2. Using New Words. Use the words given in the new *-ing* vocabulary (on pages 166–167) to open three sentences of your own. Use separate paper.

Step 3. *-ing* at the End. The *-ing* construction works nicely at the end of sentences too. On a separate sheet of paper, rewrite any five sentences you wrote in Step 1 or Step 2 above, this time placing the *-ing* word group at the end.

Sentence from Step 1: Drifting slowly across a stream, the boat returned.

Rewritten sentence: The boat returned, *drifting slowly across a stream.*

Step 4. Two *-ing* Words. Two *-ing* words at the beginning produce an effective sentence. Complete each sentence below that begins with a double *-ing* construction by adding your own complete thought.

Example:

Laughing and smiling,

Laughing and smiling, the children shouted, "Trick or treat!" _____

Hint: The first few words after the comma must tell who or what does the action of the *-ing* words. See pages 184–186 for errors that may arise in the use of the *-ing* opener.

1. Running and jumping,

_____

2. Brushing his hair and smiling into the mirror,

_____

3. Holding her stomach and gasping for breath,

_____

Infinitives as Openers

If you want to tell *why* the subject of a sentence performs some action, you can open the sentence with a word group that starts with an infinitive. (An infinitive is made up of the word *to* and the present tense of the verb: *to hope, to sing, to laugh* are just three examples.)

[This tells *why* he had the tires checked.]

To ensure the safety of his car, he had the tires checked carefully.

[comma here]

Step 5. Using Infinitives as Openers. Use each of the following infinitive word groups in front of your own complete sentence.

Hint: Use a comma after an infinitive word group when a complete sentence follows it.

Example:

1. To achieve high grades

To achieve high grades, a student needs discipline.

2. To run a marathon

_____

3. To impress a friend

_____

4. To write well

_____

Other Verb Parts as Openers

Word groups with verb parts that end in *-ed, -n, -en,* or *-t* (*past participles*) may also be used to start sentences. Again, a comma must come after the introductory word group; the first words after the comma must tell who does the action of the verb part used in that introductory word group.

Spoken in a loud voice, the announcer's words reached the whole audience.

[verb part]   [comma here]   [This tells *what* were spoken.]

[verb part]

Disgusted with the papers and beer cans on the sidewalk, Ms. Watson swept them into the street.   [comma]   [This tells *who* was disgusted.]

Step 6. Using Other Verb Parts as Openers.   Begin a sentence of your own with the following verb-part openers. Be sure you study the examples given above.

1. Pleased with his behavior

   _____

2. Stricken with grief

   _____

3. Greeted by her friends

   _____

4. Tired from all the talk

   _____

5. Delighted with the good news

   _____

Avoiding Errors with Verb-Part Openers

When you use verb-part openers, you must remember to name the correct subject (the person or thing that performs the action of the verb part) in the first few words after the opening word group. Whether or not it is intended, the first noun or pronoun after the verb-part opener is automatically the subject; this often yields strange and humorous sentences. Look at the columns below.

I Correct

1. While dressed in a new overcoat,

   [This tells who was dressed in an overcoat.]

   I brushed against a bus and soiled my sleeve.

2. Feeling fine, the little old man

   [This tells that the man was feeling fine.]

   smiled at the trees and flowers.

II Incorrect

1. While dressed in a new overcoat,

   [This shows that the bus was dressed in an overcoat.]

   a bus brushed against me and soiled my sleeve.

2. Feeling fine, the trees and flowers

   [These words tell that the trees and flowers felt fine.]

   made the little old man smile.

It is obvious that the sentences in Column II do not say what the writer wants them to say (*trees* feeling fine? a *bus* dressed in an overcoat?).

TO CORRECT THE ERROR MADE WITH VERB-PART OPENERS

1. Ask *who* or *what* is performing the action indicated by the verb part:
   Who is dressed in a new overcoat?
   Who is feeling fine?
   If necessary, rewrite the sentence so that the words that answer that question appear within the first few words after the verb-part opener.
2. Rewrite the sentence so that the subject is included in the opening word group. You will have to add a word to make a complete verb.
   Sentence 1 in Column II could be rewritten in this way:

   [added word to make a verb]

   While I was dressed in a new overcoat, a bus brushed against me and soiled

   [subject now included in opening word group]

   my sleeve.
   Sentence 2 in Column II could be written in this way:

   [added word to make a verb]

   Since the little old man was feeling fine, the trees and flowers made him smile.

   [subject now included in opening word group]

   Although this second option helps you correct errors, it also removes the *-ing* structure from the beginning of the sentence. Because *-ing* words are valuable in varying your style, try to keep them by naming the subject right after the verb-part opener, as explained in Column I on page 184.

Step 7. Making Sense with *-ing* Words. For each item below, draw an arrow from the verb part to the person or thing that the *sentence says* is the subject. Then, rewrite the sentence so that it makes sense. If the sentence is already correct, mark it *C*.

Example:

1. After failing the final exam, her father scolded her. *After she failed the final exam, her father scolded her.*

2. Running for the bus, my books fell out of my arms. _____

3. Gazing sadly out the window, the heavy rain turned my garden into mud. _____

4. While shopping for Christmas presents, the fire engines raced down the street. _____

5. After waiting impatiently for two hours, my desire to see Cathy increased greatly. _____

_____

Step 8. Checking Your Sentences. Examine the sentences you wrote in Steps 1 through 7 on the previous pages. Have you made any errors with verb-part openers? Does the sentence state clearly the subject you intended for the verb part? Correct any problems you find.

SOLVING PROBLEMS IN WRITING

Capital Letters

Step 1. What Do You Remember? Write a *full* sentence response to each question below.

1. Which football team do you think will win the Super Bowl this year?

_____

2. What river runs through your state?

_____

3. What are three subjects you enjoy at college?

_____

4. What season of the year do you find most enjoyable?

_____

5. If you could board a plane and fly anywhere, in which direction would you go?

_____

6. Which animal in the zoo do you think is funniest?

_____

7. What high school did you attend (write the words *high school* as part of your answer)?

_____

8. Which war do you think was the bloodiest?

_____

9. Which president do you think did the most for our country?

_____

10. What is the name of your favorite book, and who is its author?

_____

If you could not make up your mind about the spelling of some of your answers, study the reference charts on capital letters starting on page 187.

QUICK REFERENCE CHART: WHEN AND WHEN NOT TO CAPITALIZE

Geography

Russian River
Rocky Mountains
but
a tall mountain

Salt Lake City
but
our city

Yellowstone National Park
Market Street
but
a noisy street

Historical Occurrences, Names, and Writings

Tonkin Resolution
Boston Tea Party
Seward's Folly
Fifth Amendment
the Constitution

School Things

LaGuardia Community
College
but
a new college

Mohawk High School
but
our old high school

Coleman Junior High School
but
a junior high school

English, Spanish, French
but
American history
economics, biology, business

Hint: Languages are always capitalized. Other subjects are not, except when specific courses (usually indicated by numbers) are meant:
Economics 13.2
History 64

a sophomore in college
the senior class

Buildings and Organizations

Dime Savings Bank
Sears Roebuck and Company
Brookdale Hospital
Pathmark Supermarket
Republican Party
San Francisco Giants
Girl Scouts

The Word "I"

Always capitalize the word I
When I saw her, I was
delighted.

Days, Months, Seasons, Celebrations

Monday
April
not seasons
spring, summer, fall,
autumn, winter
Election Day
Festival of Lights
New Year's Eve

Religion, Race, Nationality

God, Lord
Bible, Genesis
New Testament
bless His Name
the Egyptian gods
Catholicism

the Jewish religion
Protestant beliefs
Negro, Indian
Dutch Reformed Church

Titles

Books, Stories, Shows, Poems

"Oh Captain, My Captain"
Love Story
A Tale of Two Cities
but
a book by Dickens

The Washington Post
All in the Family
"The Legend of Sleepy
Hollow"

People

President Carter
Judge Black
Dr. Bracken
He is the president of the
company.
Mr. Davis, President of the
company
or
Mr. Davis, president of the
company
Harriet Parsons, Ph.D.
but
a teacher, a lawyer, a
professor

Hint: If the title takes the place of a person's name, use a capital. The Mayor arrived late. The mayor's job is difficult.

Areas and Directions

Lower East Side
East-West relations

Far East
Midwest
lives in the West
**but not for
directions**
New York is six miles **e**ast
of here.
They drove **n**orth across the
bridge.

Writing Letters
Opening: Capitals for first
word and any names.
  Dear Mr. Stevenson:
  My dear Miss Trumball:
  Dear Jerry,
Closing: First word only:
  Sincerely yours,
  Yours truly,
  Very truly yours,

**No Capitals for Plants,
Animals, Games**

daisies	a vicious lion
sycamore tree	baseball
an old oak	football
bananas	swimming
a bluebird	monkeys
six sparrows	apple

The Family
I get along with Mom.
     or
I get along with mom.
This is Aunt Celia.

**No capitals to show
relationship:**
That is my sister.
Our **u**ncle is generous.
My **a**unt is very helpful.

Step 2. Making Sense with Capitals. In each of the following sentences, the first letter of several words is omitted. Decide whether you need a capital or a small letter and then fill in the blank spaces.

1. My _____ncle left his job at the _____nion _____avings and _____oan

   _____company to attend _____arvard _____aw _____chool this _____all.

2. Last _____ummer one of my _____eachers organized a trip to the _____est

   _____oast for all the _____eniors in my _____igh _____chool.

3. If you like _____merican _____istory, you should know the role of the

   _____rench _____overnment during the _____evolutionary _____ar.

4. It is not true that science—_____iology, _____hemistry, _____hysics,

   _____sychology—denies the existence of _____od; it is possible to be-

   lieve, for example, in _____reudian ideas and the _____ible as well.

5. Last _____pril just before _____aster, the _____epublican _____arty held a

   banquet at the _____ilton _____otor _____nn in _____ochester, a _____ity

   in _____estern _____ew _____ork _____tate.

Step 3. Correcting Your Errors.   Return to Step 1, page 186. Make corrections in what you wrote, based upon the reference chart on pages 187–188.

Step 4. Finding Mistakes with Capitals.   Each sentence below has the number of errors with capitals indicated in parentheses. Make the corrections directly on the page.

1. i would like to play Baseball for the chicago white soxs, but my Father insists that I become a Lawyer and work for the law firm of davis and rutter in seattle.   (10)
2. San francisco's chinatown has a number of Schools where, even during the Summer months, students can study English, Mathematics, and History.   (6)
3. when i saw the President of First National bank at a Baseball game in Shea stadium one hot august day, i was surprised because i thought he was visiting his Daughter in the midwest.   (11).

Levels of Language: Formal or Informal

Formal English is the language of professional journals, formal speeches, and most serious college writing. Informal English (the English you speak each day) is found in parts of novels, short stories, letters, books, most newspapers, articles for general readership, and advertisements. *Colloquialisms* (informal expressions used in speaking but generally not in writing) and *slang* (vivid words or phrases used because they are brief, "loose," and colorful) mark informal language and are perfectly acceptable in informal situations. Although it is effective to use such informality for special effects in your writing or as part of the quoted words you show someone speaking, for the most part informal language should be avoided in your compositions. And very often informal expressions change so rapidly that acceptable words one year are no longer used at a later time.

USING CONTRACTIONS

Putting words together by replacing letters with an apostrophe helps writers record accurately the words people speak. Thus, hearing *can't, isn't, it's, could've,* and other contractions, writers attempting to produce on paper a direct quotation would write exactly what they hear.

   Contractions are also acceptable in informal writing, even when no speaker is being quoted. Therefore, in newspapers, popular magazines, and textbooks aiming for a conversational tone, contractions work well—though never when they are excessive.

   However, most formal writing for your college courses demands that you avoid contractions wherever you can. Use the two words that led to the contraction rather than the abbreviated form of the word. Here are some examples:

Informal	*Formal*
She *didn't* look up from her page of notes.	She *did not* look up from her page of notes.
They'd have phoned if they *could've.*	They *would have* phoned if they *could have.*

Instead of these contractions:	*Write the words out:*
I'm	I am
isn't	is not
wasn't	was not
weren't	were not
aren't	are not
don't	do not
couldn't	could not

But be careful! Do not substitute for an informal expression something stuffy and unnatural, something overdone. Usually, however, students are too *in*formal in their writing.

Here are some informal expressions used in student themes and some alternatives that could be used.

Informal	*Example*	*More Formal Expression*
cool; way out; super; swell; together	It was a *cool* movie.	excellent; effective; remarkable; superior; relaxed; provocative
fun (used to describe)	We had a *fun* time.	enjoyable; uproarious; amusing; hilarious
sort of (a) kind of (a)	That policeman was *kind of* strange.	rather; somewhat
a couple of	Bring me *a couple of* books.	some; several; a few
dig on groove on	My girl friend and I were *grooving on* a record by Dylan.	enjoy; respond; appreciate; love; listen
lousy	What a *lousy* time we had.	dull; depressing
enthused	The singer was *enthused* about the piano player.	enthusiastic about or over; excited
a lot, lots of	I have *lots of* time.	much; a great deal
a fix	What a *fix* I got into with this car! I'll *fix* you!	complication; troublesome time; awkward event punish
myself yourself himself } used as subjects	Mary and *myself* were late.	I you he
real; mighty; awfully; plenty	He was *real* annoyed at me.	very; extremely; strongly

Informal	Example	More Formal Expression
faze	It didn't *faze* me in the least.	bother; disturb; annoy
sure	*Sure* I wanted to leave the house.	certainly; indeed; surely; absolutely
drag	Biology is a *drag*.	boring
do a number	My girl friend *did a number* on me.	cheat, confuse, betray

Hint: If occasionally you want to use some informal word for special effect, put the word in quotation marks:

Because of so much construction and repairs, no one but the builders can "dig" Atlanta any more.

See also "Biology Jailhouse," pages 161–162, last sentence.

Step 1. Informal to Formal.   Rewrite each of the sentence examples of informal usage on pages 190–191 into more formal language. Be careful not to make your new sentences sound too high-flown. Use separate paper.

Step 2. More Informal Sentences.   Here are several more sentences using informal language. Discuss how you would change them into sentences that would be acceptable in a formal writing activity. Do not write anything too stiff.

1. They're a cool bunch to hang out with, but my old lady flipped when she caught me.
2. I pick up lots of foxy ladies who groove on the disco scene and fancy threads.
3. Sure, Pop gave the wheels plenty of juice, but we couldn't jive those lousy couple of cops out of a ticket nohow.
4. I figure I should talk turkey if my old man hangs the accident on me. Otherwise he might think I was strung out or something, and then it's painsville for me.
5. My chick was sort of uptight when she met the tough dudes I hang out with.

Step 3. A "Square" Dictionary.   Write your own dictionary of several more informal expressions (slang, colloquialisms) that you define for someone who might not "dig" your language. Write a definition for each word; use each word in a colloquial sentence that you might speak or write; give one or two alternate words that could be used for the same effect; then, rewrite your original sentence in more formal English. You might want to define colloquial and slang expressions like *dough, kookie, wicked, uptight, with it, right on, boss, bread, gig*. Make a chart like the one below. Follow the example.

A "SQUARE" DICTIONARY

Informal Expression	Definition	My Own Sentence	Alternate Words	More Formal English
uptight	to be nervous	I was all uptight about the driving test.	anxious, worried, troubled, nervous	I was nervous about the driving test.

Word or Symbol? Using Abbreviations

When you take notes, it's often convenient to use some sign or shortened form of a word to save time. But in formal writing, you should avoid abbreviated forms of words.

What Not to Use	What to Use Instead
& or ⨎ or &	and
Feb., Apr., Wed.	February, April, Wednesday Write out the word for the day or month.
bio, psych, eco	biology, psychology, economics Write out the word for all school subjects.

thru, tho, boro
nite, lite, brite
	through, though, borough
	night, light, bright
	    Don't leave off the ends of words or make
	    up short forms.

st., h'way., ave., blvd., rd., co.	street, highway avenue, boulevard } Always write these out. road, company
ch., p., pp.	chapter page } Write these out, except in foot- pages } notes or bibliography.
lbs., oz., ft., in.	pounds, ounces } Measurements are feet, inches } spelled out.
L.A., Ill., Calif., Rocky Mts.	Los Angeles Illinois } Names of states, California } countries, cities, Rocky Mountains } geographical places are not abbreviated.
e.g.	for example
no., #	number
{ and etc. } { ect. }	etc. This is the abbreviation for *et cetera*. Do not use *ect.* or *and etc.*

Hint: Use *etc.* very infrequently.

WHEN YOU CAN USE SHORTENED FORMS

---

1. &, &, Co., Inc. only when part of an official name:
A&P, Tiffany & Co.

2. Mr., Mrs., Dr. only immediately before someone's name

3. Jr., Sr., only immediately after someone's name
is mentioned

4. Ph.D., M.D., M.A. only immediately after someone's name

5. FBI, NAACP, UN Some organizations and government depart-
ments are usually referred to by initials.
No periods are necessary after the letters.

6. A.M., P.M. when numbers appear directly before:
(or a.m., p.m.) 8:15 P.M.

Hint: If you use the word *o'clock*, write out the
number: ten o'clock *not* 10 o'clock.

7. $, No. when numbers come after:
$5.00, Booth No. 6,

Hint 1: Abbreviations usually require periods.
   2: If you don't know what an abbreviation means, consult any dictionary.
   3: It's better, in general, not to use abbreviations.

DO'S AND DON'TS ABOUT NUMBERS

Don't use the number if you can write it out in one or two words.

Use	fifty	not	50
	three hundred	not	300
	eighty-eight	not	88
	nineteenth	not	19th
	eightieth	not	80th

Do use the number if more than two words are needed to write it out.

Use 654   not   six hundred and fifty-four

Do use the number for the year and day of a date.

February 2, 1971

Hint: Don't use -st, -th, -nd, -rd after any number in a date.

Do use numbers if you need to mention a series of numbers.

On the rack hung 50 red dresses, 340 skirts, and 15 vests.

Do use the number for percentages and decimals.

Of the students, 45% were boys.
The paper measures 8.73 inches in length.

Do use the number for items in street addresses:

480 Rockaway Parkway
1874 Ninth Avenue

Hint: If the street itself is named by a number, write the word out if the number is below ten. Otherwise, use the number, *without -st, -th, -nd, -rd* at the end:

251 East 91 Street
1880 18 Street
37 Fifth Avenue

Do use the number for parts of a book.

On page *18* the author presents a graph to illustrate his point.

Don't start a sentence with a number.

Not *9 parents attended* but *Nine parents attended.*
Not *350 seats were in the room* but *The room held 350 seats.*

Step 1. Correcting Abbreviations. In each sentence below, correct whatever errors you find in regard to abbreviations. The numbers in parentheses tell how many errors there are.

1. I have lived at 1092 1st. Ave. in L.A. a no. of yrs., but I have never visited northern Calif. (6)
2. On the 2nd Thurs. nite of every month I take a bio. class at Drs. Hospital located on Madison H'way. (6)
3. On April 6, 1975, 5 children earned grades of forty-five% on their arith. tests; but Mark's bro, 8 years old, missed only No. 4. (6)

WRITING THE PARAGRAPH

Your assignment for this theme is to write a paragraph in which you discuss some vital issue concerning the growth and education of children. In order to support your ideas, you will draw upon statistics, cases, and quoted material —the details of research.

Learning from Other Students

Read the paragraphs below, written by students who investigated specific areas of child development. Discuss the answers to the questions after each selection.

Developing Reading Skills in Preschool Children

There are many excellent ways in which children can acquire the ability to read before they enter the first grade. Glenn Doman in *How to Teach Your Child to Read* advocates a system that calls upon scientifically designed materials, the child examining large red lower-case letters printed on cards. These cards progress in difficulty to normal-sized black upper- and lower-case letters as the "visual pathway" matures. Systematically, the child learns to differentiate between simple words such as "mommy" and "daddy." Later the child assimilates "self" and "home" vocabulary. And following that, "sentence structure vocabulary" develops in the context of "structural phrases and sentences." Because the alphabet is such an abstract concept, it is taught last. Another excellent approach to preschool reading is outlined by John J. DeBoer and Martha Dollman in *The Teaching of Reading*. They cite teaching three- and four-year-old children to read at the Whitby School in Whitby, Connecticut. Instructional aids include vowel shapes cut from light-colored sandpaper mounted on dark cards, and consonants and groups of letters cut out of black sandpaper mounted on white cards. Afterwards, the children select words, and eventually phrases and sentences, from baskets. Enthusiastically, they translate the words into sounds and carry out the actions that they read. Aside from these highly structured programs in schools, parents are now advised to help their children learn to read at home. Nancy Larrick stresses the point in an article called "No More Hands Off to Parents, We Need You." Parents, with their infants, are enrolling in "home-based projects" that lead directly to success in reading. Mothers and fathers learn how to read aloud and how to hold a book so that the child can see and participate. The parents also learn how to follow reading with informal converstation, how to question the child, and how to stimulate the child's interest. Carol Vukelich, in her May, 1978, article in *Education Digest*, "Parents Are Teachers," recognizes how important the child's preschool years are to later reading success. Vukelich discusses the Preschool Readiness Outreach Program (PROP) in which parents construct educational games to develop their children's talking, listening, and seeing skills. She states that "children whose parents participated actively in the program achieved significantly greater gains than those whose parents participated minimally." Therefore, parents must work with teachers in developing children's reading abilities. According to the 1971–72 National Reading Center literacy survey, at least 18 million Americans aged sixteen and over were not functionally literate, and nearly one out of every six adult Americans is handicapped with reading problems. Although these statistics are grim, with encouragement and the right program selected for each child, our future preschooler should be able to read before entering school.

—Muriel Guba

Step 1. Paragraph Review. Answer these questions about "Developing Reading Skills in Preschool Children" by Muriel Guba.

1. What is the topic? What is the writer's opinion about the topic?
2. What sources does Muriel Guba use for quoting and paraphrasing?
3. Are the statistics she uses effective? Why?
4. There are three subtopic sentences in this paragraph. What are they?
5. What is your opinion of the closing sentence? of the title?

The Advantages of Attending Kindergarten

Although many children do not attend, kindergarten is quite an advantage for five-year olds. A table in the *Digest of Education Statistics* shows that 3,024,398 American children attended kindergarten in the spring of 1970. This may appear to be a large number of children, but, in reality, it is not. James Hymes states in

Teaching the Child Under Six that "only about 60% of our five-year olds go to any kind of kindergarten: public, private, or church sponsored. About 40% go to no school at all." Hymes also gives one of the main reasons for the low rate of attendance: "Only 29 states provide state aid for kindergartens, 21 do not. And most of the 29 provide only half aid . . . ." These are discouraging figures for so important an educational experience for children as kindergarten. It improves perception, awareness, and abilities to relate to others verbally. In *The Guide to an Effective Kindergarten Program* David Mindess states that "children who have attended kindergarten show less tendency to reverse and confuse letters, have more positive work habits, do more accurate work," and they are "able to work independently as well as in groups." Mindess reports on a four-year study by researcher Loretta McHugh. Involving 709 kindergarten and 620 non-kindergarten children, the study concludes "that the verbal abilities, quantitative reasoning and phonetic abilities of the kindergarten children were superior to those of the non-kindergarten group. In the third grade the kindergarten group's total achievement was markedly superior and had more satisfactory school adjustment over the non-kindergarten group." Another advantage of the kindergarten experience is that it stresses play, allowing the child freedom of expression during a large part of the school day with classmates. According to "Education Is Play," an article in the February 1973 issue of *Childhood Education,* "Play is the . . . way the small child discovers how to use the world for his own purposes, to manipulate it. He does so by imagining in his head . . . and then externalizing those imaginings in his play." Kindergarten is also the child's first opportunity to learn from television with the aid of a teacher. *"Sesame Street:* Shaping Broadcast Television to the Needs of the Preschoolers," an article in *Educational Technology,* makes the following observations about two classes: "One class gave the program its entire attention. Down the hall a class of children the same age was only partially attentive. . . . The explanation seems to be found in the different attitudes of the two teachers. One teacher is indifferent. . . . Her colleague down the hall socializes the attitude in the opposite direction. When the program hour draws near, she enthusiastically announces, 'It is *Sesame Street* time.'" She then gets the children's attention, encourages a positive attitude toward the program, and begins a fruitful learning experience. That is what kindergarten really is, a fruitful learning experience. Kindergarten introduces children to their first formal education and prepares them for absorbing all the knowledge they have yet to gain. These are experiences for all children.

—April Wynn

Step 2. Understanding the Paragraph. Answer these questions, which are based on the selection above.

1. What is the purpose of the paragraph? Does the topic sentence effectively state that purpose?
2. What are the different sources April Wynn cites in her theme?
3. Where does she use statistics dramatically? Where does one particular case make an impressive point?

Some Topics for Child Development Themes

These suggested topics can be developed in paragraphs that use *statistics, cases,* or *quotations* as supporting details. Some of the topics are quite specific; others require that you narrow them down as suggested in the chart and Step 1 on page 198. If you need more suggestions, see Step 1, page 167. Of course you may use any topic which interests you.

open classrooms in England
the "new math"
computers and arithmetic lessons
black schools in a Southern city
child abuse
sibling rivalries
student dropouts
adopted children
teaching Chinese students English
the effects of busing
the value of *Sesame Street*
John Dewey's basic views
the gifted child
teaching the mentally retarded
the growth of student power in public high schools
constitutional rights of children
training the early childhood teacher
learning rates: boys and girls
discipline problems
day-care centers and the learning process
economics and education
teaching the slow learner to read
developing oral language for the deaf
early childhood sex education
television commercials and children
the emotional needs of children
proper nutrition for children
role models for children
how children learn
juvenile delinquency
education in foreign countries
teaching independence to children
speech disorders and the young child

Prewriting: Narrowing the Field

One of the most important goals of prewriting (see page 35) is limiting the topic. Especially when you face a topic as broad as *child development,* you must consider carefully how to narrow the subject down so that you are not overwhelmed with research. Even when you think you have selected some reasonable area within a large topic idea, you can no doubt shave the subject down even more. The chart below shows how to narrow down a topic in a series of steps.

TOO GENERAL	STILL BROAD	LESS BROAD	NARROW ENOUGH
teaching	teaching number concepts	teaching number concepts to children	teaching number concepts at home to children under five
child behavior	how children play together	how girls play together	patterns of play among four- and five-year-old girls
childhood diseases	fighting polio	vaccination in the fight against polio	the government's role in vaccination against polio
children	disciplining children	disciplining adolescents	disciplining adolescents by the methods of Haim G. Ginott

To narrow your topic, you will have to do some general research in the library, perhaps even under such broad topics as those listed in the first column in the chart above. After you decide how to narrow things down, go back to books and periodicals that deal with the specific topic you have chosen. Start gathering notes. (See pages 412–413.) If you collect lots of data, you might find an outline helpful as one of your prewriting activities. (See page 421.) When you write your first draft, your notes should already be organized in some way.

Step 1. Prewriting to Narrow the Topic. How would you narrow these topics down into reasonable areas for research?

1. busing _____

2. education and the courts _____

3. new types of classrooms _____

4. teaching machines _____

5. television and children _____

6. juvenile delinquency _____

7. child abuse _____

8. nutrition _____

Progress Reminders: A Checklist of Questions

As you write your various drafts, keep in mind these pointers—phrased as questions—to help you prepare a strong paragraph based on research. Fill in the questionnaire and submit it with your final manuscript.

1. Did I think carefully about the topic, using whatever prewriting tech- _____
niques work for me? Did I limit my topic sufficiently?

2. Did I check several library resources, including books and periodicals? _____
Did I take notes on my readings?
3. Did I organize my material before writing a rough draft? Did I change _____
language and sentence structure in later drafts? Does my final copy follow correct manuscript form?
4. Does my topic sentence tell the subject of my paragraph and my opinion _____
of or attitude toward it?
5. Did I use subtopic sentences, when necessary, to introduce each new _____
feature of the topic? Do my details support the specific points of the
subtopics?
6. Did I use adequate detail—statistics, cases, quotations, concrete sen- _____
sory images, or a combination of these? Did I study the chart on page
173 to review the correct writing of statistics?
7. Did I use transitions to connect my ideas smoothly and logically? _____
8. Did I use a variety of sentence types? Did I open sentences with subordi- _____
nators (pages 89–95); -ing words, infinitives, and other verb parts (pages
180–186); and one or two -ly words (page 53).
9. Did I read the student themes on pages 194–196 as a model for my
paragraph?
10. Did I cite any sources I used for statistics or quotations? _____
11. Did I proofread my paper carefully both before and after I prepared my _____
final draft? Did I look especially for errors in agreement, for run-ons and
fragments, for errors in capitalization, plurals, and careless errors typical
of my usual mistakes? Did I check my Theme Progress Sheet (page 429)?
12. Did I write a strong title for my paragraph? _____

THE PROFESSIONALS SPEAK

Read the selection below and answer the questions that come after it.

SOME WORDS TO KNOW BEFORE YOU READ

concede: acknowledge as true
debilitating: weakening
determinism: a theory in which causes and effects are linked together
insubordination: not giving in to authority
facilitated: made easier
analogous: similar

Why Some Schools Succeed

What makes a child learn? What keeps him from it? Is it the school building or
the pupil-teacher ratio? The mood of the classroom? The way the lessons are
taught? Or, in the long run, do things like that really not matter much, and is a
child's academic fate determined instead by such factors as his race, his family's
social class and the condition of his neighborhood?

That traditional debate has been joined by a group of British experts in an important new book that disputes some well-established theories about elementary education.

After a four-year study of 12 schools in poor neighborhoods of London, they found that the way a school is run can make a huge difference in how much a child learns and how he behaves.

Their findings, backed up with impressive statistics, fly in the face of a popular American theory that holds that if a student body has too many social disadvantages, there is not much that can be done for it educationally.

"Our study should give hope to anyone who had despaired of improving the quality of education in inner cities," said Dr. Janet Ouston, one of the four co-authors of the book, which is called *Fifteen Thousand Hours* (a reference to the total amount of time that a child spends at school). "Simply put, we found that there really are ways that the schools can be improved to make them more effective."

What matters most, the researchers found, is what they called the ethos of a school—the general tone of the place—which seemed to have more effect on pupil performance than such factors as the age of the physical plant or how strictly the children were disciplined.

The finding that schools do make a difference may seem obvious; as the book concedes, it "will come as no surprise to parents, who often go to a good deal of trouble to get their children into schools of their choice."

But regardless of what parents have thought, a good many professionals on both sides of the Atlantic have been greatly influenced over the past decade by Dr. James Coleman and Christopher Jencks, two American educators whose writings led many to the conclusion that schools in the poorest neighborhoods are unlikely to do much for their pupils until the neighborhoods are improved.

"Variations in what children learn at school," Mr. Jencks wrote in 1972, "depend largely on variations in what they bring to school, not on variations in what schools offer them," and the result achieved by a school "depends largely on a single input—the characteristics of the entering children."

That theory, and what some see as the debilitating determinism that it encourages, are disputed by the London study.

"The findings showed that school differences were not just a reflection of intake patterns, and that much of the effects of schools were linked with their features as social organizations," the authors declare, and then set out to prove it, showing how similar schools only a few miles apart can produce radically different results.

If the Jencks theory is correct, two inner-city schools that take in the same proportion of boys with behavior problems should turn out about the same proportion of boys with behavior problems. But that is not at all what happened in the schools studied here.

Fifteen Thousand Hours describes what it calls School A and School B, in each of which one-third of the incoming 10-year-olds had exhibited behavior problems, such as truancy, vandalism or insubordination. Four years later, fewer than 10 percent of the boys at School A had behavior problems, whereas the proportion at School B had risen to 48 percent.

"Clearly, one school was doing the right thing and the other was not," Dr. Ouston said. "In other words, the school did make a difference."

The research team, which was headed by Michael Rutter, a professor of child psychiatry at the University of London, came to the same sort of conclusion in regard to academic achievement. Although the schools studied tended to have pupils of about the same intellectual range, as measured by independent tests at the age of 10, there was marked variation in how the children did a few years later.

In one of its most startling findings, the University of London team reported that children in the bottom aptitude rank of the best school did as well, in final examination scores, as the children in the top rank of the worst school. In other words, a dull child entering one of the better schools had statistically the same chance to make good grades as a bright child entering one of the worst ones.

Moreover, a school that was good in one area tended to be good in others as well, reinforcing the theory that how the school is run makes a difference.

The book did not try to comprehensively assess exactly what it is that makes good schools good, leaving that to future research. But Dr. Rutter's team tentatively concluded that a major factor in making schools good was what it called "their characteristics as social institutions," including the degree of academic emphasis, the degree to which teachers got involved in lessons, the availability of rewards for students, and the extent to which children were given responsibility.

Children tended to do better, for example, in schools where the classes began on time, where teachers gave immediate and frequent praise, and where the pupils were made to feel that success was expected of them.

Naturally, good teaching was of great importance. But the study found, in comparing the schools, that "it was very much easier to be a good teacher in some schools than others."

For example, it concluded that results were better in the schools in which the disciplinary policy and the curriculum were discussed and worked out together by the teachers, rather than being dictated from above.

"It was not just that this facilitated continuities in teaching—although it did—but also that group planning provided opportunities for teachers to encourage and support one another," the book concluded.

In the best schools, though overall standards were higher, inequalities persisted. In the schools in which children of ordinary ability did better than usual, the able children also tended to do better. And it continues to be a built-in advantage to have well-educated parents.

The comparison is analogous, the book explains, to changes in body height: over the last 50 years, the height of the average British school child has increased by 9 centimeters (about 3½ inches), presumably because of better nutrition. But that does not mean, of course, that all children are now the same height. There have been "major changes in level, without any reduction in inequality."

The same thing can be done, *Fifteen Thousand Hours* maintains, with academic performance; schools can be improved to the benefit of everyone's performance.

"It is not argued that schools are the most important influence on children's progress," the book concludes. "Education cannot compensate for the inequalities of society. Nevertheless, we do suggest that schools constitute one major area of influence, and one which is susceptible to change."

—William Borders
The New York Times

1. What is the writer's main source of information? Why might you believe it to be a reliable source?
2. What statistics does the writer cite? Underline them in the passage.
3. Where has the writer quoted directly from someone else's work? Where does he paraphrase someone else's findings? How has he avoided plagiarism?
4. What cases does the writer use? Underline them.

REACHING HIGHER

Step 1. More Topics to Research. Here are several other areas in which statistical information might provide you with astonishing conclusions. Select one and prepare a well-written paragraph using the skills you have learned in this chapter.

poverty in your home state

ghetto health conditions

child beatings

dishonesty in politics

prison conditions in your city

hunger and Southern black men and women

coal mines and working conditions

deserters in the Vietnam war

casualties in the Iranian revolution

orphans in Cambodia

saving oil

rape cases in large cities

Step 2. The Perfect Child. Prepare a list of features that you think would characterize the perfect child. Include information on appearance, behavior, personality, philosophy, and any other qualities you think are important. Then, using the most outstanding features on your list, write a paragraph in which you explore the idea of a "perfect" child.

part II

THE LONGER THEME

chapter 6

A PLACE OF SPIRIT: WRITING THE LONGER THEME

INTRODUCTION TO WRITING ESSAYS

There is a place every one of us carries in our personal memories. Sometimes you cannot forget a place because you know it so well, see it so often and closely: the train station where you catch the local for school each day; a picnic site along the river; the empty lot on the corner where you played your daily game of baseball; a piece of prairie just beyond your house or town; the doctor's office with its smell of alcohol and iodine, its sounds of babies' cries. Perhaps it is a place you have not seen often, but one clear in your mind because of what happened to you there: the lake where you caught your first fish; the stable where you learned to ride a horse; the hospital emergency room; the principal's office in high school.

Your first essay assignment—a longer composition of four paragraphs—asks that you select for exploration some place both important and unforgettable to you. (If it is a place you can visit again before you write, so much the better; then, you will be able to jot down on paper the sights, colors, sounds, smells, and actions that give the place its character.) You will be able again to use your skills at narration and description—in fact, any of the paragraphs you learned about in the first part of this book can be helpful in your essay. And you will learn how to plan an essay, to avoid problems you might have had about organizing and finding enough to write. In its attempt to help you clear up problems in language, this chapter will look at some difficulties writers often have with pronouns and with punctuation.

VOCABULARY

The words in this activity will help you name sizes and shapes of things more specifically.

Step 1. Learning Words for Shape and Size. Check in a dictionary those words below that you do not know (Appendix A will help you too). Write definitions you understand in the blanks next to the words.

1. vast _____   4. corpulent _____

2. minute _____   5. amorphous _____

3. towering _____

Step 2. Sizing It Up. Write in the blanks the words from the above list which you might use to describe:

1. the sky _____   4. a speck of dust _____

2. a flat tire _____   5. the Rocky Mountains _____

3. an overweight child _____

Step 3. Sharpening the Senses. These words help name sensations of touch and smell. Check their definitions in a good dictionary (or see Appendix A for assistance) and write them in the blank lines.

Smell

savory _____

rancid _____

musty _____

pungent _____

medicinal _____

Touch

supple _____

clammy _____

gossamer _____

furrowed _____

sinewy _____

Step 4. Applying New Words. From the vocabulary above, select a word that best describes each of the following:

1. a plant of soft wood _____

2. vinegar _____

3. ridges in a forehead _____

4. the arm of an athlete _____

5. rotten eggs _____

6. turkey roasting in an oven _____

7. the feel of perspiration on a cool day_____

8. a spider's web _____

9. an old trunk opened after many years _____

10. a hospital corridor _____

BUILDING COMPOSITION SKILLS

Exploring the Topic

Step 1. Talking It Out. Complete aloud with one of your own endings any of these sentences about a place. Then speak a few more sentences to expand what you said for the rest of the class. Mention some sound or smell that you remember about the place.

1. The noisiest place I know is . . . .
2. Our campus is . . . .
3. A summer place I remember most is . . . .
4. If you saw our back yard, you would . . . .
5. A place that always scared me was . . . .
6. My brother's (sister's) room is . . . .

7. For me the park is . . . .
8. Our street corner is . . . .
9. One place I enjoy is . . . .
10. When I want peace and quiet I go to . . . .

Here is one student's response:

My sister's room is a pig sty! Silver hair curlers are piled in a heap on the dresser. Most of the drawers are opened and blouses and underwear hang out. A pile of dirty skirts sits in the corner and ten or twenty books lie all over the linoleum floor. But no one can reason with my thirteen-year-old sister Karen, the family know-it-all!

—Diane Carter

HINTS FOR STRONG DESCRIPTIONS

In earlier chapters you learned and practiced how to build images with concrete sensory detail and how to use specific words that present a scene exactly. Here are other qualities of words and some techniques for using them that will help you build strong descriptions.

Denotation and Connotation

Words mean more than their dictionary definitions. (The dictionary definition of a word is called its *denotation*.) A word can also suggest meanings to us by appealing to our emotions or by arousing associations we make about that word. (The implied meaning of a word is called its *connotation*.)

Writers who know what certain words connote can use those words to advantage, compelling a reader to respond in exactly the manner the writer wishes.

Look at these sentences:

She lifted the *glass* slowly.
She lifted the *goblet* slowly.
She lifted the *chalice* slowly.

Glasses, goblets, and chalices have very similar denotative meaning—they are vessels to drink from. But the writer who says *goblet* suggests something fancier about the action than the writer who says *glass*. There is an elegance achieved by the use of the first word. With the word *chalice*, the reader senses an even more romantic and poetic—even religious—situation: it's not an everyday drink one sips from a fine cup. By using one of these related words, a writer can create essential conditions without having to use too many modifiers.

Step 1. Explaining Connotations. The words in each numbered item have similar denotations but different connotations. Explain what each word in each group connotes. If you need to, use a dictionary.

1. wig   toupee   periwig
2. novel   romance   potboiler
3. child   youngster   adolescent
4. stallion   mustang   mare
5. advisor   counsellor   psychologist
6. coach   carriage   chariot
7. assistant   servant   maid
8. shoes   boots   galoshes

Step 2. Comparing Meanings. For each word below write a denotative definition. Then, explain the possible connotations for the word.

1. Old Glory _____

2. racism _____

3. courage _____

4. communist _____

5. religion _____

Step 3. Using Exact Meanings. In the sentences below the words in parentheses have similar denotations. However, because of what the words connote, only one of the pair is appropriate. Circle the word that suits the meaning of the sentence. Use a dictionary if you need help.

1. The (notorious, renowned) criminal made a daring escape from San Quentin prison.
2. The fashion designers admired the model's (exotic, odd) clothes.
3. When Paul popped his gum in the theater, his friend criticized his (youthful, immature) behavior.
4. The (stench, fragrance) from the gym locker was nauseating.
5. The (decrepit, frail) silent-screen actress hobbled to the stage to receive her award.

Showing versus Telling

Writers must always resist *telling* a reader how to react when they can better *show* details with strong images. Instead of words that interpret, writers try to describe clearly by naming colors, sounds, actions, sensations of touch, smell, and taste. In these two sentences, notice how the first makes a judgment whereas the second compels readers to make their own judgments based upon the detail:

He had an ugly smile.

He smiled a cold, toothless grin.

With a word like *ugly*—or any such judgmental word, for that matter—the writer is never sure that the reader sees exactly what the writer had intended. After all, what is ugly to one person may not be ugly to another.

Step 4. Showing with Clear Images. For each item below write an original image that changes the word in italics into descriptive details. Use separate paper.

Example:
The child was *happy*.
The child giggled as she shook her rattle playfully.

1. It was a *nice* day.
2. Joseph has *attractive* eyes.
3. She wore *pretty* shoes.
4. A *beautiful* tree grew on the hill.
5. I picked the *delicious-looking* pie.

Avoiding too Many Modifiers

You already know how important it is to select highly specific words in order to build successful images. Using a word like *rose* instead of *flower* or *pudding* instead of *dessert* helps you avoid using descriptive words you might not need.

But the temptation to overuse modifiers is great among beginning writers. In general, you should be cautious about using too many modifying words for the objects or people you are trying to describe. A typically weak sentence will pile up a number of descriptive words in front of a noun:

The *tall, dark-haired, blue-eyed,* quarterback spoke to his fans.

The modifiers (in italics) smother the noun *quarterback*. The sentence overwhelms the reader with detail; the reader cannot take so much in all at once in this way. By using a modifier after the noun or by expanding a modifier into a word group, the writer achieves a more desired effect:

With blue eyes smiling the tall, dark-haired quarterback spoke to his fans.
The tall quarterback, dark-haired and blue-eyed, spoke to his fans.

Removing some modifiers completely is usually one of the best ways to avoid overwhelming your reader with detail.

Step 5. Cutting Down on Modifiers. Rewrite the sentences below so that the modifiers do not all appear before the words they are describing. In some cases just shift the modifiers around. In other cases expand some of them into word groups. In others simply remove the modifier. All describing words appear in italics.

1. *A quiet, tired, dirty, young* marine wrote *a long, passionate, overdue* letter to his girl friend. _____

2. *A frail, silver-haired, tiny old* man fed *the noisy, cooing, gray and white* pigeons in the park. _____

_____

3. *A long, black, chauffeur-driven* Cadillac screeched to a stop in front of *a brand new modern glass and steel* hotel. _____

_____

4. Facing *the television* set is a *gray and white striped three piece sectional* sofa. _____

_____

5. On *a sizzling July* afternoon at *approximately twelve* noon, I shoved aboard *a crowded, musty, gray and black graffiti colored subway* car headed to Manhattan. _____

_____

_____

UNDERSTANDING ESSAY FORM

The basic difference between the theme of one long paragraph and the theme that is a four-paragraph essay is simply one of length and proportion. An essay of four paragraphs allows you to develop your ideas more, to use more details, to bring in other information you might have left out of a single-paragraph composition so it would not be too long.

For every part of the paragraph there is a similar part of the essay. In a one-paragraph theme a *topic sentence* tells the subject and your opinion about that subject. In a four-paragraph essay an *introductory paragraph* gives you more space to build up to the topic you want to discuss. One sentence of this introductory paragraph (often the last sentence) generally announces what the whole essay will be about. This is the *thesis* or *proposal sentence:* it is usually more general than a topic sentence because it must tell what the *whole essay* will deal with.

In a one-paragraph theme the first subtopic sentence introduces one aspect of the topic. In the four-paragraph essay the first subtopic sentence becomes the topic sentence of its own paragraph. It requires a transition to the proposal sentence. You develop the paragraph by using details from your own experience or from what you have read or heard. This second paragraph of your essay is the first *body* paragraph: it is the first paragraph that tries to support some aspect of the topic.

In a one-paragraph theme a *second* subtopic sentence introduces another aspect of the topic. In a four-paragraph essay, the second subtopic sentence becomes the topic sentence of its own paragraph. This topic sentence requires some brief reference to the previous paragraph for an effective transition. You develop the paragraph with the kinds of details that best support your point.

In a one-paragraph theme you need a closing sentence to tell the reader that you have achieved the purpose of the paragraph. In the four-paragraph essay you need a conclusion, a whole new paragraph which allows you more space to develop an idea related to your dominant impression.

The following chart shows how a one-paragraph theme compares with a four-paragraph essay.

FROM PARAGRAPH TO ESSAY

The One-Paragraph Theme		The Essay
Topic Sentence	P A R A G R A P H 1	*Introduction: A Paragraph* 1. Give background to your topic. 2. Make your readers feel that what you are going to say will be of importance and interest to them. 3. Set the stage for the one sentence that will tell the readers what the whole essay will be about (*proposal sentence*). 4. For your own convenience, put the proposal sentence *last* in the introductory paragraph; make sure that the proposal sentence allows you to discuss *two* aspects of the topic. 5. Take as much time with the proposal sentence as you took with the topic sentence.
Subtopic Sentence 1 *Supporting Details* *Closing Sentence*	P A R A G R A P H 2	*Topic Sentence of Paragraph 2* 1. Relate this sentence in some way to the proposal (repeat key words, use words that mean the same, use transition words, and so on). 2. Announce the one aspect of the topic that you will discuss in this paragraph. *Supporting Details* *Closing Sentence: Let the reader know you have finished with the subject of this paragraph. Bring all the information together.*

Subtopic Sentence 2	**The Body Paragraphs**	P A R A G R A P H 3	*Topic Sentence of Paragraph 3*

Subtopic Sentence 2   **The Body Paragraphs**

P A R A G R A P H
Topic Sentence of Paragraph 3
1. This sentence must relate to the proposal (the last sentence in the introductory paragraph).
2. It must tell the reader the aspect of the proposal that you will discuss in this paragraph.
3. It must also remind the reader of what you discussed in the paragraph before (paragraph 2).

Supporting Details
Closing Sentence

Supporting Details
Closing Sentence: Let the reader know that this paragraph is finished.

P A R A G R A P H 4
Conclusion: A Paragraph
1. Summarize by briefly commenting on your topic (your proposal).
2. Bring in a related idea.
3. Give a dominant impression.

BUILDING ESSAYS FROM ONE-PARAGRAPH THEMES

Step 1. Reviewing Paragraph and Essay Form. The first student sample you read in this book—"The Gloom Room" by Harry Golden—appears here for review. It is followed by Mr. Golden's four-paragraph essay on exactly the same topic. These pages should help you see clearly the basic differences between the one-paragraph theme and the four-paragraph essay. Discuss the questions after you read the two pieces.

The Gloom Room

On this dreary October afternoon in my writing class here on the second floor of Boylan Hall at Brooklyn College, a shadow of gloom hangs over the people and things that surround me. The atmosphere is depressing. There is an old brown chair beside the teacher's desk, a mahogany bookcase with a missing shelf, and this ugly desk of mine filled with holes and scratches. As I rub my hand across its surface, there is a feeling of coldness. Even the gray walls and the rumble of thunder outside reflect the atmosphere of seriousness as we write our first theme of the semester. When some air sails through an open window beside me, there is the annoying smell of coffee grounds from a garbage pail not far off. My classmates, too, show the mood of tension. Mary, a slim blonde at my right, chews frantically the inside of her lower lip. Only one or two words in blue ink stand upon her clean white page. David Harris, slouched in his seat in the third row, nibbles each finger of each hand. Then he plays inaudibly with a black collar button that stands open on the top of his red plaid shirt. There is a thump as he uncrosses his legs and his scuffed shoe hits the floor. A painful cough slices the air from behind me. I hear a woman's heels click from the hall beyond the closed door and a car engine whine annoyingly from Bedford Avenue. If a college classroom should be a place of delight and pleasure, that could never be proved by the tension in this room.

—Harry Golden

The Gloom Room

October often looks and feels dreary because school is by then in full swing. Today, a rainy Thursday, is no different. What makes it worse is that I am forced to sit in my writing class on the second floor of Boylan Hall at Brooklyn College and write a theme. It is no wonder that a shadow of gloom hangs over the things and the people that surround me in this room.

[The Proposal: It tells what whe whole essay will be about.]

[The Topic Sentence (Paragraph 2): It tells what this paragraph will be about.]

[As I look around, I see that the surroundings are old and depressing.] There is a broken brown chair beside the teacher's desk; no one will sit in it for fear of leaning back and toppling over onto the floor. There is also a mahogany bookcase with a missing shelf, and all the books are piled on the bottom in a stack of blue and yellowed covers, instead of standing in a straight row. This ugly desk of mine is filled with holes and scratches because other impatient students, no doubt, lost their tempers and took out their anger on the wooden surface. As I rub my hand across it, I feel coldness. Even the gray walls and the rumble of thunder outside reflect the atmosphere of seriousness as we write our first theme of the semester. When some air sails through an open window beside me, there is the annoying smell of coffee grounds from a garbage pail not far off. ⟨That smell is a perfect indication of our discomfort!⟩

[Details: These give concrete sensory language, statistics, cases, quotations, paraphrase, or imagery to illustrate your point.]

[Closing Sentence: It shows you are finished with this paragraph.]

[This part of the topic sentence reminds the reader about what you wrote in the last paragraph.]

→ [Aside from the unattractive surroundings,] ⟨the people around me show this mood of tension and displeasure.⟩ Mary, a slim blonde at my right, chews the inside of her lower lip. I can see by the way her forehead is wrinkled that she is having quite a bit of trouble. Because only one or two words in blue ink stand upon her clean white page, she looks around the room fearfully for some new ideas. Slouching in his seat in the third row, David Harris nibbles each finger of each hand. Then he plays with a black collar button that stands open on the top of his red plaid shirt. The tension gets to him too; drops of perspiration run slowly down his cheeks. I hear a thump as he uncrosses his legs and his scuffed shoe hits the floor. A painful cough slices the air from behind me. I hear a woman's heels click from the hall beyond the closed door and a car engine whine annoyingly from Bedford Avenue. All these signs of gloom do not help my mood at all.

[This part of the topic sentence tells the reader what you will discuss in this paragraph.] ←

[Details: These illustrate the point of the topic sentence.]

These last few painful moments make me wonder if what my friends told me about college was all true. Where are all the beautiful girls I'm supposed to be meeting and talking to in every room? Where are the freedom and relaxed atmosphere my friends bragged about? I'm supposed to be enjoying myself instead of suffering! Everybody seems to have forgotten that college is hard work too. My first days in writing class prove that delight and pleasure often disappear when assignments are due!

—Harry Golden

[Conclusion:
1. May summarize.
2. Makes transition by referring to an idea in the introduction.
3. May give a dominant impression.
4. May bring in a new—but related—idea.]

1. What is the difference between the opening sentence in Mr. Golden's one-paragraph theme and the opening paragraph in his essay?
2. How are the proposal sentence in the essay and the topic sentence in the one-paragraph theme alike?
3. How does subtopic sentence 1 in "The Gloom Room" paragraph compare to the topic sentence of paragraph 2 in "The Gloom Room" essay?
4. How do the details coming after subtopic sentence 1 in the one-paragraph composition compare with the details in paragraph 2 of the essay?
5. How does Mr. Golden's second subtopic sentence compare with the opening sentence of paragraph 3 in his essay?

6. How do the details after subtopic sentence 2 in his one-paragraph theme compare with the details in the third paragraph of Mr. Golden's essay?
7. Read the last sentence of paragraph 2 and that of paragraph 3. Are they effective as closing sentences? Why?
8. What part of the first sentence of the conclusion in Mr. Golden's essay refers back to the main idea of the essay?
9. Where in the conclusion does Mr. Golden bring in a new but related idea?
10. How does the closing sentence of Mr. Golden's one-paragraph composition compare with the concluding paragraph of his four-paragraph essay?

WRITING PROPOSAL SENTENCES

The *proposal* (or *thesis*) *sentence*—the sentence in the essay that tells what you propose or intend to discuss in the remaining paragraphs—is the most important sentence in the essay. It controls and limits your entire composition. As a good writer, you will write only about what the proposal *says* you will write about.

GUIDELINES FOR GOOD PROPOSALS

1. Make sure your proposal sentence allows you to discuss what you want to. It should announce the topic clearly. It should express an opinion. If you find as you are writing that you no longer are discussing the topic you set for yourself, *go back and change the proposal sentence.*
2. The proposal should be so written as to allow you to discuss at least two specific aspects of the topic. Notice how Mr. Golden's proposal tells *specifically* the two parts of the topic: the gloom surrounding the people and the gloom surrounding the things in his classroom. Each body paragraph, then, can pick up *one* aspect of that topic. Paragraph 2 focuses on things. Paragraph 3 focuses on people.

   But it is not essential to mention in the proposal just what each paragraph will say. An alternate proposal for Mr. Golden's essay might be this:

   It is no wonder that gloominess is everywhere.

   Notice how, in this proposal, the reader has no idea of exactly what kind of treatment Mr. Golden's essay will offer of gloominess. But still, this alternate proposal permits the writer to discuss in one body paragraph the gloomy surroundings and in the other body paragraph the gloomy people.
3. A proposal sentence may appear anywhere in the introduction, but it is much easier for you if you write it as the *last* sentence of the introduction for several reasons:

   a. You can return to it often if you know exactly where it appears; by reading the proposal often while you write, you can make sure that you are staying on the topic.

   b. You can make the transition between the proposal and the opening sentence of paragraph 2 very simple to write because the idea you must refer back

> to comes directly above your opening sentence. Mr. Golden's proposal mentions that he is in a room. The first words of paragraph 2 say "As I look around"; and because this looking around takes place in the room mentioned in the previous paragraph, the two paragraphs are thereby brought together smoothly.

Step 1. Preparing Proposals. Column I suggests the subject of an essay. In Column II, write a proposal that you think would serve to develop the ideas.

Hint: You do not need to state in the proposal exactly what each paragraph will illustrate. Just state the main purpose of your essay, the idea your whole essay will be about.

I

Example:

This essay intends to show that the writer loves the thrill of skiing although she realizes the dangers that exist.

1. This student wants to describe the differences between studying in a library and at home.

2. This essay attempts to show how proper exercise and good nutrition add years to a person's life.

3. This writer will show the pleasures and pains of raising a child.

4. This essay will defend work-study programs in colleges. Its first body paragraph will discuss the advantages for the student who comes to a college having such a program. The next body paragraph will illustrate the advantages of such programs to our society.

II

although the slopes of Vail, Colorado present certain dangers, the thrill a skier experiences is worth the risks.

5. This essay will show how the writer's kitchen is a place of great activity and also a place where the family irons out many of its problems together.

_____

_____

_____

_____

Step 2. Predicting Body Paragraphs from Proposals. These proposals all come from student's papers. Basing your selection on the topic stated in the proposal, tell briefly what you would discuss in each of the two body paragraphs.

Example:

I feel that religion serves two essential functions in our society.

Main point of paragraph 2:

religion binds a family together

Main point of paragraph 3:

religion teaches children values

1. I now realize the many problems that teachers face.

Main point of paragraph 2:

_____

Main point of paragraph 3:

_____

2. Although the majority of Americans live in big cities, many people are realizing the advantages of living on a farm.

Main point of paragraph 2:

_____

Main point of paragraph 3:

_____

3. In recent years, the major television networks have been criticized severely by their viewers.

Main point of paragraph 2:

_____

Main point of paragraph 3:

_____

4. In many ways a person's eighteenth birthday is the most important one.

Main point of paragraph 2:

_____

_____

Main point of paragraph 3:

_____

_____

5. The summers I spent on my uncle's farm
   were times of freedom and fun.

Main point of paragraph 2:

_____

_____

Main point of paragraph 3:

_____

_____

INTRODUCTION: SPARKING READER INTEREST

Aside from its purpose as the paragraph that gets the essay started by stating
the topic in the proposal sentence, the introductory paragraph must make
readers interested enough in what you have to say so that they want to read
on. Any one of the suggestions in the following list can help you write an
effective introduction to lead up to the proposal statement. Each suggestion
is followed by a sample.

Writing Top-Notch Introductions: Ideas for Starting Essays

Hint: Always write the proposal sentence before you write the introductory paragraph.

1. Tell the reader why your topic is important.

   Sample: For fifteen years I lived on East 92nd Street in Brooklyn. I made
   friends there, earned bloody noses, broke Mrs. Segal's window playing
   stickball, and nursed back to health a small, frightened sparrow in a shoe box.
   That block was mother and father to me in a way, presenting a number of
   unexpected experiences that are so important in the life of someone growing
   up without "at-home" parents—my father ran away when I was six and my
   mother worked most of the day. So the block was my teacher, and in several
   ways the lessons I learned there taught me how to think fast to survive.

2. Give background information on your topic so that readers know when
   they get to your proposal the ideas and conditions which led you to consider the point you are treating in the essay.

   Sample: For the sixteen years since the Supreme Court declared school
   segregation unconstitutional in 1954, many Americans have protested against
   the policy. We have seen governors and mayors blocking schoolhouse door-

ways, hostile police, violent white mobs, and clever legal attempts. Black parents have rightly pointed to the horribly inferior conditions in the segregated schools their children attend, showing that even "legal integration" does not always mean a fair mixing of races and an improvement of conditions. And the federal government stays neutral, giving little more than money to those schools attempting integration. Because Americans have rejected important attempts to desegregate the nation's schools, and because the government has given little real support, integration has not succeeded at all thus far.

3. Show what many people now believe is true if your proposal will attempt to suggest something else.

Sample: Education is the process by which the young people of today are trained to become functioning members of their society. This process is generally accomplished in institutions known as schools where young people become acquainted with all phases of knowledge and, after a few years, are thought ready to accept responsibility as adults. In college the usual picture is a classroom filled with excited, bright-eyed youths soaking up important lessons for living. However, the American school system has failed miserably in trying to accomplish what it sets out to do; our system of higher education does not provide a person with the necessary training to take his rightful place in society.

4. State several points that may contradict, disagree with, or disprove the point you want the rest of the essay to make.

Sample: Working hard from his childhood on, my father has grown into a hard man. He is strict and overprotective, and he screams when I tiptoe into the house at two in the morning on a Saturday. He threatens to disconnect my extension phone so he can get to make a call, but he will never give me the satisfaction of having my own number. I rarely sit down to chat with him because his opinions are so one-sided; besides, when I rush into my room and toss my books on the bed at seven o'clock after my last class, Dad's loud harsh snore already echoes through the house. Despite these difficult qualities, I am still Daddy's little girl and always will be. I am not ashamed of this either, because over the years I have grown to love my father very much and will always continue to share this unique type of love with him.

5. Ask questions to arouse the reader's interest.

Sample: Can a black lawyer, a Chinese fashion designer, and a white school teacher live happily side by side as neighbors? Can a racially integrated community achieve the dream of brotherhood and understanding? An experiment in a small town in Connecticut is providing some extraordinary answers.

6. Use an interesting quotation that helps you build toward your proposal sentence (see pages 54–55 and page 226 for writing quotations correctly).

Sample: Kahlil Gibran in *A Tear and a Smile* writes, "I looked toward nature . . . and found therein . . . a thing that endures and lives in the spring and comes to fruit in summer days. Therein I found love." This I believe to be true, because people do not "fall in love"; love that lasts is a feeling that must come gradually over a period of time and must develop only with emotional maturity.

Hint: Use quotations from your own reading of newspapers, magazines, and books, or from television, radio, or the movies. Books like *Bartlett's Familiar Quotations* and the *Oxford Dictionary of Quotations* have many quotations arranged according to subjects; often you can find a meaningful quotation there to use in your introduction.

7. Tell a brief story—an incident that helps set the stage for your proposal. Make sure the story suits the purpose of your essay: don't be funny or "cute" unless you expect to deal with matters that are not serious or unless you can work the humor into your point.

Sample: A man with one shoe and a face filled with red sores wobbles down the summer morning street cursing to himself. From his back pocket he snatches a paper bag, uncaps the bottle inside, raises it to his lips, and takes a long gulp. Then, he drops down against a brick wall and, still cursing, closes his eyes. This is the Bowery, the place of the drunkard, a place of horrors. But New York City police are now trying to reach out to these fallen men and women.

8. Tell what each body paragraph will deal with.

Sample: Solar energy devices will one day adequately replace our fossil fuels. Moreover, wind-driven turbines will also provide us with a reliable, economical source of power. Together these two important natural resources will meet the future energy needs of America.

Hint: Sentence 1 in the above introduction tells what the writer expects to develop in the first body paragraph (paragraph 2 of the essay). Sentence 2 tells the purpose of the second body paragraph. The writer has divided the topic for the reader.

9. Use a series of images to build up to your proposal.

Sample: Rocks tossed from behind trees; bottles broken on our blacktop driveway; whispering voices behind wrinkled hands at the A&P; taunts of "Kyke" and "There's a Jew" sailing at my back as I march to school alone: a Jew growing up in a small Midwestern town learns how to hate very early in life.

10. Show different aspects of the topic that you will not consider in the essay, as you lead up to the topic that you will consider.

Sample: In our society, discrimination has many different forms. There is age discrimination, which prevents a seventeen-year-old from buying a bottle of gin, and racial discrimination, which denies a black youth a job in a labor union. But another form of discrimination which is particularly unfair is sexual discrimination.

AVOIDING PITFALLS IN INTRODUCTIONS

1. Don't make your introduction too long. If each of your body paragraphs contains ten or fewer sentences, your introduction usually needs no more than four or five sentences. Longer body paragraphs may mean that longer introductions are acceptable.
2. Don't apologize for what you do not know, for your lack of experience, or for your limited abilities. Even if any of this is true, to mention it in your paragraph is to make the reader feel that you do not know what you are talking about. Don't make any of these statements:

    "Although I am not qualified to discuss this . . . ."
    "My knowledge is limited so . . . ."
    "Many people who know more than I do would disagree, but . . . ."
3. Don't think of the reader as someone who is sitting next to you as you write. Don't say:

    "Now I will tell you . . . ."
                or
    "Now I am going to show you . . . ."
4. Don't talk about the parts of the essay in your composition. Don't say
    "In my next paragraph, I . . . ."
                or
    "My introduction and my conclusion will try to show . . . ."
5. Don't write an introduction that wastes words, one that you have just thrown ahead of your body paragraphs to fulfill the requirements of essay form. Your introduction should be an important part of the essay itself.
6. Don't use overworked expressions—trite sayings or quotations that have lost their meaning because of overuse. Don't use quotations or expressions that are too general or that could be applied to hundreds of situations. To say "Too many cooks spoil the broth" in an essay about too many men at the top and giving orders in government would not really add anything of significance.
7. Don't say the same thing over and over again. If you don't have much to say by way of introduction, write only the proposal in a clear, well-planned sentence or two of some length.
8. Don't refer to your title in the introduction. A student whose essay title was "How to Save Our National Parks" would be mistaken to start the introduction this way: "It is possible in a number of ways."

Step 1. Writing Introductions to Proposals. Using any three of the proposal sentences from Step 2 on pages 218–219, write three introductions. Put the proposal sentence last. Try to write a different kind of introduction for each proposal: check the ideas for starting essays on pages 219–221. And, make sure you avoid the errors explained above.

Step 2. Reading More Introductions. Discuss the introductory paragraphs for the essays whose titles and page numbers are listed below. Are the introductions effective? Which of the items on pages 219–221 does each introduction seem to follow? How might you improve each introduction?

1. "Memories of the Australian Bush," pages 244–245
2. "Ironing for Food," pages 282–283
3. "Deprived Children," pages 318–319
4. "Women: Fragile Flowers?" pages 322–323
5. "Working Mothers," pages 321–322

Step 3. Introductions: You Be the Judge. Decide whether the introductions below would be good first paragraphs for essays. Defend you opinions. Then, make any corrections that you feel will improve the introductory paragraphs. In some cases you may have to rewrite the paragraph completely. Use separate paper.

1. Swimming is an important activity for a healthy life. I was a swimmer in high school, in college, and I will continue to swim as long as I am physically able. This essay will try to show how important swimming is and how swimmers benefit from swimming.
2. I don't drink liquor so my knowledge of its effects is limited to what I have observed at parties. Although doctors know more about this subject than I do, I would like to discuss the terrible problem of alcoholism, especially among our young people.
3. Are you fed up with street riots and automobile fumes? Are you trying to escape the summer heat of Newark and the noisy crowds that shove their way across Market Street? Well then pack a tent and a four-burner stove and head for the nearest camping grounds. Outdoor living for summer vacation is a relaxing and unusual way to spend some time with nature.
4. Working has its bad points but all people must work to earn enough money to survive. Work is hard, but if you expect to get anywhere, you have to work hard. The people were nice but the job was miserable.
5. In this introduction, I will show you the problems people encounter when they retire, for the old saying is true: "A rolling stone gathers no moss."

Step 4. More Work on Introductions. For any three of the proposals you wrote in Step 1, page 217, write three good introductions using any of the suggestions you studied.

Then take any topic sentence you wrote for any theme assignment in Part I of this book, and assume that it is the proposal sentence of an essay. Write a good introduction following the advice you learned in this chapter.

Combining Sentences for Tight Descriptions

In earlier exercises on coordination and subordination (pages 17–20 and 89–95), you learned how combining sentences often helps you relate ideas more closely. Another advantage of combining sentences is that the new word group you have created usually expresses its point more precisely and with fewer words than the original.

When two consecutive sentences discuss the same object and the purpose of one of the two is to describe the object, to identify it, or to add information about it, you can often combine the two sentences into one. Writers have many ways to achieve this effect. Sometimes words like *who, which,* or *that* help join the sentences (see pages 93–94). Sometimes special verb parts make the combination effective (see pages 180–186).

At other times a change in punctuation and the removal of some words allow you to put ideas together in a meaningful way. Look at these sets of examples.

A

(1) Henry Chin plays basketball for the county team. (2) He is a tall and supple athlete.

B

(1) Across Oakland Drive hobbled an old man. (2) He was our former gardener.

Notice how in example *A* the writer can use fewer words and can bring the descriptive details closer to the person he wants to describe:

[comma]   [comma]

(3) Henry Chin, *a tall and supple athlete,* plays basketball for the county team.

Because the words from sentence (2) now interrupt the main idea of sentence (1), the writer uses commas to signal that interruption (see pages 237–238).

Details from sentence (2) could also be added to the beginning of (1) with slightly different results:

(4) *A tall and supple athlete,* Henry Chin plays basketball for the county

[comma]

team.

In example *B* you can put at the end of sentence (1) the words from (2) in order to identify the old man:

[comma]

(5) Across Oakland Drive hobbled an old man, *our former gardener.*

You could write the sentence in this way too:

(6) Across Oakland Drive hobbled our former gardener, *an old man.*

In sentences (4), (5), and (6) a comma sets off the added details from the main idea of the sentence.

Hint: You cannot combine the sentences in examples *A* and *B* simply by removing the period between (1) and (2). That would yield run-on sentences. Why? See pages 24–31.

Step 1. Practice in Combining Sentences. In each set below, material in one of the two sentences may be incorporated into the other sentence in order to add information about or to describe an object or an idea. Using sentences (3), (4), (5), and (6) above as models, combine the two sentences into one, and write your new sentence on the blank lines. Place new material *after* the word you want to describe or identify. Use commas where you need them. Look at the example.

1. The insect repellent works well. It is a white cream.

   The insect repellent, a white cream, works well.

2. Two children sat on a fur rug. The children were well-behaved.

   _____

3. My employer bought a new pen. It is a special instrument with a built-in calculator.

   _____

   _____

4. The instructor stood angrily before the class as he announced the results of our chemistry midterm. The instructor's name is Mr. Hassan.

   _____

   _____

5. A tornado whipped across the northern plains states. It was violent and dangerous.

   _____

6. It is hard to compare my two sisters. They are both hard-working and intelligent doctors at St. Jude's Hospital.

   _____

   _____

SOLVING PROBLEMS IN WRITING
Punctuation Guidelines

AIDS TO PUNCTUATION: END MARKS

The Period (.)
1. Use a period after a sentence that makes a statement.
   I watched a crow circle over a twisted oak. Everyone was tired.
2. Use a period after a sentence that makes a mild command.
   Take the subway into Queens.
   Buy United States savings bonds.

The Question Mark (?)
1. Use question marks at the end of sentences that clearly ask questions.
   Who wrote *A Farewell to Arms?* ← [Question mark: end of question]
   "Can't you hear me?" David shouted. ← [End of sentence: no question mark.]
2. Some sentences, though

The Exclamation Point (!)
1. Use the exclamation point at the end of a sentence that shows strong emotion, sharp surprise, forceful command, or strong emphasis.
   I hate all men!
   I don't believe it!
   Call the police!
   I meant what I said!
2. Certain words and expres-

3. Use periods after initials.
   Robert E. Lee
   John F. Kennedy
4. Use periods after most abbreviations.
   Ph.D.   N.J.   etc.

Exceptions

1. Most government agencies use no periods in abbreviations: *FBI, CIA*
2. tv or TV
3. Business companies: IBM, A&P

they mention that a question is being asked, do not ask the question themselves. Such *indirect questions* are not followed by question marks.
   She wondered why he did not call. ← [Period]
   He asked who brought the station wagon. ← [Period]

sions, like *what, oh, alas, hurray, bravo,* often introduce exclamations.
   Oh! What am I going to do?
   What! You stole that car?
3. Only the individual writer can determine which sentences are spoken with strong emotion. *Do not overuse the exclamation point.*

Step. 1. A Variety of Endings. Put in correct end marks in the paragraph below. Use a capital letter to show the start of a new sentence.

My Fear of Flying

Why was I boarding this massive TWA jet that loomed ahead of me on the icy runway did I really have to fly to Washington, DC, on such a stormy day of course I did I couldn't miss my own sister's wedding she would never forgive me for not attending I wonder why I didn't take the train at least they were showing during the flight highlights of the NFL game of the week although an old W C Fields movie would have made me more relaxed, I could not concentrate on any movie Oh God, I was scared suddenly the captain's voice said, "Please fasten your seatbelts" in any case, I was trapped my body tensed, my eyes stared straight ahead, and my clammy hands squeezed the armrests I would never fly again

QUOTATION MARKS (" ")

(See pages 54–55)

1. Use quotation marks to show someone's exact words.

   "Roller skating is great!" Jane shouted excitedly.
   "When I'm in a big city," she admitted, "I miss my father's farm."
   "Why is the sky blue?" his son asked.

Hint: The exact words may be repeating what someone said in speaking; or the exact words may be a statement quoted from a book. In any case, quotation marks are needed.

2. Use quotation marks to set off the names of short stories, poems, chapters, articles, or essays that are parts of books, magazines, or newspapers.

   I read a column called "The Presidency" in *Time* magazine.

   The anonymous poem "Frankie and Johnnie" appears in *Undestanding Poetry* by Brooks and Warren.

UNDERLINING (Italicizing)

Underlining is used in handwritten sentences to show when italics are needed.

1. Underline all titles of books, magazines, movies, TV shows, and newspapers to show that these titles should be in italics.

   Most people still enjoy Gone with the Wind.

   If the sentence were printed, it would look like this:

   Most people still enjoy *Gone with the Wind*.

2. Underline names of ships, trains, and airplanes.

   My parents just returned from Bermuda on the Oceanic.

Step 2. Quotes and Italics. Use quotation marks or underlining (to show italics) as required in the following sentences.

1. Was it still raining asked Phil when you came in?
2. On the Merv Griffin show last night, Peter Benchley, author of the novel Jaws, discussed an article that appeared in The New York Times.

USING SEMICOLONS (;)

1. Use a semicolon to separate two complete sentences that are closely related (see page 18).

   The landlord painted the fence; now he is painting the steps.

2. Use semicolons instead of commas to separate items in a series if some of the items contain commas themselves. See page 234.

   On our picnic Lynette brought a whole chicken which,[comma] because of deep fry-
   ing,[comma] was a rich golden brown;[end of first item in series; semicolon used because commas already appear within the item] two pounds of potato salad that her mother
   prepared;[end of second item in series] and a basket of cold, delicious fruit.

3. Use semicolons instead of commas (see page 236) occasionally before coordinators which join complete thoughts that already contain commas.

   The landlord painted the fence around my patio;[semicolon instead of comma] but, even if he agrees to fix the plaster and repaint the whole apartment, I still intend to move.

HOW TO USE THE COLON (:)

---

1. A colon comes
   a. after the opening in a formal letter.

   Dear Ms. Stevenson: Gentlemen:

   Use a comma after informal openings.

   Dear Steve,

   b. between the hour and the minute when you write the time in numbers.

   The plane left at 6:18 P.M.

   c. between the number of the chapter and verse in the Bible.

   Matthew 6:12 is inspiring.

   d. in a title, to separate the main name of the selection from a subtitle (see page 205 for example).

   e. between act and scene in a play.
      Macbeth II:iii

2. Use a colon when you introduce a long or detailed list of items.

   [colon]
   Remember to bring to registration the following: two sharpened pencils with erasers, your admissions letter, your IBM registration card, and a check for $36.00 for student fees. [Commas separate items in series.]

Hint: Don't use the colon for a simple listing.

   [no colon]
   We bought shoes, gloves, and jeans.

3. Use a colon whenever you want to force the reader's attention to the statement that comes after the colon. That statement usually explains or clarifies the opening part of the sentence. [This part of the sentence explains the first part.]

   [colon pushes emphasis to what comes after.]
   Of this I am sure: I do not want any more life insurance.

4. Use a colon before you introduce a formal quotation.

   [colon]
   About greatness, Ralph Waldo Emerson said: "Every human being has a right to it, and in the pursuit we do not stand in each other's way."

Step 3. Semicolons and Colons in Practice. Use the semicolon or colon correctly in each sentence below. Be prepared to explain your answer.

1. The wedding will begin at 730 I will not be able to arrive on time.
2. In Shakespeare's *Hamlet* IIii Hamlet speaks these famous words "The play's the thing wherein I'll catch the conscience of the king."
3. There is one rule in tennis that must be remembered never take your eye off the ball.

PARENTHESES ( )

Parentheses are used to set off words or word groups that are not so important as the rest of the sentence. *Parenthetical expressions* add information and/or make some side comment on or about the material in the sentence.

[The information in parentheses is a side comment that adds information.]

{ Abandoned automobiles (and there are thousands throughout the country) line the roads and highways in ugly clumps.

[The information in parentheses is a side comment.]

{ If you have seen Woody Allen's *Annie Hall* (certainly you have), you know how important a good director is.

[The information in parentheses adds information about the author's birth and death.]

{ Dylan Thomas (1914–1953) read his own poetry brilliantly.

Hint: 1. Although parentheses indicate less important information, do not ignore or fail to read what appears in parentheses.

2. Commas also set off parenthetical information, but commas give the material more importance.

   a. That old man (a carpenter) works hard.
   b. That old man, a carpenter, works hard.

   The words *a carpenter* are parenthetical in both sentences, but the commas in *b* make that parenthetical information more important than it is in *a*.

3. Don't use parentheses too often in your writing.

Step 4. Your Statements in Parentheses. Add your own parenthetical information to the blank spaces in the following sentences. Use parentheses (or commas) as explained above.

1. The inflation rate _____ rose sharply in 1979.

2. The fields of corn _____ filled the Oklahoma landscape in every direction.

3. Our natural resources _____ will be seriously depleted by the end of the century.

THE DASH FOR INTERRUPTION AND SUMMARY

1. Use a pair of dashes to set off a sudden shift in thought or structure of the sentence.

[This question breaks into the complete thought expressed in the sentence.]

That old maple—did you see it?—lost all its leaves in June.

Hint: Parentheses could be used here as well. But the dash makes the information more important and stresses its sudden break into the main idea of the sentence.

2. Use a single dash before a summary of details mentioned earlier in the sentence.

Running a mile each day, exercising in a careful program, choosing food thoughtfully—these are the ways to keep weight down.

[This part of the sentence briefly summarizes
the meaning of the details in the first part.]

3. Don't use the dash too often in your writing.

Step 5. Using the Dash. Use dashes correctly in the sentences below.

1. "He is too oh you know what I mean too quiet and unfriendly," Marie said.
2. Life, liberty, and the pursuit of happiness these rights are granted to every American.
3. The airplane crash a horrible thing to witness destroyed three private homes.

THE HYPHEN AS DIVIDER

1. Use a hyphen to separate parts of certain compound words (words that are made by putting together other words).

time-consuming   president-elect
thirty-one   well-bred
self-assurance   brother-in-law

2. Use a hyphen to divide a word when there is no room on the line to finish the word.

[hyphen]

After the union leaders approved the contract, the members voted it quickly into effect.

3. Use a hyphen to separate the years of birth and death of some important figure.

Rudyard Kipling (1865–1936)

Do's and Don't's for Dividing Words

1. Don't separate the word if you can avoid it.
2. Do put the hyphen at the end of the first line, *never* at the beginning of the next line.

approved the con-
tract

not

approved the con
-tract

3. Do separate the word at the end of a syllable and nowhere else.

be-lieve	*not*	beli-eve
re-call	*not*	rec-all
per-mit-ting	*not*	pe-rmit-ting

Hint: Check the dictionary for proper syllables in words (see page 383, "How to Read a Dictionary Entry").

4. Do divide the word, if pronunciation allows, so that a consonant starts the part of the word that appears on the next line.

writ-ten   stop-ping
                    but
leop-ard   knowl-edge

5. Don't divide words of one syllable: *laugh, called, brought.*
6. Don't leave just one letter of a word at the end of the line. Write the entire word on the next line.

not   He tried to e-   *but*   He tried to
        rase his mistake.   erase his mistake.

7. Don't carry over to the next line brief word endings like *-ly* (happi*ly*), *-ed* (hint*ed*), or *-ing* (sing*ing*).
8. Don't divide people's names.

Harry, Barbara   *not*   Har-   Bar-
                          ry   bara

9. Do leave a space at the end of a line rather than fill the space with part of a word that is incorrectly broken.
10. Do learn the difference between hyphen and dash.

In writing by hand

The hyphen is a short line (-). The dash is a longer line, about the length of three hyphens (—).

In typing

The hyphen is a short line (-). The dash is typed as two hyphens with no spaces before or after them (--).

Step 6. Breaking Up Words. In the blank spaces rewrite the words that appear below to show where you would use hyphens to break the word at the end of a line. Put an X after those words you would not divide.

1. under _____   6. take _____

2. innocent _____   7. possessive _____

3. laughed _____   8. spent _____

4. illustrate _____   9. Jacob _____

5. evidence _____   10. knowledge _____

THREE USES FOR APOSTROPHES (')

---

1. Possession (see pages 271–276)
   a. If a word *does not* end in *s*, in order to show ownership add an apostrophe *s* ('s).

   boy + 's = the boy's hat
   men + 's = the men's club

   b. If a word *does* end in *s*, in order to show ownership add only an apostrophe (').

   ladies + '   The ladies' coats were soiled.
   boys + '   The boys' bicycles all fell down.

Hint: If a person's name ends in *s* and the name is to indicate possession, add *either* apostrophe *s* or just an apostrophe. Whichever you choose, however, be consistent throughout your writing.

Doris' book   or   Doris's book

2. Contractions
   To show where letters are omitted in words that are combined in contractions, use an apostrophe.

   it's = it is   I'll = I will
   doesn't = does not   you're = you are
   hasn't = has not   I've = I have

Hint: Contractions are usually informal words and should be avoided in formal compositions. Write out the two words in your themes.

3. Special plurals
   To show the plurals of numbers, letters, and symbols, use an apostrophe *s* ('s).

   There are two *t*'s in committee.
   Our address has three *5*'s in it.
   All *&*'s should be written as *and*.

Hint: Aside from these special cases, *do not* use apostrophes to show plurals.

Step 7. Correct Apostrophes. For each word in parentheses, add an apostrophe or apostrophe *s* so that the sentence is correct and write the new word in the blank. If the word needs no apostrophe, put an X in the blank.

1. _____ (Its) a shame that the disco had to close because of _____ (its) faulty electrical wiring.

2. The _____ (children) toys were left behind at Aunt _____ (Phyllis) house.

3. The preschool child practiced writing her _____(s) and _____(w).

4. The _____ (company) profits decreased last year.

5. Ms. _____ (Jones) mother _____ (couldnt) climb the stairs to our apartment because _____ (shes) a woman in her _____ (nineties).

Step 8. A Punctuation Review. Use correct punctuation in the paragraph below. Although the ends of sentences are indicated by periods, sometimes you will have to change them to exclamation or question marks. The following list indicates what punctuation you will need. Do not add commas.

What to Add

Colons: 3
Quotation marks: 4 pairs
Exclamation marks: 1
Question marks: 1
Semicolons: 2
Periods: 4

Underlining (italics): 3
Hyphens: 2
Apostrophes: 3
Dashes: 1 pair
Parentheses: 2 pairs

Conrad's Photographic Eye

One of the masters of sensory images is Joseph Conrad 1857 1925. Pictures rich in color and sound, pictures of the sea in all its beauty these fill the pages of Conrads works. Born in Poland, he settled in England in the 1890s at the age of thirty seven. Conrad came to love about the English language its musical qualities its sweet, yet harsh, sounds its rich, lively, fluid motion. Conrad knew no one can deny it the importance of the senses in creating word pictures. *My task which I am trying to achieve is, he wrote, by the power of the written word to make you hear, to make you feel—it is, before all, to make you see.** How could that be more clearly expressed. It is Conrad's power to make readers see that has led many MA and PhD students to study his novels like Lord Jim and Nostromo. What marvelous use he makes of the language. In the description of a railroad changing from the short story Heart of Darkness he says *A slight clinking behind me made me turn my head. Six black men advanced in a file, toiling up the path. They walked erect and slow, balancing small baskets full of earth on their heads, and the clink kept time with their footsteps. Black rags were wound around their loins, and the short ends behind waggled to and fro like tails. I could see every rib, the joints of their limbs were like knots in a rope; each had an iron collar on his neck, and all were connected together with a chain whose bights swung between them, rhythmically clinking.** It must be a scene like this that John Galsworthy who, incidentally, was a writer and fellow traveler journeying on Conrad's ship the Torrens thought of when he wrote *Conrads eyes never ceased snapshotting; and the millions of photographs they took were laid away by him to draw on.**

 *Start of quote.
**End of quote.

COMMAS FOR CLARITY: QUICK REVIEW CHARTS

Commas have two basic functions within our punctuation signal system. First, they help us to separate main sentence parts. Second, they help us enclose interrupters within the sentence. The following seven sections on commas illustrate those two basic functions.

I. TO SEPARATE ITEMS IN A SERIES

A. We bought eggs, bread, and cereal.
B. My mother rushed to the garage, to the car, and then to the library.
C. Larry bought a Mustang, Gina bought an old Pontiac, but Andrew bought a sleek new motorcycle.

         1   2   3
D. He was a tall, handsome, and hardworking man.

    Words 1, 2, and 3 above describe "man." Since they are equally important, can be written in any order, and would make sense if the word *and* appeared between them (He was a tall *and* handsome *and* hardworking man), you need to use commas.

                         1   2   3
    However, in this sentence, *Steve ate four small chocolate candies,* commas are not needed. You could not reverse the order of the describing words, nor could you make sense if you used *and* between the words (Steve ate four *and* small *and* chocolate candies).

Hints: 1. Each item can be either one word (as in A above) or a group of words (as in B or C above).
         2. There must be at least three items in the series.
         3. The comma before *and* or *but* is *NOT* required.
         4. To determine whether you need commas between describing words:
            a. Try to reverse their order in the sentence.
            b. Try to use *and* between the describing words.
         If you can do *a* and *b,* use commas.

Step 1. Commas and Series.   Use commas where they belong. If a sentence is correct, mark it *C.*

1. The radiator transmission and fuel pump all have to be fixed on my old Ford.
2. To create a good impression on a job interview dress neatly be courteous and be confident.
3. Down the dark wooden staircase through the empty hallways past the musty living room the old man hobbled with his cane.

II. TO SET OFF A DIRECT QUOTATION (see pages 54–55)

I said, "Sit down!"
"I'm not tired," she replied.
"But a person needs rest," I said, "even if she's not tired."

> **Hint:** If you want to use a question mark or an exclamation mark after a quotation, do not use a comma, too.
>
> "Where were you?" he asked.
> "Stand up!" she screamed.

Step 2. Commas and Quotations. Use commas correctly in these sentences. If the sentence is already correct, mark it *C*.

1. "Chicago is lovely this time of year" he admitted "but I miss the serenity of the country."
2. "Where did Daddy go?" John asked with a tear in his eye.
3. "Pull over" commanded the police officer "and show me your license."

III. TO SET OFF INTRODUCTORY SECTIONS

A. *Certain Transitions as Openers* (one word or several words).

[comma]
Nevertheless, try to speak in a loud voice.
In other words, be careful!
[comma]

B. *Certain Conversational Words* (to set off *yes, no, oh well, why,* and *now* used in conversation).

[comma]   [comma]   [comma]
Yes, he will be there. *Why,* how did that happen? *Oh,* that is awful!

C. *-ing Word or Other Verb-Part Openers* (see pages 180–186).
[-*ing* ——→ *Sailing along the lake,* I felt peace and contentment.
opener]   [comma]
[verb-part ——→ *To reach the top of the shelf,* the child stood on a chair.
opener]   [comma]
——→ *Scribbled quickly,* the note was hard to read.
[comma]

D. *Subordinated Word Groups as Openers.*

[subordinator]
Although the moon hung in the sky, the sun still shone.
[comma]

Because the vocabulary troubled us, we used a dictionary to check definitions.
[subordinator]   [comma]

Hint: Brief opening-word groups not covered in A, B, and C above usually do not have commas after them.

[no comma]
In a few months I will be twenty.

[no comma]
Beyond the tree stands a small house.

If the introductory subordinated word group is brief, you may omit the comma.
When he sang I left the room.
[no comma]

Step 3. Commas after Openers.   Put in commas where they belong. Mark the sentence *C* if it requires no commas.

1. Across the horizon flew the jumbo jet.
2. Wandering down the quaint old streets of Quebec I found my uncle's antique shop.
3. On the other hand we do carry a selection of Italian sweaters.
4. Without a substantial increase in salary John will quit his job.
5. Therefore I don't think Mr. Ross is guilty.

IV. TO HELP SEPARATE TWO COMPLETE THOUGHTS WHEN A COORDINATOR IS EXPRESSED (see pages 17–20)

Hint 1:   Coordinators are *and, or, nor, but, for.*

Memphis is considered by many as a large city, [comma] but it has few problems of traffic congestion.

Just turn the key, [comma] and you will see when the engine starts that this car is like no other you have ever driven.

Hint 2:   The comma may be left out when the two complete thoughts are very brief.

We ate [no comma] and they drank.
They flew but we drove there. [no comma]

Step 4. Commas and Coordinators.   Select a sentence from Column I and coordinate it sensibly on separate paper with a sentence in Column II, using one of the five coordinators. Use a comma when necessary.

I
1. I swim as often as possible.
2. I enjoy my college classes.
3. Fred bought a very expensive shirt.
4. My father was born in England.
5. You can join us at Steve's party.

II
1. My mother was born in France.
2. You can go to the movies with Joyce.
3. It is excellent exercise.
4. Its colors faded after the third washing.
5. The subject matter is usually interesting.

V. TO SEPARATE WORDS OR WORD GROUPS THAT INTERRUPT THE MAIN IDEA OF THE SENTENCE

A. *Transition Words to Interrupt.*
   We felt, however, that whitewall tires were unnecessary. [commas here]

   But the kangaroo, to be sure, is an unusual animal.

B. *Subordinating Word Groups to Interrupt.*

That old truck, which has ignition trouble, is hard to start.

[commas here]

Mr. Davis, who drives to work, always complains about the traffic.

[commas]

Caroline, whose voice is soft, is really charming.

The subordinated word groups in B do not give information to identify the subject, and they could be removed from the sentences without changing the meaning. We know which truck is hard to start (*that old one*) without the interrupter. We know who complains about traffic (*Mr. Davis*) without the interrupter. We know who is charming (*Caroline*) without the interrupter. Therefore, commas are needed to set off the added information.

But if the subordinating word group is needed to identify the subject, commas are not required.

[no comma]   [no comma]

A truck which has ignition trouble is hard to start.

[These words identify the truck. Without these words, we don't know which truck is hard to start.]

[no comma]   [no comma]

People who drive to work always complain about the traffic.

[Without these words it would seem that all people complain about the traffic.]

[no comma]   [no comma]

A girl whose voice is soft is speaking on the telephone.

[Without these words, we don't know which girl is speaking.]

Hint: If *that* opens the subordinating word group, you usually do not need commas.

An idea that is clever is not always good.

[no commas]

Gasoline that contains lead pollutes the air.

C. *Interrupters That Describe*

1. *-ing* word groups to interrupt

[commas here]

A shaky station wagon, laboring up the hill, backfired in a crash.

[commas]

The puppy, trembling, drew close to its mother.

2. Interrupters starting with *-ed* words or other verb parts.

[comma]   [verb part]   [comma]

Miss Kelly, *dressed* in red, ran for the bus.

[comma]   [verb part (infinitive)]

The dog, to get his food, barked wildly.

[comma]   [verb part]   [comma]

A mirror, broken in small pieces, lay on the street.

Hint: The interrupting words in 1 and 2 just add information about the subject. They could be left out of the sentence without disturbing the meaning. Therefore, commas are needed. However, when interrupting word groups like those above identify the subject, commas are not used.

[Not just any wagon backfires: this word group identifies the wagon and is essential to the meaning of the sentence.]

A wagon laboring up a hill can backfire.

[no commas]

[It is only the woman dressed in red who is attractive according to this sentence. This word group identifies the subject.]

The woman dressed in red is attractive.

[no commas]

3. Other describing words

[These words describe the driver. They could be left out of the sentence.]

The driver, a doctor, was not injured.

[commas]

The Mustang, a new white convertible, crashed into a pole.

[These words describe the car which has already been identified. The words could be left out of the sentence.]

Step 5. Commas for Interrupters. Select from Column II an interrupter that could be used sensibly within each complete thought in Column I. Decide whether or not commas are needed. Then, write each new sentence on the blank lines provided.

I	II
A student will fail.	a police captain
A news story is unprofessional.	without her glasses
An energy program is practical.	that contains the reporter's opinion
My father has just retired.	who doesn't study
Richard Nixon resigned on August 9, 1974.	our thirty-seventh President
My girl friend is practically blind.	which relies on solar energy

Example:

1. *A student who doesn't study will fail.*

2. _____

3. _____

4. _____

5. _____

6. _____

VI. SEVEN FAMILIAR PLACES FOR COMMAS

1. In dates, after everything but the month:

   On April 7, 1970, my life began.
   [commas]

   On Saturday, May 7, 1971, Alexander's Department Store had a sale on men's suits. └──[commas]──┘

2. In an address:

   [comma]
   A riot occurred in Brooklyn, New York.
   Atlanta, Georgia, has many qualities of Northern big cities.
   [commas]

3. Before and after someone's title if the title comes after the name:

   [commas]
   Carl Berkson, Ph.D., practices psychology in Los Angeles.

   [no comma]
   Dr. Smithers has retired.

4. To set off someone's name, if that person is being spoken to in the sentence:

   Carol, why don't you do your assignment?
   └────── [commas] ──────┐
   I understand, Mr. Harrington, that you cannot pay this last installment.

5. In informal letters, after the opening words and the words before the signature:

   Dear Martin,
   Dear Carl, ──────→ [comma]
   Yours sincerely,
   Very truly yours,

   Hint: In a formal letter, use a colon after the salutation.
     Dear Mr. Porter:
     Dear Senator Byrd:

6. To indicate that words are left out:

   [Comma here shows that the words "man owns" are omitted.]
   The older man owns the sedan; the younger, the convertible.

7. To set off a variety of numbers:

> [comma]
> volume four, page eighteen

> [comma]
> six feet, three inches
> 19,385 students
> [comma]

Step 6. Using Commas in Seven Ways. Fill in the commas where they are needed.

1. The lucky winner of our September 18 1979 contest is Jules Ramon M.D. who lives at 458 South Street San Francisco California.
2. Henry Davis the superintendent lives in building four apartment 12A.
3. "Would you explain Mr. Kingsley what two meters fifty centimeters is equal to in American feet and inches?"

VII. THREE PLACES NOT TO USE COMMAS

Excessive use of commas distracts the reader, especially when the writer places commas incorrectly. Based upon errors made on the papers of beginning writers, these suggestions will help you avoid using commas unnecessarily:

1. DO NOT use commas to separate subject and verb.

   INCORRECT: A small violet, grew beneath the elm.
   CORRECT: A small violet grew beneath the elm.

2. DO NOT use commas after short word groups, even if they are introductory, unless they are transitional words like *in fact, for example, however* or unless confusion might otherwise result.

   INCORRECT: Beside the fence, a calf stood grazing under a blue sky.
   CORRECT: Beside the fence a calf stood grazing under a blue sky.
   CORRECT: In fact, the child arrived after noon.
   CORRECT: From the ceiling, light flecks of plaster fell.
   [Without the comma, readers would read *ceiling light.*]

3. DO NOT use commas before coordinators when the subject of the following complete sentence is not stated.

   INCORRECT: She dug a deep hole, and planted a fir tree
               [no subject here]

   CORRECT: She dug a deep hole, and she planted a fir tree.

Step 7. Avoiding Excess Commas. Correct any errors with commas in the following sentences. Mark correct sentences *C*.

1. She saw the film, on Saturday, and failed to enjoy it.
2. Across the vacant meadow, the wind howled like a hurt dog.

3. That tall, graceful man, is my husband, but I am not surprised that you did not recognize him.
4. In any case, discarded bottles are dangerous, and are ugly to look at.
5. For a cold water and other liquids help reduce fever.

Step 8. Comma Review. Here are some sentences written by professional writers. All the commas have been left out. Put in the commas where you think they belong. In each blank space, write in the number of the review chart on pages 234–240 that tells why the comma (or commas) is needed.

_____ 1. Life like every other blessing derives its value from its use alone.
—Samuel Johnson

_____ 2. God heals and the doctor takes the fee.
—Benjamin Franklin

_____ 3. To be sure in all ages people have been afraid of loneliness and have tried to escape it.
—Rollo May

_____ 4. Stopping in her tracks she first extended her arm bent her elbow and leaned forward from the hips—all to examine the watch strapped to her wrist; then she gave a loud double-rap on the door.
—Eudora Welty

_____ 5. We pray that peoples of all faiths all races all nations may have their great human needs satisfied.
—Dwight David Eisenhower

_____ 6. Now that it was quite dark he brought his feet down to the floor and slapped the sleeping legs.
—John Steinbeck

_____ 7. In a way I suppose that the little I recall of my early childhood in Russia my first eight years sums up my beginnings what now are called the formative years.
—Golda Meir

_____ 8. I have now spoken of the education of the scholar by nature by books and by action.
—Ralph Waldo Emerson

_____ 9. On that bleak hill top the earth was hard with a black frost and the air made me shiver through every limb.
—Emily Brontë

_____ 10. With her passion for sewing knitting or crocheting baby clothes she used me as a dressmaker's dummy.
—Günter Grass

Step 9. More Review. Follow directions. Use separate paper.

1. Write a sentence that you might speak to a friend. Use his or her name at the beginning of the sentence.
2. Write a complete sentence that tells your street address, your city, and your state.
3. Write a sentence that tells the name of some well-known author. Use the words *a famous author* after the person's name.

4. Write two *complete* sentences about your favorite foods. Use the words *and* or *but* to separate the sentences.
5. Write a complete sentence that lists your *three* favorite actors. Use the word *and* only once.
6. Write a complete sentence about your boyfriend or girl friend, your husband or your wife. Use the words *who I love* somewhere in the sentence.
7. Write a quotation sentence about something you argued about recently. Use the words *I said* somewhere in the sentence.
8. Write a sentence about two sports you enjoy. Use the word *although, when, if, while,* or *because* at the beginning of the sentence.
9. Write a sentence of advice to someone who has never driven in rush hour traffic. Start your sentence with either of these word groups: *Driving in rush hour traffic* or *To drive in rush hour traffic.*
10. Use the word *however, nevertheless, on the other hand,* or *besides* after the word *voted* in this sentence: *We all voted for the Republican candidate.*

WRITING THE ESSAY

Think about some particular place that has some significance in your life: a room, an office, a school yard, a country cabin, a farm, or any other memorable place. Make sure that there are two specific aspects of this place that you can write about—one in each body paragraph. Make sure you have a strong enough feeling about the place so that you can write an effective proposal sentence. And use your highest level of concrete sensory language for details: color, sound, touch, smell, images of action will be the essential sources of support for the points you wish to make.

Suggestions for Thinking It Through

You remember that the first five chapters of this book introduced some ways paragraphs may be organized. Essays, since they are composed of paragraphs, may be organized in similar ways, each paragraph following a pattern of organization that suits the topic. Comparison, contrast, narration, several instances to support topic ideas, description, analogy, mood sketches: all these paragraph types may be extended to the essay itself. The table below makes suggestions for ways in which you can develop and organize your essay and gives you some sample proposals other students have written for the various developments suggested. But feel free to use any method you think best suits the topic you are writing about.

Possible Plan for Body Paragraphs	*Paragraph Development*	*Sample Proposal*
1. Tell about two special moments you remember about	Narration through chronology? Mood sketches?	1. In the school yard at the back of this public school

the place, one in each paragraph.

2. a. Compare and contrast the appearance of the place at two different times, or
   b. Compare and contrast the place you remember with some other place you remember.

3. One paragraph to show *several* instances that support one aspect of the place you are discussing and
   a. the other paragraph to tell *one specific moment* that illustrates another aspect of the place

   or

   b. the other paragraph *also* to show several instances that support another aspect of the place you are discussing.

4. Describe the place fully in one paragraph.

   Tell in the next paragraph about a vivid moment that occurred at the place.

Analogy in one of the paragraphs?

Narration through chronology? Comparison-contrast? Definition in images? (See pages 393–394.)

Three instances arranged through importance? Three instances arranged through chronology? Listing of instances? Narration through chronology? Mood sketch? Instances arranged through importance? Instances arranged through chronology?

Description using transitions by place? Narration through chronology? Mood sketch?

---

in Cincinnati, I remember two important lessons in sportsmanship.

2. a. The corner at Pitkin and Howard Avenues during July is two different places, one in the morning and another in the early evening.
   b. When I think back to the kitchen in our old apartment house, I realize how modern things are here in Springfield Gardens.

3. Not only did I learn in Cook County Hospital that nurses and doctors are really interested in patients, but I also saw that the patients themselves look after one another.

4. The desert near El Paso is a beautiful place, but one experience I had there shows its hidden dangers.

TOPIC TIPS FOR IMPACT

1. Select a place that is particularly clear and important to you. Perhaps you can even return there briefly before you begin writing.
2. Write about your impressions of the sounds you hear; the smells and sensations of touch you experience; the actions and colors you observe. Show the reader through details why the place is special.
3. Try to recall bits of dialogue, people's words as they participate in the place you are writing about.
4. Keep in mind the proportion of your paragraphs. Generally, introduction and conclusion should be about the same length, and both of these paragraphs should be shorter (or at least not longer!) than the two body paragraphs. A long

introduction or conclusion requires substantial body paragraphs as well. If you try *generally* for four to six sentences in your introduction and conclusion and ten to twelve sentences in each of the body paragraphs, you will have a reasonable and workable goal set for yourself.

5. If one of your paragraphs is straight description:

   a. Describe the scene from one point of view: decide where you as reporter and observer are located and show all the details from that position.

   b. Name the place, the time, and the season in which your scene takes place.

   c. Build your description by moving from objects farthest away from you to objects that are closest.

   d. Use strong and active verbs.

   e. Avoid too many modifiers.

Learning from Other Students

Step 1. An Essay on Place.   Read the sample below, an essay about a place a student remembered vividly. Answer the questions that come afterward.

Memories of the Australian Bush

From a very early age I had the urge to see what was beyond my native territory in Australia. At the tender age of eighteen I traveled half way around the world to live in the United States. Love, a new family, and boundless opportunities greeted me in this foreign country. But, I will never forget the land of my birth—Australia. There, I grew up among shady gum trees with wide open spaces for my playground. My home, a sheep station where sheep are raised for their wool, is a beautiful place to me and holds many happy memories of my childhood.

For instance, September to my sister, brother and me meant the delights of crayfishing or "yabbying" as we called it. After school we grabbed long lengths of rough, brown string, a dish of meat chunks, a chicken wire basket, and an old iron bucket. Arriving at the nearest dam, we tore off our shoes and socks. We tied large pieces of the fatty red meat securely to one end of the string. Clutching the makeshift fishing lines, we tiptoed into the mud, smooth red slime oozing around our feet and ankles. I deftly tossed the string into a dark, murky hole, causing ripples in concentric circles to break the mirror-like surface of the water. Shivering with cold and anticipation, I watched and waited for a tug on the string. "I've got one!" squealed my sister Helen. All thoughts of my own catch vanished. I dashed for the wire basket while my brother David aided my sister in the delicate process of pulling the crayfish, inch by inch, out of his hole to where I could scoop him up with my net. This process was repeated until the bucket overflowed with shining blue, purple, brown and green claws angrily snapping at each other. At this point we gloated over our fine catch; then we gleefully flung the crayfish back into the water. Tired, happy and dirty, we trudged back across the paddocks, knowing that all too soon the fierce summer sun would bake the mud dry, forcing the yabbies further into the depths of their cool, dark dungeons.

Besides the crayfishing expeditions, I loved to go out with my father on frosty June mornings to inspect the newborn lambs. Bundled up warmly in woolen hat and mittens, I sat silently as the blue utility truck bounced over the red dirt track. Arriving at a sheep camp, we slowly circled the mob, which was still dozing in the semi-darkness. Peering out from my father's brown wizened face, his bright blue eyes darted back and forth between the sleeping animals. Now and then, the urgent, high pitched bleat of a lost lamb broke the stillness of the dawn. Scurrying from one ewe to another, the lamb searched for its mother. When the comforting low reply of "Baa" sounded in the distance, I breathed a sigh of relief. That meant one less meal for the hungry foxes this morning. Suddenly, the truck stopped as my father's practiced eye discerned trouble. We plodded through the long, wet grass towards a ewe that was lying on her side with her legs flailing wildly in the air. Foxes had ripped off her udder to drink the warm, sweet milk, leaving the ewe bleeding in agony. While my father attended to the heartbreaking task of slitting the ewe's throat, I busied myself by trying to find her lamb. Huddled beside a burnt-out log, the little creature sat shaking, cold and damp with dew. As I carried it home, cradling the orphan in my arms, I pressed my cheek against the soft fuzz of its ears and smelt the musty odor of wet wool. Many times I returned from these trips bearing such a bundle, and each time I felt joyous to have a baby lamb to nurture and care for and, eventually, to profit from.

These and other fond memories I store away to relate to my children and grandchildren. It is very important for a person to have a sense of where she has come from in order to know where she is going. Pride in one's roots creates a feeling of self-worth and sets a level of attainment for each individual. It is also reflected in the way one relates to other people. Some day (before my daughter is too old) I hope to introduce her to the pleasures of living in the Australian bush.

—Muriel Guba

1. Put a check next to the proposal sentence. Is it specific or general?
2. Comment on the introductory paragraph. Is it effective? Does it tell the writer's attitude, or why the topic is important to her?
3. What action do you see most clearly in this essay? Where has the writer appealed to our sense of touch and smell?
4. Underline all of the -ing openers in this essay. Are they effective? Why?
5. How do the last sentences in paragraph 2 and in paragraph 3 serve each moment being described?
6. What part of the opening sentence of paragraph 3 tells the topic of that paragraph? What part of the same sentence refers the reader back to paragraph 2?
7. What is your opinion of the conclusion?

Step 2. Another Sample. After you read the student essay below, discuss the questions.

Practice in the High School Gym

All my life I have loved baseball. As a little boy I stood at the iron schoolyard gates and watched the ninth graders zip around the bases. I sit glued to the television and suffer with the Mets as their pitchers go limp on the mound. It is easy to understand, then, why when March comes around I look forward to the start of baseball practice in my high school gym. What I liked most about senior practice was the thrill of all my friends around me in the locker room and the activity on the gym floor.

As I dressed in the locker room, I felt the warmth and enjoyment of all my friends who played on the team with me in the previous year. Bob on my left dressed hurriedly to rush out to the gym; as team captain, he rapped on the metal lockers and yelled, "Let's get the lead out! Cut the talk and let's move!" Richard on my right stuffed his red flannel shirt and his copy of *Hamlet* into the locker as he dressed, talking continuously about winning a school championship. As I looked around, I saw all the new fellows. Trying out for the team for the first time, they struggled with their uniforms. They were so nervous that they could not even put their bright yellow shirts on straight. Then I saw Coach O'Neill flying out of his office. Even he looked excited for the oncoming season which would last until June and the championship games. As he dashed out the door to the gym he looked at me and smiled as if to say, "Isn't it great to be back with the team again?"

Then, when all the fun in the locker room was over, we charged out onto the shellacked floor of the gym. As we stood waiting for the coach to finish checking the new bats and uniforms, I could not help thinking how I felt like a father to all the new boys on the team. I looked at the brown painted stands halfway pushed out, but before we even got near to sit down, Coach O'Neill grabbed the silver whistle dangling from his neck and blew hard. His gray eyes looked mean as he barked out the drills we had to do. Then we started calisthenics because the coach said they would make us loose. As I did my push-ups to Coach O'Neill's crisp "One-two-three-four," I saw the yellow floor with its black stripes from the basketball court. Blood rushed up to my head, making me feel weak, but I still continued. Next we ran laps around the gym. As I ran I could see the huge panes of glass from the roof of the gym, the sun blinding me every time I looked up. After a loud blast from a whistle, the coach told us to stop running and to take a rest. Five minutes later we ended the workout with wind sprints in the hallway to make room in the gym for the football team on its workout session. These activities in the gym made me feel happy and healthy.

Because I have so much fun in the gym, to me exercise is a wonderful part of living. I was surprised to read in the papers about "Flabby Americans" and of the poor physical condition so many people today are in because of little activity. Maybe some worthwhile exercises and exciting workouts in high school would start more people on physical fitness programs. My friends in public school say that gym teachers leave uninterested students pretty much alone to sit and talk on the sidelines as long as there is no trouble. But I think that this is wrong: physical education teachers should be convincing all those sideline talkers that participating is the greatest part of sports.

—Thomas Albanese

1. How does the proposal sentence allow for the development of two parts of the topic in the body paragraphs?
2. How does the introduction serve to involve the reader?
3. What transitions in the opening sentence connect paragraph 2 to paragraph 1? paragraph 3 to paragraph 2?
4. How does the conclusion suit the essay? Does the closing paragraph grow logically from the main idea of the essay?

More Topics to Think About

If you have trouble thinking about a topic for your first essay on a place, try one of these as a starting point.

1. experiences at the train depot
2. hamburger stand versus a "fancy" restaurant
3. the park in your hometown
4. street-corner lessons
5. your town beach or pool
6. the high school cafeteria
7. your "hangout": bar, candy store, soda shop, street corner
8. an airport or dock
9. your church on two occasions
10. a farm you know
11. the supermarket: two experiences
12. a country resort: what you remember
13. your street at night
14. the football (baseball) stadium
15. party room blues
16. your backyard
17. the town shopping center
18. the subway car: morning and evening rush hours
19. amusement-park memories
20. a hospital room you remember

Prewriting: Timed Writing for Ideas

Timed writing is another technique that you can use to stimulate ideas. First, decide on a topic; then without pausing to correct spelling errors or to ponder an idea, write continuously for five minutes. The object is to fill up a page with complete sentences that are related to the topic. Remember, don't stop writing! If you can't think of anything to write, write "I can't think of anything" as many times as you have to. Let your ideas flow naturally. Look at one student's timed-writing exercise below.

PREWRITING: A TIMED-WRITING EXERCISE

Topic: The IRT Subway

I ride the IRT subway everyday into Manhattan. The people are jammed together like sardines. Everyone reads the morning newspaper, afraid to make eye contact. Some people doze. All types of people ride the trains: drunks, pretty, young secretaries, businessmen in their look-a-like pin-striped suits. I don't know what to write. People look fresh and alert in the morning, but are sweaty and grumpy in the evening. I don't know what to write. I don't know what to

---

write. A man once had a heart attack on the train. His wife was screaming. All the people started to push and shove. I felt trapped. Someone pulled the emergency brake and the train slammed to a stop. The noise was terrible. The air conditioners weren't working; my clothes were soaked with perspiration. I don't know what to write. So many things happen everyday. I hate the trains. They make me feel small and less than human. People get angry at each other for nothing. A guy throws a punch if someone steps on his foot. I remember the black-out in the city. I was trapped in the subway for over three hours. But that was O.K. People were friendly. Everyone helped one another. We shared someone's Coke. Kids played a guitar and we sang songs such as "A Hundred Bottles of Beer." People took turns standing up. The cops did a great job leading us through the black, stinking tunnels to the next station. I was proud to be a New Yorker. Time's almost up. I think I hate most the screeching of the wheels as the train turns and twists under Manhattan. I wish people were more friendly than they are. No one says good morning. They sit in tight little balls as if to say "Don't touch me!"

— Robert Sirola

Step 1. Reviewing Timed Writing. Answer the questions below based on the preceding paragraph of timed writing.

1. Although many ideas are mentioned in Robert Sirola's timed-writing paragraph, what two ideas might be suitable for an essay on place?
2. What are Robert Sirola's feelings about the IRT subway? Which images do you see most clearly?

Step 2. Using Timed Writing. Choose some place that you see clearly and about which you have strong feelings. Then write continuously about that place for five minutes. Use your own paper.

Your First Essay Checklist: A Questionnaire for Solid Results

As you think about this essay on place and as you plan and write your rough and final drafts, use this questionnaire as a guide. When you have prepared your manuscript, write *yes* or *no* in the blank spaces. If you have two or more no's, you should attempt another revision.

1. Did I think the topic through carefully? Did I follow some prewriting   _____
   activity that works for me, perhaps *timed writing*? (See pages 34–35 and above.)
2. Did I prepare a rough draft and any other needed drafts? Did I make   _____
   changes in language and ideas on my rough draft in order to make my ideas clearer?
3. After making changes in content, form, and sentence structure, did I   _____
   check my draft over by proofreading carefully for my usual mistakes? Did I check especially for errors in punctuation?
4. Do I have a four-paragraph essay, each body paragraph no fewer than   _____

ten sentences, the introduction and conclusion in proportion to the rest of the essay?

5. Am I sure that I understand the way an essay is put together, having _____ studied the chart From Paragraph to Essay (pages 212–213) and the sample essay written from a one-paragraph theme (pages 214–215)?

6. Have I prepared carefully a proposal sentence that will let me discuss _____ *two* aspects of my topic?

   This is my proposal sentence _____

   _____

7. Did I write an introduction *after* my proposal was clear to me? Did I _____ follow any of the suggestions in the ideas for starting essays on pages 219–223?

8. Have I planned out the essay according to one of the suggestions on pages 242–244 or have I used a logical plan of my own?

9. Have I introduced the topic of each body paragraph in the first sen- _____ tence? Have I used transitions in those sentences?

10. Have I used lively, colorful language rich in sound, smell, touch, and _____ images that use color? Do I name people, places, and times of events specifically?

11. Have I used a variety of sentence patterns?
    a. Do I have several subordinated sentences?
    b. Do I have just a few coordinated sentences?
    c. Have I used a semicolon correctly?
    d. Have I opened some sentences with words that end in *-ing* or *-ly*?
    e. Do I have a quotation sentence using someone's exact words?
    f. Did I use correctly punctuation such as the colon, the dash, the parentheses?

12. Did I try to combine sentences for tight descriptions (as explained on pages 223–225)?

13. Have I used correctly some of the new vocabulary introduced on pages 206–207 of this chapter?

14. Have I proofread (see pages 38–39) my essay very carefully, looking for the errors that appear most often on my Theme Progress Sheet? Did I check for run-on errors, sentence fragments, spelling mistakes, and especially for the kinds of punctuation errors explained in this chapter?

15. Have I written a strong title (see pages 95–97)? _____

16. Have I written a concluding paragraph? _____

THE PROFESSIONALS SPEAK

The following selection describes in rich detail the street and neighborhood of the writer's youth in the 1920s and 1930s. When you finish reading, answer the questions.

SOME WORDS TO KNOW BEFORE YOU READ

Amboys, Bristols, Hopkinsons: names of street gangs in Brooklyn
fanatical: showing extreme enthusiasm
esteem: praise, respect
one o'cat: a ball game played with a bat and two bases
triumphant: celebrating victory
pavilion: a partly open structure (usually in a park) for shelter, entertainment, etc.
compost: a mixture of decaying materials used to fertilize land
quarry: a pit from which stone or slate is removed
oppressively: harshly
remote: far away

My Block: Chester Street

The block: *my* block. It was on the Chester Street side of our house, between the grocery and the back wall of the old drugstore, that I was hammered into the shape of the streets. Everything beginning at Blake Avenue would always wear for me some delightful strangeness and mildness, simply because it was not of my block *the* block, where the clang of your head sounded against the pavement when you fell in a fist fight, and the rows of storelights on each side were pitiless, watching you. Anything away from the block was good: even a school you never went to, two blocks away: there were vegetable gardens in the park across the street. Returning from "New York," I would take the longest routes home from the subway, get off a station ahead of our own, only for the unexpectedness of walking through Betsy Head Park and hearing the gravel crunch under my feet as I went beyond the vegetable gardens, smelling the sweaty sweet dampness from the pool in summer and the dust on the leaves as I passed under the ailanthus trees. On the block itself everything rose up only to test me.

We worked every inch of it, from the cellars and the backyards to the sickening space between the roofs. Any wall, any stoop, any curving metal edge on a billboard sign made a place against which to knock a ball; any bottom rung of a fire escape ladder a goal in basketball; any sewer cover a base; any crack in the pavement a "net" for the tense sharp tennis that we played by beating a soft ball back and forth with our hands between the squares. Betsy Head Park two blocks away would always feel slightly foreign, for it belonged to the Amboys and the Bristols and the Hopkinsons as much as it did to us. Our life every day was fought out on the pavement and in the gutter, up against the walls of the houses and the glass fronts of the drugstore and the grocery, in and out of the fresh steaming piles of horse manure, the wheels of passing carts and automobiles, along the iron spikes of the stairway to the cellar, the jagged edge of the open garbage cans, the crumbly steps of the old farmhouses still left on one side of the street.

As I go back to the block now, and for a moment fold my body up again in its narrow arena—there, just there, between the black of the asphalt and the old women in their kerchiefs and flowered housedresses sitting on the tawny kitchen chairs—the back wall of the drugstore still rises up to test me. Every day we smashed a small black viciously hard regulation handball against it with fanatical cuts and drives and slams, beating and slashing at it almost in hatred for the blind strength of the wall itself. I was never good enough at handball, was always practicing some trick shot that might earn me esteem, and when I was weary of trying, would often bat a ball down Chester Street just to get myself to Blake Avenue. I have this memory of playing one o' cat by myself in the sleepy twilight, at a moment when everyone else had left the block. The sparrows floated down from the telephone wires to peck at every fresh pile of horse manure, and there was a smell of brine from the delicatessen store, of egg crates and of the milk scum left in the great metal cans outside the grocery, of the thick white paste oozing out from behind the fresh Hecker's Flour ad on the metal signboard. I would throw the ball in the air, hit it with my bat, then with perfect satisfaction drop the bat to the ground and run to the next sewer cover. Over and over I did this, from sewer cover to sewer cover, until I had worked my way to Blake Avenue and could see the park.

With each clean triumphant ring of my bat against the gutter leading me on, I did the whole length of our block up and down, and never knew how happy I was just watching the asphalt rise and fall, the curve of the steps up to an old farmhouse. The farmhouses themselves were streaked red on one side, brown on the other, but the steps themselves were always gray. There was a tremor of pleasure at one place; I held my breath in nausea at another. As I ran after my ball with the bat heavy in my hand, the odd successiveness of things in myself almost choked me, the world was so full as I ran—past the cobblestoned yards into the old farmhouses, where stray chickens still waddled along the stones; past the little candy store where we went only if the big one on our side of the block was out of Eskimo Pies; past the three neighboring tenements where the last of the old women sat on their kitchen chairs yawning before they went up to make supper. Then came Mrs. Rosenwasser's house, the place on the block I first identified with what was farthest from home, and strangest, because it was a "private" house; then the fences around the monument works, where black cranes rose up above the yard and you could see the smooth gray slabs that would be cut and carved into tombstones, some of them already engraved with the names and dates and family virtues of the dead.

Beyond Blake Avenue was the pool parlor outside which we waited all through the tense September afternoons of the World's Series to hear the latest scores called off the ticker tape—and where as we waited, banging a ball against the bottom of the wall and drinking water out of empty Coke bottles, I breathed the chalk off the cues and listened to the clocks ringing in the fire station across the street. There was an old warehouse next to the pool parlor; the oil on the barrels and the iron staves had the same rusty smell. A block away was the park, thick with the dusty gravel I liked to hear my shoes crunch in as I ran round and round the track; then a great open pavilion, the inside mysteriously dark, chill even in summer; there I would wait in the sweaty coolness before pushing on to the wading ring where they put up a shower on the hottest days.

Beyond the park the "fields" began, all those still unused lots where we could still play hard ball in perfect peace—first shooing away the goats and then tearing up goldenrod before laying our bases. The smell and touch of those "fields," with their wild compost under the billboards of weeds, goldenrod, bricks, goat droppings, rusty cans, empty beer bottles, fresh new lumber, and damp cement, lives in my mind as Brownsville's great open door, the wastes that took us through to the west. I used to go round them in summer with my cousins selling near-beer to the carpenters, but always in a daze, would stare so long at the fibrous stalks of the goldenrod as I felt their harshness in my hand that I would forget to make a sale, and usually go off sick on the beer I drank up myself. Beyond! Beyond! Only to see something new, to get away from each day's narrow battleground between the grocery and the back wall of the drugstore! Even the other end of our block, when you got to Mrs. Rosenwasser's house and the monument works, was dear to me for the contrast. On summer nights, when we played Indian trail, running away from each other on prearranged signals, the greatest moment came when I could plunge into the darkness down the block for myself and hide behind the slabs in the monument works. I remember the air whistling around me as I ran, the panicky thud of my bones in my sneakers, and then the slabs rising in the light from the street lamps as I sped past the little candy store and crept under the fence.

In the darkness you could never see where the crane began. We liked to trap the enemy between the slabs and sometimes jumped them from great mounds of rock just in from the quarry. A boy once fell to his death that way, and they put a watchman there to keep us out. This made the slabs all the more impressive to me, and I always aimed first for that yard whenever we played follow-the-leader. Day after day the monument works became oppressively more mysterious and remote, though it was only just down the block; I stood in front of it every afternoon on my way back from school, filling it with my fears. It was not death I felt there—the slabs were usually faceless. It was the darkness itself, and the wind howling around me whenever I stood poised on the edge of a high slab waiting to jump. Then I would take in, along with the fear, some amazement of joy that I had found my way out that far.

—Alfred Kazin
A Walker in the City

1. Which details of smell, sound, and color do you find most vivid?
2. Why would the author feel a "delightful strangeness" at an area not quite part of his block? Why does he like Mrs. Rosenwasser's house and the monument works?
3. Streets have personalities. What would you say was the personality of Chester Street? How do the author's descriptions give you a sense of that personality?

REACHING HIGHER

Step 1. Describing Your Street. In one narrative paragraph (see Chapter 2 for review), give an impression of your street at one particular time during one particular day. Use details of color, sound, smell, and touch as Alfred Kazin does in "My Block: Chester Street." Try to present dialogue as you hear it on your block. Look at the student's sample below. How has Ms. Boardley individualized Tompkins Avenue?

The Watermelon Man

The most pleasant memory of my youth in the slum section of Bedford-Stuyvesant in Brooklyn is the scene of the watermelon man and his crew when he drove into our neighborhood on a summer Saturday. His horse would turn first onto Tompkins Avenue. Straining under the weight of many green-striped melons, the horse chewed on its leather bit and heaved the wagon forward slowly, each step an effort. The straw hat it wore shaded its sad brown eyes. Its skin, a dirty brown and white, rippled with the stress of animal work like waves slapping some muddy shore. Patched leather straps that served as reins ran over its hide and flicked at lazy green flies; the insects buzzed in the air or hovered over the shining sample of melon, its pits winking in the sun like a thousand brown eyes. The driver and his friends too were unforgettable. The hands that held the reins were calloused and coarse, yet these overly large hands with square dirty nails held the reins with an almost regal gesture. The veins and muscles in the hands and arms of this kingly watermelon man looked like the ropes on an old homemade swing. He wore a dirty vest, a torn undershirt, and melon-splattered jeans, emblems of his trade. Suddenly, his sons and nephews in the back of the wagon laughed and grinned and started the chant, "Melon, melon, watermelon." The watermelon man, his grey hair moist with sweat, his wide mouth showing a perfect set of teeth, now took up the melody. Red bandanas and gaudy handkerchiefs waving in slight breezes, these fine men sang and hummed the chant. Finally, a transaction began. A woman from a brownstone window across the street called, "Hey, them melons fresh?"

"Yes, ma'am," cried the figures in the wagon.

"Well bring me up one," she snapped from above. "No, not you ugly. You, yeah, the cute one."

"Anything else you wants 'sides a melon, honey?" replied the "cute" one, winking at his companions in the wagon who heckled and howled at this.

"Just a melon!" screamed the hoarse voice of a man from the same window above.

I, standing in front of Jack's Candy Store on the corner of Madison Street, must have snapped that scene firmly in my mind, for I still can hear the cry of the watermelon man as it struts and dances in my ears: "Melon, melon, watermelon. Git de fresh watermelon. Melon. Melon."

—Twyla Boardley

Step 2. Point of View. In any good description—whether in a poem, a story, or an essay—we are often aware of the narrator's *point of view. Point of view* is the particular angle or perspective from which the story is told. *Point of view* is influenced by the teller's personality, background, perception, and relationship to the thing or event being described. A successful writer will be able to change *point of view* to suit a particular piece of writing. Often *point of view* is expressed by subtle choices on the writer's part: what is noted about the weather, the landscape, the colors of things around; how much is described and what is left out from the description; whether the story is told in the *first person* (where the story is told directly by one of the characters using the pronoun "I") or whether it is told in the *third person* (where the teller is not a participant in the story at all).

Try your hand at creating a strong sense of *point of view* in description. Imagine a small park. Then, in short poems or paragraphs of description, describe the station scene from two completely different *points of view*. First, write from the *point of view* of a man who has just learned that his son has died in a war. Second, describe the exact same scene (same time of day, weather, place) from the *point of view* of a person newly in love.

You may want to use either *first person* or *third person,* but in either case pay special attention to *what* the narrator describes and how he describes it. Does a grieving father see things any differently from a person who is filled with joy? Will their perceptions change according to their feelings? Try to answer these questions for yourself as you write the descriptions.

For a real challenge, in the first paragraph try not to mention death, the son, or the war; in the second, try not to mention love or the other person. By doing this, you'll find you must really determine *point of view* by carefully choosing things for description that are most appropriate to the message or mood you are trying to create.

Step 3. Study the picture on page 205, and using what you observe, write an essay that explores the meaning you find in the photograph. Use your best sensory language to portray the scene as you see it: use color, sound, smell, and action.

Step 4. With a camera prepare an essay in snapshots about some place near your home that you can observe often and at different times. Take at least fifteen to twenty pictures, and, selecting five or six of the best, arrange them in some order. Mount them one on a page. For each photograph write first a title (see pages 95–97) and then one sentence that you see as the major point of the picture: try to use in that sentence concrete images to create a scene that matches the photograph itself.

Step 5. The following essay contains thirteen sentence fragments and nine run-on sentences. Correct all the errors directly on this page. Study the run-on and fragment review charts on pages 28–29, 61, and 101.

The Key to Comfort

Rooms often portray a person's character and personality your character is displayed in the way you keep your room in order. Whether it's neat or disorganized. To me my room is the most important room in the house, the way it's kept shows the kind of atmosphere I want it helps me seclude myself when the going gets too rough at home.

The atmosphere I try to have in my room is one of solitude. I think that comes because of the way my room is decorated. Soft walls in an off-white color. Nothing but my mirror hanging on the walls. A high dark brown dresser. The desk in the far corner is walnut on the top books stand in piles. Which I keep very neat and orderly. The stereo set and my collection of albums and tapes are in the far corner. Next to my amorphous black leather reclining chair. My room is the only room in the house that is so relaxing.

Because the surroundings are so restful. I found that it served as an important place one February evening last year. When my house was filled with guests from a card party my mother was having. I had my final examination in history the next day, I knew if I did not find a quiet place to study I would fail. I excused myself from the incessant noise of my mother's guests and determined to get peace and quiet.

Marched upstairs to my room. Upon opening the door to my room. I had almost given up hope. There was still so much noise. Loud roars of laughter. People chattering. Dimes and nickels clinking on the table. I quickly slammed the door with me inside the room suddenly the noise was outside, I was trapped in a welcome silence. Because of the solitude in my room I was able to study, I passed the final examination.

Rooms help people relax and find quiet. And the appearance of a room sets the scene for relaxation. If more people would set aside a certain amount of time each day to solve their problems in a serene room of their choice. The mental pressures that many Americans suffer might disappear. Most people try to relax in an atmosphere that is more distracting than peaceful, to me, the quiet well-decorated, well-kept room is the key to comfort.

Step 6. A Collage on a Place. Using the technique of collage, try to characterize some important feeling or impression that you have about some place you know well. Look at the collage on page 115 for an example. What impression does it try to convey? What visual feature best shows you this impression? What kinds of materials has the artist used in making her collage? For your own collage, see if the people in your class can determine (without knowing in advance) what place you are portraying and what your impression of the place is.

chapter 7

YOU THE EXPERT: WRITING A HOW-TO ESSAY

INTRODUCTION TO PROCESS ANALYSIS

One of the major reasons for writing is to explain something. And perhaps no explanations are more demanding in terms of clear, precise language than those that give directions.

Of course, each of us has a well of skills and talents that allow us to perform tasks knowledgeably with our own special knack. The chores around the house, the activities you do for fun in your spare time, the part-time employment (or the full-time work) you now experience—all these give you skill in how to perform some process. You know how to clean the garage quickly, how to make sandwiches at a crowded lunch counter, how to run a busy gas station when the boss leaves early. Even if you have never worked in your life, you still have some special interest or ability that some-one else could learn from you. Or maybe you would like to *learn* so well how to do something or how something works that you can show someone else how to do it.

This theme assignment asks you for a *process analysis.* When you analyze something, you break it down into parts. When you analyze a process, you explain the various steps required to carry it out successfully. Even though the process you want to explain is one you know pretty well, *writing* about it is a special challenge. Activities on the following pages will help you meet that challenge.

VOCABULARY

Step 1. Words for Explaining Processes. The words below may be helpful as you write an essay that explains a process. In the blank spaces, and using a dictionary if you need one, write definitions for these words:

1. sequential _____

2. procedure _____

3. prior _____

4. consequence _____

5. subsequent _____

6. cyclical _____

7. reproduce _____

8. analyze _____

9. significance _____

10. synthesize _____

Step 2. Applying Definitions. In the blank spaces below write from the above list the word that best suits each meaning.

1. coming before _____

2. outcome _____

3. combine separate elements to produce something _____

4. make happen again _____

5. course of action _____

6. coming afterward in time or in order _____

7. break down into parts _____

8. following an orderly arrangement _____

9. importance _____

10. happening at regularly repeated time intervals _____

BUILDING COMPOSITION SKILLS

Exploring the Topic

Step 1. What Do You Know? Each of us has enough knowledge about (or enough interest in to find out about) procedures that we can explain to others. On this list of items put a check (✔) next to those you know well enough by first-hand experience to give instructions that someone else could follow. Put an X next to any process you might be interested enough in to investigate so that you could understand it sufficiently to explain to others. Discuss your choices with the class.

_____ 1. how to baby-sit

_____ 2. how nuclear power works

_____ 3. how to groom a horse

_____ 4. how to make a martini

_____ 5. how coal is converted to oil

_____ 6. how to make a grilled cheese sandwich

_____ 7. how to use a skateboard

_____ 8. how to meet a woman (or man) you like but don't know

_____ 9. how to adopt a child in your city

_____ 10. how to hunt big game

Step 2. Giving and Following Directions: An Experiment. To understand some of the conditions required for explaining a process that someone else should be able to reproduce, ask someone in the class to give aloud directions he or she thinks someone can follow easily. Ask another person to follow directions as the first person explains. The person giving directions should bring to class any necessary equipment.

To make this experiment work, whoever explains the process should face one of the side walls or the back wall as the other volunteer, unseen by the first but visible to the rest of the class, follows instructions. And the person following directions must do so *exactly* without taking any steps whatsoever unless specifically instructed to.

Here are some possible processes volunteers might like to explain or to follow:

1. how to cover a book
2. how to make a paper airplane
3. how to clean the chalkboards
4. how to make a peanut-butter sandwich
5. how to shave with an electric razor.

As the people in the class watch the joint performance, they should be prepared to evaluate the situation they are observing. Step 3 below will focus on that evaluation.

Step 3. Explaining Processes: Seeing the Problems. If your class is like most others, you have just observed (if you have followed Step 1 according to directions) an exercise in frustration. Even with the simplest of procedures, because there is so much room for misunderstanding, steps must be simply and clearly explained. How would you evaluate the two volunteers? What successes could you point to? When things went wrong, *why* did they go wrong? Use the checklist below by circling your answer to judge the scene you witnessed. (On the checklist, the *instructor* is the person who explained the process; the *performer* is the person who tried to duplicate it.) Discuss your responses with the class.

1. The instructor did not give enough information.	*yes*	*no*	*unsure*
2. The instructor's language was too complicated.	*yes*	*no*	*unsure*
3. The instructor assumed that the performer knew more about the process than he or she actually did.	*yes*	*no*	*unsure*
4. The instructor did not have all the materials that were needed to explain the process clearly.	*yes*	*no*	*unsure*
5. The instructor either did not explain steps in the right sequence or did not give all the steps in the sequence.	*yes*	*no*	*unsure*

Including and Arranging Details

In order to write about a process clearly—whether you are giving directions someone can follow or you are giving information about how to do or to make something—you have to include all the important details someone would need to understand what you are trying to explain.

Details in a process essay include, first, the major steps in the procedure you are writing about. People who wanted to follow your directions themselves would need to have every step included. On the other hand, you would not have to offer information with such completeness if you were simply explaining a process readers do not intend to carry out. An essay on how to make an omelet would demand full explanations; an essay on how eggs are produced and gathered could, for most readers, rely more upon general outlines and less upon absolutely complete detail.

Not only must you include all the appropriate steps in the process, but you must also mention any materials involved and any descriptive information which will instruct your readers and will hold their interest. Concrete sensory language (see pages 5–7) can add life to what otherwise might be a boring series of "do this," "do that" instructions. Also, telling readers *why* to perform a certain step keeps their attention with valuable information.

You will discover once you decide which steps to include that arranging details presents no real problems. Usually, a process paper demands a *chronological* arrangement of materials (see pages 52–53). Readers have to know what to do first in time, what to do next, and what to do after that. However, you sometimes have other options.

In explaining how to care for puppies, for example, you might offer the elements of the process in their order of *importance* (pages 84–85)—least important element first, most important element last. Or, similarly, you might first discuss the simplest element to consider in caring for puppies; and you could build to the most difficult element. Finally, you might want to tell the details of the process in order of location—that is from one point in space to another. You could tell how to care first for the puppies' eyes, then the ears, then the mouth, the digestion, the coat, the limbs and feet. Such an order is called *spatial*.

For the most part, though, a simple ordering of steps and details by chronology works best.

Read the paragraph below in which a student gives directions on how to perform a process he expects people to duplicate. Think about the steps he includes and the kinds of details he offers in order to hold the readers' interest.

An Egg Cream Delight

Anyone who has worked as a soda jerk in a New York fountain shop knows that making and drinking an egg cream take special skill. To begin select a tall, clear glass; let no colors or fancy designs hide the delicious drink that will soon fill the container. Press down three or four times on the silver squirter marked *chocolate* so that dark, sticky syrup slips down the sides of the glass to the bottom. This leaves a layer of brown about an inch and a half thick (about two heaping teaspoonfuls for the egg cream maker at home). Be careful not to do anything else until any chocolate clinging to the sides of the glass oozes its way down. Once that happens, carefully add an amount of cold milk that is twice as much as the chocolate. Now the heavy band of brown sits comfortably under a layer of white, and by taking a breath at this point, the person awaiting the drink knows how close joy really is! After this comes the most difficult stage: adding the carbonated water. Only a tiny trickle of soda water should fizz into the glass at a time so that just a small, quiet hiss sounds at the counter. (You people at home, unless you have seltzer water in dark green bottles with siphons, will have to suffer with a second-rate egg cream; popular brands of club sodas do not do the job right.) Now stir the three liquids very gently with a metal spoon that has a long handle. As the stirring continues slowly, a foamy white layer rises to the top with the thickness of cream or beaten egg whites. That is probably the reason for the name *egg cream,* even though no eggs or cream make up the drink. Beneath this snowy top sits a well-mixed liquid of the color of cocoa. Now remove the silver spoon and lick it to see if the drink is too sweet: a bit more soda water always fits in the glass. But do not add any more syrup or milk or the whole soda is ruined. The last step is to raise the glass to the lips and drink so that an equal amount of foam and liquid fills the mouth at the same time. Too much foam at the bottom after the drink disappears means the drinker has failed. But what a wonderful failure. Who will stop him from trying another time?

—Martin Berglund

Step 1. Seeing Steps in the Process. Answer the questions below about "An Egg Cream Delight." Use separate paper.

1. Name the various steps in the process. Why has Martin Berglund given such complete directions?
2. What are the materials required to follow these directions? Has the writer left any out?
3. What sensory details do you find most clear and vivid? What effect do the details have in holding your interest?
4. What order does the writer choose in which to present his information? Why has he chosen that method of organization?

Step 2. An Inventory of Materials. In explanations of processes writers must be careful to name all the materials that may be demanded for the task. Next to each process named below list all the equipment or material someone who wanted to duplicate the process would need.

1. planting bulbs

_____

_____

_____

_____

_____

2. making a hamburger

_____

_____

_____

_____

_____

3. making paper dolls

_____

_____

_____

_____

_____

Step 3. Listing Steps. For any one of the processes named below, list on the blank lines all the steps you think would be important to mention in an essay that attempted to explain the process.

1. how to baby-sit
2. how to prepare dinner in twenty minutes
3. how to register for courses
4. how to change a tire
5. how to enjoy television
6. how to eat pizza
7. how a dry cell works
8. how to play soccer
9. how to fail a test
10. how to learn a foreign language

PROCESS: _____

_____

_____

_____

_____

_____

_____

_____

Step 4. Deciding on an Order. Which method of arrangement would you use to explain the processes listed below? Tell in a brief sentence the reasons for your choice.

1. how to get from the outside of your school building to the cafeteria

   _____

   _____

2. how to become a good rock singer _____

   _____

3. how to form your own band _____

   _____

4. how the pollution problem grew out of hand in your town _____

   _____

5. how to avoid being caught for not having an assignment _____

   _____

6. how a doorbell works _____

   _____

7. how to bake a cheesecake _____

   _____

8. how it is possible to eat for a whole day on $1 _____

   _____

Step 5. Checking a Process through Research. In order to explain a process carefully, you may need to rely on sources outside your own experiences. For the topics listed below, and with the help of card catalogs, the *Reader's Guide* (see pages 400–401), and your school librarian, write the names of three books or magazine articles you could use in order to check the steps in the processes named below.

1. how a cloud chamber works

   a. _____

   b. _____

   c. _____

2. how Freud used hypnosis

   a. _____

   b. _____

   c. _____

3. how to improve your reading speed

   a. _____

    b. _____

    c. _____

4. how harps are made

    a. _____

    b. _____

    c. _____

5. how to grow vegetables organically

    a. _____

    b. _____

    c. _____

Identifying Audience

Whenever you speak to people—whether they are friends, acquaintances, teachers, fellow workers—you adjust your comments and your language to the situation in which you find yourself. What you sense about the people you are talking to tells you, first, just what topics will interest them. It also tells you how much you must say to be understood, what kinds of words to use, how strongly to make your points. Discussing rock music with your friends who know and love it demands one kind of vocabulary, one kind of talking style; discussing rock music with a neighbor or a teacher who knows little about it demands quite another.

So when you speak, you have and rely on an already keen sense of audience—the people reacting to your ideas.

Good writers, too, need to have a strong sense of audience. Of course, most of your writing at school is specifically for your instructors. But it's not a good idea to write expressly and exclusively for them. You want to aim for a more general audience, for a wider range of readers. These would be people smart enough to understand what you are writing about without having to be specialists in your topic. All writers ask themselves as part of their prewriting activity, "Who do I want to read this? Who am I writing this for?" The clearer the answer to those questions, the easier it is for a writer to pitch language to readers so that they come away with exactly what the writer wants them to have.

Although a sense of audience is important in any written work, an essay on process demands from writers a very precise idea of whom they are writing for. Just to take one obvious example, you would use completely different approaches if you wrote to explain how to make a chocolate cake to a class of newlyweds or to a group of master bakers.

Knowing your audience is critical. The box below suggests questions to ask yourself in order to identify the precise audience you are writing for in your process paper.

```
┌─────────────────────────────────────────────────────────────────┐
│ IDENTIFYING AUDIENCE: QUESTIONS TO ASK FOR THE PROCESS THEME      │
│                                                                   │
│ 1. Who am I trying to explain the process to?                     │
│ 2. Will my readers know the technical vocabulary I may have to    │
│    use? Or, will I have to define new or difficult terms?         │
│ 3. Do I expect my readers to be able to perform the process I am  │
│    writing about? If so, what steps can I assume they already     │
│    know? (Be careful. It's easy to as- sume that readers know     │
│    more than they actually do. Without talking down to your       │
│    audience, it's always best—when in doubt—to think of your      │
│    readers as having almost no knowledge of your subject.)        │
│ 4. What purpose do my readers have in reading my essay? Do they   │
│    want only to be informed, or do they expect also to be amused  │
│    or inspired or moved to action?                                │
└─────────────────────────────────────────────────────────────────┘
```

Step 1. Seeing Different Audiences. For each process below name two or three different kinds of audiences that might be interested in reading about the process. Discuss your responses with the class. What kinds of demands would each type of audience place upon the writer? Look at the example.

Process

1. how to fix flat tires on bicycles

2. how to throw a knuckleball

3. how to keep roses healthy

4. how white blood cells attack disease

Kinds of Audiences

a. *Young teenagers*
b. *Bicycle repair shop owners*
c. *people who sell tires to bicycle manufacturers*

5. how to use a power saw   _____

     _____

     _____

     _____

6. how a microwave oven works   _____

     _____

     _____

     _____

Step 2. Assessing Vocabulary. Column I below names a process. Column II names the readers the writer is aiming for. Column III offers several technical words required in the explanation. Considering the process and its intended audience, check only those terms you think the writer would have to define in his or her essay (or would have to replace with simpler words). Defend your choices. Look at the example.

I Process	II Intended Audience	III Vocabulary
1. how to stir-fry Chinese vegetables	beginning cooks	✔bok choy ✔wok ✔soy sauce tablespoon ✔peanut oil
2. how to prevent nuclear accidents	nuclear power plant managers	reactor fission geiger counter radioactivity
3. how to register for classes in college	entering college students	prerequisites program bursar registrar baccalaureate
4. how to paint a room	new homeowner	roller brush latex spackle scraper

TRANSITIONS IN THE ESSAY

Using transitions effectively in an essay helps you connect your paragraphs smoothly. The essay transition signboards below suggest key places for transitions. Before you examine the charts, review pages 211–216 on the parts of the essay.

Review Hints:
Remembering the Proposal Sentence

1. It must tell the reader the purpose of the essay.
2. It should allow you to discuss two aspects of your topic. It can state both aspects quite specifically, or it can merely suggest what these aspects are.
3. It is conveniently placed as the last sentence of the introduction.

Hint: See pages 216–219 for more about proposal sentences.

ESSAY TRANSITION SIGNBOARD I: FIRST SENTENCE OF PARAGRAPH 2

What to Do	*Why*

1. Tell what part of the proposal you want to discuss in paragraph 2 by
   a. repeating one of the two points you want to write about if you have mentioned them clearly in your proposal
             or
   b. stating (for the first time) the point you want to write about, a point based upon the suggestion made in the proposal.
	These steps help show your reader that you are moving logically from your proposal sentence to the first part of your topic.

2. Use transition words (pages 13–14, pages 86–88, pages 123–125) to help you connect the opening sentence of this paragraph with the proposal.	This makes the move from the proposal to the next paragraph smooth and not too quick.

Step 1. Analyzing Transitions in Paragraph 2.   Column I states a proposal. Decide whether or not you think the sentence in Column II would be effective as the opening sentence of the second paragraph, and tell why in Column III. Base your ideas on Essay Transition Signboard I.

I	*II*	*III*
1. Clipping the wings of a pet parakeet requires great caution.	You must first spend time in calming the bird so it feels relaxed.	_____ _____ _____ _____

I	*II*	*III*

2. I have always respected other people's property.

Once I lived in Great Falls, Montana.

_____
_____
_____
_____

3. My father has always been a friend to me.

As a boy my main love was for sports, especially baseball, and my father helped me learn the game.

_____
_____
_____

Step 2. More on Paragraph 2 Transitions.   Comment on the opening sentence of paragraph 2 in the student essays on pages 244–246.

Step 3. Your Own Opener for Paragraph 2.   For any three proposals in Step 1, page 217, write your own opening sentence for the second paragraph of an essay.

ESSAY TRANSITION SIGNBOARD II: FIRST SENTENCE OF PARAGRAPH 3

What to Do

1. Refer to the main idea of the previous paragraph (paragraph 2),
   or
   refer to the last event, instance, or proof you discussed in paragraph 2.

2. Tell what part of the proposal you intend to discuss in the paragraph by
   a. repeating the second aspect if you have mentioned it in the proposal, or
   b. stating for the first time—based upon the suggestion you made in the proposal—the part of the topic you want to discuss in paragraph 3.

Why

to show that paragraph 3 grows logically from paragraph 2,
   or
to tie together the two body paragraphs, both of which develop your proposal

to remind the reader of the whole topic of the essay

to let the reader know exactly what paragraph 3 will contain

to remind you, the writer, to stick to the topic that you stated in the proposal

Hint: 1. Coordination (pages 17–20) and subordination (pages 89–95) are especially effective in opening sentences of paragraph 3.
2. Use transitional expressions (pages 13–14, pages 86–88, and pages 123–125) as needed.

Step 4. Openers for Paragraph 3.   Read the opening sentence of paragraph 3 in each of the essays on pages 244–246. Which part of the sentence refers to the previous paragraph? Which part announces the topic of the paragraph to follow?

ESSAY TRANSITION SIGNBOARD III: FIRST SENTENCE OF THE CONCLUSION

What to Do	*Why*
1. Make some reference to the main idea of the previous paragraph (paragraph 3), or refer back to the last event, instance, or proof you discussed in paragraph 3.	to show that paragraph 4 grows logically from paragraph 3 to tie paragraph 3 more closely to the conclusion you will start to develop
2. Refer to something you wrote in the introduction (see pages 219–223).	to remind the reader about how your whole idea started
a. Pick up the idea of the proposal.	
b. Pick up a point from the background material you may have given.	to help you begin writing the conclusion, which may be based upon one of the suggestions you made in the introduction
c. Repeat why you felt your subject was important.	
d. Refer to any questions you may have asked.	
e. Refer to any quotation you may have used.	to help you make sure that the introduction is an important part of your essay
f. Pick up the idea of the story you may have told in the introduction.	
g. Refer to your title.	

Step 5. First Sentence in Conclusion. Read and discuss the opening sentence of the conclusion in each of the essays named below.

1. "The Gloom Room," pages 214–215
2. "Practice in the High School Gym," pages 245–246
3. "Memories of the Australian Bush," pages 244–245

Expanding Sentences and Changing Word Order

The words in the chart below all help show relationships between ideas and objects in sentences. Each word can introduce a word group that tells where, when, or how things happen.

WORDS THAT SHOW WHERE, WHEN, AND HOW (PREPOSITIONS)

about	except	within	between
by	under	beside	below
beneath	onto	since	upon
inside	at	as to	by means of
above	across	toward	through
for	on	at	along with

over	over	beyond	because of
outside	into	up	by way of
along	after	before	on account of
among	to	like	in spite of
of	with	below	in front of

In this sentence

An old man hobbled away.

notice how the word groups in italics expand its meaning:

A

An old man hobbled away *down the street.* The words *down the street* show where the old man hobbled.

An old man hobbled away *on shaking legs.* The words *on shaking legs* tell how he hobbled.

An old man hobbled away *before noon.* The words *before noon* tell when he hobbled.

Using word groups that tell *where, when,* or *how* in various sentence positions helps improve your sentence variety. You can shift the word group from the end to the beginning of the sentence:

B

Down the street an old man hobbled away.

On shaking legs an old man hobbled away.

Before noon an old man hobbled away.

You can also use the word group within the sentence:

C

An old man *down the street* hobbled away.

An old man *on shaking legs* hobbled away.

An old man *before noon* hobbled away.

You can use two or more word groups to expand meaning even further:

D

Down the street an old man hobbled away *on shaking legs.*

Before noon an old man *on shaking legs* hobbled away *down the street.*

Of course, you cannot simply insert the word group anywhere you'd like to in the sentence. It might not make sense, or it might not sound right to you. Also, by shifting a word group you might be changing even very slightly the meaning you had intended. For example, the first sentence in A, above, says that the man hobbled down the street. In C, the first sentence says that the man was already down the street when he hobbled away. In B, you could argue that either of those two meanings worked in the first sentence. The differences are minor, certainly; but there are differences.

Step 1. Expanding Sentences.   Select word groups from those given below and use them to expand the sentences sensibly. Use the word groups in sentence positions that you think work best for the intended meaning. Look at the example.

across the river	below the oak tree
on the lawn	at once
along the highway	with a bright smile
at noon	by five o'clock
in a sad voice	by means of courage

1. A brilliant sun had flooded the fields.

   a brilliant sun had flooded the fields at noon across the river.

2. Two children watched a spotted terrier quietly.

   _____

3. Suddenly he spoke.

   _____

4. She leaped overboard and saved the crying infant.

   _____

5. Rumbling noisily a long black train raced away.

   _____

Step 2. Changing Word Order.   Using the expanded sentences you wrote in Step 1 above, rewrite them so you shift the word group that tells where, when, or how to different sentence positions. Try for at least two new sentences for each. Look at the example. Use your own paper.

at noon a brilliant sun had flooded the fields across the river.
across the river a brilliant sun at noon had flooded the fields.

SOLVING PROBLEMS IN WRITING

Showing Possession with Nouns

a. It is the *car of the man.*
b. It is the *car belonging to the man.*
c. It is the *man's car.*

In sentence *a,* the car belongs to the man. Ownership is shown with the words *of the man.* The car is owned. The man owns it.

In sentence *b,* the car belongs to the man. Ownership is shown with the words *belonging to the man.* The car is owned. The man owns it.

In sentence *c,* the car belongs to the man. Ownership is shown by using an apostrophe s (*'s*) after the word that tells who owns the thing. The car is still being owned. The man still owns it. But in this sentence the owner is named *before* the thing that he owns. And the only way we know the owner is through the apostrophe *s.*

[owner]
It is the man's car.
[thing owned]

Sentence *a* sounds clumsy and unnatural. You would rarely say or write such a sentence. Sentence *b* is more natural, but it is wordy.

Sentence *c* is the most convenient and most usual way of indicating ownership. When we speak of *possession,* it is usually this form of showing ownership that we mean. And, because of the misunderstood apostrophe, this method often causes many difficulties.

As you practice with possession, keep in mind that ownership involves two separate ideas:

1. Somebody or something is the owner. That word will contain an apostrophe.
2. Somebody or something is being owned. That word usually comes soon after the word with the apostrophe.

Step 1. Owner and Owned. In each sentence below, circle the word that indicates who or what owns or possesses something. Put an X over the word that shows what (or who) is being owned.

Example:

       X   X
The (child's) toy fell into (Mother's) waiting arms.

1. Aunt Linda's chair collapsed in front of a neighbor's eyes.
2. Dr. Asher's patients asked whether her nurse was a friend's sister.

HOW NOT TO USE APOSTROPHES

Do not use apostrophes to show plurals. Form plurals by adding *-s* or *-es,* or by any one of the special methods explained on pages 104–107.

For example, a familiar error is one like this:

The store sells pencil's and paper's.

If an apostrophe *s* is used at the end of a word, it means that the word owns something. What, according to the sentence, do the pencil and the paper possess?

Nothing belongs to either of the two words written with apostrophes. The student who wrote the sentence wants only to indicate more than one pencil and more than one paper, so the sentence should be:

The store sells pencils and papers.

There is a minor exception, one case in which you do use an apostrophe to show plural. When you write numbers, letters, or symbols and you need to pluralize them, you use an apostrophe. (For example: "The word *membership* has two *m*'s.") However, this use is rare enough for you not to worry about but to remember instead that apostrophes do *not* usually indicate plurals.

Step 2. Spotting Wrong Possession.   Correct any incorrect use of possession in each of these sentences by changing the word to its proper plural form.

1. It cost's too much to buy doll's at toy store's these day's.
2. The heroe's of the movie had children's view's of life's problems'.
3. Her mother's friend liked the two film's about a child's love for water sports'.

HOW TO FORM POSSESSIVES: TWO SIMPLE REMINDERS

Reminder I for Possession:

If the word that names the owner *does not* end in s, add an apostrophe s ('s)

girl   The girl's dress ripped.
[apostrophe s   [This is owned by the *girl*.]
added to
girl]

senator   The senator's campaign failed.
[apostrophe s   [This is owned by the senator.]
added to *senator*]

Hint for Reminder I: It does not matter if the word is plural or singular. If the word does not end in s, add an apostrophe s.

This word is plural, ⟶ *men*   The men's cars crashed.
even though it does   [apostrophe s   [These are owned
not end in s: added to men]   by the men.]

Step 3. Possession Reminder I in Sentences.   Change the words below so that they indicate ownership. Then write your own brief sentence to use the word correctly.

Example: city   *city's*
The city's roads are crowded on weekend mornings.

1. Mr. Chan _____ _____

2. children   _____   _____

3. woman   _____   _____

4. child   _____   _____

5. women   _____   _____

Reminder II for Possession:

If the word that names the owner *does* end in *s*, add only an apostrophe (').

boys   The boys' bicycles broke.

        [an apostrophe   [These are owned
        added to *boys*]   by the boys.]

governors   The governors' meeting ended when the leader fainted.

          [an apostrophe   [This is owned by
          added to   the *governors*.]
          governors]

Hint for Reminder II: It does not matter if the word is plural or singular. If the word ends in *s*, add only an apostrophe.

This word is singular: ⟶ *Doris*   Doris' trip was canceled.

it ends in *s*.   [apostrophe   [This is owned
                           added to   by Doris.]
                           Doris]

See page 232 for an alternate method of showing possession for *names* that end in *s*.

Step 4. Possession Reminder II in Sentences. Add apostrophes to the words below so that they indicate ownership. Then write your own brief sentence to use the word correctly.

Example: nurses *nurses' The nurses' caps flew away.*

1. students   _____   _____

2. Mrs. Bernas   _____   _____

3. drivers   _____   _____

4. Nikos   _____   _____

5. ladies   _____   _____

FOUR SPECIAL CASES WITH POSSESSION

I. *Compound Words or Word Combinations:* Only the last word shows possession.

compound word: brother-in-law. My brother-in-law's cat sleeps all day.

                     [apostrophe *s* to show possession]

combination of words that name one thing: secretary of state. A secretary of state's position is important.

[apostrophe *s* to
show possession]

II. *Time and Money Words:* Words that indicate time values, in certain uses, are said to show ownership.

hour   One hour's rest is too much.

[This word is thought of as
"possessing" the rest.]

[apostrophe *s* added
to *hour* (Reminder I)]

minutes   Five minutes' rest is all you need.

[apostrophe added
to *minutes* (Reminder II)]

Words that indicate money value, in certain uses, are said to show owner-ship.

[apostrophe *s* added
to *quarter* (Reminder I)]

quarter   A quarter's worth of apples will not feed many children.

[This word is thought of as
"possessing" the worth.]

dollars   He bought three dollars' worth of chocolate.

[apostrophe added to
dollars (Reminder II)]

III. *Two People as Owners:* When both people are thought to be equal owners of the same thing, only the last word shows possession.

   McGraw-Hill's textbooks
   Standard & Poor's Index

   If two people own things individually, show possession for both words.

   Harry's and Jerome's cars crashed.

IV. *Pronouns and Ownership:* Pronouns never have apostrophes to show pos-session.

his book	*not*	his' book
That is *hers.*	*not*	hers' or her's
The pen is *yours.*	*not*	yours' or your's
Those are *ours.*	*not*	ours' or our's
Is it *theirs?*	*not*	theirs' or their's
The cat hurt *its* paw.	*not*	it's or its'

Hint: Look at the mirror words, pages 21–24.

Step 5. Practice with Special Possessives.   Underline the correct words in the parentheses.

1. In an (hour's, hours') time, (Carlos' and Maria's, Carlos and Maria's) house will be up for sale, but (their's, theirs) is not an attractive place.
2. The (editor in chief, editor in chiefs, editor in chief's) comment was, "In three (days, day's, days') time this office will no longer be (mine, mines, mine's)."
3. When (Nora and Aldo, Nora's and Aldo's, Nora and Aldo's) car slowed, they put in two (dollars, dollar's, dollars') worth of gasoline.

> **REVIEW: IF YOU THINK A WORD NEEDS AN APOSTROPHE BECAUSE IT SHOWS POSSESSION:**
>
> 1. See if you can figure out what is being owned.
> 2. See if the word in which you want to use an apostrophe is the owner of something. Usually, the thing owned appears in the sentence soon after the owner.
>
>   *Exceptions:*   It is David's.
>   We ate at Carl's.
>
>   Here the thing owned is not specifically mentioned, but understood.
>
>   David's (book)
>   Carl's (house)
> 3. Sometimes the owner is more than one. Make sure the word shows plural with the right ending.
>   *a.* If the word does not end in *s*, add an apostrophe *s*.
>   *b.* If the word does end in *s*, add only an apostrophe.
>
>   *Example:*   *a.* You want to show that a boy owns books. The word *boy* does not end in *s*. The possessive is shown this way:
>
>   the *boy's* books
>   [Add apostrophe *s*.]
>
>   *b.* You want to show that many boys are the owners of books. The word *boys* ends in *s*. The possessive is shown this way:
>
>   the boys' books
>   [Add apostrophe after *s*.]

Step 6. Adding Possessive Endings.   In the blanks at the ends of the words below, add *s*, *'s*, or simply an apostrophe (') so that the sentence is correct. For some words you need to add nothing.

1. Two women_____ stood on the bridge as a man_____ bicycle swerved

   into a post, denting it_____ surface.

2. The typewriters_____ in Richard Yee_____ office are much newer than

   your_____.

3. Shirley_____ and Jesus_____ children brought toy_____ to school;

   mine_____ brought only a book and two pen_____.

Step 7. Possession Review.   Add apostrophes wherever needed in the sentences below. Numbers in parentheses tell how many apostrophes to use.

1. Its wise to buy a dollars worth of doughnuts. (2)
2. The boss new secretary wanted two weeks pay in advance for Christmas shopping. (2)
3. "The childs books and pens are not expensive, but no one is interested in buying yours," he said. (1)

4. The womens clothes were neither at Iris house nor at Stevens. (3)
5. If its yours take it in a minutes time. (2)
6. My sister-in-laws father works at Davis and Hargoods Department Store. (2)
7. Our neighbors houses were all damaged by the winds of the last storm. (1)
8. Phyllis cat lost its bell so if youre able to get her another, her mother will pay you five dollars. (2)
9. Three hours work a week is no womans idea of full employment! (2)
10. Dickens books were a big hit with ladies as well as with gentlemen. (1)

Parallelism for Logical Expression: Right Form, Right Place

> **WHAT IS PARALLELISM?**
>
> Parts of a sentence with the same function generally need the same form. When you place sentence elements in a series or when you use certain types of connectors in pairs, you must use parallel form. *Parallelism* is a quality of correct sentence structure which balances connected parts by using the same form for ideas joined equally.

Balancing Connected Parts: Keeping the Same Form. Words or word groups in a series must match in form.

Hint: You can often recognize a series by commas and the words *and, but, or, nor.*

The homemaker liked to bake, to sew, and to cook.
[all infinitives]

not

The homemaker liked to bake, to sew, and *cooking.*

We prefer dancing and singing.
[both *-ing* words]

not

We prefer dancing and *to sing.*

[verb]   [verb]
We heard that the President spoke to his advisers, contacted reporters, and then made his announcement to the public.
[verb]

not

We heard that the President spoke to his advisers, contacted reporters, and *of his announcement to the public.*

Step 1. Making the Parts Fit.   Add a word group that completes the series with a balanced part.

1. The horse refused to eat or _____.

2. José likes swimming, diving, and _____.

3. The speaker praised the candidate, shook her hand, and _____

   _____

Balancing Connected Parts: Repeating the Series Opener.   Often you need to repeat for each part of the series the first word in the opening item of the series. The sentences on the right are clearer because they repeat the opening word.

Not

They approved his plan because it was logical and it promised to succeed.

He spoke out for the party, for its leaders, but not its principles.

But

They approved his plan *because* it was logical and *because* it promised to succeed.

He spoke out *for* the party, *for* its leaders, but not *for* its principles.

SOME SERIES OPENERS THAT OFTEN NEED REPEATING
because, for, of, by, to, at   that, so that, a (an), who, which, could

---

Step 2. Balance through Repetition.   Rewrite the incorrect underlined portion in each sentence so that it balances with the rest of the series.

1. The coach announced that athletes need special diets, that sweets add needless fat and calories, and <u>we should avoid chocolates at all costs.</u>

   that we should avoid chocolates at all costs.

2. For this course you need a textbook, <u>lab</u> manual, and <u>dissecting</u> kit.

   _____

3. He chose to withdraw his money from the bank, <u>place</u> it in a steel box, and <u>hide</u> the box under his bed. _____

   _____

4. Tomorrow we should put on our bathing suits and <u>go</u> <u>to</u> Lake Louise.

   _____

5. The governor is a woman <u>of</u> <u>talent</u> and who understands state problems.

   _____

Balancing Connected Parts: Paired Words and Matching Forms. A special effect of balance in sentences comes about through certain connectors that work in pairs. These paired connectors must be followed by words that have the same form. In the sentences below, connectors are in boldface. X's appear over words that do not match in form. Underlined words show matching forms.

The registrar is **either** working at his desk **or** visiting the dean.

not

xxxxxxxxxxxxxxxxxxxx
The registrar is **either** working at his desk **or** on a visit with the dean.

I wondered **whether** to make the telephone call **or** to see her in person.

not

xxxxxxxxxxxx
I wondered **whether** I should make the telephone call **or** to see her in person.

Words that Work in Pairs:

either . . . or	whether . . . or
neither . . . nor	not only . . . but also
both . . . and	if . . . or

Step 3. Paired Words and Forms that Match. Add a word group to each sentence below, making sure what you add matches the underlined segment.

Example:

1. We saw not only all the movies he directed,

   but also the television commercials he wrote.

2. You either should use the pliers or

   _____

3. The wind is both howling through the trees and

   _____

Step 4. Balanced Sentence Ideas: More Practice. The sentences below contain errors in parallelism like those explained in the previous pages. On separate paper, rewrite the sentences so that they are correct.

1. Titian is a painter of great skill and who uses color in dramatic ways.
2. She not only works every weekday but also is working nights.
3. On Saturdays I like visiting my aunt, taking her to the shops downtown, and to help her buy food or clothing.
4. She told him either to lower his voice or that he would have to leave immediately.

5. He enjoyed the movie for its ideas on modern life but not the photography; most, he liked the scene between a business executive and elevator operator.

Descriptive Words in the Proper Place

Words or word groups must stand as close as possible to whatever they aim to describe. Words like *only, just, even, almost, hardly*—depending upon where they are placed in the sentence—affect the meaning that the writer wishes. Look at the word *just* in five different places in the same sentence below and examine the explanation of the meanings.

Just he suggested that we leave early.
(This means he was the only one who spoke.)

He *just* suggested that we leave early.
(This means that he merely told of one idea. It also means that he made the suggestion a short while ago.)

He suggested *just* that we leave early.
(This means that he made no other suggestion.)

He suggested that *just* we leave early.
(This means that he meant nobody else should leave early.)

He suggested that we *just* leave early.
(This means that he felt we should do nothing else but leave early.)

Words placed too far from the words they describe (*modify*) often create confusing sentences. *Misplaced modifiers* are words or word groups that, because of faulty placement, do not describe the words they intend to describe. (See also pages 184–185.)

Our neighbor sold dresses to my sister without buttons.
(The *sister* has no buttons?)

At the age of five the doctor administered a smallpox vaccination to me.
(The *doctor* was five years old?)

I watched as an old car was pulled down the street that had a flat tire.
(The *street* had a flat tire?)

Here are the sentences with the describing words in the proper places.

[This word group describes *dresses:* put it close to what it describes.]

1. Our neighbor sold dresses *without buttons* to my sister.

[This word group describes *me:* put it close to what it describes.]

2. The doctor administered a smallpox vaccination to me *at the age of five.*
3. I watched as an old car *that had a flat tire* was pulled down the street.

[This word group describes *car:* put it close to what it describes.]

Step 1. Explaining Placement. Discuss the meanings created by the italicized words in the sentences below.

1. During the exam the professor told us *only* to sit two seats apart.
2. During the exam the professor *only* told us to sit two seats apart.
3. During the exam the professor told *only* us to sit two seats apart.
4. During the exam *only* the professor told us to sit two seats apart.
5. During the exam *only,* the professor told us to sit two seats apart.

Step 2. In the Right Places. Add the italicized word group in the right place in the sentence so that it expresses a logical and clear idea. Rewrite the sentences in the space provided. You may want to rearrange words.

1. *with a loud cry*

   A blue jay stood in the backyard oak. _____

   _____

2. *that swam at the top of the bowl*

   The goldfish made sucking noises at the children. _____

   _____

3. *last year*

   In history class I did not see why the settlers struggled westward in

   covered wagons to cross the desert. _____

   _____

4. *in hot water*

   Elvin washed the laundry for his neighbor. _____

   _____

Step 3. Changing Faulty Placement. In the sentences below, words or word groups do not appear close enough to the words they describe. On your own paper rewrite each sentence by putting the words in their proper places. If the sentence is correct, mark it *C*.

1. They only sleep late on Sundays.
2. We saw a giraffe in the Barcelona Zoo that had a long, long neck and sad eyes.
3. Mr. Jones is a handsome man; he has a wide forehead, a straight nose, and long brown hair with glasses.
4. We hung wallpaper in the room that was easy to apply.
5. Swiftly the fire raced through the shopping mall that stood on the outskirts of town.

WRITING THE ESSAY

Select some process you can command, and explain it in a clear essay that takes into account the principles you have been exploring in this chapter.

Learning from Other Students

Step 1. Two "How-to" Essays. Read the following samples by students and answer the questions that follow their essays.

Ironing for Food

I have never doubted the usefulness of an iron. It presses crisp pleats into my jeans and eliminates networks of tiny wrinkles in blouses I have jammed into my closet. Since coming to Penn State, however, I found that an iron is not only useful as a piece of laundry equipment but also as a fantastic cooking appliance for a dormitory room. University regulations prohibit the use of hot plates, ovens, or grills. So, when one of my cravings aroused me, I decided to experiment with my iron. Since that time I have become an expert at "iron cooking," my specialty being toasted cheese sandwiches.

When the urge for one of them strikes me, I convert my dorm room into a kitchen. I dig through the shoes and boxes at the bottom of my closet and resurrect my iron. Since I do not own a portable ironing board, I improvise. I drag my footlocker out from under my bed and place it in the center of the floor. My white bath towel serves as the cover. At the bathroom sink I fill the steam chamber of the iron with water. Examining the battered cord for exposed wires, I plug it into the outlet closest to my makeshift ironing board and turn the small black dial on the handle to the wool setting. Laying the iron down on the towel to heat, I gather ingredients for my sandwich. From our refrigerator I collect the cheese slices, bread, and pats of butter that my roommate and I smuggled out of Redifer Dining Hall. I grab a knife and a roll of aluminum foil out of my bolster cupboard and spread the supplies out on my desk.

Preliminary preparations over, I concoct my special toasted cheese sandwich. I select two slices of bread, and butter both sides of them lightly, careful not to tear holes in the bread with the knife. Melted cheese drips out of any holes in the finished sandwich and makes a gooey mess. Once I butter the bread, I tear off about one foot from the roll of foil and place it shiny side down on the top of my desk. On the foil I lay one slice of buttered bread, then two slices of cheese on it, topping these with the second piece of bread. Then, I wrap the sandwich in the foil. Crimping its edges tightly, I tear off another piece of foil and cover my sandwich with it. Secured between two shields of armor, my creation awaits the iron. I put the sandwich gently on my ironing board, and with one smooth motion I pick up the iron and touch it to the foil. Steam pours out and hisses angrily as I move the iron back and forth without pressure. (Too much pressure crushes the bread.) It takes only three minutes to grill one side; afterwards I remove the iron and wait for the steam to clear. With a washcloth potholder I flip the sandwich over and iron the other side. When the foil cools slightly, I peel it away, always burning my fingers despite my potholder. The aroma of melted cheese and warm bread pours into the room. Beneath the crisp toast melted cheese peeks out. For me, heaven is seconds away.

Using my iron, I can prepare delicious sandwiches in fewer than ten minutes, and I can satisfy my late night cravings or can escape dining hall meals with my simple technique. But, more important, here in the midst of my college education where my teachers are cramming acres of information into my brain, I have learned a little something on my own to meet my needs at the moment. I do not expect to make a career of "iron cooking"; and I am sure that my knowledge and skill will have no long-range benefits for humanity. Still, learning takes place in unexpected ways. A professor's formal lectures, as important as they are, can never replace good old necessity as the best teacher.

—Stacy Kissenger

Picking Pears

The day starts when I rise at four in the morning. Dawn has not yet broken over Kibbutz Ein Zurim. Still, the members of this Israeli commune are beginning their tasks for the day. Today, the picking of pears awaits me; inexperienced, I am both excited and worried about the job.

Preparing for it takes some time. I fumble in the darkness, finding my closet. The door creaks as I open it, and I grab my yellow T-shirt, my gray socks and slacks, and my blue sunhat. Sitting back on my bed, I dress expectantly. As I slide open the front door to go outside, the hall light stings my eyes. Then into the chill morning I stroll, ready to meet my companions and to start the day's work. I pass the bungalows of other workers as crickets murmur their sounds. Two lizards chase each other while the sun makes its way over the desert sky. As I hop onto the old bus hooked up to a tractor, its mustiness makes me cough. Around me my companions slump on the hard leather seats, resting weary heads on the window sills in last minute efforts at sleep. But the sudden, grinding sound of the tractor ends the morning's silence as we make our way down bumpy dirt roads to the pear field and our coming chores.

By the time we reach it, everyone is fully awake. We leave the bus and each of us receives a sturdy plastic bucket with a steel hook on the handle, a steel or a wooden ladder, and a small wooden square with a circle cut out in the middle. Our leader Danny instructs the group in Hebrew on which pear trees to pick. "We are to pick the fifth row of pears and when we are finished to go on to the sixth," Renee repeats in English. I follow the group to the fifth row and directly against a tree I place my ladder so its legs hit the dirt sturdily. I climb up among the massive trees with my bucket and square. Pulling one of the leafy branches downward, I hang the bucket on it with the hook. With my left hand I grab another branch full of pears and pull it closer to me. Raising my right hand, I try to slip a pear through the hole in the wooden square. The pear does not fit; that means it is big enough for picking. I give this test to each pear. If it is ripe enough, I grasp it by the bottom, lift it upward, and give it a sharp snap. If I do not do it this way, the pear might break at the bottom of the stem, and that would make the fruit unsalable. To avoid bruises further, I do not drop it into the bucket; instead, I place the pear down very carefully. When my bucket fills up, I remove it from the branch and step down the ladder. A few feet away I tenderly place the pears in a huge wooden crate. When I return to my ladder,

I see that all the pears on my tree have been picked. I grasp the ladder on both sides, tilt it horizontally, lift it, and lean it on my shoulder. Not far away, another tree needs picking, and I dig the legs of my ladder into the dirt close to the trunk. Once again I climb up to repeat the procedure.

For Kibbutz life in Israel everyone works equally. Both regular commune members and volunteers like me plant the fields and harvest the crops. Even the leaders work with us, the sun beating down on all our backs together. This group effort helps us tolerate our job. We join in songs, or we talk to our neighbors on nearby ladders. At breaks, given every two hours, we rest together on crates as we joke, gulp down water, brush off the dust on our clothing. I have a wonderful feeling of pride in this work, a feeling that comes from my playing a part in a large and important task. Too often we look at the work we do as single efforts involving ourselves alone, but I am learning that when there is a strong spirit among people, it is easy to accomplish even the most unpleasant chores.

—Myra Grossman

1. What, according to the proposal sentences, does each essay intend to show?
2. One of these essays explains a process that someone could easily duplicate; the other essay is more an explanation of how something is done, an effort to show a procedure without expecting the reader to try to do it. Which is which?
3. In each essay which words in the opening sentence of paragraph 2 help make a transition from paragraph 1? Which words in the opening sentence of paragraph 3 help connect it to paragraph 2?
4. Which details in the essays do you find most original and most clear? Find appeals to the sense of sight (color and action), sound, touch, and smell.
5. Myra Grossman's theme is a personal narrative that serves to show how a process is performed. Is her approach successful? Why?
6. For what kind of audience does each writer intend her process? How can you tell?
7. Discuss the conclusions in both essays. Do they summarize the main point of the essay? In which sentences do you find summaries? What else do the conclusions here do?

Some Topics to Think About

You might find these possible topic ideas helpful as you consider various processes and how to approach them during your prewriting. More suggested topics appear on page 258.

1. how to baby-sit
2. how to tune an engine
3. how to shovel a walk
4. how to milk a cow
5. how to take notes in Professor _____'s class
6. how to make ice cream
7. how to ride a horse

8. how Lincoln was shot
9. how a steam engine works
10. how to pick up a girl (boy)
11. how drug addiction works in the body
12. how a computer works
13. how to play soccer
14. how to sell clothing
15. how to pass English
16. how to wait on tables
17. how to play stick ball
18. how championship swimmers (boxers, gymnasts) train
19. how to make chili con carne
20. how to stop poverty
21. how to hunt big game
22. how bees make honey
23. how to ready soil for planting
24. how to camp out
25. how cheese is made

Prewriting: Making a List

Because completeness and sequence of steps are so important in a process paper, a helpful prewriting activity calls for making a list. Simply write down all the possible steps you can think of, steps required in the process you want to write about. Don't worry about whether you are repeating yourself or whether or not you have put in things that don't belong or have left out things that do belong. Just keep writing and letting thoughts develop. The point here is to get down on paper, before you attempt a draft, as much raw material as possible. And don't worry about spelling or other errors in mechanics. At this stage they are unimportant.

Once you have your list, look it over. If you've left lots of space between entries, you'll have room to add any steps or details you may have left out. You might want to rearrange some steps or to group some together logically. Little by little, the shape of your essay will suggest itself. Certain steps you'll describe in the first body paragraph because they fit together there sensibly. Other steps you will develop in the second body paragraph. Using your list and the changes you've made with it, you can then move on to your rough draft.

Look at the list below, prepared for an essay on growing roses.

Topic: planting a rose garden
1. piece of earth 15′X 5′
2. turn soil and rake it (tell them to watch out for rocks)
3. have 8-10 different rose bushes (point about variety)

4. treat soil with peat or compost or manure — lime too

5. work soil to depth of 2′

6. dig hole 1½ times as big as root ball (watch out for bud and root joint: DEFINE!)

7. cover roots with soil and water right away

8. pine bark mulch keeps weeds away

9. prevent diseases with early treatment for aphids and black spot

10. spray or dust weekly during growing season

11. feed every four weeks

12. stop feeding in mid-August

13. to protect plants against cold weather let rose flowers mature into hips

14. mulch base of plant heavily in fall

15. prune only in early spring — not fall

        —Lee Bowen

Step 1. Understanding the List. Discuss the answers to these questions about Lee Bowen's list. Or, write your responses on separate paper as your instructor suggests.

1. The announced topic is "planting a rose garden," but all the points Lee Bowen has written on his list suggest a more expanded topic. How might you restate his topic so that it allows him to deal with most of the steps he states on his list? What thesis sentence might you write as a result of that topic? On the other hand, if the writer wanted to stay with his an-

nounced topic, "planting a rose garden," what steps would you suggest he leave out?

2. Notice the little note the writer made for himself in item 2 on the list. How will the note help him expand details? What other messages has he written to himself?

3. In item 6 the writer reminds himself to define "bud and root joint." Why does Lee Bowen want to define this term? How does his wish to define it suggest the audience he wants to write for? What other words do you think he should define for that audience?

4. The items on the rough list suggest one possible grouping of steps into three categories: readying the soil, planting the bushes, caring for the new plants. If you were rewriting this list before you did your first draft, which points would you group in each of those categories? How could the grouping help you plan the body paragraphs of the essay?

Step 2. Prewriting: Making Your Own Rough List. Select a topic you think you could develop into an essay that explains a process. Then, using Lee Bowen's list as an example, on separate paper prepare your own rough list of steps the process suggests. At first, list everything that comes to mind. Skip lines between items. Later, go back to add steps or to take them away. You might want to group steps together in broad categories, as question 4 in Step 1 above suggests.

A Checklist for Your Essay on Process

As you prepare your list and do other prewriting, as you do your first and later drafts, and before you write your final copy, use this checklist so that you follow as many of the suggestions as possible. After you prepare your manuscript to hand in to your instructor, fill in the checklist and submit it with your theme.

1. Did I spend time considering the topic? Did I follow some prewriting _____ activity that works well for me? (See pages 34–35.)

2. Did I make a list of the steps in the process and then change and regroup _____ the steps in the list?

3. Did I write a rough draft and any other needed drafts before making my _____ final copy? Did I make changes in my rough drafts so that I expressed thoughts clearly and smoothly?

4. Did I write a proposal sentence that defines my topic clearly and that _____ allows me to develop two aspects of it, one in each of my body paragraphs? (See pages 216–219.)

5. Does my introduction provide a strong beginning for my essay? Does _____ my conclusion close off my point successfully?

6. Did I use transitions to tie together paragraphs one and two? two and _____ three? three and four?

7. Did I use adequate detail? If I wrote from personal experience, did I use _____ images of color, sound, action, smell, and touch? If not, did I use statistics, cases, quotations, or paraphrases as supporting detail?

8. Did I experiment with sentence structure? Did I try for one or two sen- _____
   tences with changed word order like those explained in this chapter?
   (See pages 269–271.)
9. Did I define my audience as clearly and as precisely as I could? The _____
   audience I intend this essay for is:

   _____

10. Did I try to use words from the new vocabulary on page 257? _____
11. Did I take care to include all the steps my audience needs to understand _____
    the process? Did I leave out any unnecessary steps? Did I pay special
    attention to the sequence of the steps, making sure that I discussed
    them in the right order?
12. After making changes in my drafts for clarity and smoothness, did I _____
    check my draft over by proofreading carefully for my usual mistakes?
    Did I check especially for errors in word placement and in the use of
    apostrophes?
13. Did I use a dictionary for any words whose spellings troubled me? _____
14. Did I write a strong title? _____
15. Did I read the sample themes on pages 282–284 to help me see how _____
    other students explained processes clearly?

THE PROFESSIONALS SPEAK

Among the popular forms of current nonfiction are how-to books in which
writers explain processes covering techniques for everything from improving one's life-style to flattening one's stomach. Here from *The Inner Game
of Tennis,* a best-selling book on the mental elements in successful tennis
playing, is an excerpt about how to change your stroke.

SOME WORDS TO KNOW BEFORE YOU READ

limber: loose
groove: pattern
tactile: involving a sensation of touch
inhibiting: holding back
Self 1: aspect of your personality, according to the author, that criticizes and judges
    all your actions

Making a Change in Stroke, Step by Step

Where do you want to start? What part of your game needs attention? It is not always the stroke that you judge as worst which is the most ready for change. It is
good to pick the stroke you most *want* to change. Let the stroke tell you if it wants
to change. When you want to change what is ready to change, then the process
flows.

For example, let's assume it is your serve that you decide to focus your attention on. The first step is to forget all the ideas you may have in your mind about what is wrong with it as it is. Erase all your previous ideas and begin serving without exercising any conscious control over your stroke. Observe your serve freshly, as it is *now*. Let it fall into its own groove for better or worse. Begin to be interested in it and experience it as fully as you can. Notice how you stand and distribute your weight before beginning your motion. Check your grip and the initial position of your racket. Remember, make no corrections; simply observe without interfering.

Next, get in touch with the rhythm of your serving motion. Feel the path of your racket as it describes its swing. Then serve several balls and watch only your wrist motion. Is your wrist limber or tight? Does it have a full snap or something less? Merely watch. Also observe your toss during several serves. Experience your tossing motion. Does the ball go to the same spot each time? Where is that spot? Finally, become aware of your follow-through. Before long you will feel that you know your serve very well as it is presently grooved. You may also be aware of the results of your motion—that is, the number of balls hit into the net, the speed and accuracy of those that reach the far court. Awareness of what *is*, without judgment, is relaxing, and is the best precondition for change.

It is not unlikely that during this observation period some changes have already begun to take place unintentionally. If so, let the process continue. There's nothing wrong with making unconscious changes; you avoid the complication of thinking that *you* made the change, and thus of the need to remind yourself how to do it.

After you have watched and felt your serve for five minutes or so, you may have a strong idea about the particular element of the stroke that needs attention. Ask your serve how it would like to be different. Maybe it wants a more fluid rhythm; maybe it wants more power, or a greater amount of spin. If 90 percent of the balls are going into the net, it's probably quite obvious what needs to change. In any case, let yourself feel the change most desired, then observe a few more serves.

Let's assume that what is desired in your serve is more power. The next step is to program yourself for more power. One way to do this might be to watch the motion of someone who gets a lot of power in his serve. Don't overanalyze; simply absorb what you see and try to feel what he feels. Listen to the sound of the ball after it hits the racket and watch the results. Then take some time to imagine yourself hitting the ball with power, using the stroke which is natural to you. In your mind's eye, picture yourself serving, filling in as much visual and tactile detail as you can. Hear the sound at impact and see the ball speed toward the service court. Hold this mental image for a minute or so, then ask your body to do whatever is necessary to produce the desired power.

Begin serving again, but with no conscious effort to control your stroke. In particular, resist any temptation to try to hit the ball harder. Simply let your serve begin to serve itself. Having asked for more power, just let it happen. See if your body has figured out how to produce what you want. This isn't magic, so give your body a chance to explore the possibilities. But no matter what the results, keep Self 1 out of it. If increased power does not come immediately, don't force it. Trust the process, and let it happen.

If after a short while the serve does not seem to be moving in the direction of increased power, you may want to return to Step 1. Ask yourself what is inhibiting speed. If you don't come up with an answer, you might ask a pro to take a look. Let's say the pro observes that you are not getting a maximum wrist snap at the top of your swing. He may observe that one reason is that you are holding your racket too tightly to allow for flexibility. The habit of holding the racket tightly and swinging with a stiff wrist usually comes from a conscious attempt to hit the ball hard.

So now you are ready for reprogramming. Let your hand experience what it feels like to hold your racket with medium firmness. Show your wrist what it feels like to move in a full, flexible arc. Don't assume you know just because you've been shown; let yourself *feel* the wrist motion intimately. If you are in any doubt, ask the pro to show you the motion, not tell you about it. Then, in your mind's eye imagine your serving motion, this time seeing distinctly your wrist moving from a fully cocked position, reaching up to the sky, then snapping down until it points to the court on the follow-through. After you have fixed the image of your new wrist motion, serve again. Remember that if you *try* to snap your wrist, it will probably tighten, so just let it go. Let it be flexible; allow it to snap in an ever-increasing arc as much as it wants to. Encourage it, but don't force it. Not trying does not mean being limp. Discover for yourself what it *does* mean.

—Timothy Gallwey
The Inner Game of Tennis

Step 1. Understanding "Making a Change in Stroke, Step by Step." Answer these questions.

1. You might say that this discussion deals with three main steps: observation, programming, letting it happen. What are the various elements in each of those steps?
2. What details does the author use to support the steps he offers?
3. What audience do you think Gallwey is aiming for? How do his language and sentence structure serve that audience?
4. What transitions does he use to connect the various parts of this selection?
5. What examples of imagery do you find? Where might Gallwey have appealed more to our senses of sight through color and action, our senses of sound, touch, and smell?
6. This is a selection from a longer work and stands in Gallwey's book as a complete section in a larger chapter. Do you find the ending satisfactory? If you were submitting this selection as a complete essay, what might you include in a final paragraph?

REACHING HIGHER

Step 1. A Process through Observation. Observe someone you know performing some process that the person does easily and well. Take notes on the various steps and on the details you might have to use to explain the process to someone else. After some thought, write an essay in which you describe the process that the person performed.

Step 2. A Process in Visual Terms. Take pictures of someone performing some process that interests you. You'll need to take quite a few shots. After you have the pictures developed, select the important ones, those that could serve to illustrate the major steps in the process. Arrange the steps in an appropriate order. Mount the photographs on heavy paper and write a sentence to accompany each.

Step 3. Adapting to Audiences. After your instructor returns your process essay, and after you have had a chance to correct it fully, consider how your essay would look if you were writing for a completely different audience from the one you aimed at originally. Decide on some other group who might enjoy or benefit from instruction in the process you are teaching. With that group clearly in mind, rewrite your introductory paragraph. How does it compare with your original?

chapter 8

WOMEN IN THE WORLD OF MEN: WRITING A STRONG ARGUMENT

United Nations

INTRODUCTION TO THE USE OF ARGUMENT

Since Susan B. Anthony led the fight for reform in women's rights in the late 1800s, the position of the female in American society has changed sharply. Though there are still those who would deny a woman's right to equal opportunity, the gains are clear and strong. The twentieth-century woman is moving—for some, too quickly, for others, not quickly enough—into a world once thought exclusively for men. Women doctors step through hospital corridors in greater numbers than ever before; the idea of a woman as a top business executive or college president is now accepted, even approved, by most people. And females make up 30 to 40% of America's job force. A survey of graduates with B.B.A.'s at the University of Texas revealed in 1975 that starting salaries for female graduates were higher than those for male graduates. In 1965, the average starting salary for a woman graduate in business was 75% lower than that of a male graduate; ten years later the female's salary was 4% higher. But other studies show that as men and women advance in their jobs, men usually earn more than women doing the same work. Economist Frances Hutner says, "In 1939 women earned 58 percent of what men earned. Twenty years later, in 1959, women earned 59 percent of what men earned. And in 1977, women still earned only 59 percent of what men earned."

Where do you stand on the issue of women's rights? Do you think that men and women are exactly alike and deserve complete equality? Do you think women are different from men and as a result require special treatment? Do you think women are pretty much ignored for the top jobs in our society? Do you think women *should* be ignored for top positions in business and government? This theme assignment asks you to look at your own attitudes toward women in society and their changing position in the twentieth century.

But you will have to be able to support your attitudes in some way as you write your essays. The true test of an opinion is the way in which the writer makes it convincing and believable. Anyone can scream angrily a point of view, but most educated people require solid reasons before accepting opinions. You can convince someone reasonably about your impressions by illustrating those impressions through dramatic experiences in your own personal life. Or you can try to support your opinions with information that you gather from other sources. If you choose that path, you will have to learn how to avoid the faults in reasoning beginners often show when they write essays to persuade people to change their beliefs.

In this chapter you will also learn more about tying together more closely the parts of the essay. You will examine some of the vocabulary of liberation, and you will practice with problems in writing that cause a number of difficulties: the uses of verbs to indicate time correctly.

VOCABULARY

Step 1. Familiar Words in the Women's Struggle. Much of the language of women's liberation includes words like the following. Using your dictionary, write definitions for them.

_____ 1. feminist } [These words identify people
_____ 2. suffragist } who are either for or against the
_____ 3. chauvinist } women's liberation movement.

_____ 4. hormonal } [These words name biological
_____ 5. puberty } ideas related to discussions on
_____ 6. mortality } women's equality]

_____ 7. inferiority }
_____ 8. stereotype } [Women active in the battle for
_____ 9. degradation } equality try to fight these con-
_____ 10. discrimination } ditions.]

Step 2. Matching Meanings. From the list of words in Step 1 write on the blank line the word whose meaning appears alongside.

_____ 1. a person with blind enthusiasm for a cause

_____ 2. condition of being subject to death

_____ 3. fixed ideas based upon oversimplified opinions about people

_____ 4. indicating something poor in quality

_____ 5. condition which lowers dignity or quality

_____ 6. based upon substances given off by the glands in the body

_____ 7. one who believes in the extension of women's activities in social and political life

_____ 8. favoring one person over another because of certain qualities (like sex or race) that should not enter into the act of selection

_____ 9. women who fought for the right to vote in the early 1900s

_____ 10. the stage in human development where the person becomes sexually mature

Step 3. More Words in the Struggle for Equality. Write definitions for the following words. Use a dictionary, if necessary, to write your own clear meanings.

1. oppression _____

2. downtrodden _____

3. prejudice _____

4. emancipation _____

5. activist _____

Step 4. Using Words in Freedom's Fight. From the vocabulary above, write a word that

1. means the state of freedom _____

2. describes someone who works hard for a cause _____
3. names the act of using power over someone in a cruel and unfair way

_____

4. describes people who are kept from advancing and who are ruled over severely, people who are "trampled upon" _____
5. indicates an unfavorable opinion or feeling made before any knowledge

is available _____

Step 5. Words in Your Own Sentences. On separate paper write sentences using any ten words you have learned in this chapter.

BUILDING COMPOSITION SKILLS

Exploring the Topic

Step 1. A Questionnaire on Women. The statements below examine your attitudes on women in our society.

If you agree with the statement completely, put the number 1 in the blank space.

If you agree with the statement to some degree, put the number 2 in the blank space.

If you completely disagree with the statement, put the number 3 in the blank space.

If you have no idea or feeling at all about the statement, put the number 4 in the blank space.

_____ 1. Women should not hold a position of great responsibility because they are much more emotional than men.

_____ 2. Unmarried women are not as happy as married women.

_____ 3. A woman should stay at home to raise her children.

_____ 4. Women make more sensible bosses than men.

_____ 5. Housework does not have to be dull; a woman can find her job in the house creative and rewarding.

_____ 6. The right of abortion is one that all women should be able to use if they want to.

_____ 7. Certain jobs are "women" jobs; certain jobs are "men" jobs.

_____ 8. Women enjoy being treated like little girls and being taken care of by the men who love them.

_____ 9. Supporters of women's liberation will never achieve anything by aggressive speech and actions. All that will happen is that men will stand even more strongly against women's achieving any rights.

_____ 10. If the choice for a job is between a woman whose husband works and a man who must support his family, the job should go to the man.

Step 2. Illustrating Opinions.   Select any statement from the above questionnaire for which you have written a 1 or a 3 in the margin. Discuss your reasons for believing what you do by giving an illustration from your own experience.

Step 3. Woman Talk.   These famous statements on women come from people in our time and in the past. Discuss with the class the one that you think most appropriate in today's world.

1. "The female of the species is more deadly than the male."
   —Rudyard Kipling

2. ". . . the Black movement is primarily concerned with the liberation of Blacks as a class and does not promote women's liberation as a priority. . . . The feminist movement, on the other hand, is concerned with the oppression of women as a class, but is almost totally composed of white females. Thus the Black woman finds herself on the outside of both political entities, in spite of the fact that she is the object of both forms of oppression."
   —Kay Lindsey

3. "While little boys are learning about groups and organizations, as well as the nature of the world outside their homes, little girls are at home, keeping quiet, playing with dolls and dreaming, or helping mother."
   —Germaine Greer

4. "The great question that has never been answered, and which I have not yet been able to answer despite my thirty years of research into the feminine soul, is: What does a woman want?"
   —Sigmund Freud

5. "A girl should not be too intelligent or too good or too highly differentiated in any direction. Like a ready-made garment she should be designed to fit the average man."
   —Emily James Putnam

The Interview: Gathering Your Own Statistics

For a current topic like women's rights, a topic that interests a wide range of people, you can gather ideas and details by interviewing. An interview gives you firsthand experience in collecting and comparing data; by talking to several people, you broaden your sense of the issue. Further, if you have taken notes carefully, you have lots of raw material upon which to draw as you plan and write your essay.

THE INTERVIEW: TIPS FOR GOOD TECHNIQUES

1. Write down questions about the general idea you are investigating. If you choose to interview people about whether or not women should serve in high political offices, you might prepare a list like this one:
   a. Should women get preferred treatment in political offices?
   b. What special qualities, if any, can women bring to high-pressure jobs?
   c. Would a woman make a good president of the United States?
   d. What women in politics do you admire? dislike?
   e. Are there any sex-related qualities that make men or women better suited for certain political jobs? What are those qualities?
2. Good questioning is a real skill. Try to make your questions draw out the answers you want to know.
3. Listen carefully to what people say. Take notes as they speak, eliminating any information that is not important. Be careful to get as much important material as you can as accurately as you can. If someone says "sometimes" or "maybe," make sure that you do not change those remarks into "always" or "definitely."
4. Ask everyone the same questions. That gives you a basis for comparing any differences of opinion.
5. Identify the people who agree to give information to you. Be specific so that in your essay you are able to quote somebody's exact words accurately. Say "Charles Davidson, a freshman at Fairleigh Dickinson, said '. . .'." If you want to present your interviewing results statistically in your essay, you do not need to identify every person you interview. You can say, "Seven out of the ten people I spoke to agreed that . . . ."
6. Write down exact quotations where you can. This requires very careful listening and quick writing. But often the interviewee says something so unusual or so important that you want it down exactly as it is said; then when you write up your findings in an essay, the quote can add liveliness and interest to your own work.
7. If the person you are interviewing is important, take down some details of his or her character and appearance to spark your own presentation of the person's ideas.

Step 1. Practice Interviewing. Select some aspect of women's rights that interests you, and conduct at least five interviews with people in your school or home community. Your instructor may suggest that the class break down into groups so that students can ask each other questions. Follow the tips for good techniques in the chart above.

Clear Reasoning and Evidence

When you relate from your personal experience some moment about a given topic or subject, you are not attempting to *prove* your idea. You merely demonstrate your point in that way. When you seek to argue a point by giving *proofs,* however, you often need more than just a single instance from your life. To try to prove that women are competent as doctors by basing your argument upon one experience you had with one good woman doctor would be unconvincing. For readers to agree with your point of view, you need material that is solid and plentiful, evidence that is believable, reasoning that is not faulty.

The fifteen types of poor reasoning below show some of the more familiar kinds of incorrect evidence students frequently use in essays. Each logic trap is followed by an example and an explanation alongside.

FIFTEEN FAULTS TO FAIL THE ARGUMENT

1. *Don't* give too few instances to prove a point.
   Example: Women cannot be trusted to make decisions when the pressure gets rough. My wife cries as soon as some high-pressure situation arises.

   How could one instance support the point?

2. *Don't* use famous people's names as the sole proof of your point.
   Example: Whitney Lewis, the actor, advertises that camera, so I'm sure it's good.

   How does the mentioning of the name prove that the product is good?

3. *Don't* praise or blame the *people* who state a proof you cite—and then ignore the idea.
   Example: She's such a brilliant scholar that any candidate she supports has to be good.

   Praising the woman's intelligence does not prove that the candidate is a good one.

   He's an atheist. The candidate he supports has to be weak.

   Attacking the man's religious beliefs does not prove that the candidate is a poor one.

4. *Don't* try to prove something by showing that people always believed in a certain thing.
   Example: Women have never been allowed to compete with men in professional sports. Why should we allow it now?

   People may have believed one thing a long time ago. But they can change their minds.

5. *Don't* try to prove something by showing that everyone is doing it.
   Example: Young people all over the world are using marijuana without harm. And many middle-aged people too are joining in the "pot parties" of the drug culture. How harmful can marijuana be?

   So what if everyone does it? How does that prove it is not harmful?

6. *Don't* try to prove something by saying the point over and over again.

Example: Women ought to have the same rights as men. Women's rights are just as important as men's rights, and women should receive the same treatment as men. After all, women have rights, too.

There is no proof here at all, just the same point made again and again.

7. *Don't* use a source to back up an idea unless the source is reliable and an authority.

Example: My brother Jerry says politicians are liars and cheats, and I have always trusted his judgment.

What makes Jerry an authority on politicians?

The president of Apco, a leading oil company, believes that lead in automobile gasoline is really not a polluting agent.

An oil company that has to remove lead from its fuel may have to spend large sums of money. It might be expected to try to disprove lead as a polluter.

8. *Don't* make a comparison that is weak or not true.

Example: I know I can drive a motorcycle. I can ride a bicycle, can't I?

The writer fails to realize that there are many differences between bicycles and motorcycles.

9. *Don't* appeal to a person's prejudices or unreasonable emotions.

Example: Foreign-born people should not be allowed to work at all kinds of jobs. If they are, Americans will be squeezed out of work, and you and I will be out of employment.

This writer tries to arouse the reader by appealing to personal involvement. Where is the proof that readers will lose their jobs to others?

Anyone who opposes Governor Badley's reelection is anti-American!

This writer uses a word intended to fire up emotions unreasonably. Instead of real proof, he uses a name that is designed to arouse feelings.

10. *Don't* draw conclusions that do not follow from previous information.

Example: When Astor was president of the union we really made progress. Now that Alterman has taken over, men are losing jobs and getting less and less overtime.

The writer doesn't take into account other factors. There is no proof here that the loss of jobs has anything to do with the new president.

When I went to college, I got all A's and B's. Anyone who wants to can get good grades.

The second sentence doesn't follow from the first because the writer does not take into account individual learning abilities.

11. *Don't* try to prove that someone or something is good or bad only because of associations with other "good" or "bad" things.

Example: How could he be a gangster? He goes to work in the morning, has dinner out with his family on Sundays, and is best friends with the mayor and the principal of of our high school.

This proof of innocence is built by trying to associate a person with good and solid qualities of citizenship. But it does not prove the man is no gangster. If he deals in drugs, what would his friendship with the mayor prove?

Since the dean was found guilty of robbing city funds, surely the president himself must have some illegal dealings too.

This is "guilt by association": The president is not guilty of crimes because one associate is guilty.

12. *Don't* generalize—that is, don't make one fact the source of a broad conclusion. *Don't* state the proof so strongly as to admit no possibilities of exceptions; always leave room for a margin of error.

Example: Women drivers are the worst drivers on the road.

It may be true that some women—like some men—are poor drivers, but this is certainly not true of all of them.

13. *Don't* try to show that if something happened *after* an event, that thing is necessarily a *result* of the event.

Example: Five convicted killers said that when they were younger, they enjoyed watching programs of violence on television. This proves that watching violent actions on the screen can lead to murder.

Did the killers murder *because* they watched violence on television? This might be a contributing factor, but as a proof alone, it is not very solid.

14. *Don't* state your proof in *either-or* terms.

Example: It is no wonder that he failed so many courses. College students go to school or they work; they certainly cannot do both.

What about the people who work only an hour a day, or those who work weekends or summers? This writer suggests that there are only two alternatives when there are many.

15. *Don't* ignore information that contradicts the point you wish to make.

Example: A large number of investigations suggest that legalizing heroin would be a positive step toward controlling drug abuse.

On such a controversial issue, the writer should mention studies that disagree with the statement. Much material is available on the failure of parts of the British system in which drugs have been legalized.

Step 1. Finding Foggy Thinking. Each statement below contains some error in argument such as the ones described above. Discuss the errors the writers make. Then tell how you would correct the statement.

1. Samuel Taylor Coleridge and Edgar Allan Poe both used drugs and still created great works of art. Writers should use some drug if they need stimulation for their work.
2. You mean that you dislike instant coffee? Everyone else likes it.
3. We managed very well all those years without special trade agreements with China. I don't see any reason why we should change now.
4. If foreigners do not like those conditions on the job, let them go back to their own countries to work.
5. Anyone who keeps his hair so long and who wears dungarees and sandals all the time: what could he know about politics?
6. A recent study by WKLO-TV shows no connection between actual violence and violence performed on television programs.
7. That family does not go to church on Sundays. They must all be atheists.
8. Anyone who is a communist has no love for this country, America.

9. Those boys left the party right after the diamond ring was stolen. They must have taken it!
10. How could Burkee's chicken soup be bad? Its tomato sauce, mushroom sauce, and baked beans are delicious.

Step 2. Straight Thinking, Strong Proofs. How would you go about proving or disproving each statement below? Discuss your answers, making sure to avoid the faults in argument you just learned.

1. Women's rights expanded markedly in the 1970s.
2. A father who raises children without the help of a wife does a less efficient job than a mother who raises children without the help of a husband.
3. Women executives in business are more efficient than men executives.
4. The attitude of modern single girls toward sex has not changed in the last ten years.
5. A woman competing with a man in a high-pressure political job would never stand a chance of success.
6. A major problem for women who want to get ahead in business is not men but other women.

Step 3. Proof for Attitudes on Women. Return to the questionnaire in Step 1, pages 295–296. Select any item for which you have written the number 1 or 3, and in the blank lines below show how *you would attempt to prove* your opinion.

Hint: This time do not use personal experience as proof. Plan on using other kinds of details. See crucial questions 2 to 4 on page 315.

_____

_____

_____

_____

MEETING THE OPPOSITION

If you are trying to support an idea that you know not everybody agrees on, you can defend your point of view with details of personal experience, statistics, or quotations. But you should not ignore the issues raised on the other side of the argument. What the opposition (those who disagree with you) believes can give you the content of a good solid paragraph.

> **WHY TO MENTION OPPOSITE OPINIONS**
>
> 1. Your reference to opposite opinions shows that you know what others are saying.
> 2. It shows that you are not purposely overlooking points in order to make your own ideas look stronger.
> 3. It shows that you are fair and that you do not see things in black and white only, that you are willing to consider ideas and points that do not agree with yours.
> 4. It gives you more to write about: you can go on to attack the ideas others have, if you wish.
>
> **Hint:** The introduction is a very good place in any essay to mention the points of view that oppose yours: as you discuss those ideas that do not go along with your own, you build up to your own proposal which states what you believe and what you will try to prove.

Step 1. Seeking the Opposition.   Assume that the proposal in Column I is one that you would try to support in an essay. Write in Column II three *opposing* arguments that others might raise against your point of view.

I

Example:

A. A woman's place is at home with her family.

II
1. *Women are efficient workers.*
2. *Women are creative on the job.*
3. *Some women are psychologically unfit for the dullness of housework.*

B. A woman who rises to the top of a corporation leads a life of excitement and challenge.

1. _____
2. _____
3. _____

C. There are few differences between the way men and women perform as teachers.

1. _____
2. _____
3. _____

D. Women make poorer physicians than men.

1. _____
2. _____
3. _____

Opposing Arguments: Where to Place Them

The introduction is a good place in an essay to mention the points of view that oppose yours. Using the ideas that do not go along with your own, you can build up to a proposal sentence that states what you believe in and what you will try to prove.

In the introduction below notice how the writer discusses opposing arguments. The effect here comes, of course, when the reader finally reaches the proposal sentence. It is only there made apparent that the writer's position is opposite to all the points made so far.

The jogging craze is sweeping the country. Before dawn, at noon, after dusk, men and women everywhere take to the trails and to the streets; in fancy jogging suits or in simple jeans and T-shirts these people are running to improve their health and fitness. Jogging tones the muscles, helps the heart work more efficiently, takes off unwanted poundage. Psychologically runners boast a relaxed life-style, a sense of peace with themselves. But this exercise is probably the worst form of self-torture any human being can inflict upon his mind and body.

But there are other places in the essay where you can explore your opposition.

If you know sound arguments that are raised in opposition to your proposal, you can build one body paragraph around those opposing arguments. Paragraph 2 of your essay can mention a few of the points made by people who disagree with you, and you might show with solid details the evidence these people give for believing what they do. Another possibility, if there are many arguments on the opposition's side, is to state in the second paragraph of your essay as many of the most effective arguments against your position as you possibly can. Then you can write paragraph 3 in one of two ways.

1. Try to disprove the arguments of the opposition. Give details to convince your reader that you are right and that "they" are wrong.
2. Say that the points the opposition raises are good, but that you believe differently. Give details to convince the reader that your points are just as good as the points made by those who oppose you.

On pages 320–323 you can see how opposing arguments serve in a body paragraph.

Step 2. Paragraph Practice: The Opposition in Introductions.   Select any proposal and opposing ideas from Step 1 on page 302. Write a brief introduction which mentions the opposition's points as it builds to the proposal statement. You may change the proposal somewhat. Use separate paper.

Hint: Transitional expressions like *however, but, on the other hand* will help you introduce the proposal.

Step 3. Paragraph Practice: The Opposition in a Body Paragraph.   Select any proposal from Step 1 on page 302 as the proposal of an essay, and write a brief first body paragraph in which you show what arguments could be used against your proposal. Develop just a few arguments with specific details, or mention a number of arguments that are frequently used against the proposal. Use your own paper.

Hint: In this paragraph do not try to prove that the opposition is wrong.

Sentence Combining: Changing Verb Forms to Expand Sentences

You remember from exercises in another chapter how verb parts as sentence openers help you vary your style. You can use verb parts in other positions, too, to connect logically elements in one sentence to another nearby. In some cases, eliminating all or part of a verb helps you unite thoughts. Looking over your early drafts, then, you can tighten sentence structure by manipulating verbs.

Look at this group of sentences:

(A) Charlene slumped in the driver's seat. (B) She gripped the wheel tightly. (C) Her neck was tense. (D) Her eyes were red. (E) She stared angrily through the windshield.

1. You could combine sentences A and B by changing one of the underlined verbs into an -*ing* form and by using it to open a new sentence:

   Slumping in the driver's seat, Charlene gripped the wheel tightly.

   or

   Gripping the wheel tightly, Charlene slumped in the driver's seat.

2. In another kind of combination you could keep the verb in its -*ed* form and combine A and B in this way:

   Slumped in the driver's seat, Charlene gripped the wheel tightly.

3. Sometimes you can drop the verb or part of it and can join what's left of the sentence to a sentence nearby. If you took out the verb *was* from sentence C look at how the rest of it combines with B or A or E:

   Her neck tense, she gripped the wheel tightly.
   Her neck tense, Charlene slumped in the driver's seat.
   She stared angrily through the windshield, her neck tense.

The steps numbered 1, 2, and 3 are especially helpful in allowing you to transform—transform means to change into something else—a series of complete thoughts into one sentence that combines the ideas of the several sentences. Of course, you have to decide which ideas you want to stress so that your new sentence structure emphasizes them. The kind of transformation you do depends upon the meaning you are aiming for. But transforming sentences is valuable because it means, first, that a writer can often use fewer words than otherwise necessary to make a point and, next, that a writer has more options for varying sentence structure.

By using the techniques explained in 1, 2, and 3 to combine a whole series of sentences connected in meaning like those in sentences A through E above, look at just two of the possibilities you have for expanded sentences:

Slumping in the driver's seat (A) and staring angrily through the windshield (E), Charlene gripped the wheel tightly (B), her neck tense (C), her eyes red (D).

Her neck tense (C), her eyes red (D), slumped in the driver's seat (A) and gripping the wheel tightly (B), Charlene stared angrily through the windshield (E).

In each case, before you combine you need to decide which sentence in the group you think is most important, which you want to emphasize. Keep that as the base sentence and use the other sentences, which you change by transforming their verbs, to expand and to modify it.

Hint: Be sure that the verb part you use stands close enough to the word it modifies so that you avoid illogical sentences. Instructions about verb-part *openers* on pages 184–186 go for verb parts used in any sentence positions.

Step 1. Combining Sentences by Transforming Verbs.   Create one complete sentence by combining the sentences in each group. Transform the verb into another form as you saw in the previous examples. You may have to change a noun subject into a pronoun, or vice versa.

Hint: Decide which sentence will be your base sentence; transform the verbs in the surrounding sentences only.

1. A crow sat on the branch of an oak tree. He cawed at the wind. He hopped from branch to branch. His feathers were black as tar. His eyes were small and beady.

   _____

   _____

   _____

2. My husband worked hard in the kitchen. He was sweating. His face was red and hot. He lifted the turkey. He turned it over. He pushed it back into the oven.

   _____

   _____

   _____

3. Feminism works for all people. It encourages equality among the sexes.

It is an important political philosophy for today. It brings people together on the strength of their abilities.

_____

_____

_____

SOLVING PROBLEMS IN WRITING

Verbs as Time Tellers: Using Tense Correctly

Every verb has three main forms called principal parts, and from these all the different tenses are made. The present tense, the past, and the future you usually have little trouble using; but other tenses are not so simple. Look for a moment at the verb *to laugh* and its three main parts. Underneath you will find an explanation of the tense that is made from each part.

TO LAUGH		
I laugh	*II* laughed	*III* laughed
The Present Tense	*The Past Tense*	*Tenses That Show Continuing Action*
They *laugh* too loudly. She *laughs* softly.	I *laughed also.* They *laughed* aloud.	He *has laughed without stopping.* (*This action began in the past, but may go on into the present.*)
The Future Tense They *will laugh* tomorrow. I *shall laugh* too.		She *had laughed* before they arrived. (*This action began in the past but was over before another action in the past.*)
		Before next week she *will have laughed* at all the dull jokes in the book. (*This action will be finished before some definite time in the future.*)

Hint: How to Form Tenses That Show Continuing Action:
1. Always use the third main part of the verb. (You will see later the main parts of many other verbs. These parts are always arranged in the same order as those above.)
2. Always use a helping verb:

has   had   will have
have   shall have

For *most* verbs (like *to laugh*), the principal parts are easy. All you need to know is the infinitive. If you take away the word *to*, you have the first main part of the verb (and you can form the present and future tense). If you add *-d* or *-ed* to the first main part, you have *both* the second and third main parts (and you can form the past tense and all the tenses that show actions that continue). Here are two other examples:

	I	II (add *-ed*)	III (add *-ed*)
to talk	talk	talked	talked
	They talk. She talks. We will talk. I shall talk.	I talked. They talked.	She has talked. They have talked. She had talked. They will have talked.
		(add *-d*)	(add *-d*)
to dance	dance	danced	danced
	They dance. She dances. We will dance. I shall dance.	I danced. They danced.	She has danced. They have danced. She had danced. They will have danced.

Step 1. Writing Main Parts of Verbs. From each infinitive below, make the three main parts in the same way as in the examples *to talk* and *to dance*. Write the verb parts in the columns listed.

	I	II	III
to love	_____	_____	_____
to clean	_____	_____	_____
to whisper	_____	_____	_____
to cook	_____	_____	_____
to inquire	_____	_____	_____

Troublesome Verb Parts

Unfortunately, a number of verbs do not form their parts as easily as the ones above. These verbs—called *irregular* because they are different from the usual—also happen to be among those we use most often, so it is not surprising to hear and to see a number of mistakes with them in spoken and written English. Although the list below does not include *all* the irregular verbs, it tries to indicate those most frequently used incorrectly. The starred verb is not irregular, but it still confuses many writers.

Thirty-Three Headaches: Irregular Verb Parts You Need to Know

I	II	III
Today I	*Yesterday I*	*Frequently I have*
am	was	been
begin	began	begun
break	broke	broken
bring	brought	brought
burst	burst	burst
choose	chose	chosen
come	came	come
do	did	done
drink	drank	drunk
* drown	drowned	drowned
eat	ate	eaten
fly	flew	flown
freeze	froze	frozen
give	gave	given
go	went	gone
know	knew	known
lend	lent	lent
ring	rang	rung
rise	rose	risen
run	ran	run
see	saw	seen
sing	sang	sung
sit	sat	sat
speak	spoke	spoken
steal	stole	stolen
swim	swam	swum
take	took	taken
teach	taught	taught
tear	tore	torn
think	thought	thought
throw	threw	thrown
wear	wore	worn
write	wrote	written

SOME ADVICE IN MAKING TENSES

1. If you can say *now, today, at present* before the verb, select the form from Column 1.

   Example: Now I *take* French.
   Now they will *write* a letter.
   At present she *swims* well.

2. If you can say *yesterday* before the verb, select the form from Column II.

   Example: Yesterday I *wore* a black tie.
                 Yesterday they *swam* at sea.

3. If you can say *frequently* or *often* and one of the helpers (*has, have, had, shall have, will have*) before the verb, select the form from Column III.

   Example: Often I *have done* good work.
                 Frequently they *have stolen* bicycles.

Step 1. Saying Aloud Correct Verb Parts.   Many people do not use verb parts correctly in their writing because the correct forms sound incorrect to the ear. Speak aloud each sentence below so that you learn the sound of the correct verb—no matter how strange it sounds to you.

1. Two balloons *had burst* before the Hallowe'en party *began*.
2. A cat *drowned* in Hyat's Creek yesterday.
3. She *had written* a letter before breakfast.
4. They *have* already *drunk* a case of cola.
5. After the boy *had swum* across the lake, he rested.

Step 2. Correcting Students' Errors.   Cross out any incorrect verb part in the sentences below, which have been spoken or written by college students. Put the correct verb part in the blank space on the left.

_____ 1. I seen him running away.

_____ 2. He gone to the football game.

_____ 3. Was I surprised when he brung those flowers!

_____ 4. She sung "America" in a loud clear voice.

_____ 5. Don't look at me—they done it.

_____ 6. Mary has chose the wallpaper with pretty yellow daisies.

Using *Has* or *Have* with Verbs.   You use *has* or *have* with a verb form from Column III if you want to show an action that started sometime in the past but is still continuing.

She *has laughed* for five minutes.

   [She began in the past but is still laughing now.]

If the action began in the past and ended in the past, use the past tense (Column-II verb form).

She *laughed* for five minutes.

   [She began in the past, but ended before now.]

Step 3. Verbs with *Has* or *Have*.   For each infinitive in parentheses, write the correct form of the verb in the blank space on the left.

Hint: If *has, have, had, will have,* or *shall have* appears before the verb, pick the form from Column III on page 308.

_____   1. The children have (to ring) the doorbell.

_____   2. By this afternoon I will have (to eat) four dozen clams.

_____   and Jim will have (to drink) ten cans of cola.

_____   3. Because Esteban has (to give) his time to repairing the windows, we will all be comfortable this winter.

_____   4. For the past three years a child has (to drown) in the ocean each summer.

_____   5. The class has (to come) to an agreement about the final exam.

Had as Verb Helper.   If a sentence expresses two actions in the past and one of the actions came before the other, the verb that names the earlier action needs *had* as a helper.

The man thought that he *had seen* a ghost.

[This is one past action.]   [This past action came before the man had the thought.]

Step 4. Using *Had* Correctly as Verb Helper.   Complete each sentence below by using *had* with the correct form of the verb in parentheses and any other words you need to complete the thought. Study the example.

(to come)   1. Yesterday we heard that you *had come late to class.*

(to know)   2. Before he moved into the neighborhood, I _____.

(to tear)   3. I arrived too late; she already _____

_____.

(to drink)   4. We saw the sparrow after it _____

_____.

(to rise)   5. Before the rooster crowed, an orange sun _____

_____.

Will Have, Shall Have **with Verbs.**   Use *will have* or *shall have* with a verb part if you want to show that an action will be finished before some definite time in the future.

By tonight, I *will have made* twelve telephone calls.

Hint: In formal writing, *shall* is used only with *I* and *we. Will* is used with any subject.

Step 5. Your Sentences with *Will Have* or *Shall Have.*   Use each of these word groups in a sentence of your own.

shall have spoken   will have taken
will have written   shall have seen
will have swum

Example:

By tomorrow I shall have seen your employer.

Shifting Tenses

When you write, be careful not to switch back and forth unnecessarily from present to past tense. If you are telling about an event that occurred in the past, use the past tense. Look at this sentence:

I saw my friend Thomas and he asks me, "Where are you going?"

Saw is a past-tense verb.
Asks is a present-tense verb and should be replaced by *asked,* a past-tense
    verb.
Are is not incorrect, even though it is in the present tense, because the
    writer is quoting someone's exact words. The correct sentence would be:

I saw my friend Thomas and he asked [*not asks*] me, "Where are you going?"

Step 1. Tense Shifts.   Correct the tense shifts in each sentence below. Write the verbs correctly in the spaces on the left. Write *C* if the sentence is correct.

_____   1. When I noticed him he looks the other way and runs off.

_____   2. I wanted a small pizza, but she carries out a large one and

_____   hands it to me. I decided to keep it.

_____   3. I told him the bench was wet, but he sits down without

_____   listening and then gives a loud yell of anger.

_____   4. After he awakens he prepares breakfast before he showers

_____   and dresses for work.

Some Confusing Verbs

Lie **and** *Lay.*   The words *lie* and *lay* are two different verbs.

To lie means *to rest or to recline.*
To lay means *to put or to place something.*

Here are the three main parts of *to lie* and the tenses that are made from them.

lie	lay	lain
I lie in bed.	He lay down for a nap.	The cat has lain in the
The book lies there un-	She lay there quietly.	driveway for hours.
noticed.		She had lain in bed for
Tomorrow we will lie		hours before the doc-
in the grass.		tor arrived.

Hint: The past tense of *to lie* is the same as the present tense of *to lay.* That is the source of much of the confusion.

The *-ing* form of *to lie* is *lying.*

The flowers *are lying* on the table.
A cat *is lying* in the yard.

Here are the three main parts of *to lay* and the tenses that are made from them.

lay	laid	laid
I lay the pencil on the	The cowboy laid his	She should have laid
desk.	gun on the bar.	the carpet on the
The child usually lays		hallway floor.
his head on a small		After Lynn had laid out
pillow.		the map, directions
		were easier to follow.

Hint: There must always appear after the word *lay* or any of its forms the thing that is being put somewhere. Also, if you can use the word *put* or *place* for the verb you want, select a form of the word *lay.*

The -ing form of *to lay* is *laying.*

He was laying out his clothes on the bed.

Step 1. Using *Lie* **and** *Lay.*   Follow directions. Use your own paper.

1. Write a sentence using the words *he lies* to mean *he rests.*
2. Write a sentence in which you use *lay* to mean *put* or *place.*

3. Use *has lain* correctly in a sentence.
4. Use in a sentence the word *lay* so that it means *rested* or *reclined.*
5. Use the word *laid* in a sentence so that it means *put* or *placed.*
6. Use the words *has laid* correctly in a sentence.
7. Use in a sentence the word *lying* to mean *resting.*
8. Write a sentence in which you use the word *laying* correctly.

Raise and *Rise.*

Raise means *lift up.*
Rise means *get up* or *go up.*

Hint: There must always appear after the word *raise* or any of its forms the thing that is actually being raised.

Here are the main parts and the tenses of *to raise.*

raise	*raised*	*raised*

[thing being raised]

He raises his hand.   She raised our scores.   He has raised enough
I raise the flag at dawn. ____ [thing being raised]   money to start a
                    [thing being raised] business.

-ing form: raising

The farmer was *raising* beans.

Here are the main parts and some of the tenses of *to rise.*

rise	rose	risen

Everyone rises when   He rose to shake our   The sun has risen
 the judge enters.   hands.   earlier than usual.
I will rise when he
 speaks.

-ing form: rising

We were just *rising* to leave.

Step 2. *Raise* and *Rise:* **Which Is Right?**   Pick out the correct word in the parentheses and write it in the blank space.

_____ 1. After the sound of a trumpet an old soldier had (risen, raised) the American flag.

_____ 2. An eagle (rose, raised) its wings against the pale sky.

_____ 3. The students had (risen, raised) before the instructor rushed into the room.

Sit **and** *Set.*

Sit means *to take a seat.*

sit	sat	sat
I sit in the last row.	They sat in the office.	The dog has sat there
She sits quietly.		without moving.
		She had sat down before
		they asked her to.

Set means *to place* or *to put.*

Hint: There must always appear after the word *set* the thing that is being put somewhere.

set	set	set
[thing being put somewhere] ↓		
I set my dictionary where I can reach it easily.	Yesterday she set her coat in the closet. ↗ [thing being put somewhere]	By the time he had set the pot on the stove, ↗ we were not hungry [thing being put somewhere] anymore.

Step 3. Completing Sentences with *Sit* or *Set*. Write the correct form of *sit* or *set* in the blank spaces below.

1. After I had _____ down, the telephone rang.

2. After I had _____ the glass down, Stella arrived.

3. Why will the children not _____ on the floor without talking?

4. _____ your packages here on the table.

5. Let me _____ awhile before I leave.

Leave **and** *Let.*

To let means *to allow.*
To leave means *to go away from.*

Let me speak to you.   We want *to leave* early.
          not
Leave me speak to you.

Stay **or** *Stand.*

To stay means *to remain.*
To stand means *to be in a straight up-and-down position.*

I stayed in bed with a cold.
          not
I stood in bed with a cold.

I should have *stayed* home.
          not
I should have *stood* home.

Can or *May*.

Can asks whether or not you are able to do something.
May asks whether or not you will get permission to do something.

Can I drive the car? (This question means: Do I have the ability to drive the car?)

May I drive the car? (This question means: Will you give me permission to drive the car?)

Step 4. *Leave, Let; Stay, Stand; Can, May.*   Circle the correct words in the parentheses:

1. If you (leave, let) me go early, I will visit my aunt in the hospital.
2. I (stood, stayed) in the house waiting for your call.
3. "(Can, May) I (leave, let) my car on this side of the street?"
4. She (stood, stayed) in bed with a cold for a week.

WRITING THE ESSAY

Suggestions for Thinking It Through

Think about some point of view you hold about the trends in women's liberation—perhaps something suggested in the early pages of this chapter or in the list of suggested topics on page 324. Use some prewriting techniques (see page 35) that work successfully for you. You might try the *subject tree,* explained in this chapter on pages 324–326.

Once you think you know what topic you want to write about, and once you can prepare a proposal that states what it is that your essay will discuss, your concern is then with details: how can you illustrate your point to the reader? If you ask yourself these questions before you begin the essay, you will know before you write just what source of supporting details you will use.

ON THE HUNT FOR DETAILS: FOUR CRUCIAL QUESTIONS TO ASK YOURSELF

1. What moments have I experienced in my own life that can help me illustrate my reasons for believing what I do about the topic?
2. What have I read recently in books, newspapers, or magazines—or what can I read quickly and easily before I write—that can help me support my reasons for believing what I do about the topic?
3. What have I learned from the television, the movies, or the radio that can help me support my reasons for believing what I do about the topic?
4. What have I learned from reliable friends, parents, relatives, teachers that can help me support my reasons for believing what I do about the topic?

Suppose, for example, you believe that as drivers of automobiles, women are very competent. And you can remember two specific moments in your life which will illustrate to readers why you feel the way you do, moments which might even persuade them to believe what you believe. After you write an introduction (see pages 219–223), you might show in each body paragraph one of those moments expanded with concrete sensory details. You will not have *proved* that women are excellent drivers or that they are better drivers than men; but you will have *illustrated* to the readers how your own experiences explain the opinion you hold. That is a very effective way to build an essay.

But you may want to use several reasons to back up your opinion. Make a list. Eliminate any ideas you think would be hard to illustrate or prove. Then perhaps your list will look something like this:

1. Women think very quickly in times of danger.
2. Women are very cautious on the road.
3. Women are courteous drivers.
4. Women are particularly familiar with safety regulations.
5. Women rarely drink before they drive, so they have fewer fatal accidents than men.
6. Women have fewer accidents, in general, than men.

Consult now the Four Crucial Questions on page 315. Did you live through incidents which could illustrate any of these reasons? Did you, on the other hand, see important statistics about women drivers and their safety record? Did you read an article about women drivers (and could you quote or paraphrase accurately from this article)? Did you hear on one of the radio or television talk shows an interview in which you learned about the driving patterns of women and the effects of these patterns on insurance rates? Of course, you will have to decide how to arrange the details effectively.

Whatever points you decide to develop, your essay should have some kind of support. If you feel that you have a great deal of support to offer for *two* of the reasons above, fine. Forget about the other four. Discuss one of the two points in the first body paragraph (paragraph 2 of the essay), using support you think convincing. Discuss the other point in the next paragraph. There too, you need to use as many details as you think will convince the reader that you are right.

But perhaps you want to discuss in your essay *all* the reasons listed above. Fine. First try to pick out the reason for which you have the most solid and convincing support. Save that one until later! In the paragraph that comes after the introduction, discuss all the *other* reasons, giving brief support for each that you mention. In the third paragraph, discuss the one most important reason you have. By saving the most important reason for last and for treatment in its own paragraph, you impress the reader with your most striking evidence.

Perhaps you want to show in the paragraph after the introduction the arguments many people give when they say women are *not* good drivers (see pages 301–304). In paragraph 3, then, you can go about trying to show why all those reasons are in your opinion, wrong. You would support the points you made with some strong details. Or you can say at the beginning of paragraph 3 that you think there is some truth in what others say; and then go on to develop your own reasons for believing what you do about women drivers.

These are only suggestions: *you* decide what you want to include in each paragraph, how many points you want to discuss, whether you want to stress certain ideas more than others. You will need to think about the various ways of developing paragraphs (explained in Part I of this book) so you can figure out which method will be best for your essay. As one of your options you might consider writing a definition of a key word in a body paragraph or in the introduction. After you examine pages 393–395 in the Minibook, you might want to define a word such as *woman, freedom,* or *masculinity.* But you must have answers to one or more of those crucial questions on page 315 so that you will know just what details to use before you write, and so that you will not run out of things to say. Everyone has opinions (you have hundreds of your own about the status of women), but the details that illustrate your opinions are what will convince readers that you know what you are talking about.

HANDY PAGES FOR REVIEWING DETAILS

1. Imagery and Sensory Language	pages 5–7, 208–211
2. Using Statistics and Cases	pages 168–173
3. How to Paraphrase	pages 173–176
4. How to Use Quotations	pages 173–176

Step 1. Practice Planning for the Essay.   Read the proposal sentences below. Consult the list of Four Crucial Questions. Then tell briefly what you might discuss in each body paragraph and what kinds of details you would use. Study the example.

1. Even in the field of hard physical labor, women should not be overlooked.

Body Paragraph 1
Discussion of women laborers in Russia. Statistics from New York Times Almanac.

Body Paragraph 2
American women overlooked for jobs of hard physical labor. Paraphrase of TV interview with Women's Liberation leader. More statistics from Labor Department.

2. Women excel in profes-
   sional competitive sports.

   ———————————————— ————————————————

   ———————————————— ————————————————

   ———————————————— ————————————————

   ———————————————— ————————————————

   ———————————————— ————————————————

   ———————————————— ————————————————

3. In high-level executive
   positions, women are not
   without problems of
   stress.

   ———————————————— ————————————————

   ———————————————— ————————————————

   ———————————————— ————————————————

   ———————————————— ————————————————

   ———————————————— ————————————————

4. Because of past discrimination, women should be
   allowed special privileges
   for jobs and education.

   ———————————————— ————————————————

   ———————————————— ————————————————

   ———————————————— ————————————————

   ———————————————— ————————————————

   ———————————————— ————————————————

Learning from Other Students

Step 1. Arguing from Personal Experience. Although the theme below offers no *proof* for its main arguments, dramatic illustrations serve to explain to the reader just why the writer holds the opinions she does. Read "Deprived Children" and discuss the questions after the essay.

Deprived Children

An untrained observer watching a group of children at play may see no real difference between them. The child sitting in the sand pile looks similar to the one squealing happily down the sliding pond. Yet a closer look might reveal many differences. Each child has her own physical appearance; each has her own mental abilities; each has a home life that may not resemble the others'. A few people do notice, however, that some children appear insecure and unhappy; I believe that these are frequently the children of working mothers.

Children of working mothers are deprived of the security of a healthy and loving environment. As a young child with a working mother, I felt her absence deeply. On my first day in third grade, for example, a violent storm shook the streets of Brooklyn. Happy at the idea of a new teacher and new friends, the class grew even more excited by the trees whipping back and forth across from our first floor windows and the sound of September rain pounding against the glass. However, this happiness soon wore off when streets flooded and winds of sixty miles an hour soaked the sidewalks. All the classes moved to the basement, and the principal, Mr. Greenwalder, announced that only children whose parents came for them could go home. Nervously hugging my new notebook to my thin jacket, I prayed somehow my mother would get to me. A slow line of mothers holding yellow raincoats and black umbrellas and boots trudged in to pick up their nervous children while I stared at a speck on the floor. The hours unfolded gradually, and soon I stood in the midst of the huge gray basement, alone except for my faithful teacher, Mrs. Timmins. The fear of a trip home in the hurricane disappeared in the pain and shame I felt that day by not having a mother at home like everyone else. As a child of a working mother I often felt that sense of loss and shame.

The results of such feelings in the children of a working mother can be very serious as the example of my brother Richie clearly illustrates. My older brother, younger sister, and I grew up in the care of indifferent housekeepers. At eleven years old, Richie often left the house for hours at a time with no excuses or explanations of his absences. No one really knew his friends, and my mother's own daily battle with tiredness after work kept her from questioning Richie's activities. As we grew older, Mother's continued absence became an accepted part of our family life, and neither my sister nor I could detect the gradual change in our brother. Richie grew into a sullen, moody, overweight teen-ager. He failed miserably in school, finally dropping out. He rarely spoke to anyone in the house. Although these signs all pointed to tragedy, I was too busy with my own problems to pay any attention— and Mother just was not around. One night a call from a far off hospital told us that Richie's condition was fair after a drug overdose. My mother's eyes looked confused as if to say, "How did it happen?" when we sped to the hospital, but through the shock I *knew* the cause. Richie survived and is now in the midst of costly psychiatric care. But in my opinion, this whole tragedy might have been avoided through the presence and guidance of a mother. My mother was never there.

In many cases, then, a working mother's child is under great stress. She must become independent early in life and must learn to accept the loss of a parent. She can easily fall under bad influences and must be strong enough to resist if she wants to stay out of trouble. At a very young age she must learn the difference between right and wrong and must often face the difficult chore of choosing alone. These tasks present a challenge to the child of a working mother, and one can only hope that she will succeed in mastering them.

—Phyllis Gold

1. What, according to the proposal sentence, does the essay try to illustrate? How does the purpose of paragraph 2 differ from the purpose of paragraph 3?
2. Has the writer convinced you that what she believes is true? If she has,

what kinds of details has she used to do so? Which images do you find most appealing?

3. Do you find any examples of the kinds of poor reasoning described on pages 298–300?

Step 2. Themes that Meet the Opposition. The student samples below use in body paragraphs arguments made against their own proposals. Read the essays and answer the questions that appear below.

Job Discrimination for Women?

Several years ago, Betty Friedan, author of *The Feminine Mystique* and activist in the Women's Liberation Movement, stated, "Women are not being brought into the mainstream of American society in equal partnership with men. The oppression of females is especially noticeable in our economic structure." Are women really the object of discrimination and exploitation by employers?

In recent years, the Women's Liberation Movement screamed out "Yes!" as it challenged discriminating practices against women. For instance, airlines forced stewardesses to retire at the age of thirty-five when no such requirement existed for males. Further, a study by Professor James White, author of *Women in the Law,* showed how of all women law school graduates in the years 1959 to 1968, approximately half have been objects of discrimination by employers. For example, the average income differed sharply based on sex. After eight years, male law graduates earned an average of $18,000 while female law graduates earned only $10,000. Women have also argued about discriminatory practices against them when both female and male applicants show equal qualifications for jobs. Employers usually hire males because males do not leave jobs to have babies and raise families. Like Robin Morgan, editor of *Sisterhood Is Powerful,* many argue that "women are an oppressed class. They are exploited as domestic servants and cheap labor" and "men have controlled all political, economic and cultural institutions. They have used their power to keep women in an inferior position."

In spite of the cries of the Women's Liberation Movement, women make up a substantial part of the work force in the United States, so what are they crying about! Today, nearly half the women in the United States work; that amounts to more than 33 million women, representing 40 per cent of the work force. Obviously, a woman's place is no longer in the home, and any real effort to discriminate against women would have dropped that total considerably. Dr. David Gilbert, chief economist for the First Pennsylvania Corporation, described the changing female role in *Nation's Business Magazine.* He stated, "Over 63 per cent of the female labor force participants are married. From 1948 to 1970, the labor force participation rates of married women rose from 22 per cent to 40 per cent." Significantly, the greatest percentage increase in married female job holders over this period occurred among women with children. Working women today also tend to be better educated than females years ago. In the period 1952 to 1970, a Federal survey shows that the median number of years of education in the women's labor force had risen from 12.0 to 12.4. Historically, women selected clerical work as a major occupational area. However, with more education, more women today assume professional and technical positions of importance. I believe that with the increasing number of women completing college and obtaining higher degrees, this trend should continue. Even in jobs thought only for males, women have advanced. A recent article in the *New York Daily News* showed that the female policewoman is equal to her male counterpart. Just as the males on the police force serve in every area, the females too work all types of beats and receive the same pay as men. It is not so strange on a New York City street to see a female in a blue uniform while she drives a police patrol car, her partner, a male, sitting and chattering away next to her.

Although some complaints about discrimination may be true, I believe current evidence shows great strides for women in the job world. What then are women crying about? Why instead of stressing the advances do they scream about the continued failures? I think this is really a question about human nature, one that has nothing to do with sex. Men and women seem rarely to be happy with what they have. People earning $20,000 a year wish for $40,000. Single men long for marriage; married men dream of being single. Women with children feel crushed by the burdens of responsibilities; single women hope for marriage and children. Children pray to be older; older people wish they had back their youth. In the winter we complain of the cold and wish for summer; in the summer we moan about the heat and wish for winter. It seems to me that dissatisfaction is just another of the traits that make human beings what they are.

—Richard Tomasuolo

Working Mothers

"Toward the end of World War II," reports economist Dr. Eli Ginzberg, "large numbers of wives and mothers entered the labor force, but the experts were sure that when peace came, the mothers would return to their traditional ways, leaving the work force to devote themselves exclusively to child-rearing, homemaking, and volunteer activities." Time proved the experts wrong. The percentage of working wives and mothers kept on accelerating through the 50's, 60's, and 70's. "Today," he says in 1977, "about two out of every five women with a child under six is working at an outside job." Those are strong figures. Millions of mothers are pushing their way into the job market, and are dealing successfully with responsibilities as parents, workers, and homemakers.

It is easy, however, to understand the feelings of many mothers who refuse to work, mothers who quit their jobs to stay at home and devote their full time to raising children. In a special issue on working mothers by *Parents' Magazine* (April, 1977) Ellie Brock explained that it is her sole responsibility as wife and mother to take care of her three-year-old daughter Lauren, her husband Richard, and their home in Arlington, Virginia. An attorney, Richard is busy all week and unable to help. No paid housekeeper or sitter, Ellie is convinced, could devote more time and energy than she herself could. No longer teaching high school students, she is less tired and, therefore, she feels, more interesting to her husband. Many working women like the freedom being at home offers. They can do things they had no time for when they worked, reading for an hour on a living room chair, taking courses in yoga or tennis or dance at the neighborhood health club, tinkering around the kitchen with a chocolate cream pie or a Caesar's salad. My own mother, a "floor lady" in a pocketbook factory for thirteen years, quit her job twenty years ago for the coming birth of her first child, my older brother Salvatore. Three more babies came in the next seven years, and Mom feels that her staying at home all this time kept the family strong.

Although many women choose to stay home and care for their families, increasing numbers of working mothers have made new lives for themselves outside the home. In the same issue of *Parents' Magazine* Eleanor Seale, mother of three-year-old Archie, tells of a life filled with active, money-making work. During the day she is secretary to Justices Thomas Dickens and Clifford A. Scott of the New York State Supreme Court. Between eight and ten at night, she keeps the books, does ordering and inventory work, and serves customers at the Seale's new, family-owned store. "We weren't born with silver spoons in our mouths," she says. "We want certain things for our family and we have to struggle to achieve them." Women like Eleanor feel that their jobs make them more attractive, more interesting to their husbands. With the money earned by a working mother the family enjoys things they otherwise could not: a shiny new sedan, perhaps, a summer vacation on the West Coast, an assured college education for the children. These mothers believe that carefully selected day-care centers, nursery schools or at-home sitters enrich the child's life with experiences no parents alone can offer. Perhaps children have much less time with a working mother than they do with a mother close by all day long; but the quality of the time is what is important. In a single hour a thoughtful working mother can give to her child as much love and attention as a mother at home all the time can give to her child in a full day.

Because of the attention to women's rights, many mothers who in the past might have felt trapped in their homes have seized opportunities to use their energy and potential in stimulating careers. Yet there are women at home who see their work there as more important than anything. The point in all this, as I see it, is that the society must be made to tolerate choices so that no one is locked into a hateful life simply because someone expects him or her to behave in a required way. People must be free to choose the lives they believe are best for themselves and must have enough opportunities to change their minds if they make mistakes.

—Carmelyn Martini

Women: Fragile Flowers?

Whenever people discuss the idea of women in the world of men, a male voice always cries out that women are biologically different from men, even in the animal kingdom. Such was the case last Tuesday when a hot discussion on "women's lib" filled our freshman English class. With an air of authority George Kerman rattled off biological "facts" to back up his statements on how women are "different." Although I felt that I wanted to contradict him, I knew better. I had no biological statistics to back up my beliefs, just a bit of pride that hurt when he compared women to female peacocks. But now I can stand my own ground well assured of my resources. Women are not the weaker sex.

Many like George would paint a pretty picture of womankind as a fragile flower easily bent. The argument that women are biologically different from men always hints that women are *inferior* to men, inferior in terms of stamina, stability, and thinking. A number of scientists argue that males are sturdier and able to withstand stress more admirably than females. Dr. Edgar Berman, a former surgeon and one-time State Department consultant on Latin American health problems, agrees with George. "Women should be excluded," Dr. Berman says, "from high executive positions because of their monthly raging hormonal imbalances." People like Dr. Berman point out that women cry while men keep a stiff upper lip, meaning that women have poor responses to life's problems. There are also statements on record that women usually have lower I.Q.'s than men do, and that this accounts for the low percentage of women in professional jobs. All these remarks certainly do seem to point a finger at women as delicate butterflies, needing protection and care and not needing positions of responsibility in the world today.

But the finger is pointing in the wrong direction because *men* lack all the important biological features. The term "biologically different" used against women tries to be impartial but it still is an expression of a male's prejudice. In fact, men are the weaker sex. The female of almost any species is sturdier than the male. Dr. James Hamilton, an endocrinologist, shows that from worms to humans the male is less able to tolerate life's everyday stresses. "There can be little doubt that the male has a higher mortality rate in almost all forms of animal life studied." Even during the first week of life, the death rate for infant males is 32% greater than that of females. Later on in life the society puts strain on the man to compete, produce, and succeed; this also affects the survival rate. Another part of the problem of male mortality is the male hormone testosterone which brings about a higher metabolic rate in most tissues, wearing them out faster. But there is no proof that the woman's monthly "hormonal imbalance" is a sign of inferiority. True, many women do experience some discomfort each month; some even are quite ill for a day or two. But most women do not suffer with any reactions. Federal surveys in every job category show that women take off the same amount of time from work as men. Although crying is often another "proof" of a woman's difference from man, United States Public Health data show that females have a much lower suicide rate—less than half that of males. Isn't it better to cry? And there are no sex differences in regard to I.Q. On all forms of intelligence tests the female I.Q. is not significantly different from the male's. Women are, in my opinion, biologically superior to men.

Woman has not been able to prove she is not the weaker sex because the society has assigned her to an inferior position. Few brilliant women have tried to develop their talents simply because there has been a small market for brilliant women in this country. The few who have bothered to develop their creative talents find that the world views them as "odd balls." The stereotype of a brilliant woman is that of a horsefaced, flat-chested female in support shoes, one who has hidden all her sexual instincts in her search for a career. It may be fun being treated like a fragile flower by a boyfriend or a date, but there's a time and place for everything. It is time society stopped giving out positions based on stereotypes. We women must develop and make use of our wasted female brain power.

—Stella Tesoriero

1. Richard Tomasuolo states his proposal as a question. Do you think that is an effective technique? If you were to change his proposal to a statement, what would it be?
2. What kinds of evidence does he offer to show that women have been discriminated against? How does he then support the idea that women have *not* suffered discrimination in jobs? Which do you find most convincing, paragraph 2 or paragraph 3?

3. What, according to the proposal in "Women: Fragile Flowers?" is Stella Tesoriero's purpose in writing her essay? What details in paragraph 2 does she use to show why people think women *are* the weaker sex?
4. Where does Carmelyn Martini argue against her own proposal?
5. What kinds of details does each of the writers use to support points in the body paragraphs? Which writer uses the highest degree of sensory language? Which writer might have used more sharply visual language?
6. Comment on the transitions each writer uses to connect the second paragraph to the first, the third to the second, the fourth to the third.

Some Topics to Think About

In case you have trouble finding a topic, here are some possibilities for topics for this theme assignment.

1. equal sex standards for everyone
2. alimony: reverse discrimination?
3. the Chinese woman versus the American woman
4. I don't want to be liberated.
5. my experience with a woman doctor (lawyer, salesperson, dean, insurance agent)
6. my views on abortion
7. the image of women in advertising
8. women politicians
9. women as artists
10. women drivers
11. prejudice against women in competitive athletics
12. women football players? men baby nurses? how far will it go?
13. women in the work force
14. pornography: degrading the modern woman
15. women in the military

You may wish to challenge one of the statements in Step 3 on page 296. You may wish to write about a topic suggested in the questionnaire on pages 295–296.

Prewriting: Making a Subject Tree

As with free association (see pages 110–111), the subject tree is a prewriting technique that helps you move from one level of suggestion to another as your mind considers the topic. In this way you follow your thoughts as they develop into higher and higher levels of specificity. The final product looks like a tree with branches reaching out toward possibilities for focused writing. After you consider what your tree includes, any one branch can serve as a starting point for the development of other ideas, for expanding and grouping details, and, ultimately for writing a first draft. Look at the following example.

PREWRITING: A SUBJECT TREE

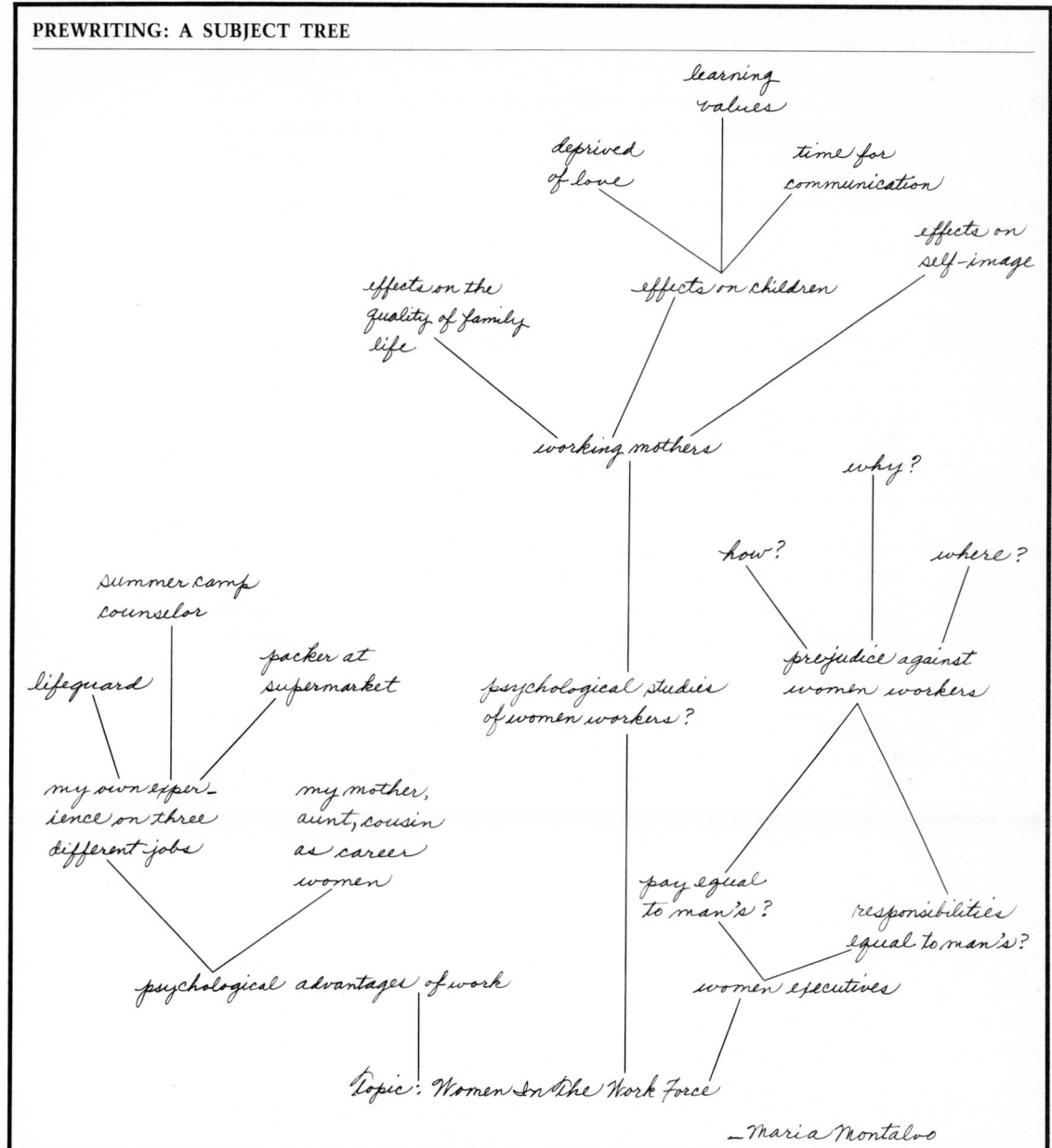

learning values

deprived of love

time for communication

effects on self-image

effects on the quality of family life

effects on children

working mothers

why?

how?

where?

summer camp counselor

lifeguard

packer at supermarket

psychological studies of women workers?

prejudice against women workers

my own exper- ience on three different jobs

my mother, aunt, cousin as career women

pay equal to man's?

responsibilities equal to man's?

psychological advantages of work

women executives

Topic: Women In The Work Force

— Maria Montalvo

Step 1. Examining a Subject Tree

1. What are the three general topic ideas Maria Montalvo uses to start branching into specific areas?
2. If she chose to write about the psychological advantages of work, accord-

ing to her subject tree, what kinds of details might she use? How do you know? If she chose to deal with working mothers, what kinds of details might she use?

3. Select any one of the topic ideas on her subject tree. What proposal sentence could you develop for it? How might some people argue against that topic? What points could you make in each of the body paragraphs?

Step 2. Your Own Subject Tree.   Using a topic from the list on page 324 or one of your own, develop a subject tree in which you explore by branching out a number of different possibilities for your basic idea.

Your Views on the Woman's Place: A Checklist of Requirements

As you prepare a subject tree or do other prewriting for your essay, as you do your first and later drafts, and before you write your final copy, use this checklist so that you can follow as many of the suggestions as possible. After you prepare your manuscript to hand in, fill in the checklist and submit it with your theme.

1. Did I consider the topic carefully before writing anything? Did I use   _____
   some prewriting activities that work particularly well for me?
2. Did I write a rough draft and any other needed drafts before making my   _____
   final copy? Did I make changes in my rough drafts so that I expressed
   thoughts clearly and smoothly?
3. Is my proposal clearly stated?   _____
4. Did I use smooth transitions as explained in the Essay Transition Sign-   _____
   boards I, II, and II on pages 267–269?
5. Did I avoid the traps in logic and clear reasoning by studying the Fif-   _____
   teen Faults to Fail the Argument on pages 298–300?
6. Did I consider carefully the types of details I want to use in my essay   _____
   by asking myself the Four Crucial Questions explained on page 315?
   Do I know the difference between *illustrating* my opinion and *proving*
   my opinion is correct?
7. Did I use a variety of sentence patterns: coordination and subordina-   _____
   tion, sentences with verb-part openers, sentences joined by transforming verbs (see pages 304–306)?
8. Did I try to use strong verbs, clear expressions, and images that appeal   _____
   to the senses?
9. If I used statistics, cases, or opinions expressed by others, have I men-   _____
   tioned the source of my information? Have I used reliable sources?
10. Did I read carefully the themes on pages 318–323 to help me see how   _____
    other students presented their ideas on women's rights?
11. After making changes in my drafts for clarity and smoothness, did I   _____
    reread my essay, looking for errors, especially in the use of possession
    and in the kinds of mistakes I usually make? Did I examine my own
    Progress Sheet?

12. Did I try to use some of the new vocabulary introduced in this chapter? _____
Here from my theme is a sentence that uses one of those words:

_____

_____

THE PROFESSIONALS SPEAK

This selection from *The Female Eunuch,* one of the most important books of the early 1970s in the modern woman's movement for liberation, uses statistical details to prove women's difficulties in the job market. Discuss the questions that appear beneath it.

The Woman as Worker

In England women form thirty-eight percent of the workforce; in the U.S.A. the proportion is only slightly smaller, around thirty-five percent. This means that in both countries half the women between the ages of sixteen and sixty-four work outside their homes. Of the seventeen million married women in the U.S. who go out to work, ten million have children under the age of seventeen. The average wage of an Englishwoman doing administrative, technical or clerical work is less than £12 ($28.80) a week, while men in the same industries earn an average wage of £28 a week. Male manual workers earn an average wage of £20 a week; women, £10. The same disparity between the earnings of the sexes is visible right across the board in the United States, where male professionals and technicians can expect to earn $9,370 annually and females, $5,210. Male clerical workers can expect to earn $6,380, women $3,844. While a sales*man* can live on a respectable $6,814, his female counterpart must do with $2,116. The skilled operator, who is nearly always a man, nets about $7,224 annually; skilled women may expect $3,826. Men in the service industries get paid an average wage of $4,532 annually for more important work than the women waitressing, cleaning and answering the telephone for the starvation wage of $2,076. The average male employee in the United States earns $6,610 a year; his sister $3,157, less than half.

—Germaine Greer

1. What conclusion does Greer want the reader to draw about the way women are treated in paid occupations?
2. What statistics does the writer use to compare English women and English men?
3. What details illustrate the disparity between the earnings of the sexes in America?

The following article shows how differently school books portray boys and girls. Use the questions after the selection as a basis of discussion.

SOME WORDS TO KNOW BEFORE YOU READ

overwhelmingly: to an overpowering degree
predominate: be the stronger, controlling element
implication: suggestion
depicted: portrayed; shown
constrained: held back
domain: area under control
epitome: high point
prototype: model
deprecate: express disapproval of
perpetuate: carry on and on

Sex Bias in Textbooks

Textbooks have always been a cornerstone of our education system. Although the main function of textbooks is to convey specific information, textbooks also provide the child with ethical and moral values. Thus, at the same time that a child is learning history or math, he or she is also learning what is good, desirable, just.

This second type of information—which sociologists refer to as the "latent content" of textbooks—provides standards for how men, women, boys, and girls should act. This latent content was the focus of research we carried on for the last three years. During that time, we have analyzed the latent content of the most widely used textbook series in the United States in each of five subject areas: science, arithmetic, reading, spelling, and social studies. (A grant from the Rockefeller Family Fund supported the research.) Through computer analysis, we obtained data on the sex, age, racial distribution, and activities of the texbook characters by grade level and subject area.

This article will summarize the ways in which the two sexes are portrayed and the type of behavior encouraged for each.

Sex Distribution. Since women comprise 51 percent of the U.S. population, one might expect half the people in textbook illustrations to be females. However, males overwhelmingly predominate in all series: Females are only 31 percent of the total, while males are 69 percent. Of over 8,000 pictures analyzed, more than 5,500 are of males. Girl students using these books are likely to feel excluded.

Sex Differences by Grade Level. The percentage of females varies by grade level. In all series combined, females comprise a third of the illustrations at the second grade level, but only a fifth of the total on the sixth grade level. In other words, by the sixth grade, there are four pictures of males for every picture of a female. This contrast is vividly illustrated in the accompanying figure. Thus, as the textbooks increase in sophistication, women become less numerous and, by implication, less significant as role models.

This decline in female role models makes it harder for a girl student to identify with the textbook characters and thus may make it harder for her to assimilate the lesson. Covertly, she is being told that she, a female, is less important as the textbook world shifts to the world of adults—to the world of men.

This declining representation of females is particularly striking in some of the series. For example, in the second grade spelling series, 43 percent of the illustrations are of females, but in the sixth grade series, the percentage has declined to a mere 15 percent.

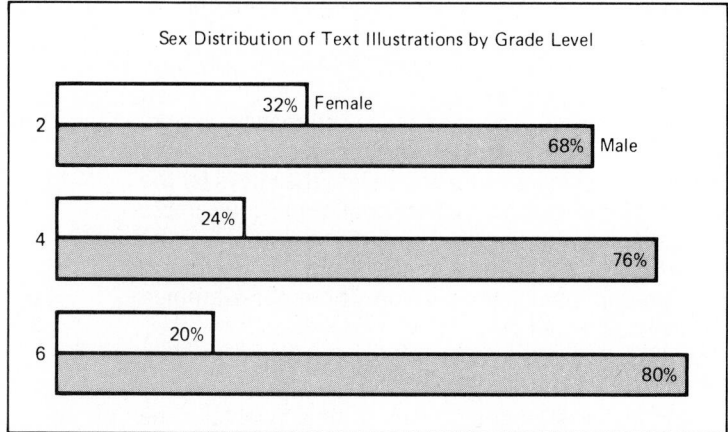

Sex Distribution of Text Illustrations by Grade Level

Sex Differences in Activities.   The pictures of children show three striking differences between the boys and girls. First, boys are portrayed as active, skillful, and adventuresome; girls are typically shown as passive—as watching and waiting for boys.

Second, while boys are depicted as intelligent and as mastering work-related skills, girls are shown engaging in domestic activities or in grooming themselves, trying on clothes, and shopping. Third, girls are depicted as affectionate, nurturing, and emotional, but boys almost never embrace or cry. Thus, the young boy is taught that to be manly he must control his emotions. In the same way that girls are constrained by images which stereotype them as pretty and passive, boys are constrained by images which stereotype them as strong and unemotional. The textbooks thereby encourage both sexes to limit their development.

Adult men and women in textbooks are even more sex-stereotyped. While only a few women are shown outside the home, men are portrayed in over 150 occupational roles. A young boy is told he can be anything from a laborer to a doctor. He is encouraged to imagine himself in a wide variety of roles and both to dream about and plan his occupational future.

In contrast, the future for young girls seems preordained: Almost all adult women in textbooks are housewives. In reality, however, 9 out of 10 women in our society will work at some point in their lives. By ignoring women workers, the textbooks fail to provide the necessary occupational role models for girls and thus unnecessarily restrict future horizons.

Sex Differences in Subject Areas.   There are systematic differences in the treatment that girls and women receive in different subject areas. The percentage of females in illustrations varies from a high of 33 percent in social studies to a low of 26 percent in science. These subject differences are important in understanding why children like certain subjects and want to major in them—or why, in contrast, they feel unwelcome because of the covert messages they receive.

In science, the most male-oriented series, 74 percent of the pictures are of males. The science texts seem to imply that the world of science is a masculine domain. When boys are shown, they are actively involved in experiment—looking through microscopes and pouring chemicals. In contrast, when girls are shown, they observe the boys' experiments. The epitome of the male prototype in science is the astronaut. But only boys are pictured as astronauts and, in the text, only boys are told to imagine that they can explore the moon.

In mathematics textbooks, many problems are based on sex-stereotyped roles, with men earning money and women dividing pies. Further, despite the Equal Pay Act of 1963, we found math problems in which girls were paid less than boys for the same work. (It would be hard to imagine a textbook publisher allowing an example in which a black child is paid less than a white child.)

In the reading series, story titles provide a good indicator of the relative importance of males and females. Boys predominate in every grade. The series examined had 102 stories about boys and only 35 about girls.

Even the female heroines reinforce traditional female roles. For example, Kirsten, the heroine of a third grade story, wins over the girls who have rejected her by making Danish cookies and having the most popular booth at the school fair. The moral in this story is that girls can succeed by cooking and serving. But Kirsten slights herself and the very skill that had earned her favor when she says, "It's easy; even I can do it, and you know how stupid I am." Thus, even when girls succeed, they tend to deprecate themselves. In contrast, boys show a great deal of confidence and pride.

Both the reading and spelling series demonstrate a surprising amount of antagonism and hostility toward females. In the spelling series, female characters are yelled at and pushed around. In the reading series, they are shown as stupid and clumsy three times as frequently as males.

In social studies, the best series studied, women were often skillful and important. Here, mothers play a crucial role in passing on their cultural tradition to their daughters. Although we applaud these positive pictures of women, it should be noted that mothers in the series teach only their daughters, not their sons. Similarly, fathers teach only sons. Thus, traditional sex roles are perpetuated. Today, boys need to learn to manage in the home and to be parents, and girls need to learn about vocations and the outdoors. Textbooks could expand rather than contract children's potential.

Although this series has the largest percentage of females in pictures, still 2 out of 3 are pictures of males. Women are in the section on the home but are absent from the sections on history, government, and society.

After studying these textbooks for three years, one cannot help but conclude that children are being warped by the latent messages in them. We urge teachers to examine the textbooks they use and to check the ways in which sex roles are stereotyped. Only teachers can change the impact that these books will have on our young people and on the next generation of adults. Teachers can tell their girl students about the world and the real options they have in it. Teachers can encourage them to dream and can help them plan.

What is sorely lacking in textbooks and thus desperately needed in the classroom is a new image of adult women and a wide range of adult role models for young girls. Girls—and boys too—should learn about the history of women in this country, about suffrage and the current women's liberation movement, and about female heroines of our country and the world. What a difference it would make if young girls could point to adult women with pride and feel that they themselves have an exciting life ahead.

While we must all create pressure to change the textbooks, in the meantime, it is up to teachers to counteract the latent messages in them and to create positive images of adult women in the minds of students.

—Lenore J. Weitzman and Diane Rizzo

1. What is "latent content" in regard to textbooks?
2. What are some of the latent messages the authors see in textbooks? How do the numbers of males shown in textbook pictures compare with the numbers of females? How are the activities of boys shown to differ from activities of girls? How does the story of Kirsten effectively show how girls deprecate themselves even when they succeed?
3. Although they praise the social studies texts they have examined, the writers find some fault there. What is it? Do you agree that sex roles are perpetuated by such presentations?
4. What evidence do the authors give to support the idea that children are being hurt ("warped," the writers say) by the latent sex messages in textbooks? What evidence might you give?
5. Do you agree that teachers can counteract latent messages in textbooks and can create positive images of adult women in the minds of students? How can this be done?
6. This piece appeared in the mid-1970s in *Today's Education.* Are the points made here still valid today? Is there still sex bias in textbooks schoolchildren use? What evidence can you offer to support your point of view?
7. The authors have used subheadings (in italics) to divide their work into smaller parts. None of the subheadings is a complete sentence. Rewrite each of them so that it:
   a. is a complete sentence
   b. provides an effective transition from the previous section
   c. states clearly the purpose of the section that follows it
8. Is the essay a good example of argumentation? Why or why not?

REACHING HIGHER

Step 1. Analyzing Photographs.   Look at the picture on page 292, and write an essay in which you compare and contrast the situation in the picture with modern attitudes toward women in your town or city.

Step 2. An Essay in Pictures and Words. Using a camera you can easily operate, take a number of pictures (on or near the college campus) which show either the advances made by women in a man's world or the way in which women are kept down in a man's world. Take pictures of women (a relative, a friend, a stranger) at work, women at leisure, women on their way to their jobs or at the supermarket or in their homes. Select the ten best pictures, and for each write one sentence which summarizes the main point of the snapshot.

Step 3. More Topics on Liberation. The struggle for freedom and equality over the centuries knows no sex or nationality. Using any effective kinds of details, develop one of these liberation ideas in a four-paragraph essay:

the black people's struggle in South Africa today

the Jew and equality in large cities

a slave revolt in the South

the Italians' charge of prejudice today

Palestinian rights

machismo—myth or reality

busing in Boston for racial equality in schools

the American Indian and equal opportunity

the Irish immigrant in the New York City of 1900

unfair treatment of Mexican-Americans

freedoms in the Republic of China

Step 4. A Collage to Present a Point. Using old magazines, newspapers, paint, ink, pieces of advertisements for captions, and any other materials, develop a theme in a collage that presents an argument. You may want to focus on an idea such as women's rights, ecology, overpopulation, violence, or some other pressing problem in the world today. You might want to answer a question in your collage. In any case, what you should try to do is to persuade someone to agree with your point. Use colors and visual images of action carefully to help make your point.

chapter 9

**REVEALING CHARACTER:
A PERSON YOU KNOW**

Christopher Lukas/Photo Researchers, Inc.

INTRODUCTION TO CHARACTERIZATION

What person has had a major influence on your life? Is it a wife or husband who urges you on, who talks out problems with you, who sacrifices goals and needs so that you can advance? Is it a father or mother who ignores you, who by his or her absence has made you feel angry or unsure of yourself? Was it a teacher who developed your thinking or a special talent? Was it—is it—a boyfriend or girl friend who added a glow of love to your life or who brought you misery, tension, and pain?

In this theme assignment you will reveal the character of some person who affected your life greatly. Naturally, you will explore your own feelings for this special someone, feelings you need to illustrate through sharply drawn experiences. And in order to make the person come alive, you need to turn to the tools you use every day for judging the character of people you meet. How does the person look? What do the eyes, the shape of the head, the curve of the mouth reveal? What do the quality of the voice and the things the person says tell you? How do actions, or "body language"—the way the person gestures or steps across a room—give you clues to his or her character? The clothing—the length of a skirt, the shine on a pair of shoes, the number of buttons opened at the neck—what do they suggest?

The writer, then, uses action, detailed description, and dialogue as the proven techniques to reveal character.

VOCABULARY

Step 1. Words to Name Relationships among People. In the blank spaces below write definitions for the words. Check a dictionary for any word you do not know; Appendix A gives added help.

peer _____ kin _____

contemporary _____ fraternal _____

familial _____ conjugal _____

sibling _____ paternal _____

comrade _____ maternal _____

Step 2. Naming Relationships. Each item in Column I names or describes a relationship. In Column II write, from the vocabulary above, the word that you think best expresses the relationship. Each word is used only once.

I   *II*

1. a person who acts like a mother to other people   _____

2. a brother or a sister   _____

I   *II*

   3. someone of the same rank as someone
else   _____

   4. an intimate friend or associate   _____

   5. a marriage relationship   _____

   6. fatherly   _____

   7. living at the same time   _____

   8. a family relationship   _____

   9. one's relatives   _____

10. brotherly   _____

Step 3. Your Own Sentence.   For any words that are new to you in the list
above, write your own sentences. Use separate paper.

Familiar Words, New Uses

The describing words below are familiar to you in the way they are usually
employed. But these words when used in an unusual way create original
pictures. A word like *icy* to describe a lake or a street is not unusual; but to
say *an icy smile* lets the reader see a different and expressive picture.

Step 4. Writing Original Pictures.   Each word in Column I appears in Column II in its most usual use. Check in a dictionary for any meanings you are
not sure of. (See Appendix A for further help.) In Column III, use the word in
an unusual way to describe some aspect of appearance or personality. Study
the two examples below.

I	*II*	*III*
1. foggy	*foggy* afternoon	*a foggy thought*
2. hollow	a *hollow* tube	*a hollow laugh*
3. shining	a *shining* light	_____
4. bright	a *bright* light	_____
5. metallic	*metallic* jewelry	_____
6. proud	a *proud* father	_____
7. murky	a *murky* lake	_____
8. fiery	a *fiery* blaze	_____
9. leather	*leather* suitcase	_____
10. arid	an *arid* field	_____

I	II	III
11. velvet	*velvet* dress	_____
12. upright	an *upright* piano	_____

Step 5. Writing Sentences.   For any five word groups you wrote in Column III, write complete sentences. Make sure to use the words in an unusual way. Use separate paper.

BUILDING COMPOSITION SKILLS

Exploring the Topic

Step 1. Character in Faces: A Brief Talk.   A person's face is a miracle of expressions and feelings and often reveals the personality that lies beneath. Many times people say, "He looks mean" or "She's really clever." Rightly or wrongly, the faces of people in our lives do reveal impressions of their character. Think of someone you know, someone whose face is vivid in your mind. (You might wish instead to look at one of the pictures of faces on page 117.) Select a face which gives you a certain feeling or impression, a face which expresses some feature of character: is it *pain, delight shame, peacefulness, anger, pride*? Once you can name the impression, decide what aspects of the face give the impression you have. Are the eyes fierce or soft? Are the lips heavy, or thin and pale? Once you have thought this out, discuss your ideas briefly with the class.

Step 2. A Person in a Sentence.   Ask a volunteer to stand and to speak before the class for a few minutes. On the blank lines below write *one* sentence which describes the volunteer in the midst of some action. See how many senses you can use in the one sentence: appeal to color, sound, touch, and smell. Use a lively word to show action. Study the student samples below. When you have finished, read your own sentence aloud.

[color]   [action]   [touch]   [color]
Staring through wire gold-framed glasses, Jean brushes a soft strand of brown

[sound]   [action]
hair off her forehead and then coughs nervously into a trembling hand.

—Beth Anna Winters

His hairy arms stretching from black pants pockets, a yellow shirt hanging loosely over a worn leather belt, Danny breathes deeply cold morning air and whispers, "I don't know what to talk about."

—Albert Leone

_____

_____

_____

_____

How to Write Conclusions

The concluding paragraph of an essay is very much like the closing sentence of a paragraph. It should do all the things you learned in Chapter 5. A good conclusion should therefore

- tell the reader that your essay is coming to a close, and
- give the reader a feeling that you have accomplished what you set out to do.

But a closing paragraph permits the writer to develop some larger application for the topic. A good conclusion applies the topic of the essay to a broader issue. In a conclusion you can illustrate that the subject you have written about has importance beyond the ideas developed in your body paragraphs. You show that you have used what you have written to help you think about other ideas. This is not an easy chore. You run the risk of sounding too "important," too philosophical, too much like a show-off. As a result, the concluding paragraph needs especially careful thought and must often progress through several rewritings. But the finished product is well worth it: it helps the reader see that the narrow topic you developed has relevance in other critical areas. It gives you an opportunity to develop an idea that has an important relationship to your topic, but is new in the frame of the essay itself.

Let us examine the conclusion of an essay you read earlier and the relationship of the conclusion to the rest of the theme. Stella Tesoriero wrote in "Women: Fragile Flowers?" (pages 322–323) this proposal sentence:

Women are not the weaker sex.

In her second paragraph she tried to show how others would argue against her proposal. (She brings up the arguments of women's inferiority in stamina, stability, and thinking.) The third paragraph answers these arguments by presenting proof that they are incorrect and that women have a biological superiority to men. Here is Stella Tesoriero's conclusion; as you read, try to determine how she has worked upon her previous paragraphs to develop a broad issue in her last paragraph:

Woman has not been able to prove she is not the weaker sex because the society has assigned her to an inferior position. Few brilliant women have tried to develop their talents simply because there has been a small market for brilliant women in this country. The few who have bothered to develop their creative talents find that the world views them as "odd balls." The stereotype of a brilliant woman is that of a horsefaced, flat-chested female in support shoes, one who has hidden all her sexual instincts in her search for a career. It may be fun being treated like a fragile flower by a boyfriend or a date, but there is a time and place for everything. It is time society stopped giving out positions based on stereotypes. We women must develop and make use of our wasted female brain power.

This conclusion shows why women have not advanced in society. That is *not* an idea that is clearly part of the writer's proposal sentence:

Women are not the weaker sex.

Yet, by bringing in the related idea of stereotyping and the reasons for woman's inferior position in today's world, the writer offers a new significance for the topic. From the topic idea of woman's superiority to man, Stella Tesoriero moves into a larger application: the reason why women have for so long been kept down in society. She is showing the reader how the ideas she developed in paragraphs 2 and 3 (the superiority of man or woman) suggest a broader, more general application for the topic (the reasons why women do not show their superiority).

Her new application works effectively in the essay, but it is not the only possibility she could have chosen. The conclusion—based upon the proposal and the supporting body paragraphs—might have treated any one of these broader issues:

- women in the future replacing men in high-pressure jobs
- women as top political leaders
- the failure of male scientists to treat women fairly in experimental data
- a world in which men stay home to raise children and do housework

This list is not complete, but any of these points, developed with sufficient supporting details, might nicely suggest a wider and more general truth for the ideas proposed in the rest of the essay.

Notice, furthermore, that the first sentence of Stella Tesoriero's conclusion refers back to the ideas developed in previous paragraphs by mentioning the topic that the writer set out to develop. Look at the two sentences side by side:

Proposal	*First Sentence of Conclusion*
Women are not the weaker sex.	*Woman* has not been able to prove she *is not the weaker sex* because the society has assigned her to an inferior position.

The italicized words in the first sentence of the conclusion act as a transition because they bridge the conclusion to the topic as stated in the proposal. In addition, these words help summarize the topic for the reader who has read two full paragraphs since last seeing the proposal. This device of summary is excellent early in the conclusion because it reminds readers of what the essay set out to do, and permits them to evaluate the writer's success in developing the proposal.

TIPS AND REMINDERS FOR DRAMATIC CONCLUSIONS

(See pages 178–179, Some Closing Sentence Pointers.)
1. Remind the reader that you have achieved what you set out to do and that your essay is drawing to an end.
2. Strive to establish a new, a larger, a more general application for your topic.
3. Summarize briefly the main point of your essay.

4. Make the conclusion an important part of the essay, not an afterthought you glued on to add more words.
5. Do not:
   - start a whole new topic
   - contradict your entire point
   - make obvious or overused statements
   - apologize for your lack of knowledge
   - end suddenly with a one-sentence conclusion such as, "That's all I have to say."
   - draw conclusions that are absolute or too general (make sure that you allow for possibilities of exceptions)
   - talk about other parts of your own essay by mentioning words like "my introduction," "so my conclusion is," "my proposal sentence said"

Step 1. Essay Conclusions. Examine the essays listed below, paying special attention to the concluding paragraphs. Write in the blank lines below the title the writer's proposal (you may have to restate it in your own words so it is clear when you remove it from the essay). Then, in the blank space alongside, write the broader issue that the writer tries to develop in the conclusion. Study the example.

*Larger Application
(Broader Issue) in
Conclusion*

1. "Deprived Children," pages 318–319.
   Proposal: *children of working mothers are frequently insecure and unhappy.*

   what children left on their own must learn.

2. "Practice in the High School Gym," pages 245–246. *Proposal:* _____

3. "Ironing for Food," pages 282–283.
   Proposal: _____

4. "Working Mothers," pages 321–322.
   Proposal: _____

_____   _____
_____   _____

5. "Some Disappointments," pages 359–
   360. *Proposal:* _____

_____   _____

_____   _____

_____   _____

6. "Memories of the Australian Bush," pages
   244–245. *Proposal:* _____

_____   _____

_____   _____

_____   _____

Step 2. Finding New Areas of Relevance.   For each essay you have reread in connection with Step 1 above, suggest some *other* area of importance the writer could have developed in the conclusion. Base your suggestions on the proposal sentence and the two body paragraphs. Use separate paper.

Transforming Sentences: Active-Voice Verbs for Strong Meanings

Many verbs can express the same thought in two different ways. Which of these sentences do you find more satisfactory?

1. The tired employee locked the office door.
2. The office door was locked by the tired employee.

If you selected sentence 1, you probably realized, correctly, that the extra words needed to make sentence 2 really added nothing of importance to the sentence. Why take more words to say exactly what you could say with fewer words?

   Notice further that in sentence 1 the subject (*the tired employee*) performs the action of the verb. (It is he who *locked the office door.*)

   But in sentence 2 the subject (*the office door*) does not do anything. In fact, something happens to *it* (it was locked by the tired employee).

   Because the subject of sentence 1 actively performs the action of the verb, we say the verb is in the *active voice.*

   Because the subject of sentence 2 is acted upon by the verb, we say the verb is in the *passive voice.*

Hint: In most cases choose the active voice over the passive.

It is easy to transform passive-voice sentences to active ones. Just remember these pointers.

1. Passive-voice sentences always use some form of *to be* in combination with the verb. Look for word groups like *is seen, will be observed, can be cleaned, was done, should have been bought, would have been eaten.* You will have to remove the *to be* part to write an active-voice sentence.
2. Decide who performs the action of the verb. Usually the performer appears after the word *by.* Make that word the subject.

Passive:

The pencil was sharpened *by* Harriet.
           [This is a clue   [This is who
           to who performs   performs the
           the action.]   action of the
                                verb *sharpen.*]

Active: [*Was* is removed.]
Harriet sharpened the pencil.
    [The person who performs the
    action is now the subject
    of the verb.]

Step 1. Passive into Active. In the spaces provided, change the passive-voice sentences into active-voice ones.

Hint: Sometimes the person who performs the action is not mentioned in the passive-voice sentence. You will have to determine the performer of the action before you write the active-voice sentence. Study the example.

Example: The two employees were quickly brought before the manager.

(Here we do not know who actually brought them to the manager. Decide who you think performs the action and then rewrite.)

The guards quickly brought the two employees before the manager.

1. The rose bushes were planted in the garden by my sister Consuela.

   _____

2. A new Chevrolet was purchased by my wife and me.

   _____

3. It was decided that the office would close at noon.

   _____

4. We were told to eat fresh strawberries.

_____

5. The old woman's eyes were filled with fear and suffering.

_____

6. We were given as much help as we needed at Center Hardware Store.

_____

7. The blazing Montana sunset can be seen from Len Anderson's ranch.

_____

8. At Glacier National Park we were visited by mountain goats at our campsite.

_____

9. The rule about early bedtimes was expected to be obeyed in our home.

_____

10. Roses were delivered to Susan Wo Tan at five o'clock in the afternoon.

_____

SOLVING PROBLEMS IN WRITING: PRONOUN PRACTICE

Pronouns as Subjects

PRONOUN CHART I: SUBJECT PRONOUNS	
Singular Pronoun Subjects	*Plural Pronoun Subjects*
I it	we you
he you	they
she who	

You remember from your work in subject-verb agreement that the pronouns that appear above may be used as subjects of verbs.

_____ *run(s)*.

Any of the pronouns you see in the chart could be used in the blank space in the sentence above.

Example: I run.
He runs.
They run.

Although you would never say or write *Me run* or *Him runs*, when you use two subjects (one of which is a pronoun) for the same verb, you can forget to use the subject pronouns from this chart. The following sentences from student papers fail to use pronouns correctly. Alongside the incorrect sentence you will see the sentence written with the right subject pronoun.

Incorrect
1. My father and *me* never got along.
2. *Him* and *me* watched fireworks from across the bay.

Correct
My father and *I* never got along.
He and *I* watched fireworks from across the bay.

HINTS FOR CORRECT PRONOUNS WHEN YOU USE TWO SUBJECTS FOR THE SAME VERB

1. Always pick a pronoun you want to use as a subject from Pronoun Chart I on page 342.
2. Test each subject *alone* before you decide which pronoun to use. For example, suppose you do not know whether to use *her* or *she* in the blank space in this sentence:

   Her mother and _____ rushed into the house.

   First say:
     a. Her mother rushed into the house.
   Then say:
     b. Her rushed into the house.
   That would never sound right.
   Then say
     c. She rushed into the house.
   That is correct. Now combine the two subjects from *a* and *c*.
   Her mother and *she* rushed into the house.

Step 1. Speaking about Two Subjects. Combine any one of the subject pronouns (*he, I, she, it, we, they, you, who*) with the name of someone you know to tell about a place you recently visited. Speak your answers aloud.

Example: Jim and she saw that group at a concert.
My father and I drove into Waco last night.

Step 2. Filling in Pronoun Subjects. Fill the blank spaces with any pronoun subjects that make sense to you. Use different pronouns in each sentence.

1. Mrs. Chandler and _____ fixed the flat tire.

2. Charlotte and _____ dance well together.

3. _____ and her aunt own a health food store.

4. After _____ and their children finished painting, the whole house looked bigger.

5. His father and _____ share all the cooking.

PRONOUNS AFTER TO BE _____

[part of *to be*]

a. Everyone thought it was her.

b. Everyone thought it was she.

If you had to choose between *a* and *b*, you would probably select *a* as the sentence that you hear more frequently. However, sentence *b* is correct, and in writing, you want to remember this suggestion:

After a form of the verb to be *use a subject pronoun.*

The verb *to be* has many forms, a number of which appear below:

am	has been	should have been
is	have been	should be
are	had been	could be
was	will be	may be
were	must have been	
	could have been	

Hint: The expression "It's me" (It is me) is not correct formal English: "It is I" is what formal writing requires. However, "It's me" is used in conversation and is acceptable.

Step 3. Pronouns after *to Be*. Complete each sentence below by writing a correct *pronoun* after the verb. Circle the pronoun you use. You may add any other information you like.

Example:

1. It was ~~he who sang~~ _____.

2. We know it is _____.

3. The lawyer could have been _____.

4. It must have been _____.

5. It will be _____.

Step 4. Selecting Pronouns. Choose *subject pronouns* in the parentheses below to make the sentences correct.

1. The other actors and (he, him) didn't want to do the play.
2. Although it was (he, him) who was absent often from class, the instructor still gave him an A for the course.
3. (He, Him) and (me, I) went to the health club together.
4. Both (him, he) and his brother believed it should have been (they, them) who received the jobs.

Pronouns in Other Places

PRONOUN CHART II: NONSUBJECT PRONOUNS (OBJECTS)

Singular	*Plural*
me	us
him	them
her	whom
whom	

Hint: The words *it* and *you* may be used as subject or nonsubject pronouns.

The pronouns above are not subject pronouns and do not appear as subjects in sentences. Yet these words are usually found in two important sentence positions.

1. Pronouns After Verbs

[verb] [pronoun]
Give **me** the book.

[verb] [pronoun]
Bonnie selected **him** as her dancing partner.

[pronoun]
You *told* **whom** about the riot?
[verb]

Although you would never write

Give *I* the book

or

Bonnie selected *he* as her partner

whenever you use *two* words after the verb (one of which is a pronoun), you probably have some difficulty selecting the correct pronoun. Look at these sentences; is *a* or *b* correct?

[verb]   [verb]
a. The instructor praised Harriet and _I_ for   *b.* The instructor praised Harriet and *me* for
    our creativity.   our creativity.

You remember that *I* can be used only as a subject. In sentence *a*, the subject is *instructor* (for the verb *praised*). Since the pronoun you need comes *after* the verb *praised*, select the pronoun from the chart above. Since *me* appears in the chart, sentence *b* is correct.

HINTS FOR CORRECT PRONOUNS AFTER VERBS

1. Select the pronoun from Pronoun Chart II, page 345.
2. If two words must come after the verb, test each word alone before you decide which pronoun to use. Suppose you do not know whether to use *he* or *him* in the blank in this sentence.

   The teacher praised his brother and _____ for their cooperation.

   First say
     a. The teacher praised *his brother.*
   Then say
     b. The teacher praised *he.* That wouldn't sound right. Then say
     c. The teacher praised *him.*
   That is correct. Now combine the words after the verb in *a* and *c*:
     The teacher praised *his brother* and *him* for their cooperation.

Step 1. Writing Pronouns after Verbs. On separate paper write sentences for any ten of the following verbs. Use *two* words after each verb, one a noun and the other a correct pronoun. Write about things that really happened and use as many different pronouns as possible. Look at the example beneath the list of verbs.

noticed	accused	resisted
hurried	begged	drove
told	replaced	pretended
allowed	annoyed	frightened
questioned	brought	
chased	left	

Example:

The movie left my sister and me with an unpleasant feeling.

2. Pronouns After Connecting Words that Show Relationship

Aside from their use after verbs, the pronouns in Chart II above are used after certain connecting words that relate one word or word group in the sentence to some other sentence part. First, look at some of the connecting words that show relationship.

a. We read a *book* **about** *teenagers.*

The word *about* relates the words *book* and *teenagers* to each other by showing the kind of book.

b. Charlene *ran* **toward** *David.*

The word *toward* relates *ran* and *David* by showing where the action was performed. Now, if you wanted to use a pronoun instead of *teenagers* and instead of *David,* you would need a word from Pronoun Chart II (page 345):

We read a book **about** *them.*

Charlene ran **toward** *him.*

There are many connecting words like *about* and *toward* that show relationships. Here is a list of several of the most important. (See pages 269–271.)

SOME CONNECTORS THAT SHOW RELATIONSHIP			
about; by; beneath; inside; above; for; over; outside; along; among; of	except; under; onto; at; across; on; over; into; after; to; with	within; beside; since; as to; toward; at; beyond; up; before; like; below	between; below; upon; by means of; through; along with; because of; by way of; on account of; in spite of; in front of

Step 2. Remembering Connectors. Study the connectors above. Then, after covering the chart, write from memory as many as you can in the blank space below.

You probably would not have trouble writing *one* correct pronoun after the connector words mentioned above. No one would write

Give the book to *I.*

  or

The boy ran toward *he.*

But as soon as *two* words are used after the connector, students have difficulties.

Give the book **to** Mary and (I, me).

The boy ran **toward** the child and (he, him).

Since the pronoun you need comes after a connecting word that shows relationship (*to* and *toward*), you must select a pronoun from Pronoun Chart II. The words *I* and *he* are not correct because they are subject pronouns (Pronoun Chart I) and must be used as subjects of verbs. Correctly written, the sentences above become:

Give the book to Mary and *me*.

The boy ran toward the child and *him*.

HINTS FOR PRONOUNS AFTER CONNECTORS THAT SHOW RELATIONSHIP

1. Select the pronoun from Pronoun Chart II, page 345.
2. If *two* words come after the connector word that shows relationship, test the words one at a time before you decide which pronoun to use. If you don't know whether to use *I* or *me* in this sentence:

   The dean spoke about Joe and _____ .

First say

   a. The dean spoke about *Joe.*

Then say

   b. The dean spoke about *I.*

That doesn't sound right.
Then say

   c. The dean spoke about *me.*

This is obviously correct.
Now combine the results in *a* and *c* above.

   The dean spoke about *Joe* and *me.*

Step 3. Pronouns for You to Choose. Fill in both blanks in each item below. Use a pronoun in at least one of the blanks. You can use a noun *or* another pronoun in the other blank. Look at the example.

1. toward *him* and *me*
2. for _____ and _____
3. beyond _____ or _____
4. except _____ and _____
5. between _____ and _____
6. at _____ and _____
7. because of _____ and _____
8. in spite of _____ and _____
9. below _____ and _____
10. instead of _____ or _____

Step 4. Writing Sentences with Connectors that Show Relationship. Use five of the subject-verb combinations below in sentences of your own. After each subject-verb combination, use correctly one of the completed word groups from Step 3 above.

Subject-Verb Combinations

you speak   a bird flew
he played   the child laughed
they drove   he watched
they included   everyone saluted
a motorcycle roared

Example:

1. *They drove toward him and me.* _____.

2. _____.

3. _____.

4. _____.

5. _____.

6. _____.

A Special Problem

Some of the words listed as connectors that show relationship also act as subordinators or coordinators. You remember that subordinators and coordinators (see pages 17–18 and 89–94) introduce subject-verb groups which are connected to complete sentences. So, it *is* possible to find a subject pronoun after one of the words listed as connectors that show relationship. But notice how differently the word is used in each of these sentences:

A   *B*
My brother ran <u>before</u> me.   <u>Before</u> <u>I</u> <u>ran</u> away, my brother left home.

In *A*, the word *before* is a connector that relates the word *ran* and *me* by showing where the action took place.

In *B*, the word *before* is a connector that subordinates the subject-verb word group *I ran away* to the complete thought *my brother left home.*

Step 5. Connectors in Two Ways. Fill in each blank after the connector with the correct pronoun from either Pronoun Chart I or Pronoun Chart II.

Hint: 1. If the pronoun is the subject of a verb, use Pronoun Chart I.
2. Study the hints on pages 343–344 and 348.

1. They brought the tools for my girl friend and _____.

2. We were very thirsty, for my brother and _____ ate hot sauce.

3. After Delores and _____ cooked the frankfurters, they raced to the lake.

4. A lonely dog followed Charles and _____.

How Pronouns Agree

a. The girl kissed her mother.
b. The boys brought their gloves.

In these two sentences the underlined word is a pronoun that takes the place of the noun to which the arrow is drawn. In sentence *a*, the word *girl* is singular and the pronoun that refers back to it must be singular (*her*). In sentence *b*, the word *boys* is plural and the pronoun that refers back to it must be plural (*their*). It is easy to see that *boys* is plural and *girl* is singular.

c. She kissed her mother.
d. They brought their gloves.

In sentence *c* and *d* the underlined pronoun takes the place of another pronoun. *Her* takes the place of *she;* since *she* is singular, *her* must be singular. *Their* takes the place of *they;* since *they* is plural, *their* must be plural too. But with words like *boys, girl, they,* and *she,* it is easy to decide whether the word is singular or plural. Several pronouns—although they may look plural—are always singular. If another pronoun later on in the sentence refers back to one of these special singular pronouns, that pronoun must be singular too.

SPECIAL SINGULAR PRONOUNS

anyone	everyone	someone	one
anybody	everybody	somebody	neither
each	either	no one	none
		nobody	

Hint: If a pronoun refers to one of these words, the pronoun must be singular.

Everyone	should bring	*his* own assignment.
Each	of them packed	*his* own bag.
Anybody	may raise	*his* own hand.
Either	of the boys can drive	*his* own car.
Anyone	can love	*his* own country.
One	of them sold	*his* own camera
None	of them helped	*his* own country.

[This pronoun refers to one of the special singular pronouns.]

HIS **OR** *HER*?

His is used as a pronoun even when the group contains men and women. *Her* is used when the group is clearly all women.

    Everyone of them drove *her* own car.
    Either of them can make *her* own clothes.

> Many writers who are sensitive to sex stereotyping try to avoid using *his* to refer to mixed groups that contain men and women. Sometimes plural forms help avoid choosing *his*.
>
> *Examples:*
>
> | *Singular* | *Plural* |
> |---|---|
> | Everyone should bring his own assignment. | All the students should bring their assignments. |
> | Each of them packed his own bag. | They all packed their own bags. |
>
> Some writers use the form *s/he* to refer to mixed groups, but it has not won wide popular approval.

Step 6. Selecting the Right Pronoun. Write in the blank spaces the correct word in the parentheses. Or, rewrite the sentences so they use plural forms.

Example: Everyone sharpened ___*his*___ pencil (his, their).

1. Each of them should have driven _____ car more safely (her, their).

2. Everybody likes taking pictures of _____ vacation trips. (their, his).

3. All the drivers started _____ engines at the same time (their, his).

Pronouns that Point Out (Demonstrative Pronouns)

This book is mine.
These papers ripped.
That girl fell.
Those cars sped along the highway.

Only *this, these, that, those* point out.

Don't Use **Them** *to Point Out.*
Not: *Them* windows look dirty
but: *Those* windows look dirty.

Since *this* and *that* are singular, the words they point out must be singular.
Since *these* and *those* are plural, the words they point out must be plural.

[singular] [singular]
This kind of book is stimulating.

    not

[plural] [plural]
These kinds of cars save money on gasoline.

[plural] [singular]
These kind of books is stimulating.

Step 7. Pointing Out with Pronouns. Fill in the blanks with *this, that, these, those,* or *them.*

1. Never eat _____ kind of sandwich.

2. _____ type of lock never opens easily.

3. With _____ sort of friend you always have someone to turn to.

4. _____ kinds of people buy many books but never read _____.

5. _____ kind of movie annoys me.

For the steps below, use the review charts. Make sure that you know the connectors listed on page 347.

REVIEW

PRONOUN CHART I	PRONOUN CHART II
Subjects	*After Verbs and after Connectors That Show Relationship*
I we he she they it you you who	me us him her them it you whom
After "to be," use subject pronouns.	If you need a pronoun as one of two words, try one word at a time.
Use *this, that, these, those* to point out. Don't use *them!*	He asked Barry and (I, me). He asked *I.* [wrong] He asked *me.* [right]
these boys not *them* boys	Then: He asked Barry and me.

Hint: Use a singular pronoun to refer to a special singular pronoun like *anyone, everyone, anybody, someone, no one, neither, either, each.*

THE USE OF THE PRONOUN *YOU*

In many informal writing situations, where the writer is actually addressing the reader, the pronoun *you* works nicely. However, it sometimes creates problems in style when *you* includes the reader unintentionally. In the second of the two sentences below, the writer addresses the reader as if the reader were present:

My room is a restful place. When you look out the window you can see tall pines against the gray sky.

The use of *you* in the second sentence is too informal and, hence, not appropriate to essay writing. The *you* assumes that the reader can join the writer in the actual experience.

One way to avoid the informal *you* is to use *I* (or *we,* if it works), a more accurate pronoun under the circumstances:

My room is a restful place. When *I* look out the window, *I* can see tall pines against the gray sky.

Although American writers (as opposed to British, say) do not always feel comfortable with the pronoun *one, one* can serve well for more formal effects than *I:*

My room is a restful place. When *one* looks out the window, *one* can see tall pines against the gray sky.

Another solution is to use a word like *person* or some other noun that works in the sentence:

My room is a restful place. When a *person* looks out the window, *he* can see tall pines against the gray sky.

Finally, a writer could combine sentences to eliminate the pronouns for a smoother, fuller, more descriptive sentence:

My room is a restful place because out the window tall pines nestle against the gray sky.

Step 8. Avoiding *You* in Sentences. Rewrite the sentences below for formal papers by removing the pronoun *you.*

Hint: If you use *one,* make sure that your new sentence does not sound strained.

1. The car is only one year old. You wouldn't know it by looking at it though. _____

   _____

2. In Rose of Lima Church you can see the stained glass windows just above your pew if you look to your left. _____

   _____

3. An old brown chair stands near the door. If you're tired you can sit down and rest your feet. _____

   _____

Step 9. Pronouns in Your Sentences. On separate paper, use the following word groups correctly in sentences.

1. my family and me
2. the girl and I
3. the author and us
4. you and them
5. Sandy and me
6. those kinds
7. Maria and who
8. Greg and me
9. him and me
10. he and I

Name _____ Class _____ Date _____

Step 10. Reviewing Pronoun Usage. Write on the blank line in the margin the correct pronouns you select from parentheses. Look at the example.

Is College Worth It?

1. _𝓘_   Sometimes I wonder if college and (me, I) were meant for each
2. _____ other. These days, many people say that (they, them) think a col-
3. _____ lege diploma is worth only the paper it is written on. (Them, Those)
4. _____ people may be right. My father tells me that all his friends and (he, him) have done just fine without college degrees. In many ways he
5. _____ and (them, they) are very successful. To anyone who measures
6. _____ (their, his) success by big cars, large houses, and fancy clothes, a
7. _____ college degree may not be worth (his, their) time. However, for my
8. _____ friends and (I, me) success means something else. Every one of us
9. _____ wants more for (his, their) life than just material things. Sure, (them,
10. _____ those) symbols of status are very nice and comfortable, but against
11. _____ (it, them) we'll compare even one finely tuned mind. So, although
12. _____ we may never have Cadillacs and diamonds, the people whom I re-
13. _____ spect and (me, I) will always have our knowledge. (You, One) can
14. _____ lose (your, one's) riches, but knowledge remains.

Step 11. Pronouns in Review. Circle the correct pronouns in the parentheses.

1. None of the children brought (their, his) pens.
2. The musician gave lessons to Marian and (me, I).
3. Was it really (her, she)?
4. George gave (them, those) tickets to Anna and (I, me).
5. Sally and (I, me) loved to sketch people in the park.
6. The doctor and (he, him) agreed on the diagnosis.
7. Between (he, him) and (I, me), there was never a loss for words.
8. (That, These) kinds of oranges taste sweet.
9. Ellen and (she, her) said it was (they, them) who sent the card.
10. Someone left (his, their) briefcase full of money in the taxi.

DEGREES OF COMPARISON

Words that Compare: Which Form to Use

When we use describing words, we can often compare one thing with another merely by changing the ending of a word. For example:

One boy is tall. Another boy is tall*er*.

Parker is the tall*est* boy at the party.

You have to be careful, however, to use the correct ending.

Use *-er* at the end of a word if you want to compare only two items.
Use *-est* at the end of a word if you want to compare three or more items.

Examples:

One person or thing is	Of two people or things, one is	Among three or more people or things, one is
short	shorter	shortest
quick	quicker	quickest
silly	sillier	silliest

If the word you are using to compare has *three or more* syllables:

Use *more* in front of the word if you want to compare only two items.
Use *most* in front of the word if you want to compare three or more items.

Hint: If you are not sure how to make the correct form of the word, use your dictionary.

One person or thing is	Of two people or things, one is	Among three or more people or things, one is
attractive	more attractive	most attractive
enormous	more enormous	most enormous
done quickly	done more quickly	done most quickly

Some words do not form comparisons in the usual way; these you have to memorize because they are irregular.

One person or thing is	Of two people or things, one is	Among three or more people or things, one is
bad	worse	worst
done badly	done worse	done worst
good	better	best
done well	done better	done best
little	less	least
many	more	most
much	more	most

Some words may not be compared at all because their meanings do not allow for degrees in comparison:

unique	empty
perfect	full

Step 1. Correct Comparison. Fill in the spaces in the three columns below. The word you write must make sense in the blank line that appears in the sentence on top of the column. Look at the example.

Hint: For some words you have the choice of either adding an ending (*-er* or *-est*) or using *more* or *most*. But remember, use one or the other—*not both*.

Wrong: She is more thriftier than her friend.
Right: She is more thrifty than her friend.
        or
      She is thriftier than her friend.

The teacher is _____.	Between Professor Merryl and Professor Grace, Professor Grace is _more_. _attractive_	Of all the teachers I have had, Professor Grace is _most attractive_.
1. attractive		
2. witty	_____	_____
3. understanding	_____	_____
4. productive	_____	_____
5. messy	_____	_____

Hint: Check spelling rule 2 on page 377.

Step 2. Changing Wrong Comparisons. Each sentence below uses a comparison incorrectly. Draw a line through the wrong word, and write in the blank space at the right the word or words that you would use to make the sentence correct.

Example: He runs the ~~most~~ fastest on the team.   _fastest_

1. Of the two boys Juan and David, David is tallest.   _____
2. Nina was the talentedest of all the photographers.   _____
3. Mr. Chin is the most smartest teacher I ever had.   _____

Step 3. Your Own Comparisons. Use correctly in a sentence of your own each of the following words or word groups. Use separate paper.

1. least
2. better
3. more quickly
4. best
5. nastiest

WRITING THE ESSAY

Suggestions for Thinking It Through

From all your associations with people, select one individual who has had a deep and important effect on your life—a relative, a friend, an acquaintance—and write a four-paragraph essay in which you explore this effect.

Although you may choose any suitable method of development for each of the *body* paragraphs (paragraphs 2 and 3, that is), the most forceful presentation will probably be one dramatic, full, expanded moment in each paragraph. In that way specific events serve to illustrate the character of someone close to you. Perhaps you will want to show how your feelings toward someone you know changed, or how someone you know can show opposite qualities: in that case, compare and contrast two specific moments which show the reader these opposite qualities.

But if you do not want to use narration—the story-telling device—you have a number of other possibilities for developing paragraphs. Perhaps you will want to use several instances to explore one specific aspect of the character of someone close to you (Chapter 3). You might want to use one of many devices of comparison and contrast within one paragraph: one of the three patterns explained on pages 127–135; the analogy (pages 161–162); or the mood sketch (pages 159–161). You might want to analyze a particular personality trait of someone close to you: you could try to explain *why* the person has such a trait, and what the causes were for the development of such a personality. A vivid essay usually makes use of a combination of techniques.

In any case, make sure that each paragraph expands through clear details one aspect of your topic. The four crucial questions you ask yourself before you write (see page 315) will help you pinpoint the kinds of details you will need to use. You might repeat your favorite author's exact words; you might say in your own words what you remember of what someone said on television; you might even use numbers, percentages, or case studies to illustrate your idea on the subject you have chosen. You will also need to interpret certain objective facts as you see them in order to determine their significance to your essay. For example, you might observe a certain gesture used by the individual you choose to write about. You must also decide what that gesture *means* about the person's character.

Several topics for you to consider appear after the student samples.

Learning from Other Students

Read the samples below. In the first selection Karl Joreid explores his own character and that of his father. Barbara Pomerantz shows her brother's character as she illustrates two specific moments she remembers with him.

My Father Teaches Me to Cry

Cried? Certainly I've cried before, I cried the time a bumble bee stung my earlobe, the time a branch of an oak on 116th Avenue cracked and dropped me to the ground, the time a brown squirrel at Forest Park mistook my finger for a peanut. I cried when a policeman fished me out of the black waters of Jackson Pond and the time my brother Al, getting even for my locking him outside the house during a thunderstorm, chased me around the yard with a spider in his hand. Crying as a little boy was a way of saying "Hug me Mommy, I'm hurt." But it also earned me a frown from my father, a thunderous slap on the back, and a "What are you crying for? Big boys don't cry." And thus gradually I learned from my father how *not* to cry, keeping this instruction all through my teens. Even when I checked Dad into Fort Hamilton's Veterans Hospital that winter afternoon, I did not cry. Even during his operation for cancer and the awful suffering afterwards I held back my tears, only to learn crying again the day after he died.

With such good training in holding back it was frighteningly simple to stay near him, alone and dry eyed every day, and to comfort Mom at home, too frightened to see him. On December 13, a week after the operation to remove cancerous tissue from beneath his tongue, pneumonia set in. I stood at his bedside, tightly gripping with one hand the cold railing around his bed. With my other hand I gently grasped his. The lids of his eyes cracked open. He squeezed my fingers and tried hard to speak, but with half a tongue and with a jaw rebuilt with wires, it was impossible. His words hissed through a tube draining liquid from his lungs. Prepared, I had brought a yellow pencil and a sheet of white paper. My father's massive hand scrawled out two words. I thought I saw a tear hanging in the corner of his eye, as he handed me the note. It said, "I'm afraid." I smiled weakly and patted him on his shoulder. "Hey, don't worry. Everything'll work out fine, you'll see." I said the same words to Mom when I returned from the hospital as she sat in the dark kitchen, chewing her lip, drumming her fingernails on the wooden table. Each time I tried to speak her eyes would fill with tears and she would turn away from my stare. At five minutes to midnight the eerie ringing of the telephone echoed through the still rooms. Dead.

Having stayed manly in my sorrow and through the ordeal of his dying, I prayed to cry even as I drove to Veterans Hospital to claim my father's things. As I dragged my feet across the parking lot I wished for a gust of wind to start my tears. I thought of the night before, and how I had sat in the living room amid my mother's sobs slumped into the couch, rubbing circles in the dust on the black phone, my eyes stinging but dry. I hadn't even been able to release my feelings at the news of my father's death. As I worked my way through the stark hospital corridors to the claim desk, the medicinal stench of ether and alcohol surrounded me. Slowly, efficiently, a tall nurse brought me to a room lined with metal shelves; reaching up, she brought down a paper bag and gave it to me. So that was all that was left! I clutched the bag as she handed me a brown wooden cane tipped with a cup of black rubber. I held the warm wood; the gentle curve of the cane felt awkward in my grasp. I saw my father again poking his cane along the frozen ground, struggling from the car and limping painfully to his death in a hospital bed. Unable to keep in my tears this time, I finally collapsed onto a cold metal chair and sobbed miserably, the bag crushed to my chest. I cried as I thought of my father's last words on a sheet of white paper; I cried as I saw Mom trembling in the large empty house; I cried for all the tearless pain and anger and frustration building up inside me over the years.

Why did it have to take the death of someone I loved to put me back in touch with my feelings? The idea of being unmanly kept back in me the expression of such a basic emotion as sorrow for the death of a loved one. The whole idea of required behavior based upon sex seems unfortunate to me now, and I support the push nowadays toward equality between the sexes, especially as children grow up. Little girls should learn to play baseball, should have instruction in mowing lawns and hunting, should be praised for showing strength and courage and force. Little boys should learn to love dolls, should be taught about cooking, sewing and cleaning, should earn rewards for showing that they are sensitive and are often hurt. Children growing to adulthood who learn to explore many interests and feelings in spite of society's stereotypes will not run the risk of facing serious emotional problems.

—Karl E. Joreid

Some Disappointments

My girl friends always envied the fact that I had an older brother, and until about two years ago, their envy was understandable. Gary taught me everything about life until I was old enough to learn for myself. Having a brother three years older had its little advantages. I not only knew all about baseball, but I could also name every single New York Yankee on the team and every team in both leagues. Gary forced me to watch "boy" TV programs like *Combat* and *Battleground,* but now I switch on such shows myself without a second thought. It was Gary who tried to stop me from reading girlish romance magazines so that I could read more important literature. And he tried to get me to like classical music, although I stuck with the Beatles. As I grew older I followed in the path he laid for me, but Gary suddenly changed. I can remember two distinct moments when my faith in my brother was shattered—when I discovered that he was not the very special person I thought him to be, but instead, someone quite ordinary.

I realized the change in Gary one winter Saturday when I rushed excitedly into his room to talk about *The Red Badge of Courage,* a book I had just read and loved. "Let me read you this part," I shouted. "You'll just love it." Gary lay on the wrinkled sheets of his bed, eyes shut, humming along with the song drifting from the radio. "I'm not interested," he replied, returning to his dreamy thoughts about the lyrics. Those three words stung me deeply and I felt an angry reply jump to my lips. Instead I tried to look away from Gary, to seek comfort in the familiar surroundings of his room. But this depressed me. Musty old newspapers lay scattered on the bare floor. One dim bulb threw shadows on the walls and in the dark corners. Rows and rows of books stood forgotten on the scratched mahogany shelves, gathering dust. A white shirt with rolled-up sleeves hung on the closet doorknob; one black sock stretched from under the bed. A poster of Uncle Sam stared down from the wall, pointing his finger and telling me he wanted me for the United States Army. When I saw Gary's spotless radio and his beloved collection of "soul" records, I exploded. "You're never interested in good books anymore. You're all wrapped up in yourself. You listen to that creepy jazz all the time and if you read the back of a cereal box, that's your reading for the day. What's wrong, Gary?" With his eyes still closed and a sly smile crossing his face, he said, "I've seen the light." I fled from the room, wondering if I had dreamed what had just occurred. Was that stranger in there my brother?

That moment in Gary's room was mild, though, when compared to the changes I saw in his temper. I will never forget the way he looked one weekend evening as he stalked to the front door on his way out. He wore a blue-denim shirt unbuttoned halfway down his chest, revealing a clump of black hair; faded bell-bottomed jeans clinging tightly to his hips; a green army jacket, worn out at the elbows. Gary's blonde hair was uncombed and his moustache pointed downwards, giving him the look of the bad guy in an old western. Those warm gray eyes that once encouraged and helped me now looked confused and distant and cold. "Where are you going so late?" my mother called from the kitchen above the clatter of dishes. "Get off my back!" he snapped. "I'm twenty years old, and if I want to stay out all night, I will." I stood rooted to the floor, shocked at his outbreak. Through the door, out of the house, down the front porch steps Gary stormed. The sharp smell of after shave lotion still hung about the room. As the door slammed, my mother rushed into the living room. We looked helplessly at each other. "What's happened to him?" she moaned. "It wasn't easy raising two children all alone after your father died. Gary should have become the head of the family and look what's become of him! Is it my fault?" Wishing desperately to relieve her, I could only remain silent. There have been many times since when my mother and I have stood shocked at one of Gary's outbursts, unable to say a word and wondering why this was happening.

I often wonder why Gary had to change so drastically; I was very fond of him the way he was. As a child I had a brother unlike any others, but now he is just like anyone else who thinks that bad language and sloppiness will cure the ills of society. Gary has also announced to my mother—who turned sick and cried when she heard it—that he no longer believes in God. I have tried to tell him during these past few years that his way will not work, but as usual, he does not listen. Strangely enough, however, even with my brother's awful new behavior, he is still helping me. Gary has shown me that his course in life is wrong and that mine is better and more effective. He sees all the ugliness in life, but I look for and find beauty. In his denial of God, I strengthen my own faith. I see his restlessness and I seek a purpose.

—Barbara Pomerantz

Step 1. Review Your Reading. Discuss these questions about the essays you have just read.

1. What, according to the proposal sentence, does each writer set out to illustrate?
2. For each essay, outline the incidents or images that develop the reader's sense of the characters.
3. How does each writer's conclusion support or contradict the proposal sentence for each essay?

Some Essay Titles for You to Consider

Here are some titles which may suggest essay topics for you.

1. Love Means Trouble
2. The Forgotten Relative
3. The Refugee
4. A Handicap Overcome
5. You'll Never See Me Again
6. A Remarkable Neighbor
7. My Father's Shame
8. Grandmother: A Burden *or* a Blessing

9. A Friend Who Turned Against Me
10. The Liberated Man
11. We Don't Get Along at All
12. My Mate Is My Security
13. My Child Learns
14. Nobody Believes _____ (fill in name)
15. My Husband's Return

Remember that titles are made to catch the reader's attention. You may adapt any of these titles (or one of your own) to suit the needs of your own essay.

Revealing Character: A Checklist of What to Aim For

Before you write this theme, examine the checklist below. Then, after you are satisfied that your theme is in its final form, fill in the answers to the questions and submit this list with your essay.

1. Did I make use of the prewriting techniques I learned in previous chapters? Which of the following techniques did I use in taking this essay from my ideas to its final form? (Also think about which techniques were the most effective in making your writing better.)

sensory list (pages 35–36) _____
brainstorming (pages 66–67) _____
free association (pages 110–111) _____
scratch outline (pages 152–153) _____
narrowing the topic (pages 197–198) _____
timed writing (pages 247–248) _____
making a list (pages 285–287) _____
subject tree (pages 324–326) _____

2. Did I write a complete rough draft which I revised before handing in the finished product? _____
3. Did I select for the subject of my essay a person who means a great deal to me, someone who has affected me strongly? _____
4. Does my proposal sentence allow me to explore two significant aspects of the person I wrote about? _____
5. Does my introduction logically and smoothly lead up to my proposal sentence? Study pages 219–223 for ideas on introductions. _____
6. Have I chosen one moment to expand on in each paragraph and have I made sure to fill in some details of the setting by mentioning time and place? Notice how Barbara Pomerantz describes Gary's room. _____
7. Have I used vivid details based in sensory language to give the reader a clear idea of the sights, the colors, the sounds, and the smells of the moment? Karl Joreid makes the hospital smells very real. _____
8. Have I made sure to include at least one description of my subject in action? _____
9. Are my transitions careful and flowing, especially at the openings of paragraphs 2 and 3? _____

10. Have I used at least one line of spoken details? Ms. Pomerantz writes: _____
    "With his eyes still closed and a sly smile crossing his face, he said, 'I've
    seen the light.'" See pages 125–126 for hints on expressive quotation
    sentences.

11. Have I made sure to use a variety of sentence openers to vary the style _____
    and rhythm by trying to write sentences like those explained on pages
    304–306? Have I written active voice sentences (pages 340–342)?

12. Have I used some of the new vocabulary explained on pages 334–336? _____

13. Did I review my Theme Progress Sheet for errors I made in my last few _____
    papers in order to correct them in this essay?

14. Have I used the suggestion on pages 337–339 in order to write a more _____
    effective conclusion?

15. Have I reread this essay first for clarity and smoothness and then for _____
    errors, and have I spent sufficient time rewriting the problem spots?

16. Did I make sure to read the student themes on pages 358–360 to get a _____
    clearer idea about how to reveal character most effectively?

THE PROFESSIONALS SPEAK

The stories below present interesting and effective character studies. Discuss the questions after each selection.

Birthday Party

They were a couple in their late thirties, and they looked unmistakably married. They sat on the banquette opposite us in a little narrow restaurant, having dinner. The man had a round, self-satisfied face, with glasses on it; the woman was fadingly pretty, in a big hat. There was nothing conspicuous about them, nothing particularly noticeable, until the end of their meal, when it suddenly became obvious that this was an Occasion—in fact, the husband's birthday, and the wife had planned a little surprise for him.

It arrived, in the form of a small but glossy birthday cake, with one pink candle burning in the center. The headwaiter brought it in and placed it before the husband, and meanwhile the violin-and-piano orchestra played "Happy Birthday to You" and the wife beamed with shy pride over her little surprise, and such few people as there were in the restaurant tried to help out with a pattering of applause. It became clear at once that help was needed, because the husband was not pleased. Instead he was hotly embarrassed, and indignant at his wife for embarrassing him.

You looked at him and you saw this and you thought, "Oh, now, don't *be* like that!" But he was like that, and as soon as the little cake had been deposited on the table, and the orchestra had finished the birthday piece, and the general attention had shifted from the man and woman, I saw him say something to her under his breath—some punishing thing, quick and curt and unkind. I couldn't bear to look at the woman then, so I stared at my plate and waited for quite a long time. Not long enough, though. She was still crying when I finally glanced over there again. Crying quietly and heartbrokenly and hopelessly, all to herself, under the gay big brim of her best hat.

—Katharine Brush

1. What does the story reveal about the husband? About the wife?
2. Why is the husband embarrassed? How does he show his embarrassment? Can you understand how he feels? What about the way the story is written makes it hard to sympathize with him?
3. The writer has used sensory language sparingly but very effectively. Which images do you find most successful? Why?
4. Discuss the last two sentences. How do they summarize in an image all the contradictions of the moment?

The selection below develops through details of one specific moment the character of both the narrator and someone he meets in the park. Write the answers to the questions that appear after the story.

SOME WORDS TO KNOW BEFORE YOU READ

togs: clothing
Perstando et Praestando Utilitati: Latin phrase, meaning "Persevering and Excelling in Practicality"

The Stick Up

I felt good. I think the park had something to do with it. Trees, grass, bushes—everything in brand-new togs of shining green. The warm yellow sunlight sifting down through the trees, making my face feel alive and healthy and casting shadows on the paved walks and the unpaved walks and the wooden benches. Slight breezes tickling my nostrils, caressing my face, bringing with them a good clean odor of things new and live and dripping with greenness. Such a good feeling made me uneasy.

The park breathing with people, old and young. Playing checkers and chess, listening to portable radios—the Dodgers leading the Giants. I walked to the end of the park and stood near the wading pool where the water spurted skyward.

Little children in their underpants, splashing the water and pretending to swim, and throwing water at each other and yelling and shouting in wild childish happiness. One Negro child with a soft dark face and big brown eyes pretended to enjoy herself, but her big black eyes gave her away—anxious and uneasy. As if she were not sure that all of a sudden the other children would not turn on her and bite her like a bunch of mad dogs. I knew that feeling—even now. Barefoot women sat round the pool watching the children, reading books, trying to get brown without the expense of a Florida vacation. A little blonde-headed girl got smacked in the face and ran bawling to her black-haired mother. A double-decker Fifth Avenue bus passed to the east, with curious passengers looking from the top deck. The tall buildings of New York University looked over and down upon a noisy humanity playing in the park. *Perstando et Praestando Utilitati* —

The kids were having loads of fun and it made me think back. I substituted a country woods for the beautiful city park. I made believe the wading pool was the swimming hole on old man Gibson's forbidden grounds. And something turned over and over in my stomach and ran like a chill through the length of my body, leaving a funny taste in my mouth. I took a sudden trip into the past. Meeting kids I had known many years ago, as if they had remained kids and had never grown up. My face tight and full now as I swallowed a mouthful of cool green air. It was the first time I had been homesick in many years. Standing there trying to recall names, faces and incidents. After a moment I shrugged it off. I could never really be homesick for the country woods and the swimming holes of Georgia. Give me the city—the up-north city.

I turned and started walking back through the park, passing women, young and old, blond and brunette, and black and brown and light brown in white uniforms, pushing various types of baby carriages. I had almost reached the other end of the park, when a big lumbering giant of a white man came toward me. I tried to walk out of his way, but he maneuvered into my path and grabbed me by the shoulders. He was unshaven, his clothes were filthy and he reeked of rot-gut whiskey and days and nights without soap and water. He towered over me and coughed in my face and said in a deep rasping voice—"This is a stick up!"

I must have looked silly and startled. What was he up to, in broad open daylight? Oh—no—he must be kidding. And yet, crazier things happen every day in this crazy world of New York City. Especially in the Village.

He jabbed his big forefinger into my side, causing me to wince. Then he nudged me playfully and said, "I'm only kidding, buddy. But cheesuz christmas, I do need just four more cents for the price of a drink. How about it, professor? It's just four lousy cents. Didn't hardly take me no time at all to hustle up the rest of it this morning, but seems to me I just can't get this last four cents don't care how hard I try. It's a goddamn shame!"

I made a show of feeling in my pockets. I had no loose change and knew it. I wanted to say, Well, you sure won't get it from me, but I said instead, "Gosh, I don't have it. I'm sorry."

I started to walk away from him. He put his big arms around me, surrounding me with his foul odor. His shirt was dirty and greasy, smelled like sour food and whiskey vomit. A deep gash started near his right eye and beat a trail down into his mouth. An awful cloud came between me and the springtime, blotting out the breeze, the sunshine, the freshness that had been everywhere.

"Look, buddy, I ain't no ordinary bum you meet on the street. I want you to know that. I'm just down on my luck—see?"

I wanted to shrug my shoulders, wanted to say, I don't give a damn what you are! Through the years I had built up a resistance against people like him, and I thought I was foolproof. He rambled on, "I know—you—you think I'm just one of them everyday bums, but it isn't so. I'm just as educated as the next feller. But I know what you think though. I—"

My nostrils quivered, my neck gathered sweat. I wanted to be away from him. "You don't know what I think!"

He leaned heavily on my shoulder. My body sagged under his enormous weight. My knees buckled. "You don't have to be that way, mate. Just because a feller is down on his luck. Can't never tell when you'll need a favor yourself. Listen, I'm an educated man. Look, I used to be a business man too."

I kept thinking angrily to myself, of all the people in the park, most of them white, why did he single me out? It wasn't the first time a thing like this had happened. Just a week before I was on the subway and a white drunk got on at Thirty-fourth Street. He looked around for a seat and there were plenty available next to other people. But he finally spied me, the only Negro in the half-empty car, and he came and sat down beside me, choosing me to be the benefactor of his infinite wisdom and his great liberal philosophy and his bad-liquored breath.

I tried to pull away from this one in the park but his huge hand held me by the shoulder. With his other hand he fumbled in his shirt pocket, then in the back pocket of his trousers. He fished out a dirty ragged snapshot. "Look," he said, "that's me and my family. I used to be a business man out west. Had a good business too. Yes indeed."

It would have been comical had it not been so tragic, the way pride gleamed in his eyes as he gazed at the picture. I suppose it was he, although you had to stare at it hard and stretch your imagination. He looked like a million dollars, posing with a wife and two fine-looking children. I began to wonder what had happened to him along the way—what had become of his family—then caught myself going soft. Oh—no—none of that sentimental stuff. I glanced at my watch deliberately. "Look, my friend," I said, "I've got—"

His eyes were like red flint marbles. He coughed like he would strangle to death and directly into my face. My entire being came up in revolt against everything about him, but still he was a human being, and he might have gotten his four cents, maybe more, if he hadn't made his next pitch the way he did.

"Look, professor, I don't think I'm any better than you or anybody else. I want you to know that. We're all fighting together against them goddamn gooks in Viet Nam, ain't we? You look like an intelligent young man. I'm an educa—How about it, professor? Just four little old lousy cents—"

All of my inner resentment pushed outward as I squirmed and wrested myself angrily from his hold. "I've got to go! Goddamnit—I don't have any four cents for you!"

I started walking away from him toward the street corner trembling with anger, but uplifted by the fresh air rushing into my entire body. I stood at the intersection waiting for the light to change. Something made me turn and look for the big man. I saw him lumbering toward me again. My body became tense. A flock of cars were passing. Why in the hell didn't the light change to green? But then he stopped and sat down heavily on the last bench in the park. Amid a fit of coughing I heard him mumble—"Damn. This is getting to be a helluva country, when you can't chisel four lousy pennies off a prosperous-looking nigger!"

My hands clenched unconsciously. I smiled with a bitter taste in my mouth. The light changed to green. I started across the street.

—John Oliver Killens

1. What images does the narrator use to show the environment?
2. Why in the first paragraph does the narrator say he feels "uneasy"?
3. What does his reaction to the Negro child (paragraph 3) tell you about his own personality? How does the child relate to the narrator's "uneasiness"?

4. What details give you the best picture of the "big lumbering giant of a white man"?
5. What does the man want? What does he say or do to work on the narrator's sympathies?
6. How do the narrator and the man he meets differ in their positions in society?
7. Why do you think the narrator does not want to give what the drunkard asks for?
8. What other important difference is there between the two men? Did you realize this difference before the very obvious statement of it by the drunk at the end of the story? Where?
9. The narrator, early in the story, says "Give me the city—the up-north city." After the incident do you think he would still choose the city over his early life in Georgia? Why?
10. Does the narrator seem any more "at ease" as he starts across the street? How or why?
11. Write one sentence in which you tell what you think is the main idea of this short story.

REACHING HIGHER

Step 1. Pictures of Expressive Features. Decide which feature of the human body you think best expresses emotion or personality—the eyes, the hands, the head, the nose, the lips. Then, from pictures in newspapers and magazines, cut out and mount a number of these features in different aspects of expression. When you show your mounted selections to the class, ask students to identify the particular emotion or personality each picture presents.

Step 2. Putting Voices on Record. The human voice is a clue to a person's background and character. Using a cassette recorder, ask five people to speak the same sentence into the microphone. (You can use any sentence you like—make up one or take it from a book.) Play the tape back to your class to see how other students describe the quality of the voices and the nature of the people who speak.

Or, pick some controversial topic (welfare, government controls in business, busing for balanced integration, legalizing marijuana) and let five different people speak out for two or three minutes each. Then see what students in the class can determine about the speakers.

part III

A MINIBOOK
OF NINETEEN SPECIAL SKILLS

1. IMPROVING SPELLING

HOW TO BE A BETTER SPELLER

---

1. Keep a list of the words you usually have trouble with: write the word correctly spelled; underline the troublesome letters; and make up some way of remembering the word. Start your list on page 382 after you examine the sample.
2. Write troublesome words several times, saying the letters aloud.
3. Trace the letters with your fingers after you think you know the spelling.
4. Use a dictionary to find correct spelling. Note the syllables.
5. If you cannot find the word in a dictionary, don't assume that the dictionary left out the word you are looking for. Try as many possible letter combinations as you can. For example, let us imagine that you had real trouble spelling *conscious.* You look first under the letter *k* (it often makes the same sound as *c* at the beginning of a word), but when you find no *kon* combination, you have to look for another possibility: *con* starts many words. If you had trouble with letters after *con,* you might look next at *sh* (it makes the same sound as *sci* here). But when you find no *consh,* you need to think of other possibilities: maybe even *consch.* If you follow these suggestions, you will often locate the correct spelling. When you find the spelling that looks right to you, *read the definition* to make sure that the spelling offered is the correct one for the word you want.
6. Learn the spelling demons, words most frequently misspelled by many people. One hundred and fifty appear below.
7. Learn spelling rules for the most difficult problems.

Spelling Demons: Group A

1. *abundance*   Have <u>a</u> <u>bun</u>; then <u>dance</u>.
2. *accommodate*   two <u>c's</u>, two <u>m's</u>
3. *achievement*   <u>i</u> before <u>e</u>
4. *adolescence*   -<u>scence</u>
5. *allowed*   Look for <u>all</u>.
6. *analyze*   -<u>yze</u>
7. *apparent*   double <u>p</u>; -<u>ent</u>
8. *appreciate*   double <u>p</u>; <u>iate</u>
9. *arrangement*   Don't drop the <u>e</u>.
10. *attendance*   two t's; end in <u>dance</u>
11. *available*   <u>Ail</u> is in this word.
12. *becoming*   Drop the <u>e</u> in <u>become</u>; one <u>m</u> only.

13. *benefited*   Look for the <u>fit</u> after <u>bene</u>.
14. *business*   The <u>bus</u> is <u>in</u> so add -<u>ess</u>.
15. *category*   an <u>e</u> between <u>cat</u> and <u>gory</u>
16. *cigarette*   two <u>t</u>'s surrounded by <u>e</u>'s
17. *competition*   Make the last <u>e</u> in <u>compete</u> an <u>i</u>; add -tion.
18. *conscious*   <u>sc</u> + <u>ious</u>
19. *cruel*   <u>u</u> + <u>e</u>
20. *dependent*   -<u>ent</u> ending
21. *dilemma*   <u>Emma</u> has a <u>dilemma</u>.
22. *discipline*   -<u>sci</u>
23. *eliminate*   <u>e</u> + <u>lim</u> + <u>i</u> + <u>nate</u>
24. *environment*   <u>nm</u> combination
25. *exaggerate*   two <u>g</u>'s
26. *existence*   <u>exist</u> + <u>ence</u>
27. *familiar*   The word <u>liar</u> is in <u>familiar</u>.
28. *grammar*   **Hint:** <u>ram</u> and <u>mar</u> are the same letters reversed.
29. *guiding*   Drop the <u>e</u> in <u>guide</u>.
30. *hoping*   only one <u>p</u> in <u>hope</u>
31. *independence*   -<u>ence</u> at the end
32. *jealousy*   Jealousy is <u>lousy</u>!
33. *loneliness*   lonel<u>y</u> + ness (i)
34. *management*   Add <u>ment</u> to <u>manage</u>.
35. *mischief*   The Indian <u>chief</u> does <u>mischief</u>.
36. *organization*   drop the <u>e</u> in organize; add -<u>ation.</u>
37. *particular*   <u>i c u</u> are <u>particular</u>.
38. *persuade*   Add -<u>suade</u> to <u>per</u>.
39. *precede*   pre + <u>cede</u>
40. *presence*   If you are <u>present</u> make your <u>presence</u> known.
41. *proceed*   The church needs the <u>proceed</u>s.
42. *receive*   <u>i</u> before <u>e</u> except after <u>c</u>

43. *rhythm*   <u>rhy</u> + <u>thm</u>
44. *satisfied*   -<u>fied</u>
45. *separate*   Separate means <u>part</u>.
46. *sincerely*   Keep the last -<u>e</u>.
47. *succeed*   two <u>c</u>'s, two <u>e</u>'s
48. *thorough*   a <u>rough</u> word to spell
49. *thought*   -<u>ought</u>
50. *unnessary*   two <u>n</u>'s, two <u>s</u>'s

Step 1. Practice with Group A Words. Fill in the blanks with correct letters to complete the words below.

1. We must all pro_____d to el_____m_____te the un_____c_____ary pollution of the env_____n_____nt if we are ever tho_____r_____ly to ap_____c_____te our ex_____st_____ce.

2. We must encourage sincer_____y courses such as gram_____r, which have ben_____f_____ted people in the past.

3. That p_____rti_____lar musical r_____t_____m satis-f_____d my lon_____l_____ness, and I was glad the pro-c_____ds of the performance would help the organi_____tion in beco_____ing strong.

4. A f_____l_____r dil_____ma of adoles_____n_____e is a choice between the need for ach_____v_____t and ind_____-p_____ce on the one hand and for dis_____pline and comp_____-t_____t_____n on the other hand.

5. We rec_____ve complaints annually about ci_____ar_____tes from those trying to p_____rs_____de us to stop smoking in public places.

Spelling Demons: Group B

1. *acceptance*   accept + <u>ance</u>
2. *accompanied*   two c's + -<u>ied</u>

3. *acquaintance*   ac + quaint + ance

4. *advertisement*   tise

5. *all right*   two words like "all wrong"

6. *annually*   double n

7. *appearance*   An ear is part of your appearance.

8. *approach*   a double p before the roach

9. *article*   -le ending

10. *attitude*   double t

11. *basis*   ends in is

12. *behavior*   Don't forget the i.

13. *breathe*   We breathe to take a breath.

14. *career*   two e's

15. *certainly*   cer-tain-ly

16. *coming*   Drop the e in come.

17. *condemn*   Don't forget the silent n.

18. *convenience*   con + ven + ience

19. *deceive*   i before e except after c

20. *description*   des

21. *disappoint*   dis + appoint

22. *discussion*   discuss + ion

23. *embarrass*   two r's, two s's

24. *equipment*   Look for the *quip*.

25. *excitable*   Drop the e in excite; add -able.

26. *experience*   -ence at the end

27. *fascinating*   sc after the a and before the i

28. *guaranteed*   guar as in guard; two e's at the end

29. *height*   -ei in the middle

30. *hungrily*   Make the y in *hungry* an i; add -ly.

31. *intelligence*   Can you tell he has intelligence?

32. *knowledge*   Did you know the ledge was there?

33. *losing*   Drop the e in lose.

34. *marriage*   marry + age (with "i" above)
35. *morale*   <u>Ale</u> will lift a soldier's morale.
36. *parallel*   Are <u>all</u> lines par<u>all</u>el.
37. *peculiar*   A <u>liar</u> is pecu<u>liar</u>.
38. *pleasant*   Drop the <u>e</u> in pl<u>ease</u> and add an <u>ant</u>.
39. *preferred*   Start with <u>pre</u>; double -<u>r</u> at the end.
40. *principle*   A principle is a ru<u>le</u>.
41. *psychology*   <u>psy</u> to open
42. *recommend*   one <u>c</u>, two <u>m</u>'s
43. *ridicule*   <u>rid</u> + <u>i</u> + <u>cule</u>
44. *schedule*   <u>s</u> + <u>ch</u>
45. *significance*   -<u>ance</u>
46. *studying*   study + <u>ing</u>
47. *surprise*   no <u>z</u> in this word
48. *tragedy*   no <u>d</u> before the g
49. *valuable*   Drop the <u>e</u> in value; add <u>able</u>.
50. *weather*   I can't b<u>ear</u> the w<u>ea</u>ther.

Step 2. Practice with Group B Words. Unscramble the following list of jumbled letters in order to spell correctly the words, all taken from the above list. (Hint: The first letter of each word is in boldface; the second letter is underlined.)

1. c e m <u>e</u> r d m o n _____

2. a e <u>c</u> a n t q a c n i u _____

3. l <u>u</u> n i y **h** g r _____

4. l l e l <u>a</u> r **p** a _____

5. r e a <u>u</u> n t e g a d _____

6. e <u>e</u> e v c i **d** _____

7. h o y g l <u>s</u> **p** y c o _____

8. b <u>a</u> l a v u l e _____

9. t e e h a r **b** _____

10. <u>n</u> l e t i l i e g c n e _____

Step 3. More Group B Practice: Looking for Smaller Words. In the above list, there are many words that contain another word of five letters or more. Write nine of these words below and underline the smaller word contained in each.

Example:

1. _acceptance_ _____   6. _____
2. _____   7. _____
3. _____   8. _____
4. _____   9. _____
5. _____   10. _____

Spelling Demons: Group C

1. ac<u>c</u>ident<u>all</u>y   two c's, two l's
2. ac<u>c</u>ustom   double c
3. admi<u>tt</u>ance   two t's
4. a<u>gg</u>ravate   two g's
5. am<u>a</u>t<u>eur</u>   e u r
6. apo<u>log</u>i<u>zed</u>   Look for the <u>log</u>; add i z e d
7. ap<u>p</u>l<u>y</u>ing   two p's. Don't drop the y at the end!
8. ar<u>g</u>ument   Drop the e in argue.
9. ath<u>let</u>e   Don't forget the e in "let." No e after h.
10. au<u>die</u>nce   At such a bad show the au<u>die</u>nce almost <u>died</u>.
11. beaut<u>i</u>ful   y in beauty changes to i
12. bel<u>ieve</u>   Don't bel<u>ieve</u> a <u>lie</u>.
13. bri<u>ll</u>iance   two l's + <u>iance</u>
14. ca<u>rr</u>ied   double r.
15. chang<u>e</u>able   Leave the e in <u>change</u>.
16. co<u>mmittee</u>   two m's, two t's, two e's
17. con<u>scien</u>tious   A <u>scien</u>tist is conscientious.
18. criti<u>cize</u>   -cize
19. de<u>finite</u>ly   Look for the <u>finite</u>.
20. di<u>ff</u>er<u>ence</u>   two f's; <u>ence</u>

21. *disastrous*   no e between the t and r
22. *efficient*   -ient after c
23. *emphasize*   Does it emphasize your size?
24. *especially*   This word has something special: double l.
25. *exercise*   no -z here!
26. *extremely*   The m stands between two e's.
27. *genius*   -ius not ious
28. *guidance*   Put gui before dance.
29. *heroes*   Add es to hero.
30. *ignorance*   He ran in ignorance.
31. *interest*   in + ter + est
32. *leisure*   -ei + sure
33. *magnificent*   magnif*y* + i + -cent
34. *miniature*   mini + a + ture
35. *noticeable*   Was not ice able to freeze the lock?
36. *paralyze*   -yze
37. *performance*   -ance after *perform*
38. *possession*   two double s's
39. *prejudice*   Look for the dice.
40. *privilege*   Privilege is vile.
41. *pursue*   two u's
42. *relieve*   Lie down to relieve your pain.
43. *sacrifice*   sacrifice
44. *seize*   The -e comes before the -i.
45. *similar*   ilar
46. *sufficient*   double f; -cient
47. *transferred*   two r's
48. *unusually*   three u's all in one word
49. *villain*   The villain had lain on the street.
50. *writing*   Drop the e in write.

Step 4. Group C Practice. In each of the following sets of words, one is misspelled. Write that word, correctly spelled, in the space provided at the left.

_____	1. beautyful	amateur	criticize	heroes
_____	2. pursue	admittance	writting	seize
_____	3. audience	athelete	possession	difference
_____	4. privilege	villain	argument	paralize
_____	5. efficient	ignorance	definately	exercise
_____	6. performance	unusually	genius	leisure
_____	7. transferred	noticeable	aggravate	guidence
_____	8. brilliance	beleive	conscientious	accustom
_____	9. apologized	committee	similiar	interest
_____	10. magnificent	priviledge	sufficient	changeable

Step 5. Mastering Spelling Demons. Fill in the blanks to complete correctly the words (taken from Groups A, B, and C) in the following phrases.

1. the b_____ is for ac_____vement

2. to anal_____e the ar_____ment

3. unable to acco_____date the
   aud_____nce

4. an amat_____ ath_____te

5. a successful b_____iness car_____r

6. appl_____ng the princip_____

7. a be_____t_____ful des_____iption

8. to criti_____e the commit_____e

9. to exa_____erate the
   d_____le_____a

10. a d_____ast_____us
    exper_____nce

11. to el_____m_____ate
    compet_____ion

12. the p_____chology of human
    behav_____

13. to s_____ze val_____ble gems

14. the man_____ment of an
    organ_____tion

15. a cr_____l ex_____t_____nce

16. a fa_____inating
    per_____m_____nce

17. to rid_____le pre_____dice

18. her magn_____cent appe_____nce

19. must have suff_____ent exer_____e

20. an eff_____ent sch_____d_____le

21. a pecul_____r vill_____n

22. to surp_____e her
    ac_____dent_____y

23. pl_____sant w_____ther

24. a di_____us_____ion about

    mar_____age

25. the e_____pment is

    gu_____ant_____ed.

26. the pr_____v_____lege of his

    a_____uaint_____nce

27. It was cert_____nly a great

    tr_____edy.

28. to p_____sue knowl_____e

29. con_____entious stud_____ing

30. a cigar_____te advert_____ement

31. to rec_____ve their

    indep_____nd_____nce

32. the lon_____l_____ness of

    adol_____c_____nce

33. to proc_____d with the

    ar_____ang_____ment

34. an ext_____mely good

    env_____ro_____ent

35. hop_____ng to suc_____d

36. to sac_____f_____ce his

    pos_____e_____ion

37. They are def_____nit_____ly

    sim_____l_____r.

38. a chang_____ble a_____itude

39. We conde_____ his

    j_____lo_____sy

40. He al_____o_____ed them to

    sep_____r_____te.

41. sat_____sf_____d with his grades

    in gra_____r

SOME SPELLING RULES FOR DIFFICULT PROBLEMS

Rule 1. Solving -*ie* Headaches

1. *i* usually comes before *e*.

   Examples: f*ie*ld   y*ie*ld   ach*ie*vement   bel*ie*ve

2. If the letter immediately before the -*ie* combination is *c*, the *e* usually comes before the *i*.

   Examples: dec*ei*ve   rec*ei*ve   conc*ei*ve

3. The *e* also comes before the *i* if the combination of letters sounds like the *a* in *say* or *clay*.

   Examples: n*ei*ghborhood   w*ei*ght   *ei*ght

   —— [This sounds like *a* in *say* so the *e* comes before the *i*.]

EXCEPTIONS: FOR YOU TO MEMORIZE	
*ei*ther	l*ei*sure
for*ei*gn	sc*ie*nce

*se*i*ze*   h*ei*ght
n*ei*ther   effi*ci*ent

The following jingle will help you to remember the above rule:

i before *e* except after *c*,
or when sounded like *a*
as in *neighbor* and *weigh*.

Step 1. Using -*ie* Correctly. Fill in *ie* or *ei* in the words below.

1. dec_____ve
2. rec_____pt
3. bel_____vable
4. l_____surely
5. w_____rd
6. w_____ght
7. n_____ghborhood
8. s_____zure
9. rec_____ve
10. misch_____vous
11. effic_____ntly
12. r_____gn
13. y_____ld
14. rel_____f
15. n_____ther
16. n_____ce
17. for_____gn
18. sc_____ntific
19. sh_____ld
20. conc_____ved

Rule 2. Changing *y* to *i*

1. If a word ends in *y* and the *y* is directly preceded by a consonant (any letter other than *a, e, i, o,* and *u*), the *y* is changed to *i* before an ending (suffix) is added.

   Examples: fly + *es* = flies   carry + *ed* = carried
   [The *y* is preceded by the consonant *l*.]   [This is the new ending.]

2. However, when the ending begins with *i* as in -*ing*, the *y* is *not* changed.

   Examples: study + *ing* = studying   try + *ing* = trying

EXCEPTIONS: FOR YOU TO MEMORIZE

lay + *ed* = laid   say + *ed* = said   pay + *ed* = paid

Step 2. Adding to Words that end in -y. Using the above rule, add the suffixes indicated to the following words.

	-ed	-ing	-(e)s
1. apply	_____	_____	_____
2. marry	_____	_____	_____
3. stay	_____	_____	_____
4. try	_____	_____	_____
5. destroy	_____	_____	_____

Step 3. More Practice. Add the indicated endings to the following words.

1. carry + *ed* _____
2. destroy + *ed* _____
3. supply + *ing* _____
4. lonely + *ness* _____
5. bounty + *s* _____

6. beauty + *ful* _____
7. rely + *ing* _____
8. portray + *ed* _____
9. scurry + *ing* _____
10. deny + *al* _____

Rule 3. Words that Drop the Final *e*

1. Words ending in silent *e* usually drop the *e* before a suffix beginning with a vowel.

   Examples: use + -*ing* = using   use + *able* = usable

2. However, the silent -*e* usually remains before a suffix beginning with a consonant.

   Examples: use + *ful* = useful   use + *less* = useless

EXCEPTIONS: FOR YOU TO MEMORIZE

argue + *ment* = argument
judge + *ment* = judgment
true + *ly* = truly
notice + *able* = noticeable

change + *able* = changeable
courage + *ous* = courageous
canoe + *ing* = canoeing
mile + *age* = mileage

Step 4. Working with the Final -*e*. Using the above rule, add the suffixes indicated to the following words.

	-ing	*-ment*	*-able*
1. arrange	_____	_____	_____
2. achieve	_____	_____	_____
3. state	_____	_____	_____
4. manage	_____	_____	_____
5. advise	_____	_____	_____

Step 5. More Practice. Add the suffixes to the following words:

1. prescribe + *ing* _____   6. judge + *ment* _____

2. love + *ly* _____   7. replace + *ing* _____

3. excite + *able* _____   8. outrage + *ous* _____

4. name + *less* _____   9. write + *ing* _____

5. survive + *al* _____   10. safe + *ty* _____

Rule 4. Doubling the Final Consonant

1. When you add a suffix to a word, the final consonant of that word is doubled if the following are true:

   The suffix begins with a vowel.

   Examples: rot + *-ing* = rotting

   The word is one syllable *or* is accented on the last syllable.

   Examples: sit + *-ing* = sitting
   (This word is one syllable.)
   control (con-trol) + ed = controlled
   (The accent is on the last syllable.)
   offer (of-fer) + ed = offered
   (The accent is *not* on the last syllable and so the final consonant is *not* doubled.)

Step 6. Doubling Practice. Add the indicated suffixes to the following words.

1. quit + *ing* = _____   6. forget + *ful* = _____

2. prefer + *ed* = _____   7. swim + *ing* = _____

3. occur + *ed* = _____   8. big + *est* = _____

4. begin + *ing* = _____   9. profit + *able* = _____

5. depend + *ence* = _____   10. lessen + *ing* = _____

11. plan + *ing* = _____   16. commit + *ed* = _____

12. benefit + *ed* = _____   17. beg + *ed* = _____

13. admit + *ing* = _____   18. visit + *ing* = _____

14. whip + *ed* = _____   19. travel + *ing* = _____

15. stop + *ed* = _____   20. forbid + *en* = _____

Step 7. Mastering the Spelling Rules. Test your mastery of the preceding spelling rules by adding the indicated suffixes to the following words. The numbers in parentheses refer to the spelling rule that applies to that word.

1. study + *ing* _____ (2)   21. portray + *ed* _____ (2)

2. judge + *ment* _____ (3)   22. offer + *ed* _____ (4)

3. spare + *ing* _____ (3)   23. beauty + *ful* _____ (2)

4. manage + *ing* _____ (3)   24. profit + *able* _____ (4)

5. differ + *ence* _____ (4)   25. destroy + *ed* _____ (2)

6. accompany + *ed* _____ (2)   26. transfer + *ed* _____ (4)

7. benefit + *ed* _____ (4)   27. entire + *ly* _____ (3)

8. lonely + *ness* _____ (2)   28. arrange + *ment* _____ (3)

9. unwit + *ing* _____ (4)   29. prefer + *ed* _____ (4)

10. move + *able* _____ (3)   30. receive + *ing* _____ (3)

11. annoy + *ed* _____ (2)   31. pay + *ed* _____ (2)

12. argue + *ment* _____ (3)   32. write + *ing* _____ (3)

13. forbid + *en* _____ (4)   33. admit + *ing* _____ (4)

14. deny + *al* _____ (2)   34. true + *ly* _____ (3)

15. event + *ful* _____ (3)   35. forget + *ful* _____ (4)

16. slip + *ed* _____ (4)   36. apply + *ing* _____ (2)

17. try + *ing* _____ (2)   37. care + *ful* _____ (3)

18. concur + *ed* _____ (4)   38. equip + *ment* _____ (4)

19. use + *ing* _____ (3)   39. excite + *ing* _____ (3)

20. spy + *es* _____ (2)   40. bury + *ed* _____ (2)

Fill in *ie* or *ei* in the words below. To check your spelling, refer back to rule 1.

1. f_____ld   3. n_____ghbor

2. aud_____nce   4. l_____sure

5. rec_____ve   8. dec_____ve

6. bel_____ve   9. s_____ze

7. sl_____gh   10. f_____gn

YOUR OWN DEMON LIST: WORDS YOU MISTAKE

Fill in the columns on page 382, as indicated, with your own troublesome
spelling words. Study the examples. Continue your list, if necessary, on
your own paper.

2. LEARNING VOCABULARY

HOW TO LEARN NEW WORDS

The following steps will help you build your vocabulary:

1. Look up new words in a reliable dictionary.
2. Read definitions carefully. Pick only definitions which explain words as you
   want to use them or as they are used in what you have read.
3. Write each word on a small index card. Put definitions on the other side.
4. Categorize study words in related groups: *size* words, *liberation* words, *space-
   age* words, and so on.
5. Study words briefly on many occasions rather than for long periods on few
   occasions.
6. Say words and meanings aloud.
7. Write sentences using the words.
8. Add new words to your speaking vocabulary.
9. Use new words in writing sentences.
10. In reading, if you see an unfamiliar word, try to figure out its meaning from:

    the way it is used in a sentence

    the prefix, root, or suffix that you see

    the words that may be put together to make up the new word

    a smaller word you recognize within the new word

Step 1. Predicting Meanings.   Try to determine the meanings of the underlined words below in any way you can. Write definitions in the blank spaces.

1. underestimate
2. unsuitable
3. keepsake
4. paramedical
5. heartfelt
6. lowland
7. irrevocable

Word Correctly Spelled	Confusing Letters Underlined	A Way to Remember
You're accommodate	You're accommodate	You're = you + are double c, double m

8. spittoon

9. For that <u>laudable</u> plan you deserve all the praise and thanks the committee can give.

10. The idea angered him so that he overcame his usual <u>passivity</u> and screamed, "That's the stupidest thing I've ever heard!"

3. READING A DICTIONARY ENTRY

Most instructors encourage you to use dictionaries to check meanings and spellings even when you write a test or essay in class. Although pocket dictionaries give simplified entries for words, you still need to understand the several parts of each entry. Here are samples from the *New Merriam-Webster Pocket Dictionary:*

[The word is a noun. Other abbreviations and symbols of parts of speech (vb., adj., adv., etc.) are explained in dictionary.]

[History of the form of the word. "OF" means Old French. Check key in front or back of book for abbreviations.]

[Pronunciation: all symbols explained in front of dictionary or on bottom of pages]

[This stands for same form of word as main entry.]

[Main entry]

[Period between syllables shows where to break word at end of a line]

¹forge \'fōrj\ *n* [OF, fr. L *fabrica,* fr. *faber* smith] : SMITHY
²forge *vb* 1 : to form (metal) by heating and hammering 2 : FASHION, SHAPE 〈~ an agreement〉 3 : to make or imitate falsely esp. with intent to defraud 〈~ a signature〉 — forg·er *n* — forg·ery *n*
³forge *vb* : to move ahead steadily but gradually
for·get \fər-'get\ *vb* -got; -got·ten *or* -got; -get·ting 1 : to be unable to think of or recall 2 : to fail to become mindful of at the proper time 3 : NEGLECT, DISREGARD 〈*forgot* his old friends〉 — for·get·ful *adj* — for·get·ful·ness *n*

[Past forms of verb: only irregular forms appear]

[Words that come from main word]

Step 1. Understanding Dictionary Entries. Using the *New Merriam-Webster Pocket Dictionary* or some other handy pocket dictionary, look up the word *episode.* Write the answers to the following questions.

1. What languages did the word come from? _____

_____

2. What syllables make up the word? _____

_____

3. What part of speech is the word? _____

_____

4. How is the word pronounced? _____

_____

5. How many definitions appear? _____

_____

6. What suffix can combine with it? What new word is created? _____

_____

7. Which definition is new to you? Write it here. _____

_____

4. USING WORD PARTS AS CLUES TO MEANINGS

Important Prefixes and Suffixes

A prefix is a letter or group of letters placed at the *beginning* of a word to contribute to its meaning.

A suffix is a letter or group of letters placed at the *end* of a word to contribute to its meaning.

If you know some of the prefixes and suffixes used most frequently, it is often possible to determine the definition of a word, or at least to get an idea of the kind of word being used, without using the dictionary.

For example, if you saw the word

asocial

and you knew that the letter *a* placed at the beginning of a word means *not,* you could figure out easily that *asocial* means *not social.* If you saw the word

heroism

and you knew that *-ism* added to a word means *the quality of,* you could conclude easily that *heroism* means *the quality of being a hero.* And suppose, in your reading, you saw a sentence like

The doctor prescribed an *antirheumatic* medicine.

If you knew that the prefix *anti-* means *against,* you could figure out that *antirheumatic* means *against* some rheumatic disease.

Here are some of the most common prefixes:

> **PREFIXES THAT SAY NO**
>
> *a-*: not (asocial)
> *an-*: not (anarchy)
> *un-*: not (unattractive)
> *im-*: not (impossible)
> *in-*: not (insecure)

non-: not (nonviolent)
mis-: wrongly (mistreated)
ir-: without, not (irresponsible)
il-: not (illegible)
mal-: bad or wrongful (maladjustment)
anti-: against (antimissile)
contra-: against (contradict)

PREFIXES THAT SHOW PLACEMENT

ab-: from or away from (abstain)
circum-: around (circumference)
com-: with, together (commission)
trans-: across (transport)
dis-: away (displace)
sub-: under (submarine)
inter-: among or between (interlocking)
intra-: within, inwardly (intramurals, introvert)
in-: in or on (invest)
de-: down from (deflect)

PREFIXES THAT TELL TIME

ante-: before (antedate)
pre-: before (predict)
post-: after (postdate)
ex-: former or out of (exconvict)
re-: again, back (repeat)

PREFIXES THAT TELL DEGREE

hyper-: too much (hypertension)
super-: above or highest (superman)
poly-: many (polyangular)
pro-: in favor (proponent)
semi-: half (semicircle)
extra-: beyond, outside (extracurricular)

PREFIXES THAT MEAN ONE

uni-: single, one (uniform)
homo-: same (homogenize)
self-: one's own person (self-propelled)
mono-: one (monologue)
auto-: self, same (autograph)

Step 1. Making Words with Prefixes. Select the correct prefix that has the meaning described and use it before the word or word part that appears. On your own paper write the new word and a definition. Check your dictionary to make sure that the word you have written is correct.

1. (bad or wrongful) + practice
2. (under) + way
3. (not) + proper
4. (again) + educate
5. (against) + aircraft
6. (one) + lateral
7. (within) + state
8. (among) + state
9. (the same) + -nym
10. (before) + date
11. (out of) + -hale
12. (across) + continental
13. (together, with) + mingle
14. (one) + cycle
15. (not) + possible

SUFFIXES TO SIGNAL MEANINGS

Relating to or Pertaining to
-al (formal)
-ic (sonic)
-ance (performance)
-ence (permanence)

Able to Be
-ible (terrible)
-able (capable)

State or Quality of
-ship (statesmanship)
-ment (management)
-ion (tension)
-ness (happiness)
-ism (terrorism)
-hood (manhood)
-tude (aptitude)

Someone Who
-er (speaker)
-or (debtor)
-ist (florist)

Filled with
-ous (joyous)
-y (juicy)
-ful (sorrowful)

Without
-less (mindless)

Step 2. Suffixes for Correct Words. Change the words in italics in the sentences below to the proper form by adding a correct suffix. You may have to change the final letters of the starting word before you add an ending. Write at *a* the new word and at *b* the meaning of the suffix you added. Check the dictionary for spelling. Study the example.

Example:
1. On *chill* days we run home quickly.

1. a. *chilly*
   b. *filled with*

2. The *neighbor* grew old and shabby as more and more buildings fell to ruin; the sight was *awe*.

2. *a.* _____

 b. _____

 a. _____

 b. _____

3. The *jewel* showed us a *shine, flaw* di-diamond.

3. *a.* _____

 b. _____

 a. _____

 b. _____

 a. _____

 b. _____

4. *Adult* is not necessary measured by age, but by *achieve* and *intellect mature*.

4. *a.* _____

 b. _____

 a. _____

 b. _____

 a. _____

 b. _____

 a. _____

 b. _____

Ten Roots to Rescue Meanings

Roots—or stems—are those parts of words to which pieces may be added at the beinning or end. Several roots, coming from Greek, Latin, or other languages, appear frequently in English words; therefore, to know a select number of roots is to improve your skill with word recognition. The ten roots below play an important part in our vocabulary.

			Example
Roots of the Senses	spect, spic	means "look"	spectator
	loqu, locut	means "speak"	eloquent
	tang, tact	means "touch"	tangent
	vid, vis	means "see"	vision
	voc, vok	means "call"	vocal
Roots of Action	vers, vert	means "turn"	divert
	pos	means "place"	position
	port	means "carry"	porter
	mor, mort	means "die"	moratorium
	mit, mis	means "send" or "put"	admit

Step 3. Roots for Definitions. Underline the root in each word in italics below. In *a* write a meaning of the word based upon your knowledge of the root. In *b* write the definition given by the dictionary. How close do the two come in meaning?

1. There sounded a *moribund* howl, then silence.

    a. *dying*

    b. *on the verge of death*

2. One hundred clowns marching down Broadway created quite a *spectacle.*

    a. _____

    b. _____

3. The employer *dismissed* all her part-time workers.

    a. _____

    b. _____

4. *Circumlocution* weakens arguments.

    a. _____

    b. _____

5. The child *reverted* to bad behavior.

    a. _____

    b. _____

Step 4. Prefix, Root, and Suffix in Combination. Each word below is made from prefix, root, and suffix. Write below the word the meaning of each part and then a suitable definition of the entire word in Column I. Use a dictionary if you need to. Look at the example.

Example:

I

1. submitter

    under put one who

    someone who gives in to someone else

2. circumlocution

    _____
    _____

3. irrevocable

    _____
    _____

4. intermission

    _____
    _____

5. comportment

    _____
    _____

6. intangible

    _____
    _____

7. universal

_____

_____

8. revisionist

_____

_____

9. disposal

_____

_____

10. introspection

_____

_____

5. USING A THESAURUS

A *thesaurus* is a dictionary of synonyms. You can look up a word like *humorist* (given below), for example, and find fifteen or twenty words, which are in some way related in meaning to that word.

WHEN TO USE THE THESAURUS

when you repeat the same word too often
when a word does not sound right in your sentence
when you write slang or nonstandard expressions and you want more formal
  language
when you learn new words and you want to see other words used in a similar
  way

Two Hints for Thesaurus Use

1. Different methods of organization are used in preparing a thesaurus. One thesaurus groups synonyms according to ideas or subject categories. There, you look up words in the back of the book, find the section numbers in which the word you want appears, and then turn to a specific section, which gives the synonyms that interest you. Other thesauruses are alphabetically arranged, like dictionaries.
2. Not all synonyms listed for any word have the same meaning. And the thesaurus rarely tells the difference in shades of meaning among the synonyms offered. Therefore, know definitions of any words you select. Don't pick words just because they are unusual, impressive in length, or new to you. Use a dictionary to check out differences in meanings.

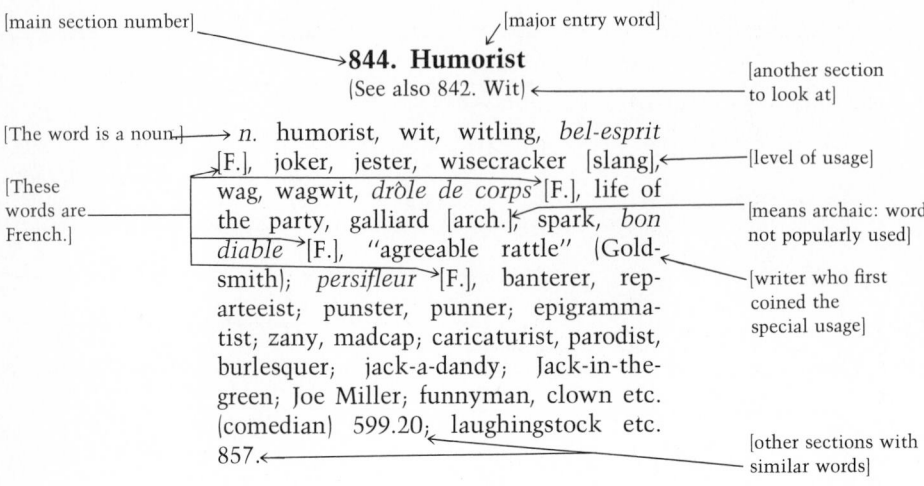

[main section number]

[major entry word]

844. Humorist

(See also 842. Wit) ←——————————— [another section to look at]

[The word is a noun.] ——→ *n.* humorist, wit, witling, *bel-esprit*

[These words are French.]

[F.], joker, jester, wisecracker [slang], ←——— [level of usage]
wag, wagwit, *drôle de corps* [F.], life of
the party, galliard [arch.], spark, *bon* ←——— [means archaic: word not popularly used]
diable [F.], "agreeable rattle" (Gold-
smith); *persifleur* [F.], banterer, rep- ←——— [writer who first coined the special usage]
arteeist; punster, punner; epigramma-
tist; zany, madcap; caricaturist, parodist,
burlesquer; jack-a-dandy; Jack-in-the-
green; Joe Miller; funnyman, clown etc.
(comedian) 599.20; laughingstock etc. ←——— [other sections with similar words]
857.

Step 1. Thesaurus for Synonyms. Use a thesaurus to look up the words
below. For each word select and write down three synonyms whose meanings you do not know. Then, using a dictionary, write definitions of the
three new words. Look at the example. Use your own paper and make three
columns.

Example:

Word	*Synonyms*	*Definitions*
happy	1. *opportune*	1. *coming at the right time*
	2. *auspicious*	2. *favorable; suggesting success*
	3. *joyous*	3. *full of delight*

1. fear
2. to observe
3. obedient
4. peaceful
5. to say

6. WRITING DEFINITIONS: THREE BRIEF EXERCISES

I. A Strong One-Sentence Definition

In order to write a logical definition that is clear and easy to understand,
write a sentence of four parts:

1. Name the term to be defined.
2. Use the word *is.*
3. Name the general group of things to which the term belongs.

4. Name some specific characteristic that identifies the term from the rest of the group.

You will have to use your dictionary or encyclopedia as a starting point in the preparation of accurate and precise meanings.

Examples:

[term] ["is"] [general group to which term belongs] [specific characteristic: shows the special use of the plot of ground]

A garden is a plot of ground for cultivating plants.

[term] ["is] [general group to which term belongs] [special characteristic: shows how this pardon is different from any other kind]

Amnesty is a pardon for offenses against a government.

[term] ["is"] [general group to which term belongs]

A church is a building for public Christian worship.

[specific characteristic: shows the special nature of the building]

TOWARD ACCURATE DEFINITIONS

Don't use *where* or *when* after *is.*

Wrong: A closet is *where* you store clothing, food, or tools.

Right: A closet is an enclosure for storing clothing, food, or tools.

Don't use in your definitions the word (or one of its forms) you are attempting to define.

Wrong: Anger is the act of being angry.

Right: Anger is a feeling directed at someone who performs a real or imagined wrong action.

Don't use negatives in your definition.

Wrong: Sadness is *not* being happy.

Right: Sadness is a feeling characterized by sorrow or depression.

Exception: Sometimes negative qualities are the specific characteristics of words. In those cases, negatives are acceptable parts of definitions.

Example: An orphan is a person *without* parents.
[negative]

Step 1. A Definition in a Sentence. Fill in the blanks below to create logical one-sentence definitions. Use your dictionary. Study the examples above and below.

The Term	Is	General Group ,	Specific Characteristic
1. A silkworm	*is*	*a caterpillar*	*that spins a fine thread to make a cocoon.*

2. An emerald   _____   _____   _____

_____

_____

3. Freedom   _____   _____   _____

_____

_____

4. Seniority   _____   _____   _____

_____

_____

5. An engineer   _____   _____   _____

_____

_____

6. An aside   _____   _____   _____

_____

_____

7. Photosynthesis   _____   _____   _____

_____

_____

8. An aardvark   _____   _____   _____

_____

_____

9. A sanction   _____   _____   _____

_____

_____

10. A bill of lading   _____   _____   _____

_____

_____

11. Neurology   _____   _____   _____

_____

_____

II. A Brief Paragraph as Definition

Often you need to expand a one-sentence definition into a paragraph so that the reader can identify more completely the thing you are defining. Your paragraph should begin with a one-sentence definition, as you have already learned, with significant features added in five or six more sentences. The dictionary, encyclopedia, or reference text can help you with your definitions.

MAKING THE CONCRETE DEFINITION GROW

Some questions you should try to answer as you expand your definition are:
1. What are the physical features of the object: size, shape, color?
2. What may the object remind readers of? Does the object look like any other object?
3. What materials contribute to the object?
4. What is the object used for?

What Is Rayon?

Rayon is a synthetic fiber produced from cellulose and used to weave fabrics. Chemicals dissolve the cellulose (wood pulp or short cotton fibers), which machines then force through tiny holes. The dissolved material, hardened in warm air or liquid, forms filaments which may be either twisted into threads or cut and spun. Spun filaments of rayon may look like wool, linen, or cotton. Because yarns with new features are developed all the time, rayon now has a variety of uses: it appears in automobile tires, in grease-proof cellophane sheets, in sponge rubber as a substitute for cellulose, and in special glass that cannot be shattered.

—Caroline Narby

Step 2. Your Paragraph Definition. Using whatever reference material you need, write a one-paragraph definition of any of the words below. Use separate paper.

1. ghetto
2. impressionism
3. narcissism
4. gymnastics
5. grudge
6. anxiety
7. novella
8. astrolabe
9. metaphor
10. sonnet

III. Definitions through Images

An effective way to define difficult words—especially abstract ones—is by means of imagery (see pages 6–7). The dictionary defines *love*, for example, as "the attraction, desire, or affection felt for a person who arouses delight or admiration." Although this is surely an adequate definition, anyone who has experienced love knows how incomplete the dictionary meaning is. A great number of words in the language suggest through our own experiences a number of definitions that go beyond what the dictionary says. This is what is meant by the *connotation* of words: the ability to suggest or hint at meanings that are not part of what the word actually points out. The actual dictionary definition of a word (like the definition given above of the word *love*) is called *detonation*. (See pages 208–209.)

In this paragraph of definition, define any word you wish through a series of strong images based upon your own observations. Select a word that is rich in image responses for you, a word that calls up a string of pictures of happiness, tension, delight, or pain. Use sensory details to make each picture sharp and clear.

Read the student sample below as an example.

Old: A Spider's Web, An Attic Trunk

Old: a lump of coal in a dark, moist corner of my basement, an abandoned spider's web still clinging to its gritty surface; the metallic smell of a coin, its date rubbed silvery smooth; that gray-brown chunk of oak in my backyard, its bark as cold as stone on my fingers; the scent of photographs when I open the brown shoe box, and the slick, glossy feel of the yellowing snapshots inside; the squeal of the attic trunk as with dust-covered hands my brother Al and I push back the lid to eye Mom's rotting silks and satins; the musty aroma of a book from my childhood, *Peter Pan*, whose brown-stained pages crackle as I turn them; that brown mahogany chair Aunt Polly once owned, the one with the grinning face carved into it, the one with the cold wooden tongue that licks at my spine whenever I lean back; the craggy folds surrounding grandma's smile as she carefully knits pink yarn into a blanket for her first great-grandchild, my brother's new baby; the breath of my dog, Pepper, who looked up at me with milky eyes as I stroked his fur for the last time.

—Karl Joreid

TIPS FOR THE PARAGRAPH DEFINITION IN IMAGES

1. Select a word that suggests many definitions for you, a word that calls pictures into your mind. *Your success in the paragraph depends on the selections of a word that has important meanings to you.*
2. Write at least ten images that you associate with the word. Make your images rich in color, sound, smell, and touch.
3. Mention the names of specific places and people.
4. Vary the length of the images. Make some images long; write one or two brief images of strong visual quality.
5. Use a colon after the word that you are attempting to define.
6. Use a semicolon after each image.

> **Hint:** Each image is a fragment, not a complete sentence. Notice that the verb used in most of the images is an *-ing* or an *-ed* verb part. Some of the images contain no verb part at all. But the *-ing* adds a certain liveliness to your picture, so try to use it often in the imagery.
>
> 7. Make up a title that uses both the word you are defining and a piece of your favorite image or two. What images do the words after the colon in Mr. Joreid's title come from?

Step 3. Words for Image Definitions. Here are some words that might suggest to you a series of sharp pictures. You can use one of these, if you wish, in your paragraph definition.

1. hope
2. blue (or any color)
3. fear
4. May (or any month)
5. Saturday (or any day)
6. loneliness
7. autumn (or any season)
8. football
9. maturity
10. breakfast
11. peace
12. ecstasy

7. CONFUSING WORDS: A GLOSSARY

accept, except

  accept—means to *receive,* to *welcome,* to *say yes.*
   We *accept* your offer of help.
  except—means *leaving out, excluding.*
   Everyone *except* Barry ate together.

affect, effect

  affect means 1. to *assume* or *pretend.*
   He *affected* a smile of agreement.
   2. to *influence* or *act on.*
   Good study habits *affect* learning speed.

Hint: Think of the **a** in *affect* as a signal to act.

  effect means 1. to *bring about.*
   His disposition *effected* a change in our mood.
   2. *result* or *outcome.*

Hint: Think of the **e** in *effect* as a signal for result.

   The *effect* of her speech cannot be measured.

Hint: If *the* or *an* comes before the word, you must choose *effect.*

all ready, already
>   *all ready*—means *fully prepared.*
>   The team was *all ready* to play.
>   *already*—means *by this time* or *before a set time.*
>   When you arrived, I had *already* eaten.

among. See **between.**

amount, number
>   *amount*—refers to things in large masses, things that cannot be counted.
>   A large *amount* of water filled the tub.
>   *number*—refers to countable things.
>   He received a *number* of parking tickets.

bad, badly. See **good, well.**

barely. See **hardly.**

being that—avoid this expression. Use *since* or *because.*
>   *Because* (not "being that") I felt tired, I went to sleep.

between, among
>   *between*—used to name relationships between *two* people or things.
>   *Between* you and me that book is dull.
>   *among*—used to name relationships referring to *three* or more people or things.
>   *Among the* students only Carol answered.

could have, could've, could of
>   *could have*—correct for all forms of written or spoken expression.
>   We *could have* studied more carefully.
>   *could've*—a contraction, good for informal writing or speaking.
>   "You *could've* been more careful," Sandra replied.
>   *could of*—incorrect! *Could've* sounds like *could of* but this last form is not correct in writing. Also, for the following words,

> use *should have*   *not* should of
>   *would have*   *not* would of
>   *might have*   *not* might of

> If you need a contraction, use *should've* for *should have,*
>   *might've* for *might have,* and
>   *would've* for *would have.*

But remember, contractions appear most of the time in informal writing only.

different from, different than
>   *different from*—the preferred form, although *different than* is sometimes used when a subject and verb follow it.
>   That pen is *different from* mine.

effect. See **affect.**

except. See **accept.**

fewer, less
>   *fewer*—used for things that can actually be counted.
>   He has *fewer* books than I have.
>   *less*—shows worth, quantity, or degree.

That cigarette has *less* tar than yours.

His car costs *less* than hers.

former, latter

former—between two objects, *former* refers to the first thing named.

latter—between two objects, *latter* refers to the second of two things named.

Neither the car nor the motorcycle would start; the *former* because of a bad carburetor, the *latter* because of faulty ignition.

Hint: If three objects are involved, do not use *former* and *latter;* use *first, second* (or *next*), and *last.*

A dog, a cat, and a horse appeared in the cartoon; the *first* did a tap dance while the *last* played a guitar.

good, well; bad, badly

good, bad—describe things or people.

A *good* movie is hard to find.

What a *bad* idea!

well or *badly*—describe actions named by most verbs.

She reads *well.*

She dances *badly.*

> *not*

She reads *good.*

She dances *bad.*

Hint: After one of these verbs use *good* or *bad: is, am, are, were, have been, look, remain, appear, taste, smell, feel.*

She looks *bad.*

The soup tastes *good.*

The news was *bad* this morning.

If you want to indicate someone's health, use *well* or *bad* with one of the above verbs.

I feel *well* today.

hanged, hung

hanged—shows someone's life was taken by execution.

The mob *hanged* the criminal without a trial.

hung—refers to things, not to people.

We *hung* the mirror on the wall.

hardly, scarcely, barely

Since these words are already negative, do not use them with *never, not,* or with verb contractions ending in *n't.*

I could *hardly* breathe.

> *not*

I couldn't *hardly* breathe.

hung. See **hanged.**

in, into

> *in* —movement within one place.
>> He ran *in* the room. (This means he was already inside the room when the action began.)
>
> *into* —movement from one place to a position within.
>> He ran *into* the room. (This means he was not already within the room when the action began.)

irregardless   Avoid! See **regardless.**

latter. See **former.**

learn, teach

> *learn* —means *gain information or knowledge.*
>
> *teach* —means *give information so that someone else learns.*
>> He *taught* me right from wrong.
>>> *not*
>> He *learned* me right from wrong.

less. See **fewer.**

might have, might've. See **could have.**

myself

> Use *myself* to stress the word *I* in a sentence or to show that the subject and the receiver of the action are the same.
>> I *myself* will judge.
>> I shaved *myself* this morning.
>
> Avoid using *myself* as a substitute for *I* or *me.*
>> It was Larry and *I.*
>>> *not*
>> It was Larry and *myself.*
>> She took Beverly and *me* to the Dean.
>>> *not*
>> She took Beverly and *myself* to the Dean.

number. See **amount.**

regardless, irregardless

> Use *regardless* only; *irregardless* is incorrect.
>> *Regardless* of our suggestions, he voted in his own way.

scarcely. See **hardly.**

should have, should've. See **could have.**

somewhere, somewheres

> Do not use an *s* at the end of any of the compound direction or time words. Use

somewhere	*not*	somewheres
anywhere	*not*	anywheres
nowhere	*not*	nowheres

teach. See **learn.**

well. See **good.**

would have, would've. See **could have.**

Step 1. The Right Words in Your Sentences. Write a brief sentence of your own that uses correctly each word or word group.

1. different from
2. among
3. could hardly
4. fewer
5. badly

6. into
7. somewhere
8. affect
9. well
10. all ready

Step 2. Correcting Sentences. Several sentences below contain errors. Underline each mistake and write a correct word or word group to replace it. If the sentence is correct, mark it *C*. Use separate paper.

1. For a child she plays the piano very good.
2. Johnny Cash's last record is much different than his earlier ones.
3. He learned his son how to chop wood.
4. Supposedly, there are less people in this college than in my high school, but I myself do not see how that can be true.
5. The bank robbers divided the loot between the four of them.
6. "I could of been a contender!" is a line spoken by Marlon Brando in the movie *On the Waterfront.*
7. I simply will not except your excuse for poor grammar!
8. At the park concert the musicians played loudly enough, but I couldn't barely hear.
9. The temperature on Thursday was anywheres from 70 to 85 degrees.
10. That suit looks well on you.

Step 3. Making the Words Work. Follow instructions.

1. Tell in a sentence what happens to your own personality when you get very little sleep at night. Use the words *the effect* in your sentence.

_____

_____

2. Tell in a sentence what kind of music you dislike. Use *accept* or *except* correctly. _____

_____

_____

3. Use *regardless* in your own sentence. _____

_____

4. Use *hang* or *hung* in a sentence about a man's conviction in a murder case. _____

5. Write a sentence about a diver and the ocean or a lake. Use *in* or *into* correctly. _____

6. Use *affected* to mean *pretended* in a sentence. _____

7. Use *affect* or *effect* in a sentence that tells how a friend's decision about something led to a certain unexpected result. _____

8. Write a sentence about dividing found money with friends. Use *between* or *among* correctly. _____

9. Correct this sentence: *He had to return his tickets for the high school reunion game being that his mother was sick.* _____

10. Write a sentence about the long-range effects of chocolate on the teeth. Use *amount* or *number* correctly in your sentence. _____

8. USING THE *READER'S GUIDE*

The *Reader's Guide to Periodical Literature* is a semimonthly report giving the names of authors and the titles of articles in many important magazines like *Time*, the *Atlantic*, *Saturday Review*, *Harper's*, and *The New Yorker*. The reports are bound together in volumes each year.

HOW TO USE THE *READER'S GUIDE*

1. To find articles on any given subject, look up the subject in the index. Several authors, titles, and names of the magazines in which they appear are listed.
2. To find an article written by an author whose name you know, look up the author's last name in the index.

Sample Subject Entry

FIREFLIES
[the subject of the article]
[article has illustrations]

Midsummer night's gleam.   R. Telander. il
[title of the article]   [author's name]

Nat Wildlife   17: 34–5, Ag '79 ← [date of issue]
[name of periodical] [volume   [pages on which
                     number]   article appears]

Sample Author Entry

[author's name]

FLINK, Steve
[title of the article]   [illustrations]   [volume number]

Keeping an eye on the kids   il   World Tennis   27:
[page number]
                          [name of the periodical]

36+, S '79 ← [date]
[article continued on later pages]

Hint: All abbreviations appear in a key at the beginning of the *Reader's Guide.* Look up any abbreviations you do not understand.

Step 1. Looking for Articles and Essays.

For each subject below, check the latest volume or issue of the *Reader's Guide* and copy from it one magazine reference on the line provided. Be prepared to explain the abbreviations in your entries.

1. hunger in Asia _____

2. rock music _____

3. Soviet Jews _____

4. television advertising _____

5. Edward Kennedy _____

9. PREPARING A BIBLIOGRAPHY

Whenever you do research about a topic, readers expect to find a *bibliography,* an alphabetical list of the sources you have consulted or quoted from in your paper. When you prepare a bibliography, keep in mind these guide-lines:

1. The bibliography appears on a separate page at the end of the paper.
2. Items are *not* numbered but are listed alphabetically according to author's last name.
3. Write author's last name first, then first and middle name.
4. List alphabetically according to title other works by the same author, directly under the first entry for the author's name.
5. For works by more than one author, list the entry under last name of first author, giving other writers' names in regular order (first name, middle, last).
6. List works with no authors alphabetically according to the first important word in the title.
7. Do not give pages for books. Do give pages on which essays and articles in periodicals, encyclopedias, and newspapers appear.
8. The first line of each bibliography entry starts at the left-hand margin. Indent all other lines.
9. Double-space all entries but separate one entry from another by triple-spacing.

SAMPLE BIBLIOGRAPHIC ENTRY FOR BOOK

[author's last name first]   [title (underlined)]

Malamud, Bernard. Dubin's Lives. New York: Farrar

[comma]   [period]   [period]   [colon]

[comma]

Straus Giroux, 1979. ←—[period]

[publisher's name]   [date of publication]

SAMPLE BIBLIOGRAPHIC ENTRY FOR ARTICLE IN PERIODICAL

[period]

Sisk, John P. "The Tyranny of Harmony." The American

[author's last name]   [title of article (in quotes)]   [title of periodical (underlined)]

[parentheses]   [comma]   [period]

Scholar, 46 (Spring, 1977), 193–205.

[comma]   [season or month of publication]   [pages on which article is found]

[volume]   [year]

Here is the bibliography April Wynn prepared for her theme, "The Advantages of Attending Kindergarten" on pages 195–196.

Bibliography

Courtney, Richard. "Education Is Play." Childhood Education, 49 (February

1973), 246–250.

Grant, Vance W. Digest of Education Statistics. Washington D.C.: U.S.

Government Printing Office, 1975.

Hymes, James L. Jr. Teaching the Child Under Six. Columbus, Ohio:

Charles E. Merrill Publishing Company, 1968.

Mindess, David. Guide to an Effective Kindergarten Program. New York:

Parker Publishing Company, Inc., 1972.

Palmer, Edward L. "Sesame Street: Shaping Broadcast Television to the

Needs of the Pre-schooler." Educational Technology," 11 (February

1971), 18–22.

"Play." World Book Encyclopedia, 1969.

Step 1. A Bibliography Exercise. Using the resources of your college library, prepare on a separate sheet of paper a bibliography of *five* entries for one of the topics below. Make sure that at least one of your entries is for a periodical.

1. health foods
2. anti-nuclear power protests
3. illegal adoptions
4. Cuban community in Florida
5. teenage alcoholism

10. WRITING SIMPLE FOOTNOTES

Sometimes you need to tell in footnotes the source for a statement you are quoting from someone else's work. Each quotation or paraphrase in an essay with such requirements, then, should be consecutively numbered slightly above the line and at the end of the statement you are borrowing from someone else's writing. At the bottom of the page or at the end of the essay, give the information about your source for each numbered quotation.

Compare these sample footnote entries with bibliographic entries for the same book and periodical by turning to page 402.

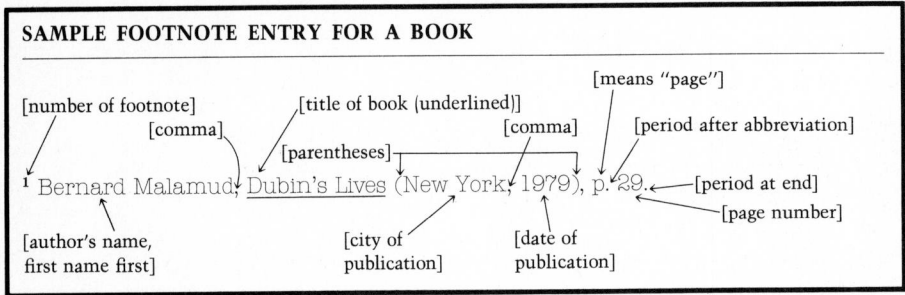

SAMPLE FOOTNOTE ENTRY FOR A BOOK

[number of footnote]
[comma]
[title of book (underlined)]
[parentheses]
[comma]
[means "page"]
[period after abbreviation]

[1] Bernard Malamud, Dubin's Lives (New York, 1979), p. 29. ← [period at end]
[page number]

[author's name, first name first]
[city of publication]
[date of publication]

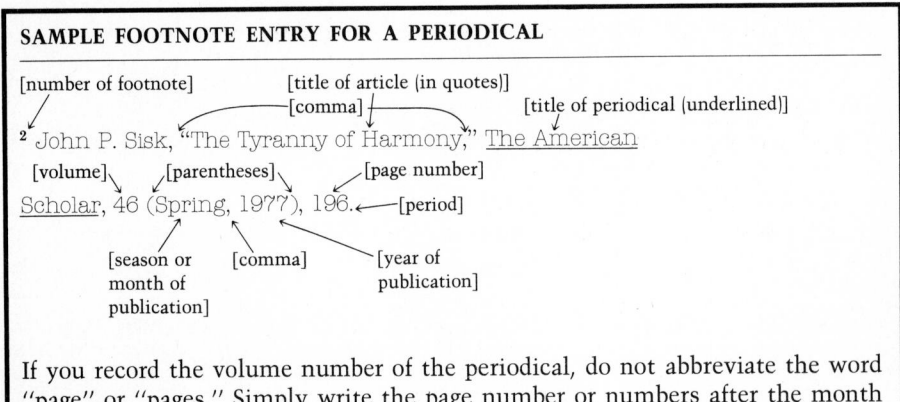

SAMPLE FOOTNOTE ENTRY FOR A PERIODICAL

[number of footnote]
[title of article (in quotes)]
[comma]
[title of periodical (underlined)]

[2] John P. Sisk, "The Tyranny of Harmony," The American

[volume]
[parentheses]
[page number]

Scholar, 46 (Spring, 1977), 196. ← [period]

[season or month of publication]
[comma]
[year of publication]

If you record the volume number of the periodical, do not abbreviate the word "page" or "pages." Simply write the page number or numbers after the month and year of publication, as shown above.

If you quote from a book or article and the very next quotation you use in your paragraph comes from the same book or article, do this:

[capital letter]
[This means *pages.*]
[period]
[the page numbers]

[3] Ibid., pp. 29–30. ← [period at end]

[comma]
[period]

[This is an abbreviation for the Latin *ibidem,* meaning *in the same place.*]

If you quote again from a writer's book or article that you have described in an earlier footnote but not in the immediately preceding footnote, do this:

[This means *pages*.]

[period]

⁴ Malamud, pp. 58–59. [page numbers]

[comma]

[author's last name]

Step 1. Understanding Footnotes.   Look at the footnotes at the bottom of the paragraph on page 406. Explain the reasons for each of the entries.

11. QUOTING FROM BOOKS

1. If the passage you select to quote has fewer than one hundred words, work the quotation smoothly into your own sentences. Use a colon or a comma before the quotation. Use quotation marks at the beginning and at the end of the statement you are quoting. (Example *a* below)
2. If you quote a longer passage (three or more typed lines or more than one hundred words), block the quotation off from the rest of the text by leaving several spaces from the margin on each side. If you type, this longer quotation should be single-spaced (the rest of the paragraph or essay is double-spaced). Do not use quotation marks when you set off this longer passage. (Example *b* below.)
3. If you want to leave out any words of a sentence in the selection you are quoting, use three dots (. . .). If a complete sentence precedes the omission, use four dots (. . . .). See *c* below.

Here is part of a student's paragraph on understanding reading problems. Note the correct use of quotations.

Every teacher and psychologist knows that emotional factors play an important part

in the way a child reads; but specialists are still unsure of how emotional problems

really affect reading skills. No one knows whether or not the problems are there to

prevent the child from reading properly or come after the child sees that he

[quotation marks]

cannot learn the way others do. One teacher of readings says, "Some writers have

[comma]

gathered evidence to support the view that emotional upsets are perhaps caused   a.

[quotation mark]

by reading failure."[1] Failure affects the way we all regard ourselves, and reading

failure would have an emotional effect on a student.[2] Even if this is true, however, there does not seem to be any pattern in how personality affects reading competence.

Analyzing the findings in some recent studies, a leading specialist concludes:
[no quotation mark]   [colon]

[single-spaced]
> If one hopes for consistent grade-to-grade findings in these results one is bound
> to be disappointed. However, and this is my first point, if one takes a develop-
> mental approach, one discovers that relationships between reading and per-
> sonality found at the primary level become inconsistent at the intermediate
> and junior high school grades, and so far as the evidence is concerned, seem
> completely to disappear at the high school and college levels. Of course, there
> may be many possible explanations, such as the increased selectivity of stu-
> dents, the unreliability and use of different types of tests, etc.[3]

b.

[no quotation mark]

But no matter how these factors work in the reading process, no one can disagree

that "Students who are . . . disturbed by major fears and anxieties should be re-   c.

ferred to persons qualified to help them. . . ."[4]

—Steve Lederman

[Footnotes
to show
sources
see pages
404–405]
> [1] Robert Karlin, <u>Teaching Reading in High School</u> (Indianapolis,
> 1964), p. 29.
> [2] <u>Ibid.</u>, pp. 29–30.
> [3] Jack A. Holmes, "Personality Characteristics of the Disabled Reader,"
> <u>Journal of Developmental Reading</u>, 4 (Winter, 1961), 1961, 112.
> [4] Karlin, p. 29.

12. FORMAT OF A BUSINESS LETTER

An important on-the-job demand, once you graduate from college, is the
writing of clear business letters. When you write you need to observe several
principles agreed upon by the business community. In this letter requesting
information (page 410 presents a letter of job application), the parts of the
letter and some suggestions appear in the margin.

Step 1. Letter Writing.   Follow the suggestions below to write a letter requesting information. Use separate paper.

1. Write to a college out of the state for a copy of the college bulletin, or for
   copies of campus publications.
2. Write to a local newspaper requesting a back issue that deals with drugs
   or pollution in your neighborhood.
3. Write to the U.S. Department of Interior asking for information about
   the standard of living for American Indians.
4. Write to the chamber of commerce of a city or state you want to visit.
   Ask for information about hotels, amusements, places of interest.

[heading
(your address)]   [no abbreviations]

[comma] 847 Ditmars Boulevard
        Astoria, New York   10001

[date]→February 2, 1981
                    [comma]

[inside
address] → Office of Admissions   [no abbreviations]
Fordham University
Rose Hill Campus
Bronx, New York   10458
          [comma]

[salutation]→Dear Sir or Madam:←[colon]
              [capital]

[body of
letter:
clear
concise
correct
courteous
complete]

I would like some information on the possibilities of my transferring to Fordham University from LaGuardia Community College after I complete my Associate of Arts degree this June. At LaGuardia I am a liberal arts student with the equivalent of a B− or C+ average; I would like to major in urban government at Fordham. Do you have an urban government program? If you do, would I be eligible for admission to it as a two-year transfer student?

If you have an up-to-date college bulletin, a schedule of tuition fees, and an application for admission, I should like to have that information too. And any materials you could send along about housing and dormitories would be very helpful.

[capitalize   [complimentary
first word──→Yours very truly,   close]
only]   [comma]

Russel Kise ←[signature]

Russel Kise ← [name typed below signature]

RÉSUMÉ

<u>Personal Data</u>

Susan E. Davis
18–28 Deegan Road
Elmhurst, New York   11373
Telephone: (212) 481-9998

Age: 18
Height: 5 ft., 1 in.
Weight: 100 lbs.
Marital Status: Single

<u>Career Objective</u>: Junior Accountant

<u>Educational Background</u>: Long Island City High School
(Commercial Diploma: June, 1978). La Guardia Community College
(Major: Accounting; A.A.S. Degree expected June, 1980).

<u>Major Courses</u>: Accounting, data processing, statistics, insurance, business organization
and management, writing for business, bookkeeping, business law, economics,
stenography, typing.

<u>Special Skills</u>: Typing (65 W.P.M.); stenography (40 W.P.M.); machine experience: IBM
electric typewriter, IBM 029 and 129 Keypunch.

<u>Honors and Awards</u>: Perfect attendance award (1977–1978); certificate for highest yearly
average in bookkeeping (1978); outstanding service award (1977).

<u>Extracurricular Activities</u>: Business Honor Society (1975–1976); Program Committee
(1975–1976).

<u>Experience</u>

Pantry Pride Supermarket
82-66 Broadway
Elmhurst, New York   11373
Manager: Mr. Micelli

August 1974 to present
Cashier and Office Worker
Duties: Recording sales in the ledger book.

F. W. Woolworth Company
976 Third Avenue
New York, New York   10002
Manager: Mr. Pastore

April 1974 to August 1974
Part-time Cashier
Duties: Pricing merchandise and filling
shelves.

Abraham & Straus
Fulton Street and East Broadway
New York, New York   11201
Section Manager: Mr. Murray

November 1973 to January 1974
Sales Clerk
Duties: Recording cash and charge sales
and displaying merchandise.

<u>References</u>

Mr. John Micelli, Manager
82-66 Broadway
Elmhurst, New York   11373

Mr. John Weigel, Asst. Professor/Coordinator
Division of Cooperative Education
Fiorello H. LaGuardia Community College
31-10 Thomson Avenue
Long Island City, New York   11101

Hint: Be sure to ask permission from those people whom you want to list as sources of
recommendation.

5. Write to your state board of education for material on special programs in education for minority-group students or students in poverty areas.

13. APPLYING FOR A JOB YOU WANT

Preparing a Résumé

When an advertisement for some good job appears in a local paper, the employer often receives hundreds of responses. If you are one of those interested in such a position, you will want to make sure that your response attracts the employer's interest. Your answer should be brief but to the point; and your qualifications should be clearly stated. A convenient method of presenting your qualifications is through a résumé, a statement of your particular accomplishments in summary form. In a résumé, a prospective employer can see at a glance just why you feel he or she should select you for the job opening.

Notice in the résumé on the facing page how the writer groups information together for easy reference to show clearly her qualifications as an accountant's assistant.

HOW TO WRITE YOUR RÉSUMÉ

1. Include your name, address, and telephone number.
2. Sometimes an office will advertise several available positions, so make sure to indicate the job for which you are applying.
3. If you have a specific salary in mind, include it in the résumé.
4. Include honors or awards that show your qualifications for the job you want. Otherwise leave out this part.
5. Include all your job experience. Any job can give you skills which may be helpful in the position you are seeking.
6. Extracurricular activities show your interest in voluntary service and often reflect skills that might be handy on the job. Susan Davis' membership in the Business Honor Society suggests that her skills are advanced.
7. Show whatever specific training you have had that makes you eligible for the job.
8. List two or three references—their names and addresses—so that information about your character and abilities is easy to obtain. Make sure you include people who know you well enough to give a fair evaluation of your character. It is a good idea to ask someone's permission before giving that person as a reference.
9. *Type* your résumé on sturdy typing paper. Avoid errors and erasures.

Step 1. Writing Your Résumé. Prepare a résumé about yourself on a separate sheet of paper. Assume that you want to apply for a job for which you feel well qualified. Résumés often include additional information, such as

108 East 93 Street
Brooklyn, New York   11212
October 5, 1980

Mr. Harry Koster
Chief of Division of Receipts
Comptroller's Office of the City of New York
New York, New York   10007

Dear Mr. Koster:

Your advertisement in the <u>New York Chief</u> yesterday called for a part-time accountant's assistant to help in the processing of city income tax forms. Because of my interest in accounting and city government, I think I am well qualified to apply for the job you are advertising.

You will see from my résumé that I have had both training and experience in the field of accounting. My course of study at college is designed to qualify me as an accountant after graduation. My interest and skill in mathematics contribute to my qualifications for this job.

My schedule at college now requires me to attend classes late in the afternoon; for this term I am available for work from 9 a.m. to 11:30 a.m. every day but Wednesday when I can work from 9 a.m. to 11:00 a.m.

May I please come for an interview any morning during the week? I will telephone your office to arrange a time convenient to you. You will find me an eager and cooperative worker.

Very truly yours,

Darrel M. Farnsworth

Darrel M. Farnsworth

travel experience, military status, bilingualism or other language skills, hobbies, involvement in sports; many of these may be appropriate for your résumé. The kind of job always determines the range of information to be included.

A Letter of Application

The letter that you send along with your résumé should be a brief and sincere attempt to arouse the employer's interest in you. Paragraphs in a business letter (see page 407 for the correct format) are often just three or four sentences long, making the letter easy to read quickly.

The first paragraph usually includes a statement about how the job came to your attention and expresses your interest in the position. The second paragraph mentions briefly the highlights of the résumé which you send along with the letter: if you are not planning to send a résumé, the second paragraph (and the third as well, if you need more space) should indicate all your special qualifications for the job.

Another paragraph can indicate any special conditions you may have to present. If you are not sending a résumé, name your references in this paragraph. Another brief paragraph should show your willingness to come for an interview—suggesting a convenient time and a day. On the facing page appears the letter that will accompany Darrel Farnsworth's résumé.

14. FILLING OUT APPLICATIONS

Whether you are interested in getting a job, a checking account, a life insurance policy, or a driver's license, you have to make out application forms that give important data about yourself. Filling out these forms correctly requires care, attention, and some preparation beforehand.

FILLING OUT AN APPLICATION: SOME GUIDELINES

1. Look the whole application over carefully before you begin writing answers.
2. Print all your answers clearly in ink. If you can, type your responses.
3. Answer all questions required of you. If you have no answer to one or more of the questions, do *not* simply leave a blank space. Put in a dash (–) or write *NA* (not applicable); such a response shows that you have read the question but that it does not pertain to you.
4. Answer all questions honestly. Leaving out required information can only hurt your chances of getting what you are applying for.
5. Some applications have special boxes or sections for office workers' notations. Those sections often say: *DO NOT WRITE IN THIS SPACE* or *FOR OFFICE USE ONLY*. Follow instructions. Leave those lines blank.
6. Try to use available space to answer questions on the form. If, however, you see that the space is too small for your answer, don't try to squeeze in in-

formation by writing in very small letters. Instead, attach a sheet of paper on which you can respond fully. Make sure that you indicate on the form that you have added a sheet; and be sure to number your answers on that sheet so they correspond to numbered questions on the application.

7. To be prepared, try to anticipate the kind of information you might be asked for. A job application, for example, will always ask for information about your education and about other jobs you've held. Make a list at home of your graduation dates, your previous employers and their addresses, the dates you worked for them. With the list in hand as you fill out your application, you'll have all the data you need at your fingertips. What kind of information might you be asked for on an application for life insurance? for a loan?

Step 1. Filling Out a Job Application

Using the application form on pages 414–415, fill in the blanks carefully as if you were applying for a job of your choice with L. L. K., Inc., Insurance.

15. TAKING NOTES

Few people remember accurately what they read. That is why note taking is such an aid to the student who is frequently asked to read a great deal of material for exams, reports, and term papers.

NOTES ON READINGS: SIX STEPS TO EXCELLENCE

1. Write down the names of the author and the book, article, essay, or story you need to take notes on.
2. Take notes on one paragraph at a time.
3. Look up any words you do not know.
4. Write in your own words the main idea of the selection.
5. Write in your own words the subtopics of the selection if they are clearly stated.
6. Jot down briefly the key words, most important facts, illustrations, details, or statistics. Use the author's own words for special key ideas.

Read the paragraph "Racism in Education" on pages 174–175. Then look at the notes below, taken by a student as he read.

Notes on paragraph "Racism in Education," by
  Maude White Katz
Main Idea: Racist beliefs make Negro appear "subhuman or only semi-human."
Subtopics and Important Details
  The Establishment, through colleges and mass media, gives racist philosophy

Black child can be educated
  intelligence tests dishonest
  when intelligence of whites differs many reasons given as possible expla-
    nations
  when Blacks and whites differ, reason is genetic
Other instances of racism
  Blacks excluded from trade schools
  Craft union officials keep Blacks out of schools
  Sheet Metal Workers Union Local 28 in New York has 3,300 white members,
    no Blacks: State Commission on Human Rights finds union guilty

—Geoffrey Hunte

UNDERLINING

If you own the book, underlining is a very good method of note taking because it saves time. Remember these tips about underlining:

1. Underline the main points, subpoints, and the key supporting details.
2. Write notes to yourself in the margin: jot down a question; say an idea more simply than the author has, using your own words; write down an idea the author's writing makes you think about.

Step 1. Note Taking on Your Own. Reread the paragraph by William Shannon on pages 169–170. Take notes on your reading, using separate paper.

Step 2. Underlining. Read "Why Some Schools Succeed" on pages 199–201, underlining as you read. Follow the suggestions above.

16. WRITING A SUMMARY

Much college writing—especially brief reports and homework questions—is summary writing. A summary gives a brief idea of material you have read. It is usually a statement you write from your notes or from your underlining. Good summaries focus on main ideas, major subtopics, and only *important* details.

FOR CLEAR SUMMARIES THAT MAKE THE POINT

1. Read carefully. Take notes as explained on pages 412–413. Look up words you do not understand.
2. Your first sentence should state the main idea of the selection you are summarizing.
3. Use your own words in repeating details. Use the author's exact words for certain key ideas.
4. Repeat information accurately.

L.L.K., Inc. Insurance
Employment Application

An Equal Opportunity Employer
L.L.K., Inc., policy and federal law prohibit discrimination because of race, religion, age, marital status, sex, disability, or natural origin.

Date _____

Personal Data

Applying for position as _____ Salary required _____ Date available _____

Name: _____
      (Last)   (First)   (Middle)   (Maiden)

Present address _____
      (Street)   (City)   (State)   (Zip)   (How long at this address)

Permanent address _____
      (Street)   (City)   (State)   (Zip)   (How long at this address)

Telephone number _____ Social Security number _____
    (Area code)

Are you a U.S. citizen? ☐ Yes ☐ No   If non-citizen, give Alien Registration No. _____

Check appropirate box for age: Under 16 ☐, 16 or 17 ☐, 18 through 69 ☐, 70 or over ☐

Person to be notified in case of emergency:

  Name _____ Telephone _____

  Address _____

Will you consider relocation? Yes ☐ No ☐   Domestic Yes ☐ No ☐   International Yes ☐ No ☐

Educational Data

Schools	Print address for each school given	Date	Type of course or major	Graduated (yes or no)	Degree received
High School		From____ To			
College		From____ To			
Graduate School		From____ To			
Business, Correspondence, Night, or Trade School		From____ To			
Other		From____ To			

Approximate scholastic average: High School _____ College _____

Activities

Do not name organizations that will reveal race, religion, age, sex, or national origin.

School and college activities _____

Special interests outside of business.   1._____   Indicate the amount of time devoted to each.   1._____

    2._____   2._____

    3._____   3._____

Skills

List any special skills you may have _____

What foreign languages do you:
☐ Speak _____ ☐ Speak _____ ☐ Speak _____
☐ Read _____ ☐ Read _____ ☐ Read _____
☐ Write ☐ Write ☐ Write

Business machines you can operate _____

Typing speed _____ words per minute ☐ Electric Steno speed _____ words per minute Method _____
☐ Manual

References

List names, addresses, and telephone numbers of three people who can attest to your character.

	1.	2.	3.
Name			
Address			
City, State, Zip			
Phone Number			

Employment Data Begin with most recent employer. List all full-time, part-time, temporary, or self-employment.

Company name _____ Employed from Mo-Yr ___ To Mo-Yr ___

Street address _____ Salary or earnings Start Finish

City _____ State ___ Zip code ___ Telephone (Area code) ___

Name and title of immediate supervisor _____ Your title ___

Description of duties

Reason for terminating or considering a change _____

Company name _____ Employed from Mo-Yr ___ To Mo-Yr ___

Street address _____ Salary or earnings Start Finish

City _____ State ___ Zip code ___ Telephone (Area code) ___

Name and title of immediate supervisor _____ Your title ___

Description of duties

Reason for terminating _____

I agree that after accepting employment I will complete a medical exam by a physician recommended by L.L.K., Inc. Insurance.

Date _____ Signature of Applicant _____

Personnel Interviewer _____

Do Not Write Below This Line

Interview number _____

Reference check 1. _____
2. _____
3. _____

Applicant employed as _____ Will begin work

on _____ at a salary of $ _____ per _____

Salary Code

Signed _____ Date _____

Title _____ Dept. _____

Additional approval _____

5. Follow the author's development in the selection you are summarizing. If information is arranged chronologically or by importance; if material is presented through comparison-contrast, narrative, several examples—your summary should reflect the author's pattern.
6. Revise your first draft so that your sentences flow smoothly. Use subordination to tighten ideas.
7. Summaries should be brief, usually not more than a third of the total number of words in the original.

Here is a summary written from the notes, taken by Mr. Hunte, that appear on pages 412–413.

Summary of "Racism in Education"

Racist beliefs make many Americans view Negroes as "subhuman or only semi-human." The Establishment (higher education and mass media) is responsible for this philosophy. Yet Blacks *are* educable, in spite of dishonest intelligence-test results. Although valid reasons appear for intelligence differences among white children, Blacks are said to differ from whites for genetic reasons. Proof of racism in education appears in the exclusion of Blacks—through craft union officials—from trade schools. The New York State Commission on Human Rights found guilty the Sheet Metal Workers Union Local 28 because none of its 3,300 members was Black.

—Geoffrey Hunte

17. WRITING ABOUT LITERATURE

Often in your courses you will have to report on assigned reading. In your English class you may have to give your responses to a novel, perhaps, a short story, a play, or a poem. As with all writing assignments your first step as part of prewriting activity is to limit your topic. Of course, there are many possibilities for writing that each piece of literature itself suggests, but with an idea of some *possible* approaches to take you might find it easier to prepare an essay on a literary work. Below appear some suggestions that singly or in combination may help you focus your discussion.

Approaches to Writing about Literature

1. Write about the *theme.* The theme in a poem, novel, play, or short story is its main idea, the dominant point the writer had in mind for the work. Because the writer rarely states the theme outright—it is almost always implied—you have to figure out the main idea by thinking about the people, the characters, the events in what you have read. Is the writer trying to make a point about human behavior? about social conditions?

about religion or morality? about personal psychology? about humanity's place in the universe? How does the work of literature reveal one or several of those points? Once you have an idea about the theme, you will have to support that idea with specific details drawn from the work itself.

2. Write about one *character* or about several of the characters. Explain what you think their motives are; discuss their behavior and the results of it; show how characters interact; examine their personal psychologies. Are the characters realistic? Do they change through the course of the work or do they remain constant? Pages 418–419 explore in greater detail some approaches to writing about characters in books or poems.

3. Write about the *action*. Although you may need occasionally to summarize some details of the plot (the story line, the events that take place), writing a report that is almost entirely a summary is not a good idea because it reveals none of your abilities to evaluate. Therefore, in writing about action you must avoid a simple plot summary. You might want to discuss the climax of the action, its major turning point; you might show how various incidents are connected to each other; you might show how characters are forced to behave in certain ways because of events; you might point out the elements that cause suspense; you might show how the events are rooted in historical occasions.

4. Write about the *structure* of the work. How does the writer put the pieces together? How is the work similar to or different from other examples of literature like it? If you are writing about a love poem, for example, how does the poet conform to what readers expect to find in such poems? How does a writer make a work special, however? How do the different stages (or chapters or acts or scenes) interact with each other?

5. Write about the *tone* of the work. What is the writer's attitude toward the subject? Is it serious or mocking? What attitude does the writer show toward the characters? Is it admiration or dislike or pity?

6. Write about the *language* in the work. What is the quality of the writer's use of words. Are the images particularly clear and vivid? Are figures of speech used (see pages 120–123) with any special skill? Are there any patterns that you can figure out about the images? Does the writer have special talents in writing dialogue? Does the language portray actions clearly? Does any special strength lie in the use of details?

An Essay on a Book Character

The pages of novels and biographies are rich in unforgettable characters who make exciting topics for book reports. One approach to take to an essay on character is to select *two* dramatic moments that illustrate something significant about an important person in your book. Then, you can expand each moment in a body paragraph as you try to illustrate your proposal. Study the guidelines and the student model on the next pages before you write.

ESSAY GUIDELINES FOR BOOK CHARACTERS

1. Decide on some important personality trait of the hero in your book. Is the person *brave, mean, thoughtless, loving, pitiful?* Write a proposal sentence that indicates that personality trait.
2. Let each body paragraph relate one specific moment that illustrates from the book the impression you stated in the proposal sentence.
3. Select moments that are important in the growth and development of the hero. A moment that focuses on the hero in the midst of a crisis or a turning point (especially where some important decision must be made and acted upon) is especially emphatic for the reader.
4. Make the sounds and colors and smells of each moment alive. Show the actions of the character. What is he or she doing, thinking about, or saying?
5. Follow the suggestions on pages 219–223 for writing good introductions: be sure also to include the author's name and the title of the book in your first paragraph.
6. Make sure that you use in your essay a quotation right from the book. This may be a sentence or two that describes an action or it may be something said by one of the characters.

In the student essay below, notice how the two body paragraphs effectively support the proposal sentence.

Antonia's Strength

History books are filled with words of praise for the pioneers who settled the West. But the struggle with personal hardships by the courageous families who cleared Nebraska and Kansas come to life in Willa Cather's *My Antonia.* In the novel the heroine, Antonia Shimerda, faces familial hardships with unusual strength.

She shows it first after her father's suicide. A girl in her early teens, Antonia loved her father deeply. When Jim Burden, the narrator of the novel, arrives at the house for the burial, Antonia rushes out to him and sobs, her heart almost breaking. But at the funeral she is much more controlled. Her dead father lies in the coffin with his knees drawn up. "His body was draped in a black shawl," writes Cather, "and his head was bandaged in white muslin, like a mummy's; one of his long, shapely hands lay out on the black cloth; that was all one could see of him." Yet Antonia, in spite of that awful figure, follows her mother up to the coffin and makes the sign of the cross on the bandaged head of her dead father. When Antonia's mother, a woman with little maternal softness, pushes her youngest daughter Yulka up to the body, the child cries wildly. After a neighbor insists that the child not touch the body, it is Antonia who puts her arms around the younger girl and holds her close. I'll never forget the warmth of that scene: Antonia, herself so sad, comforting her little sister as a fine, icy Nebraska snow falls outside.

That quiet moment of courage Antonia matches later on with physical strength. On an April afternoon after Mr. Shimerda's death, Jim Burden rides out to the house; he has not seen Antonia for three months. When he spots her as the sun drops low, he watches her drive a team of horses up to the windmill. She wears her father's boots, his old fur cap, and an outgrown cotton dress with sleeves rolled up. Antonia has taken upon herself to work the fields in her father's absence. Although she cries briefly at not being able to attend the sod schoolhouse, she states in her broken English, "I ain't got time to learn. I can work like mans now. . . . School is all right for little boys. I help make this land one good farm." Jim is disappointed at her mannish ways: she yawns at the table, eats noisily like a man, and boasts often of her strength and the chores she can perform. But this is just an outgrowth of what is really strength of character. To accept the challenge of the soil as a man in her father's place is certainly an act of courage.

Antonia's courage should be a lesson for women of today. Living the soft life, I and many of my contemporaries complain about the slightest trouble. We complain when the washing machine is broken or when we have to walk to the bus. We complain if we have to wash dishes by hand or if the garbage barrels need pushing out to the street. Antonia Shimerda would look these minor inconveniences in the eye and say, "I can work like mans now."

—Phyllis Dubin

OTHER APPROACHES TO LITERATURE ESSAYS ON CHARACTER

Compare and contrast two characters with different traits, showing a dramatic moment to illustrate each personality.

Show how the hero changes by relating two different instances, one from an early part of the book and one from a later part.

Show how the hero responds to a moment of crisis and then show how a moment in your own life was similar to or different from the hero's. Or, show how you would have behaved in the hero's place.

Show how a moment in a book compares with the same moment in a movie about the book.

---

18. ANSWERING ESSAY EXAMINATION QUESTIONS

Midterm or final examinations in college courses usually ask—in addition to short-answer questions—that you answer some questions in *essay* form. Although the word *essay* in this sense is used loosely, it usually means some longer response to a question that requires extended thought and development.

Hint: If the exam asks you to answer more than two or three *essay* questions, a one-paragraph response is often adequate for each question.

If the exam asks you to answer only one or two questions, plan to write a four-paragraph essay to develop your responses.

MAKING THE GRADE: HOW TO ANSWER ESSAY QUESTIONS

1. Think about the question before you write. Take clues for the development of your paragraph or essay from the question itself.

   If the question says *compare and contrast,* use comparison-contrast methods of development.

If the question says *how,* show how something is done or how something works. If the question says *explain, tell, illustrate, discuss,* use any method of development that uses facts, statistics, paraphrases, or quotations in order to back up your point.

If the question says *define,* write a paragraph or essay that uses substantial details to illustrate the meaning of a word, idea, or theory.

If the question says *list,* it is often enough just to write your answer by numbering 1 through 10, for example, and by writing some fact for each number. But you can also "list" ideas in paragraph form.

If the question asks *why,* make sure you understand what conclusion the instructor wants you to reach. Then, give as many details as you can to explain the *causes* for the result you are asked to explain.

2. Repeat the main part of the question in your topic sentence (for one-paragraph answers) or in your proposal sentences (for four-paragraph essay responses).

3. If you answer in a four-paragraph essay, your introduction and conclusion may be much briefer than those urged in other parts of this book. But do not abandon other requirements of the well-constructed essay.

Make sure your proposal sentence allows you to discuss two aspects of the topic your instructor asks you to write about.

Make sure the proposal sentence comes *last* in paragraph 1.

Make sure to use a clear transition in the first sentence of paragraph 2.

Make sure that in the first sentence of paragraph 3 you refer back to the topic in paragraph 2 and that you introduce the new aspect of the topic of paragraph 3.

4. In your conclusion, say again your main point by summarizing the topics of paragraphs 2 and 3. Then, apply your topic to some general principles, if possible (see pages 337–340).

5. Use a number of details to illustrate or to prove whatever points you make in your paragraphs. In this book you have learned how to use the following kinds of details and illustrations:

a single moment from your life experience
concrete sensory details
figurative language and imagery
statistics
quotations and paraphrases
illustrative moments from fiction
cases

Step 1. Understanding Questions. These essay-type questions all come from college textbooks. Explain on a separate sheet of paper how you would go about answering them; tell what methods you would use in developing your paragraph or essay.

1. Discuss the growth of trade unions in the 1930s in America.
2. List the basic features of the open classroom.
3. Compare *realism* and *naturalism* in literature.
4. Discuss Freud's Oedipal theory.
5. Compare and contrast Marxism in Europe and Latin America.

19. MAKING A SIMPLE OUTLINE

To sort out ideas on a complicated topic, we often use the sentence outline before writing an essay. An outline allows you to see the main ideas of each paragraph at a glance; it also shows how major details (and subtopics) relate to each main idea; and it illustrates quickly just how each body paragraph relates to the proposal sentence. Writing each outline entry in a full sentence allows you to express main thoughts fully and to avoid writing fragments in the essay itself.

Hint: Outlines are designed to help you write and are useful only so long as they serve that function. Even after you prepare an outline you may change your subtopic or even main-idea sentences in the essay.

Here is a simple outline for the essay "Antonia's Strength" that appears on pages 418–419. You will find in the margin explanations of the letters and Roman numbers.

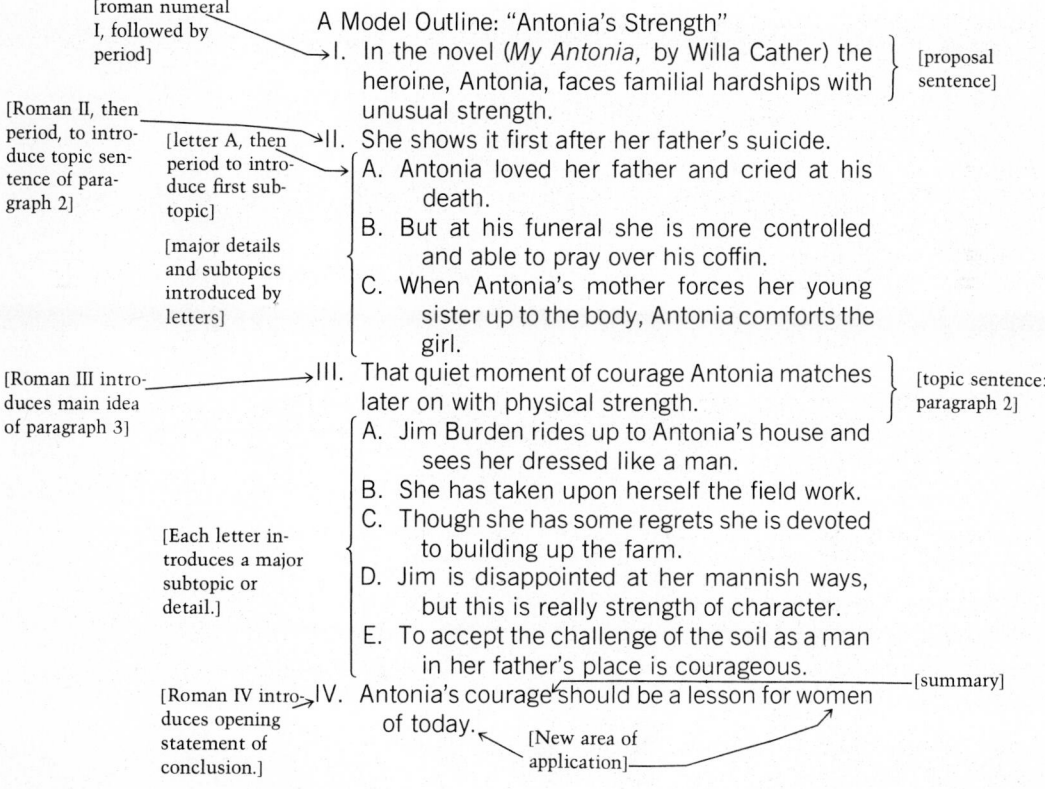

[roman numeral I, followed by period]

A Model Outline: "Antonia's Strength"

I. In the novel (*My Antonia*, by Willa Cather) the heroine, Antonia, faces familial hardships with unusual strength. } [proposal sentence]

[Roman II, then period, to introduce topic sentence of paragraph 2]

[letter A, then period to introduce first subtopic]

[major details and subtopics introduced by letters]

II. She shows it first after her father's suicide.
  A. Antonia loved her father and cried at his death.
  B. But at his funeral she is more controlled and able to pray over his coffin.
  C. When Antonia's mother forces her young sister up to the body, Antonia comforts the girl.

[Roman III introduces main idea of paragraph 3]

III. That quiet moment of courage Antonia matches later on with physical strength. } [topic sentence: paragraph 2]
  A. Jim Burden rides up to Antonia's house and sees her dressed like a man.
  B. She has taken upon herself the field work.
  C. Though she has some regrets she is devoted to building up the farm.
  D. Jim is disappointed at her mannish ways, but this is really strength of character.
  E. To accept the challenge of the soil as a man in her father's place is courageous.

[Each letter introduces a major subtopic or detail.]

[summary]

[Roman IV introduces opening statement of conclusion.]

IV. Antonia's courage should be a lesson for women of today.

[New area of application]

HOW TO MAKE THE OUTLINE HELP:

1. Check Roman numerals II and III to see if they clearly follow from the proposal you wrote for Roman numeral I.
2. Check subtopics A, B, C, etc. under each Roman numeral: make sure each subtopic relates to the topic sentence.
3. Leave out minor details.
4. Don't elaborate on the proposal or the introduction in the outline. You can do that in the essay itself.
5. Check to see if the transitions in the opening sentences of paragraphs 2 and 3 are clear and obvious.
6. Make sure that every entry you have written is a full sentence.

Step 1. Seeing an Outline Work.   Write an outline for "Some Disappointments," the essay by Barbara Pomerantz on pages 359–360. Use separate paper.

Step 2. Putting an Outline Together.   Select a topic suggested in any chapter in this book and, on separate paper, prepare an outline following the form and suggestions given on page 421.

appendix a

VOCABULARY EXERCISES: DEFINITIONS BY CHAPTER

CHAPTER 1

A. Words to Describe Situations

1. boisterous: noisy in an active way
2. amiable: friendly
3. regal: kingly; royal
4. malevolent: wishing harm to others
5. dismal: dreary; causing gloom
6. hushed: very quiet
7. hectic: marked by excitement
8. tranquil: peaceful
9. cluttered: piled up in a disorderly way
10. effervescent: bubbling with excitement

B. Words that Name Sounds

1. guffaw: laugh in a loud burst
2. clamor: loud outcry or shouting
3. inaudible: incapable of being heard
4. bellow: utter in a loud, powerful voice
5. resonate: echo back with vibrations

CHAPTER 2

A. Words for Actions

1. grimace: show disapproval with the face
2. stagger: move unsteadily with loss of confidence
3. trot: walk fast; jog
4. swagger: walk conceitedly
5. saunter: stroll
6. plunge: enter violently
7. careen: lurch, swerve without control
8. mutter: say something unclearly
9. squirm: wriggle; move like a snake
10. spurn: reject with scorn

B. How People Do or Say Things

1. irresponsibly: in a way that is not dependable; unreliably
2. contemptuously: scornfully
3. sullenly: gloomily
4. spontaneously: impulsively; without any thought
5. irritably: in an annoyed and angry manner
6. brazenly: loudly; shamelessly
7. precariously: dangerously
8. painstakingly: with great care
9. meekly: with patience and humility; mildly
10. vehemently: forcefully; with passion

CHAPTER 3

A. Words for the Past

1. reminisce: recall and tell of past experiences
2. nostalgia: a longing for things, persons, or events no longer present
3. memorable: worth being remembered
4. evoke: to call forth memories
5. recollect: remember
6. discern: detect; perceive the distinctions
7. interlude: a period of time that comes between events
8. remembrance: something remembered
9. contemplate: consider thoughtfully
10. retrospect: a review of things in the past

B. Words for Unforgettable Personalities

1. compulsive: acting as if compelled by irresistible impulses
2. domineering: ruling like a tyrant over others
3. reticent: shy
4. gregarious: sociable
5. volatile: explosive

CHAPTER 4

A. Words for Opposite Physical Qualities

1. dexterous: skillful in the use of the hands
   awkward: clumsy
2. diminutive: tiny
   massive: bulky; solid
3. rotund: plump
   slender: gracefully slim
4. swarthy: having a dark or sunburned complexion
   pallid: having a pale complexion
5. petite: small and trim
   statuesque: stately; graceful and dignified

B. Words for Contrasting Moods

1. benevolent: kindly
2. confident: assured
3. affectionate: loving
4. serene: peaceful
5. exuberant: overflowing with joy
6. irate: angry
7. spiteful: full of ill will prompting an urge to hurt or humiliate someone
8. sluggish: slow; inactive
9. masochistic: deriving pleasure from being hurt
10. depressed: saddened

CHAPTER 5

A. Words for Growth

1. phase: stage of development
2. retarded: delayed in progress
3. accelerate: to make happen sooner than expected; speed up
4. enrichment: something that adds value
5. maturation: the process of becoming fully developed

B. Words for a Child's World

1. naïve: lacking sophistication
2. vulnerable: unprotected from danger; easily hurt
3. nurture: promote growth and development; educate
4. puerile: immature; childish; juvenile
5. peer: a person who has equal standing with another in age, rank, or class

C. -ing Words for Liveliness

1. sputtering: speaking in an explosive way
2. asserting: claiming
3. familiarizing: making acquainted with
4. lauding: praising
5. assenting: agreeing

CHAPTER 6

A. Words for Size and Shape

1. vast: very great in size
2. minute: tiny
3. towering: noble; reaching high intensity
4. corpulent: excessively fat
5. amorphous: without definite shape

B. Sharpening the Senses

1. savory: something with special flavor
2. rancid: rotten smell or taste
3. musty: moldy; smelling or tasting of dampness
4. pungent: sharply stimulating
5. medicinal: relating to medicine
6. supple: able to bend easily without breaking
7. clammy: damp, sticky, and cool
8. gossamer: thin, sheer fabric
9. furrowed: filled with wrinkles or grooves
10. sinewy: physically strong

CHAPTER 7

A. Words for Explaining Processes

1. sequential: characterized by an order of events or steps
2. procedure: a way of performing or effecting something
3. prior: occurring before
4. consequence: result
5. subsequent: following in time order
6. cyclical: moving in an order in which a regular event (or a sequence of events) takes place
7. reproduce: make happen again
8. analyze: break down into basic parts
9. significance: importance; meaning
10. synthesize: produce by putting together or combining elements

CHAPTER 8

A. Familiar Words in the Women's Struggle

1. feminist: one who believes a woman's activities should be extended in social and political life
2. suffragist: a woman who believes women should have the right to vote
3. chauvinist: anyone who has blind devotion to any cause
4. hormonal: relating to substances given off by certain organs in the body
5. puberty: sexual maturity; the age at which a person is able to have children
6. mortality: the condition of being subject to death
7. inferiority: the state of being lower in rank
8. stereotype: a fixed idea about a person or thing based upon oversimplified points of view
9. degradation: the state of being lowered in quality or estimation
10. discrimination: a distinction or preference in favor of or against some thing or person

B. More Words in the Struggle for Equality

1. oppression: the use of power over others in a cruel way
2. downtrodden: trampled upon; ruled over severely
3. prejudice: an unfavorable opinion formed beforehand, without knowledge
4. emancipation: the act of setting free
5. activist: an especially enthusiastic worker in a political cause

CHAPTER 9

A. Words to Name Relationships among People

1. peer: an equal
2. contemporary: living at the same time
3. familial: pertaining to a family
4. sibling: brother or sister

5. comrade: companion; associate; friend
6. kin: family; relatives
7. fraternal: brotherly
8. conjugal: pertaining to marriage or to the mutual relations between husband and wife
9. paternal: fatherly
10. maternal: motherly

A MINIBOOK OF NINETEEN SPECIAL SKILLS

A. Roots for Definitions

1. moribund: on the verge of dying
2. spectacle: public performance or display
3. dismissed: discharged; sent away
4. circumlocution: roundabout, evasive speech or writing
5. revert: return to a former condition or belief

B. Prefix, Suffix, Root in Combination

1. submitter: one who gives in
2. circumlocution: a roundabout way of speaking
3. inversion: the act of reversing in position; turning upside down
4. intermission: recess; period between acts in a performance
5. comportment: behavior; bearing
6. intangible: unable to be touched
7. universal: pertaining to or affecting the whole world
8. revisor: someone who changes or modifies something
9. disposal: act of putting something away in its place
10. introspection: act of looking into one's self and examining one's own mental state

appendix b

THEME PROGRESS SHEET

After your instructor grades and returns your themes, count up and enter the number of errors you make in each category listed on top ot the chart. Before you write each following composition, study this sheet so that you know your errors and so that you can avoid them in your writing. The symbols for the errors and the page numbers on which to discover how to make specific corrections appear on the inside covers of this book.

Date	
Title of composition	
RO	
Frag	
Agr	Grammar
Vb	
Pro	
Ms	
Cap	Mechanics
It	
Abbr	
,	
;	
'	
"	
./	
!/	Punctuation
?/	
:/	
–/	
( )/	
-/	
Sp	Spelling and vocabulary
Voc	
Us	Diction
Ef	
Var	
Ord	
//	Strong sentences
mm	
Dang	
¶	
¶ Det	Paragraphs and essays
¶ Dev	
E	

appendix c

RECORD OF TEACHER-STUDENT CONFERENCES ON COMPOSITIONS

Date	Discussion points	Follow-up assignment

ACKNOWLEDGMENTS

William Borders, "Study Indicates Why Some Schools Succeed," *The New York Times*, July 24, 1979. Copyright © 1979 by The New York Times Company. Reprinted by permission.

Claude Brown from *Manchild in the Promised Land.* Copyright © 1965 by Claude Brown. Reprinted by permission of The Macmillan Company.

Katharine Brush, "Birthday Party." Reprinted from *The New Yorker*, March 16, 1946. Copyright © by Thomas S. Brush.

Pearl S. Buck, from "The Frill," copyright © 1933 by Pearl S. Buck. Renewed. Reprinted by permission of Harold Ober Associates Incorporated.

James F. Fixx, *The Complete Book of Running*, pages 96–98. Copyright © 1977 by James F. Fixx. Reprinted by permission of Random House, Inc.

Selma H. Fraiberg, "Why Does the Baby Smile?" Excerpt from "Why Does the Baby Smile?" is reprinted from *The Magic Years* by Selma H. Fraiberg with the permission of Charles Scribner's Sons. Copyright © 1959 by Selma H. Fraiberg.

W. Timothy Gallwey, *The Inner Game of Tennis.* Copyright © 1974 by W. Timothy Gallwey. Reprinted by permission of Random House, Inc.

Germaine Greer, from *The Female Eunuch.* Copyright © 1971 by Germaine Greer. Reprinted by permission of the publisher, McGraw-Hill Book Company.

Langston Hughes, "Mother to Son." From *Selected Poems*, by permission of Alfred A. Knopf, Inc. Copyright © 1926 by Alfred A. Knopf, Inc., and renewed 1954 by Langston Hughes.

Maude White Katz, from "End Racism in Education: A Concerned Parent Speaks." Reprinted from *Freedomways Magazine*, vol. 8, no. 4 (fourth quarter), 1968.

Alfred Kazin, from "The Block and Beyond" in *A Walker in the City*; copyright © 1951 by Alfred Kazin. Reprinted by permission of Harcourt Brace Jovanovich, Inc.

John Oliver Killens, "The Stick Up" from *The Best Short Stories by Negro Writers.* Copyright © 1967 by John Oliver Killens. Reprinted by permission of International Famous Agency.

Edna St. Vincent Millay, "Lament," from *Collected Poems*, Harper & Row. Copyright © 1921, 1948 by Edna St. Vincent Millay.

The New Merriam-Webster Pocket Dictionary; copyright © 1971 by G. & C. Merriam Co., publishers of the Merriam-Webster Dictionaries. Entries reprinted by permission.

Newsday, "How Teens Are Spending Vacations" (table), August 8, 1979, Part II, page 2. Copyright © 1979 by Newsday, Inc. Reprinted with permission.

George Orwell, from *Such, Such Were the Joys.* Copyright © 1953. Reprinted by permission of Harcourt Brace Jovanovich, Inc., and Mrs. Sonia Brownell Orwell.

Robert Phillips, "The Mole," *The New Yorker*, August 13, 1979, page 62. Reprinted by permission; © 1979 The New Yorker Magazine, Inc.

John R. Regan, "My Room at the Lilac Inn," from *The Purple Testament*, ed. Don M. Wolfe. Copyright © 1946 by Don M. Wolfe. Reprinted by permission of Don M. Wolfe.

Roget's International Thesaurus. Copyright © 1946 by Thomas Y. Crowell Company. Entries under the word "humorist," #844, reprinted by permission of the publisher.

Carl Sandburg, "Mag," from *Chicago Poems.* Copyright © 1916 by Holt, Reinhart, and Winston, Inc. Copyright © 1944 by Carl Sandburg. Reprinted by permission of Holt, Reinhart, and Winston, Inc.

Dick Schapp, "Boxing—That Thrilla in Manila," *The Washington Star*, 1975. Reprinted by permission of the Sterling Lord Agency, Inc. Copyright © 1975 by Dick Schapp.

William Shannon, "Our Lost Children," *The New York Times*, September 10, 1975, op-ed page. Copyright © 1979 by The New York Times Company. Reprinted by permission.

Andrew Siscaretti, "What Am I? West Clapton and Flynn," from "Media Compositions: Preludes to Writing" by Harvey S. Wiener, in *College English*, February 1974. Copyright © 1974 by the *National Council of Teachers of English.* Reprinted with permission.

Betty Smith, *A Tree Grows in Brooklyn.* Copyright © 1943, 1947 by Betty Smith. Reprinted by permission of Harper & Row, Publishers, Inc.

Lenore Wietzman and Diane Rizzo, "Sex Bias in Textbooks," *Today's Education*, January-February 1975. Reprinted by permission of *Today's Education* and the authors.

INDEX